Living in the Flesh by the Spirit

Living in the Flesh by the Spirit
The Pauline View of Flesh and Spirit in Galatians

Brian H. Thomas

WIPF & STOCK · Eugene, Oregon

LIVING IN THE FLESH BY THE SPIRIT
The Pauline View of Flesh and Spirit in Galatians

Copyright © 2020 Brian H. Thomas. All rights reserved. Except for brief quotations in critical publications or reviews, no part of this book may be reproduced in any manner without prior written permission from the publisher. Write: Permissions, Wipf and Stock Publishers, 199 W. 8th Ave., Suite 3, Eugene, OR 97401.

Wipf & Stock
An Imprint of Wipf and Stock Publishers
199 W. 8th Ave., Suite 3
Eugene, OR 97401

www.wipfandstock.com

PAPERBACK ISBN: 978-1-5326-6545-5
HARDCOVER ISBN: 978-1-5326-6546-2
EBOOK ISBN: 978-1-5326-6547-9

Scripture quotations marked ESV are from the ESV® Bible (The Holy Bible, English Standard Version®), copyright © 2001 by Crossway, a publishing ministry of Good News Publishers. Used by permission. All rights reserved.

Scripture quotations marked NASB are taken from the New American Standard Bible® (NASB), Copyright © 1960, 1962, 1963, 1968, 1971, 1972, 1973, 1975, 1977, 1995 by The Lockman Foundation. Used by permission. www.Lockman.org.

Scripture quotations marked NIV are taken from the Holy Bible, New International Version®, NIV®. Copyright © 1973, 1978, 1984, 2011 by Biblica, Inc.™ Used by permission of Zondervan. All rights reserved worldwide. www.zondervan.com The "NIV" and "New International Version" are trademarks registered in the United States Patent and Trademark Office by Biblica, Inc.™

Scripture quotations marked RSV are from Revised Standard Version of the Bible, copyright © 1946, 1952, and 1971 National Council of the Churches of Christ in the United States of America. Used by permission. All rights reserved worldwide.

Scripture quotations marked NRSV are from New Revised Standard Version Bible, copyright © 1989 National Council of the Churches of Christ in the United States of America. Used by permission. All rights reserved worldwide.

Quotations from the Apocrypha marked RSV are from Revised Standard Version of the Bible, Apocrypha, copyright © 1957; The Third and Fourth Books of the Maccabees and Psalm 151, copyright © 1977 National Council of the Churches of Christ in the United States of America. Used by permission. All rights reserved worldwide.

Manufactured in the U.S.A.   01/31/20

To my Lord who has saved me,
To my wife who has walked with me,
To my son who has enriched me,
To my church who has supported me,
To my mentors who have guided me.

Contents

List of Tables | viii
Acknowledgments | ix
Abbreviations | xi

1 Introduction | 1
2 The Old Testament Background to the Theme of "Flesh" | 25
3 *Kata Sarka* and *En Sarki* Relations, Identity, and Values in Paul | 68
4 Preliminary Theoretical Issues Regarding Paul's *Sarx-Pneuma* Antithesis | 87
5 Paul's Supplementary Salvation-Historical Framework of *Sarx*: Romans 6–8 | 102
6 Paul's *Sarx-Pneuma* Antithesis and the Schema of Overlapping Ages | 127
7 The *Sarx*, the *Pneuma*, the Gospel, and the Letter to the Galatians | 151
8 The *Sarx* and Walking by the Spirit in Galatians 5:13–26 | 178
9 Conclusion | 209

Bibliography | 213
Author Index | 227
Subject Index | 231
Ancient Document Index | 233

Tables

1. Linguistic and Conceptual Parallels of Genesis 12, 20, and 26 with Genesis 6:2 | 52
2. Five Elements of the Flood Narrative | 58
3. The Current Body vs. The Resurrection Body | 121
4. Antitheses in Galatians 2–3 | 168
5. Living by the flesh vs. Living by the Spirit | 177
6. Chiastic Structure of Galatians 5:13–26 | 179
7. Exegetical Diagram of Galatians 5:13–26 | 179
8. The Vices of Galatians 5:19–21 | 195
9. Galatians 5:24 and Its Intra-epistolary Parallels | 199

Acknowledgments

This book is a revision of my 2015 Doctor of Theology thesis from Trinity Theological College (Singapore). I wish to express my gratitude first of all to my advisor Dr. Tan Kim Huat for his patient guidance, and his wisdom which kept me from making some embarrassing errors while nonetheless allowing me to follow my convictions. I would also like to thank my thesis readers, Dr. Leonard Wee of Trinity Theological College and Dr. G. Walter Hansen of Fuller Theological Seminary, for their kind assessment of the work, and their encouragement to publish it.

I must also acknowledge my indebtedness to Dr. Walter B. Russell of Talbot School of Theology, who first introduced me to this fascinating topic in my first semester as a seminary student. I benefitted tremendously from Dr. Russell's warm and wise teaching in the art of reading Scripture well. His insights into Paul and the flesh have challenged me ever since. Though I had originally intended to research the Johannine usage of the flesh concept and its implications for our understanding of the incarnation, I could not escape the gravitational pull of the perplexing issue of Paul's treatment, and the growing conviction that there were new things to say about it. Though some of my conclusions differ from Dr. Russell's own, I am grateful for his insightful work, which made mine possible.

I would also like to acknowledge the encouragement of Dr. Mark Chan as both a pastor and friend throughout my time in Singapore and my doctoral studies. Also, without the generous financial support of Evangel Christian Church in Singapore, I would not have been able to pursue my DTh studies which became the basis for this book, as well as for my current academic ministry. I am deeply grateful for the church's support, both for my theological education and for my family in manifold ways during our time in Singapore. I also must express my thanks for the encouragement and accommodation of my dean and faculty colleagues at Singapore Bible College which enabled me to complete the writing of the thesis in the final year of my DTh program, and the first year of my teaching at SBC. I count it a joy and a privilege to be a part of this team at SBC, in partnership to teach such wonderful students and faithful servants of Jesus Christ.

The love, joy, and companionship of my wife and son, I'Ching and Craig, refreshed me every step of the way and motivated me to persevere until the end of my research and writing. I am profoundly thankful to them, and to God for them.

Finally, I offer my praise and thanksgiving to the triune God for saving me through the work of the Son, and for giving me life through the indwelling Holy Spirit. It is my prayer that this book will bring glory to Jesus Christ and serve his people in the seminary and the church by helping them to read and understand his word, in spite of whatever errors I may have made in judgment or execution. By God's grace, may those deficits be overlooked and forgotten, and may what Paul intended to communicate long ago be heard afresh by God's people again.

Abbreviations

AB	Anchor Bible
BBR	*Bulletin for Biblical Research*
BBB	Bonner Biblische Beiträge
BDAG	Bauer, Walter, Frederick William Danker, W. F. Arndt, and F. W. Gingrich. *A Greek-English Lexicon of the New Testament and Other Early Christian Literature*. 3rd ed. Chicago: University of Chicago, 2000.
BDB	Brown, Francis, S. R. Driver, and Charles A. Briggs, eds. *The Brown-Driver-Briggs Hebrew and English Lexicon: With an Appendix Containing the Biblical Aramaic*. Oxford: Clarendon, 1907. BibleWorks 8, 2009.
BECNT	Baker Exegetical Commentary on the New Testament
BJRL	*Bulletin of the John Rylands Library*
BNTC	Black's New Testament Commentary
CBQ	*Catholic Bible Quarterly*
DLNT	*Dictionary of the Later New Testament and Its Developments*. Edited by Ralph P. Martin and Peter H. Davids. Grand Rapids: InterVarsity, 1997.
DPL	*Dictionary of Paul and His Letters*. Edited by Gerald L. Hawthorne and Ralph P. Martin. Grand Rapids: InterVarsity, 1993.
HALOT	*The Hebrew and Aramaic Lexicon of the Old Testament*. Ludwig Koehler and Walter Baumgartner. Translated and edited under the supervision of M. E. J. Richardson. 5 vols. Leiden: Brill, 1994–2000.

HTR	*Harvard Theological Review*
IBC	Interpretation Bible Commentary
ICC	International Critical Commentary
IVPNTC	InterVarsity Press New Testament Commentary
JBL	*Journal of Biblical Literature*
JETS	*Journal of the Evangelical Theological Society*
JPS	Jewish Publication Society
JSNT	*Journal for the Study of the New Testament*
JSNTSup	Journal for the Study of the New Testament Supplement Series
JTS	*Journal of Theological Studies*
LN	Louw, Johannes E., and Eugene A. Nida. *Greek-English Lexicon of the New Testament: Based on Semantic Domains.* 2nd ed. 2 vols. New York: United Bible Societies, 1989.
LSJ	Liddell, Henry George, and Robert Scott. *A Greek-English Lexicon.* 9th ed. Revised by Henry Stuart Jones with Roderick McKenzie and with a Supplement by E. A. Barber. Oxford: Clarendon, 1968. BibleWorks 8, 2009.
MNTC	Moffatt New Testament Commentary
NAC	New American Commentary
NIBCNT	New International Bible Commentary on the New Testament
NICNT	New International Commentary on the New Testament
NICOT	New International Commentary on the Old Testament
NIDNTT	*New International Dictionary of New Testament Theology.* Edited by Colin Brown. 4 vols. Grand Rapids: Zondervan, 1986.
NIDOTTE	*New International Dictionary of Old Testament Theology and Exegesis.* Edited by Willem A. VanGemeren. 5 vols. Grand Rapids: Zondervan, 1997.
NIGTC	New International Greek Text Commentary
NIVAC	NIV Application Commentary
NovT	*Novum Testamentum*

NTS	*New Testament Studies*
OTL	Old Testament Library
PNTC	Pillar New Testament Commentary
RevExp	*Review and Expositor*
SBJT	*Southern Baptist Journal of Theology*
SBL	Society of Biblical Literature
SBLMS	Society of Biblical Literature Monograph Series
SNTSMS	Society of New Testament Studies Monograph Series
SNTW	Studies of the New Testament and Its World
TDNT	*Theological Dictionary of the New Testament.* Edited by Gerhard Kittel and Gerhard Friedrich. 10 vols. Grand Rapids: Eerdmans, 1964–76.
TWNT	*Theologische Wörterbuch zum Neuen Testament.* Edited by Gerhard Kittel and Gerhard Friedrich. 10 vols. Stuttgart: Kohlhammer, 1932–1979.
TWOT	*Theological Wordbook of the Old Testament.* R. Laird Harris, Gleason L. Archer Jr., and Bruce K. Waltke. 2 vols. Chicago: Moody, 1980. BibleWorks 8, 2009.
TZ	*Theologische Zeitschrift*
TZT	*Tübinger Zeitschrift für Theologie*
UBS	United Bible Society
VT	*Vetus Testamentum*
WBC	Word Biblical Commentary
WMANT	Wissenschaftliche Monographien zum Alten und Neuen Testament
WTJ	*Westminster Theological Journal*
WUNT	Wissenschaftliche Untersuchungen zum Neuen Testament
ZECNT	Zondervan Exegetical Commentary on the New Testament
ZNW	*Zeitschrift für die neutestamentliche Wissenschaft und die Kunde der älteren Kirche*
ZThK	*Zeitschrift für Theologie und Kirch*

— 1 —

Introduction

This thesis revisits Paul's understanding of "the flesh" (σάρξ, sarx), especially in the epistle to the Galatians, and culminates in the exegesis of Galatians 5:13–26. The word σάρξ is a multifaceted anthropological term in Paul that is used to express diverse theological truths. It is the Greek equivalent of the Old Testament Hebrew term בָּשָׂר (bāśār), which itself had a wide range of meaning, and was employed in many different ways in the Old Testament as a result. This complexity was multiplied in the writings of Paul as this OT concept was applied to new circumstances after the work of Christ at Calvary and the advent of the Holy Spirit at Pentecost. This resulted in an enlarged scope of referents for σάρξ, such that the precise nuance and object intended is often unclear. This has led to what has seemed to be, to modern readers, vague and apparently contradictory statements. Unsurprisingly, this has led to long-standing controversy among scholars, who have proposed different religious-historical backgrounds in addition to the Old Testament, as well as divergent understandings of Paul's overall theology, resulting in a wide and contentious spectrum of opinion regarding the significance of σάρξ. To this day there is little consensus on this issue, particularly the use of σάρξ in Galatians.

The argument of this thesis is as follows. First, three background elements are necessary and sufficient to account for Paul's view of σάρξ in its most profound theological senses: (1) the Old Testament; (2) the revolutionary new work of God through Jesus Christ and the Holy Spirit which was experienced personally by Paul in his own conversion; and (3) the Judaizing controversy that is immediately behind the letter to the Galatians. Other proposed religious-historical backgrounds, such as Qumran, rabbinic Judaism, or Hellenistic influence, are either of doubtful significance, or are insufficient in comparison to the three elements cited above. To say that a proposed background is of doubtful significance means that the similarity between Paul and the alleged background is arguably due instead to a third factor, the common OT heritage, and that a dependence relationship between Paul and the alleged background has not been clearly demonstrated. To say that a proposed background is insufficient, it is meant that that the alleged background on closer examination seems incongruent with Paul's thought in general, or his use of σάρξ in particular.

Second, two Pauline theological frameworks are necessary and sufficient for the interpretation of σάρξ in Paul's letters. The first is that "flesh" is a fundamental and definitive anthropological term from the Old Testament, and that it continues to be so for Paul. That is, "man is flesh" is part of Paul's inherited OT anthropological framework, and this anthropological sense of σάρξ remains an underlying constant for Paul. The second framework essential to understanding Paul's use of σάρξ is the salvation-historical change wrought by Christ and the resultant work of the Holy Spirit. This change both enables Paul to make a profound comparison before and after Christ, and also engenders much of the controversy on the terms of gentile inclusion in God's people in which σάρξ is such a relevant term. It is Paul's contrastive use of "flesh" and "Spirit" with reference to salvation-history, combined with his simultaneous use of "flesh" as an anthropological constant, that results in the difficulty of the σάρξ passages. Failure to fully accommodate this twofold use of σάρξ leads to the inadequate treatment of this aspect of Pauline thought.

History of Research

A survey of the various scholarly views on Paul's flesh-spirit antithesis in the modern period can be broadly organized according to two considerations: (1) the scholar's understanding of the source, background, or influence for Paul's conception of the flesh; and (2) the scholar's understanding of the substantive content of Paul's view of the flesh. It should also be pointed out that both (1) and (2) are strongly influenced by the intellectual currents of the scholar's time, a phenomenon that Herman Ridderbos observed to occur with great regularity in Pauline studies; indeed, this tendency at its worst involves the modern scholar merely substituting his own background philosophical influence—which we could enumerate analogously as (1a)—for the content of Paul's doctrine (2).[1]

Given the lack of consensus on the meaning of Paul's flesh-Spirit antithesis and the sheer volume of interpretive proposals, it is difficult to summarize the history of research briefly with neat categories. Even limiting ourselves to the two considerations mentioned above admits many complications in the

1. Ridderbos, *Paul*, 14–15.

picture: there are many instances where scholars agree on the background but argue for different substantive understandings of the content; or have a similar understanding of the content, though they consider it to be derived from different backgrounds. There are also many proposals which straddle categories. Accordingly, in what follows we attempt to make note of the major streams of interpretation with representative scholarly proponents, while avoiding arbitrary groupings, redundancy, or omission. In the survey that follows, for the sake of brevity we will frequently abbreviate "Paul's view of the flesh-spirit antithesis" by simply referring to "Paul."

Generally Hellenistic Understandings of Paul

One major question that divided scholars in the modern period was whether it was a Jewish or Hellenistic source that provided the most relevant conceptual background for Paul. Within each of these camps there were a variety of views regarding the meaning of Paul's antithesis. Generally, the Jewish view has prevailed over the Hellenistic one, however, it is recognized that various strands of Jewish thought admitted varying degrees of Hellenistic influence.[2]

F. C. Baur and the Tübingen School: The Paul of Hegelian Idealism

Ferdinand C. Baur initiated modern critical study of Paul in the early nineteenth century. In 1831 he argued[3] that there was a fundamental division in the Corinthian church between Paul and Peter, which reflected a schism in the early church in general. Peter represented the "Christ party," a particularistic, Law-oriented form of Jewish Christianity, which was opposed by Paul, who represented a more universal, Law-free, gentile Christianity with a gospel shaped to some degree by Hellenistic thought. These competing strands were reconciled in the form of a third party of "early Catholicism" led by the apostle John. In this understanding of the three factions, we may observe the form of the dialectic of Hegel, with the above factions playing the respective roles of the thesis, antithesis, and synthesis.[4] Much of Baur's

---

2. Dunn, *Theology of Paul the Apostle*, 54–55.

3. Baur, "Die Christuspartei in der korinthischen Gemeinde," 61–206; cited by Hafemann, "Paul and His Interpreters," 666–68.

4. Hafemann, "Paul and His Interpreters," 666–68; Harris, "Baur, Ferdinand Christian (1792–1860)," 34–35; Neill and Wright, *Interpretation of the New Testament*, 20–30; Barclay, *Obeying the Truth*, 182–83; Ridderbos, *Paul*, 16–17; Frey, "Impact of the Dead

work was thus based on "an irrelevant and unproved presupposition."[5] By virtue of this dialectic structural conception of the factions, Paul must be understood in a Hellenistic fashion as the antithesis to Peter's Jewish Christianity. Baur serves as the prelude to the consensus of liberal theology which understood Paul in increasingly Greek terms as the proponent of a universal rational and ethical religion.[6]

In Baur's view, Paul's understanding of the flesh-spirit antithesis is the center of Paul's preaching.[7] In terms of its substantive meaning, Baur interpreted the antithesis in accord with the Hegelian idealist tradition. He thus identified Paul's flesh concept as that which was finite, "merely outward," sensuous, or material, particularly the material body. In that way, σάρξ could be a synonym for σῶμα (sōma), both of which opposed man's πνεῦμα (pneuma) (or νοῦς [nous]), which Baur defined as the principle of consciousness linking man and God.[8] In this way, the flesh-Spirit opposition is not merely internal to man, but operates in the cosmic sphere as two powers standing above man.[9] This reflects the Hegelian notion of absolute Spirit or Mind (either can be intended by the German Geist) as the underlying immanent dynamic of particular historical events, persons, and social realities, such that individual consciousness finds its ultimate fulfillment in absolute Spirit.[10] In this way, Baur's flesh-Spirit antithesis can refer to both individual anthropological realities as well as to more extra-individual, corporate, or even cosmic realities. As Ridderbos summarizes:

> In the spirit man has a share in the Spirit of God himself, by which he is freed from the finite and relative and attains absolute freedom. In this idealistic scheme Christianity for Baur is the absolute religion and Paul is the one in whose doctrine of freedom and reconciliation the absolute consciousness of the unity of man with God in the Spirit has been embodied.[11]

Sea Scrolls on New Testament Interpretation," 455n185; Frey, "Die paulinische Antithese," 46–47; Dunn, *Beginning from Jerusalem*, 31–36; Wilkens and Padgett, *Faith and Reason in the Nineteenth Century*, 79–86, 99–106.

5. The evaluation of Neill and Wright, *Interpretation of the New Testament*, 23.

6. Jewett, *Paul's Anthropological Terms*, 51; Baur, *Paul*, 2:123–26; Ridderbos, *Paul*, 16–17.

7. Ridderbos, *Paul*, 16.

8. Baur, *Paul*, 2:126–29; Barclay, *Obeying the Truth*, 182–83.

9. Jewett, *Paul's Anthropological Terms*, 51.

10. Wilkens and Padgett, *Faith and Reason in the Nineteenth Century*, 82–85.

11. Ridderbos, *Paul*, 16.

The Liberal Interpretation: The Paul of Hellenistic Ethical Struggle

Baur was followed by some prominent scholars in the second half of the nineteenth century who further developed the liberal interpretation of Paul, defining his flesh-Spirit antithesis as a Hellenistic conception of the personal moral struggle that characterizes life "in Christ." This "in Christ" relationship was a kind of ethically oriented mysticism that was central to Paul's theology. The most noteworthy representatives of this general interpretation were Carl Holsten, Hermann Lüdemann, Otto Pfleiderer, and H. J. Holtzmann.[12] Holsten developed more than any of his predecessors the idea that the flesh-spirit antithesis was a Greek philosophical concept in which the flesh was identified with the body as the source of sensuality, weakness, and sin.[13] Although there was some variation in their exposition of the details, Lüdemann, Pfleiderer, and Holtzmann all followed Holsten in this basic conception of Paul's antithesis and the significance of the flesh.[14]

In addition to their shared views on the flesh and the Hellenistic origin of the antithesis, these writers held varying positions on related issues which influenced later scholars. Regarding the spirit side of the antithesis, Holsten insisted that Paul was referring to the divine Spirit, and never the human spirit.[15] Lüdemann, Pfleiderer, and Holtzmann, on the other hand, held the view that both the human spirit and the divine Spirit are involved in the struggle with the flesh, with Pfleiderer also identifying the Spirit as Christ.[16] Holsten pointed to Paul's religious experiences of failure under the Law and his subsequent conversion experience as the impetus for the development of his flesh-spirit antithesis, which many scholars followed, including Holtzmann.[17] Holsten argued, however, that Paul's conception blended strands from the contradictory anthropologies of Jewish and

---

12. Holsten, *Zum Evangelium des Paulus und des Petrus*; Holsten, *Das Evangelium des Paulus*; Lüdemann, *Die Anthropologie des Apostels Paulus*; Pfleiderer, *Der Paulinismus: Ein Beitrag zur Geschichte der urchristlichen Theologie*; Holtzmann, *Lehrbuch der Neutestamentlichen Theologie*; cited in Stacey, *Pauline View of Man*, 41–42; and Jewett, *Paul's Anthropological Terms*, 51–55.

13. Stacey, *Pauline View of Man*, 41–42; Jewett, *Paul's Anthropological Terms*, 51–52; Ridderbos, *Paul*, 17–18, 22; Frey, "Die paulinische Antithese," 47.

14. Stacey, *Pauline View of Man*, 41–43, 166–71; Jewett, *Paul's Anthropological Terms*, 52–57; Ridderbos, *Paul*, 17–22; Matlock, *Unveiling the Apocalyptic Paul*, 29–30; Barclay, *Obeying the Truth*, 183; Russell, *Flesh/Spirit Conflict*, 154.

15. Jewett, *Paul's Anthropological Terms*, 51.

16. Jewett, *Paul's Anthropological Terms*, 52–56; Stacey, *Pauline View of Man*, 174; Barclay, *Obeying the Truth*, 183; Pfleiderer, *Paulinism*, 1:199–215.

17. Jewett, *Paul's Anthropological Terms*, 51–52, 56–57.

Hellenistic thought. Later writers would wrestle with this contradiction. Lüdemann understood Paul as exhibiting a diachronic development from a Jewish anthropology and conception of the flesh to a more Hellenistic one that attempted to blend both together, yet resulted in an incongruous synthesis. Lüdemann argued that Paul presented a Jewish view of the flesh in Romans 1-4, in which the flesh represents man as a whole in his weakness, such that his neutral "inner man" is unable to obey the Law, and therefore man must be saved by the imputation of Christ's ideal righteousness by faith. However, in Romans 5-8, Paul expresses the Hellenistic view that the flesh is a material substance which is stimulated by the Law to enslave man under the curse and death; deliverance comes when the Spirit destroys the flesh. As a result, Lüdemann sees in Paul two views of flesh, two anthropologies, and two soteriologies. Pfleiderer and Holtzmann likewise posited that Jewish and Greek views on these matters coexisted simultaneously in Paul's thought, resulting in the contradiction that the flesh is merely human weakness in Paul and at the same time it is intrinsically evil and sinful, such that the flesh is a sufficient condition for sin, which consequently follows from the flesh by necessity.[18]

After Holtzmann, this general approach to Paul began to wane. It had always been resisted by those scholars who maintained a Jewish background for his thought. Additionally, the explicit contradiction in Paul's anthropology came under increasing criticism, such as by Albert Schweitzer. Finally, the History of Religions School posited a new view of the background of Pauline thought that was regarded as more compelling.[19]

The History of Religions School: The Paul of Hellenistic Mystery Religions and Gnosticism

In the turn of the nineteenth into the twentieth century, the *religionsgeschichtliche Schule* centered at the University of Göttingen led the search for the historical antecedents of Christian theology and practice (i.e., of the sacraments) away from Greek philosophical thinking towards the more syncretistic form of Hellenistic popular religion found in the mystery religions and Gnosticism. Hermann Gunkel argued that this influence was imported into Christianity

---

18. Jewett, *Paul's Anthropological Terms*, 51-57; Stacey, *Pauline View of Man*, 42-43, 166-7; Neill and Wright, *Interpretation of the New Testament*, 169-70; Baird, *From Jonathan Edwards to Rudolf Bultmann*, 111-12, 120-22, 217-20; Barclay, *Obeying the Truth*, 183; Matlock, *Unveiling the Apocalyptic Paul*, 29; Russell, *Flesh/Spirit Conflict*, 154; Ridderbos, *Paul*, 18-20.

19. Jewett, *Paul's Anthropological Terms*, 56-57; Barclay, *Obeying the Truth*, 183; Ridderbos, *Paul*, 20-22; Hafemann, "Paul and His Interpreters," 668-69.

via the medium of a more syncretistic Hellenistic Judaism.[20] More prominently, Wilhelm Bousset argued that Paul was exposed to the mystery religions in the Hellenistic Christian communities, particularly Antioch. As a result he developed a syncretistic blend of Christianity in which the mystical idea of Jesus as the risen Christ who was the *Kyrios* present in the church was derived from the Hellenistic mystery cults. The *Kyrios* was mystically experienced as the Spirit in the Hellenistic church, especially in the observance of the sacraments. In Bousset's view, the Spirit was a power that completely overcame the human will, for man was by nature opposed to it. The basis of this opposition was the flesh, which Bousset defined as the principle of sin and sensuality in man which was radically evil and beyond reform, and thus essentially opposed to the Spirit. Bousset argued that Paul's antithesis was an instance of Hellenistic syncretistic dualism. It also parallels the gnostic myth of the Primal Man, a cosmic power which sinks down into matter and produces the mixture of good and evil elements in man which generates the experience of the inward struggle.[21] Paul's conception of the flesh-spirit antithesis places at least "one foot on the soil of dualistic Gnosticism."[22] Bousset's basic view was followed by Kirsopp Lake—who would transmit these ideas into British scholarship—and C. G. Montefiore.[23]

Another scholar from the *religionsgeschichtliche Schule*, Richard Reitzenstein, studied deeply in the mystery religions and Gnosticism and concluded that Paul was deeply influenced by both, but particularly by Gnosticism. In his view, Paul, who was "the greatest of all the Gnostics," taught that man was by nature imprisoned in the material world, but is released by receiving the divine Spirit. Paul used the terms ψυχικός (*psuchikos*) and σαρκικός (*sarkikos*) synonymously to describe a man who has received the Spirit but has not yet had the *gnosis* formed in him that the Spirit brings and which brings release from the world and human limitations. This proposal stimulated exegetes of the next generation to interpret Paul's flesh-spirit

---

20. Gunkel, *Zum religionsgeschichtlichen Verständnis des Neuen Testaments*, cited in Ascough, "Historical Approaches," 157-59; Dunn, *Beginning from Jerusalem*, 36-40; Baird, *From Jonathan Edwards to Rudolf Bultmann*, 239.

21. Bousset, *Kyrios Christos*, 186-200, 254-55; Neill and Wright, *Interpretation of the New Testament*, 175-77; Baird, *From Jonathan Edwards to Rudolf Bultmann*, 243-47, 249-50; Stacey, *Pauline View of Man*, 45-46; Jewett, *Paul's Anthropological Terms*, 63; Ridderbos, *Paul*, 22-27; Schnelle, *Apostle Paul*, 116; Frey, "Die paulinische Antithese," 47; Frey, "Impact of the Dead Sea Scrolls," 455n185; Dunn, *Beginning from Jerusalem*, 39-40; Yamauchi, *Pre-Christian Gnosticism*, 21.

22. Bousset, *Kyrios Christos*, 255.

23. Lake, *Earlier Epistles of St. Paul*; and Montefiore, *Judaism and St. Paul*; both cited in Stacey, *Pauline View of Man*, 46; Neill and Wright, *Interpretation of the New Testament*, 177-78.

antithesis in these terms, and this influence can be seen in the later work of Rudolf Bultmann as well.[24] However, the history-of-religions approach to Paul and the New Testament faltered upon the recognition that the alleged connections between mystery religions and the New Testament were doubtful, and that no evidence was forthcoming to support the existence of Gnosticism prior to the second century.[25]

Generally Jewish Understandings of Paul

From the time of Baur, most scholars outside of Germany had been opposed to the German critical scholarship attributing various kinds of Hellenistic backgrounds and meanings to Paul and his flesh-spirit antithesis. This was particularly true in Britain, where J. B. Lightfoot led the opposition, with B. F. Westcott and F. J. A. Hort, against Baur and his disciples.[26] In the early-to-middle twentieth century, Anglophone scholars like H. St. J. Thackeray,[27] H. W. Robinson,[28] H. A. A. Kennedy,[29] Ernest D. W. Burton,[30] J. Gresham Machen,[31] W. D. Davies,[32] John A. T. Robinson,[33] and W. David Stacey[34] continued to argue strongly for a Jewish conceptual background to Paul's thought, and that Hellenistic influence was incidental and insubstantial. Additional support for this view came in the form of Albert Schweitzer's survey and criticism of German Pauline scholarship from the time of Baur

24. Reitzenstein, *Die hellenistischen Mysterienreligionen*; cited in Ascough, "Historical Approaches," 157–58; Jewett, *Paul's Anthropological Terms*, 62–63; Stacey, *Pauline View of Man*, 43–44; Neill and Wright, *Interpretation of the New Testament*, 172–75; Frey, "Die paulinische Antithese," 47; Frey, "Impact of the Dead Sea Scrolls," 455n185; Ridderbos, *Paul*, 27–29; and Yamauchi, *Pre-Christian Gnosticism*, 22–26.

25. Hafemann, "Paul and His Interpreters," 668–69; Schnelle, *Apostle Paul*, 116; Baird, *From Jonathan Edwards to Rudolf Bultmann*, 241, 268–69; Yamauchi, *Pre-Christian Gnosticism*, 170–86, 243–49.

26. Hafemann, "Paul and His Interpreters," 668–69; Neill and Wright, *Interpretation of the New Testament*, 26–27, 34–40, 56–60; Baird, *From Jonathan Edwards to Rudolf Bultmann*, 71–73, 82–84; Dunn, *Beginning from Jerusalem*, 33–34.

27. Thackeray, *Relation of St. Paul*.

28. Robinson, *Christian Doctrine of Man*.

29. Kennedy, *St. Paul and the Mystery-Religions*.

30. Burton, *Spirit, Soul and Flesh*.

31. Machen, *Origin of Paul's Religion*.

32. Davies, *Paul and Rabbinic Judaism*; cited in Baird, *From C. H. Dodd to Hans Dieter Betz*, 293–96; Stacey, *Pauline View of Man*, 53; Jewett, *Paul's Anthropological Terms*, 78; Russell, *Flesh/Spirit Conflict*, 155.

33. Robinson, *Body*.

34. Stacey, *Pauline View of Man*.

onwards which had advocated a Hellenistic Paul. Schweitzer would argue for a thoroughly Jewish and eschatological Paul.[35]

Anthropological-Ethical Views of the Flesh-Spirit Conflict as an Internal Dualism

H. W. Robinson and Ernest D. W. Burton were influential early-twentieth-century representatives of a consensus of Anglophone scholarship on Pauline anthropology which remained relatively stable to the late twentieth century, and which even now remains one of the major interpretive positions.[36] Let us consider them jointly with W. David Stacey, a prominent mid-twentieth-century defender of this position.[37] They argue that Paul's view of the flesh and the flesh-spirit antithesis were Jewish and ultimately of Old Testament origin, as opposed to any major strand of Hellenistic thought. Paul's entire range of meaning for σάρξ is ultimately derivable from the OT meanings of בָּשָׂר. This even holds true for Paul's flesh-spirit antithesis, which these scholars interpreted according to an "ethical" sense of σάρξ. However, they also acknowledged that Paul's flesh-spirit antithesis is far more developed than what is found in the Old Testament, and the extreme to which Paul pressed this view of σάρξ demands some explanation sufficient to account for the degree of Paul's innovation.[38] Dunn rightly indicates that this is the crux. Is there such a possible explanation to account for the Pauline development of the flesh-spirit antithesis within the basic OT understanding of בָּשָׂר? Proponents of this view insist that there is, while those who find their proposals inadequate appeal to a more apocalyptic conception of the σάρξ as a hostile cosmic power as the necessary basis for understanding Paul's flesh-spirit antithesis, as we shall see below.[39]

Despite the general consensus among Robinson and his followers that there *is* a sufficient explanation to account for this development, there is a great diversity of opinion about *what* the proper explanation is, and consequently, the exact significance of the antithesis that results from the development. Robinson himself appealed to Paul's own intense personal experience of both the power of the flesh and of the Spirit as the impetus for his development of the flesh-spirit antithesis. The resulting understanding

---

35. Schweitzer, *Paul and His Interpreters*.
36. Jewett, *Paul's Anthropological Terms*, 77–80; Dunn, *Theology of Paul*, 66n68.
37. Jewett, *Paul's Anthropological Terms*, 78.
38. Robinson, *Christian Doctrine of Man*, 24–25, 104–5, 111–31; Burton, *Spirit, Soul and Flesh*, 186–98, 205–7; Stacey, *Pauline View of Man*, 50–51, 161–62.
39. Dunn, *Theology of Paul*, 66, and 66n68.

is of an internal moral conflict that is generated by sin taking advantage of the weakness of the flesh or the lower element of man's nature. Though this included man's physical impulses, the sins of the flesh were not restricted to sensual ones, but also included sinful attitudes and ways of thought as well, as can be seen from a careful examination of the "works of the flesh" in Galatians 5:19–21, as well as the reference to "the mind of the flesh" in Colossians 2:18. This contrasts with Hellenistic dualism, in that it is sin that is the ultimate spiritual enemy, as opposed to "the flesh" or the body, or materiality in general. If the Hellenistic conception of the intrinsic evil of the flesh or material body were attributed to Paul, passages like 2 Corinthians 7:1 would be rendered nonsensical, for it would be impossible to cleanse the flesh of all defilement if it were intrinsically corrupt. Nonetheless, though not intrinsically evil, the flesh is weak before the power of sin, and it is only the competing power of the indwelling Holy Spirit in the believer that gives the victory over sin. The key passages describing this internal moral conflict are Romans 7:14—8:11 and Galatians 5:16–26.[40] The view of Burton is nearly identical, though he sees in Galatians 5:16–26 an understanding of the flesh as a nonphysical, inherited impulse to evil, which, however, is not coercive but is resistable by the power of the Spirit.[41]

Stacey's conception of the Pauline flesh-spirit conflict is also similar, but with a few unique aspects that are worthy of note. Stacey acknowledges that what is distinctive to Paul's use of the flesh is the intensity of his flesh-spirit antithesis. However, he insists that the essential starting point for understanding Paul's antithesis is with the background OT conception. If one starts directly with Paul's antithetical passages, one is likely to misinterpret Paul in accordance with a kind of dualistic view in which the flesh is intrinsically evil. Stacey argues that those passages represent the furthest extension of the flesh concept that is rooted in the Old Testament.[42] With this basic point, we are in agreement. However, when Stacey proceeds to account for this development in Paul, he opens himself up to criticism. He argues that the persistence of sin suggests a principle of sin in each man, that is, a lower sinful nature. This came to be identified with the flesh, which became a synonym for the lower sinful nature. When Paul speaks of sin and the flesh as synonymous, as in Romans 7, he is speaking in an extreme way out of desperation, due to the anguish of his own personal struggle with sin. Stacey argues that we must take this as an exaggeration, not a sober account of

---

40. Robinson, *Christian Doctrine of Man*, 104–5, 111–18, 122–31; Stacey, *Pauline View of Man*, 50–51.

41. Burton, *Spirit, Soul and Flesh*, 191–98; Russell, *Flesh/Spirit Conflict*, 155; Stacey, *Pauline View of Man*, 52.

42. Stacey, *Pauline View of Man*, 191–92.

Paul's own view, otherwise a contradiction in Paul's thought is unavoidable.[43] However, this explanation itself seems desperate, and has been criticized by Barclay as evading the problem, and by Jewett as question-begging.[44] This criticism strikes us as entirely just; Stacey's explanation for the Pauline development of the flesh-spirit antithesis is inadequate.

Another explanation for this development was offered by W. D. Davies, who shared the view that Paul's concept of the flesh is entirely a Jewish development of the OT concept of בָּשָׂר. Davies sought to defend Paul from the argument of C. G. Montefiore that, as a Diaspora Jew, Paul's Judaism was thoroughly tainted with Hellenism, from which the Hellenistic mystery religions served as the inspiration for Paul's flesh-spirit antithesis. Davies rejected the argument that Palestinian Judaism was devoid of Hellenistic influence, and that Diaspora Judaism was Hellenized to the point of the nullification of what is recognizably Jewish. Davies argued that Palestine had long been subject to Greek influence, and therefore we could not speak in dichotomous terms of Palestinian vs. Hellenistic Judaism, but must speak in terms of relative degrees of interpenetration and mixture of Hellenistic and Jewish thought. Therefore Davies anticipated some of the conclusions of Martin Hengel.[45] We must acknowledge this state of affairs, and in speaking of a Jewish Paul as opposed to a Hellenistic one, we do not wish to suggest that these were hermetically sealed categories, but merely that the general distinction could be drawn to indicate that Paul's understanding owes more to the Old Testament and the Jewish heritage, rather than to Hellenistic sources like Plato, the mystery religions, or even Gnosticism.

Davies explained Paul's development of the flesh-spirit antithesis from its OT background by means of Paul's rabbinic training. In Davies's theory, Paul combined the OT view of the flesh and Spirit with the rabbinic ideas of the יֵצֶר הָרַע (*yēṣer hārā'*; the evil impulse) and the יֵצֶר הַטּוֹב (*yēṣer haṭṭôb*; the good impulse). In dismissing the alleged parallel from Hellenistic thought, Davies pointed out that Hellenistic dualism was never expressed in terms of σάρξ and πνεῦμα, yet these terms are prominent in

---

43. Stacey, *Pauline View of Man*, 163–65, 172–73.

44. Barclay, *Obeying the Truth*, 192n36; Jewett, *Paul's Anthropological Terms*, 78–80 (note that "question-begging" is not Jewett's term, but is my descriptive summary of Jewett's criticism).

45. Davies, *Paul and Rabbinic Judaism*, and Montefiore, *Judaism and St. Paul*; both cited in Stacey, *Pauline View of Man*, 53–54, 160–61; Neill and Wright, *Interpretation of the New Testament*, 316–17; Matlock, *Unveiling the Apocalyptic Paul*, 55n58; Barclay, *Obeying the Truth*, 184. See also Hengel, *Judaism and Hellenism*, 310–14; Koester, *History, Culture, and Religion*, 214–15. For a perspective advocating a blend of both Jewish and Hellenistic influence, but slightly more direct Hellenistic influence than Hengel allows, cf. Schnelle, *Apostle Paul*, 70–83, esp. 82n127.

the Old Testament.⁴⁶ However, Davies's own explanation of Paul's development of the Old Testament's בָּשָׂר to his σάρξ-πνεῦμα conflict by way of the יֵצֶר הָרָע is faced with an analogous counter-argument: Paul sticks with the basic "flesh"-"spirit" language of the Old Testament, rather than speaking in terms of an "evil inclination."⁴⁷ All we are left with is a formal parallel, without it being clearly established that Paul intended the same meaning or derived it from the יֵצֶר הָרָע.⁴⁸ Davies's own admission that the rabbis did not develop "the ethical connotation that *basar* had in the Old Testament"⁴⁹ would also seem to sever the link he has proposed from the OT concept through the rabbis to Paul.

Regardless of how the move from the Old Testament's בָּשָׂר to Paul's σάρξ-πνεῦμα conflict is explained, there is a broad consensus among many interpreters regarding the final result: Paul is describing an anthropological reality in which man's weakness, fallenness, and sinfulness results in opposition to the Spirit of God and a tendency towards sin and evil in various forms. There is some ambiguity whether the flesh is to be understood as referring to the man himself, i.e., what the man, considered as a whole, *is*, or whether it is referring to some faculty or aspect of the man, distinguishable from the man, that the man *has*, variously characterized as a sinful or evil impulse⁵⁰ or inclination, a sinful nature,⁵¹ or an unregenerate human nature. This results not only in differences *between* commentators but also inconsistency *within* the accounts of individual commentators, for example, the following explanation by George E. Ladd: "While Paul makes a sharp and absolute contrast between being 'in the flesh' (unregenerate) and being 'in the spirit' (regenerate), there remains in the believer a struggle between the flesh and spirit. If 'flesh' means unregenerate human nature, the believer still possesses this nature even though she or he has received the Spirit."⁵² This is at best lacking in conceptual clarity, and, in fact, seems to be a flagrant

---

46. Davies, *Paul and Rabbinic Judaism*, cited in Stacey, *Pauline View of Man*, 171; and Jewett, *Paul's Anthropological Terms*, 78. Others have also argued a similar point, such as Robinson, *Body*, 11–16.

47. However, it must be granted that there does not appear to be a strictly corresponding Koine term for the Hebrew יֵצֶר. In the LXX, the Hebrew term is rendered by a variety of phrases, e.g.: Gen 6:5, πᾶς τις διανοεῖται ἐν τῇ καρδίᾳ αὐτοῦ; 8:21, ἔγκειται ἡ διάνοια τοῦ ἀνθρώπου ἐπιμελῶς ἐπὶ τὰ πονηρά.

48. Note also the criticism of Jewett, *Paul's Anthropological Terms*, 78.

49. Davies, *Paul and Rabbinic Judaism*, 20; cited in Robinson, *Body*, 24n1.

50. E.g., Burton, *Spirit, Soul and Flesh*, 197, refers to the flesh as "an inherited impulse to evil." We have already seen Davies's explanation in terms of the יֵצֶר הָרָע.

51. E.g., the NIV (1984) translation of σάρξ as "sinful nature" throughout Rom 7–8 and Gal 5–6.

52. Ladd, *Theology of the New Testament*, 515.

contradiction in terms. In many cases there is an analogous ambiguity over whether the πνεῦμα in question is the Spirit (i.e., the Holy Spirit), or the spirit of a regenerated person.

Regardless of the particulars, advocates of this general view are in wide agreement that Paul is describing an internal battle within the person between the flesh and the Spirit (or spirit). Russell cites this as the predominant view and lists many advocates, including Ladd, Eduard Schweizer, Alexander Sand, David J. Lull, and Charles H. Cosgrove; and among the commentators on Galatians, C. K. Barrett, Heinrich Schlier, Pierre Bonnard, Franz Mussner, Hans Dieter Betz, F. F. Bruce, Gerhard Ebeling, Ronald Y. K. Fung, R. Alan Cole, Richard N. Longenecker, G. Walter Hansen, and Timothy George.[53] This view has also been very prevalent among laymen in the churches.

Rudolf Bultmann vs. Ernst Käsemann on the Flesh-Spirit Antithesis

At the same time that this strand of Anglophone scholarship was developing, an alternate stream of interpretation was evolving in European scholarship. In the aftermath of the breakup of the idealistic liberal theological approach to Paul and the flesh, Rudolf Bultmann proposed a gnostic background to Paul's thought that was in line with the history of religions school, a perspective also initially shared by Bultmann's student Ernst Käsemann. However, the significance of their respective views of Paul's background was eclipsed by the compelling power of their accounts of the meaning of Paul's flesh-spirit antithesis. Their debate over the meaning of the flesh continued to command scholarly attention long after the appeal of gnostic background theories had dimmed. In fact, their accounts of the Pauline theology of the flesh could easily be adapted to other background theories. Hence, Bultmann's theory won favor also among some who advocated a Jewish background for Paul, such as J. A. T. Robinson. In a similar way, Käsemann originally developed his account of Paul's flesh-concept with a background of gnostic influence, but subsequently nested the same

---

53. Schweizer, "σάρξ, σαρκικός, σάρκινος," 7:130–35; Sand, *Der Begriff "Fleisch" in den Paulinischen Hauptbriefen*, 165–218; Lull, *Spirit in Galatia*, 113–28; Cosgrove, *Cross and the Spirit*, 154–67; Barrett, *Freedom and Obligation*, 275; Schlier, *Der Brief an die Galater*, 279–312; Bonnard, *L'Epitre de Saint Paul aux Galates*, 108–17; Mussner, *Der Galaterbrief*, 364–96; Betz, *Galatians*, 271–95; Bruce, *Epistle to the Galatians*, 239–58; Ebeling, *Truth of the Gospel*, 247–61; Fung, *Epistle to the Galatians*, 243–78; Cole, *Letter of Paul to the Galatians*, 202–23; Longenecker, *Galatians*, 235–67; Hansen, *Galatians*, 162–82; and George, *Galatians*, 374–407; all cited in Russell, *Flesh/Spirit Conflict*, 5–6.

account in the background of Jewish apocalypticism.⁵⁴ Therefore, we shall for the most part set aside any further consideration of the history-of-religions background and focus on the accounts of Paul's flesh-Spirit antithesis given by Bultmann and Käsemann.

Rudolf Bultmann: The Antithesis as Anthropological-Existentialist-Individualist Choice of Life-Orientation

Bultmann's interpretation of Paul's anthropology was heavily colored by the existentialism of Heidegger such that his emphasis was heavily upon the individual, his self-conception, his relationship to himself, and to the possibilities that lay open to him in the present that may be determined by his decision.⁵⁵ According to Bultmann's Paul, a man's nature is not determined by his substance or qualities, but by the sphere in which he moves, which "marks out the horizon or the possibilities of what he does and experiences."⁵⁶ The two possible spheres which man must choose are "in the flesh" or "in the Spirit." Human beings as subjects are uniquely capable of acting with respect to themselves as objects, which makes them responsible for themselves because they have the power of decision. They can choose to come under the mastery of one sphere or another. Bultmann denied the existence of an anthropological dualism behind Paul's flesh-spirit antithesis, but posited instead a dualism of decision—choosing a "spurious life" in the sphere of the flesh, or an authentic life as a gift from God in the sphere of the Spirit.⁵⁷

---

54. Jewett, *Paul's Anthropological Terms*, 64–72; Barclay, *Obeying the Truth*, 192–202; Baird, *From Jonathan Edwards to Rudolf Bultmann*, 106–16, 131–32, 138–40; Frey, "Impact of the Dead Sea Scrolls," 455n185; Frey, "Die paulinische Antithese," 47; Robinson, *Body*, 24–26.

55. Barclay, *Obeying the Truth*, 194–98; Neill and Wright, *Interpretation of the New Testament*, 244–46, Baird, *From C. H. Dodd to Hans Dieter Betz*, 86–92, 96–97. Note, however, that this characterization of the vector of ideas has been challenged by Johnson, *Origins of Demythologizing*, who has argued that the Neo-Kantianism prevalent at Marburg, and the theology of his mentor Wilhelm Hermann was more influential; or, alternatively, that the interchange of ideas between Bultmann and his friend Heidegger was more reciprocal than it is typically characterized; cited by Congdon, "Eschatologizing Apocalyptic," 134n44. We are actually indifferent to the question; our concern, ultimately, is *what* is, or, *whether* there is, any connection at all between these ideas and Paul's thought.

56. Bultmann, *Theology of the New Testament*, 1:235.

57. Bultmann, *Theology of the New Testament*, 1:236; Matlock, *Obeying the Truth*, 101–2, 188; Barclay, *Obeying the Truth*, 192–93; Russell, *Flesh/Spirit Conflict*, 5, 154.

Bultmann defined the range of meaning for σάρξ to include "man's material corporeality," his "weakness and transitoriness," and asserted that "all that is 'outward' and 'visible,' all that has its nature in external 'appearance' belongs to the sphere of 'flesh.'" Thus, "flesh" could be taken as synonymous with "world" (κόσμος, *kosmos*) which "denotes the world of created things which is the stage and the life-condition for 'natural' life."[58] To live in this "world," or to live *in the flesh* (ἐν σαρκί, *en sarki*), is to live in the natural earthly sphere, which in and of itself is not sinful. However, when one takes the stage of living ἐν σαρκί as a norm, it becomes living *according to the flesh* (κατὰ σάρκα, *kata sarka*), which is sin, for it entails turning from the Creator to the creation, trusting in himself to procure life for himself in his own strength apart from the Creator, rather than receiving it from the Creator as a gift.[59]

Having defined life κατὰ σάρκα in this manner, Bultmann could apply this description to a life both of sensual vice and lawlessness, stereotypical of gentiles, as well as to Jewish attempts to establish their own righteousness through keeping the Torah and thus boasting in their own flesh. The ability of Bultmann's characterization of life according to the flesh to describe both of these tendencies corresponded with what Paul wrote in Galatians and other key σάρξ passages (Gal 3:3; 5:19-21; Phil 3:3-9; Rom 8:3-9; 13:14).[60] This characterization also sounded rather Augustinian and Lutheran. Accordingly, it was adopted by many theologians and commentators.[61]

Two final aspects of Bultmann's interpretation must be considered: (1) his view of Paul's eschatology and apocalyptic framework, and (2) his view of demythologization. Paul presented his doctrine of redemption in the language of traditional Jewish and Christian teaching about eschatology and the apocalyptic expectation of the last judgment which will end the old world, or age, of sin and begin the new one of salvation and life. However, Bultmann argued that these are mythical traditions which must be demythologized to get at the existential heart of Paul's doctrine. Accordingly, responding to the proclamation of the Christ event in faith puts the individual between the times, simultaneously living in the old and the new age. Thus, the cross is not an apocalyptic event which changes the cosmos

---

58. Bultmann, *Theology of the New Testament*, 1:233-35 (quotes from 235).

59. Bultmann, *Theology of the New Testament*, 1:232-39; Barclay, *Obeying the Truth*, 192-3; Stacey, *Pauline View of Man*, 164-65.

60. Bultmann, *Theology of the New Testament*, 1:239-43; Barclay, *Obeying the Truth*, 193-4.

61. Barclay, *Obeying the Truth*, 195n40, 196, cites J. A. T. Robinson, Alexander Sand, Eduard Schweizer, W. G. Kümmel, Anthony T. Thiselton, Pierre Bonnard, Heinrich Schlier, Franz Mussner, and Robert Jewett as examples.

itself, but brings about the "turn of the ages in the life of the individual," as Käsemann characterized Bultmann's position.[62] Another implication of Bultmann's demythologization is that Paul's references to the flesh and Spirit as external spheres of power, between which a man may choose one to master him, are mythical as well, and once correctly interpreted, what remains is the individual person with the power of choice within him. Man "bears the sole responsibility for his own feeling, thinking, and willing . . . He is not, as the New Testament regards him, the victim of a strange dichotomy which exposes him to the interference of powers outside himself."[63] This is a position that Käsemann would reject.

Ernst Käsemann: The Antithesis as Opposed Cosmological Apocalyptic Corporate Power Spheres

Käsemann, taking up Schweitzer's insistence on the centrality of Pauline eschatology,[64] refused to subordinate or demythologize what he considered to be Paul's eschatological and cosmological emphases to his anthropology. W. G. Kümmel had already attempted to develop a coherent description of the flesh as both a cosmic power and an anthropological corporeal reality grounded in the old aeon.[65] Initially, when Käsemann had perceived gnostic theology as influential to Paul's thought, he described Paul's conception of flesh as both a cosmic power and an anthropological reality, and referred to it as something like a gnostic aeon. Käsemann had reasoned that the phrase ἐν σαρκί could not have been derived from the Old Testament, for the OT assumes that man *is* flesh. Neither could this notion have come from Hellenistic thought, which held that man *has* flesh. To make sense of being "in the flesh," then, Käsemann argued that the flesh and Spirit were cosmological realities, cosmic spheres of power that determined man's existence. Subsequently, Käsemann grounded these conceptions in Jewish apocalyptic theology rather than gnostic thinking, but the basic content remained the same. God was involved in a cosmic conflict over the ownership of the world, and humanity is caught up in that conflict. Redemption is not just

---

62. Käsemann, *New Testament Questions of Today*, 13–14, cited in Matlock, *Unveiling the Apocalyptic Paul*, 188. See also Boer, "Paul's Mythologizing Program in Romans 5–8," 3–5; Matlock, *Unveiling the Apocalyptic Paul*, 102–3.

63. Bultmann, "New Testament and Mythology," 6; see also Dunson, "Individual and Community in Paul's Letter to the Romans," 24–25.

64. Matlock, *Unveiling the Apocalyptic Paul*, 47–53, esp. 52n52.

65. Kümmel, *Römer 7 und die Bekehrung des Paulus*; Kümmel, *Das Bild des Menschen im neuen Testament*; cited in Jewett, *Paul's Anthropological Terms*, 69–70.

about the individual. Käsemann thus criticized Bultmann's anthropological over-emphasis and the individualism of his interpretation.[66]

Käsemann sets Paul's anthropology in the context of Christ's apocalyptic seizure of power as the "Cosmocrator," or world ruler. Accordingly, he denied that the term "body" supported an individualistic interpretation.[67] Rather, he asserted that the essential thing is that "this individual be regarded as the concrete piece of worldly reality that I myself am."[68] In submitting to Christ, a believer turns over to him that "piece of the world" which he is, and thus participates in the cosmic warfare for Christ's lordship of the world, and ultimately, God's triumph in becoming all in all (1 Cor 15:28). He also commits himself to being integrated into "the Spirit," conceived of as that heavenly sphere which will determine his existence. The Spirit is in opposition to the sphere of the flesh, which determines man in his rebellion, and thus implies both worldliness, and ultimately the demonic. Thus, the terms "flesh" and "spirit" speak of corporate and cosmic realities.[69] As Matlock explains,

> Against Bultmann's emphasis on the continuity and identity of an individual self, Käsemann sees in Paul's anthropology discontinuity in a corporate self defined by its spheres of influence, a discontinuity both in terms of the self within the course of its own life and in terms of the breaks in the course of salvation history. For Paul a human being is radically embodied and radically bound up in structures of solidarity—under the lordship of sin, flesh, law, the "powers," or the lordship of Christ—not free and free-floating.[70]

Käsemann offered an explanation for the way Paul uses "flesh" both as an anthropological reality and as a cosmic power that opposes the Spirit. Furthermore, since the apocalyptic war for Christ's lordship has not yet been won, it makes sense that the flesh remains a continuing threat and

---

66. Ernst Käsemann, "On Paul's Anthropology," 7, 10–14, 19–29; Jewett, *Paul's Anthropological Terms*, 70–72; Barclay, *Obeying the Truth*, 199–200; Matlock, *Unveiling the Apocalyptic Paul*, 188; Boer, "Paul's Mythologizing Program in Romans 5–8," 5–6; Neill and Wright, *Interpretation of the New Testament*, 418–20; Baird, *From C. H. Dodd to Hans Dieter Betz*, 131–33, 138–40, 144.

67. Käsemann, "On Paul's Anthropology," 20–23; Matlock, *Unveiling the Apocalyptic Paul*, 190.

68. Käsemann, *New Testament Questions of Today*, 60, cited in Barclay, *Obeying the Truth*, 200.

69. Barclay, *Obeying the Truth*, 200–201; Matlock, *Unveiling the Apocalyptic Paul*, 188–90; Boer, "Paul's Mythologizing Program in Romans 5–8," 6n21.

70. Matlock, *Unveiling the Apocalyptic Paul*, 211.

temptation that must be resisted by the believer as he fights the ongoing eschatological conflict by his daily obedience of walking in the Spirit (Gal 5:16–26). Another element of the quote above is the discontinuity and the "breaks" in salvation history. Käsemann was vigorously opposed to the notion of salvation history, and viewed it as incompatible with an apocalyptic theology of the cross centered on the cosmic lordship of Christ, in which the two aeons are no longer conceived of as successive but simultaneously existing in a dialectical relationship.[71]

This apocalyptic reading of Paul has been influential and has continued to be developed by Käsemann's theological descendants, such as Peter Stuhlmacher, J. Christiaan Beker, and especially J. Louis Martyn.[72] Other scholars like John M. G. Barclay advocate a more moderate blend of the apocalyptic framework and its cosmic aspects with the anthropological realities evident in passages like Galatians 5:16–26.[73]

It is significant to underscore here three aspects of Käsemann's understanding of the flesh. First, Käsemann sees a twofold conception of σάρξ at work in Paul: as an anthropological reality and as a cosmic power. Second, Käsemann affirms the continuing threat that the σάρξ poses in the life of a Christian, and attributes this to the persistent opposition of the flesh as a cosmic power against the Spirit. Third, we note Käsemann's opposition to the salvation-historical approach. We believe that Käsemann is correct that Paul employs a twofold conception of σάρξ, one of which is an anthropological reality, and that in one sense the flesh does pose a continuing threat in the life of the believer. However, we will later argue that the secondary aspect of the σάρξ is to be understood, not as an apocalyptic cosmic power, but as a salvation-historical reality. We will further argue that it is the anthropological sense of σάρξ which is a continuing threat; σάρξ as a salvation-historical reality speaks of a discontinuity with the Spirit, conceived of in temporal or horizontal terms, not a static reality of antagonism between two spheres, coexisting temporally in spatial opposition. It is this meaning that is typically in view when Paul contrasts being ἐν σαρκί with being ἐν πνεύματι (*en pneumati*).

---

71. Käsemann, "On Paul's Anthropology," 20–23; Barclay, *Obeying the Truth*, 200–201; Käsemann, *New Testament Questions of Today*, 18, 46, 50–51, 65–68, 71–76, cited in Matlock, *Unveiling the Apocalyptic Paul*, 213–18, 226.

72. Stuhlmacher, *Gerechtigkeit Gottes bei Paulus*; cited in Hafemann, "Paul and His Interpreters," 676–77; Beker, *Paul's Apocalyptic Gospel*; Martyn, *Galatians*; Martyn, *Theological Issues in the Letters of Paul*.

73. Barclay, *Obeying the Truth*, 202–15.

Paul and Qumran

The publication of the Dead Sea Scrolls beginning in the 1950s renewed efforts to find the historical and conceptual background to Paul's flesh-spirit antithesis in the hopes that the discoveries at Qumran would hold the key. In that decade, a series of scholars attempted to make that case. Karl George Kuhn, Sherman Johnson, Siegfried Schulz, David Flusser, and Otto Betz argued for strong and direct parallels between בָּשָׂר in the Qumran literature and Paul's flesh-Spirit antithesis. These arguments were rebutted by Friedrich Noetscher, H. Huppenbauer, W. D. Davies, and R. Meyer. Reviewing the discussion, Jewett argued that these rebuttals were inconclusive, and insisted that some parallel or relationship must obtain between Paul and the Qumran view of the flesh.[74] However, Barclay rightly advocated caution and sensitivity in handling superficial parallels, lest we overlook more significant differences in theology between these sources.[75]

More recently, Jörg Frey has argued against the view of Egon Brandenburger that the dualistic Hellenistic Jewish wisdom literature of Philo and the Wisdom of Solomon contained uses of *flesh* and *spirit* comparable to Paul's. Frey and others have noted that the theology of flesh and Spirit in these writings is very different from Paul's. Instead, Frey has argued that some of the nonsectarian wisdom texts in the Qumran collection have more promising parallels, and indicate that the roots of Paul's negative use of σάρξ are to be found in Palestinian Jewish wisdom traditions which Paul may have studied in the course of his education as a Pharisee.[76] We would argue that this parallel is not all that surprising, because it most likely represents parallel development of a common, inherited OT theme. We reject the suggestion that Paul's heightened "flesh" language is as qualitatively different from that in the Old Testament as it has often been presented. It differs by degree, of course, and that difference requires some explanation, but we do not believe it differs in kind. We will argue that Paul's view of

---

74. Kuhn, "New Light on Temptation," 94–113; Sherman Johnson, "Paul and the Manual of Discipline," *HTR* 48 (1955) 157–65; Schulz, "Zur Rechtfertigung aus Gnaden in Qumran," 155–85; Flusser, "Dead Sea Sect and Pre-Pauline Christianity," 215–66; Betz, *Offenbarung und Schriftforschung in der Qumransekte*; Noetscher, *Zur theologischen Terminologie der Qumran-Texte*; Huppenbauer, "Fleisch in den Texten von Qumran," 298–300; Davies, "Paul and the Dead Sea Scrolls," 157–82; and Meyer, "Fleisch im Judentum," 109–18; all cited in Jewett, *Paul's Anthropological Terms*, 82–88.

75. Barclay, *Obeying the Truth*, 187–89.

76. Brandenburger, *Fleisch und Geist*; cited in Frey, "Impact of the Dead Sea Scrolls," 451–58; Frey, "Die paulinische Antithese," 45–48; Frey, "Notion of 'Flesh' in 4QInstruction," 197–200; see also Jewett, *Paul's Anthropological Terms*, 88–93; Barclay, *Obeying the Truth*, 184–87; Goff, *Worldly and Heavenly Wisdom of 4QInstruction*, 19.

the flesh can be explained by a stable Jewish anthropology that meets with a second factor, the salvation-historical changes wrought by the work of Christ and the Spirit.

Herman Ridderbos, Walter B. Russell, and the Redemptive-Historical Approach

Finally, we have alluded to the salvation-historical approach a number of times. Hermann Ridderbos and Walter B. Russell have argued that the σάρξ-πνεῦμα antithesis is a redemptive-historical or salvation-historical contrast between two conflicting eras or modes of existence characterized by two different mind-sets. The old aeon was that of the flesh, characterized by creaturely weakness, but Christ has initiated the new creation, in which the mark of the people of God is the Spirit and his power. Therefore, the σάρξ-πνεῦμα antithesis is not an internal conflict within believers but an external one between an old mode of existence that passed away in virtue of the new way Christ inaugurated. However, some people—e.g., the Judaizers—retain the mindset of the flesh even though Christ has come, which results in an external conflict between them and those whose mindset is after the Spirit. This external conflict is Paul's actual topic of discussion in Romans 8:1–11 and Galatians 5:16–26 and similar passages, rather than an intra-individual dualism of natures, impulses, or decisions of life orientation.[77]

We have already shown our hand to reveal our conclusion that salvation-historical considerations are highly relevant to correctly understanding the σάρξ-πνεῦμα antithesis. It is interesting to consider how this stance may or may not be compatible with other approaches. On the one hand, Russell denies that (or at least greatly diminishes the idea that) the flesh can be predicated of Christians now in an anthropological sense in a way that is ethically relevant to the individual believer already settled in a community that has left behind Torah observance in favor of reliance on the Spirit. This can be noted in the way Russell acknowledges that there continues to be a struggle in the Christian life, but it is a struggle against the effects of the "former condition" of being "in the flesh."[78] However, it remains an open question for us whether an adequate appreciation for Paul's redemptive-historical argumentation forces us to deny the anthropological sense to the extent that Russell does. Furthermore, we doubt that an appreciation for the ethical-anthropological aspects of the flesh in Galatians 5 necessitates that we understand it in a

---

77. Ridderbos, *Paul*, 65–68, 93–105; Russell, *Flesh/Spirit Conflict*, 1–11; Russell, "Apostle Paul's View of the 'Sin Nature' / 'New Nature' Struggle."

78. Russell, "Apostle Paul's Redemptive-Historical Argumentation," 356–57.

problematic "two natures" manner. If our suspicions are correct, then it may be the case that Russell is more "doggedly consistent"[79] than Paul himself is on the use of σάρξ in the passage, if we understand such consistency to mean a strictly univocal use of the term.[80]

On the other hand, we have seen above that Ridderbos and Russell freely use terms associated with the apocalyptic interpretation of Paul such as those put forward by Käsemann and Martyn. Thus Russell adopts Martyn's apocalyptic view that the cross delivers us from the present evil aeon (Gal 1:4), which is equated with the cosmos that is crucified (Gal 6:14–15) and establishes the new creation in its place. In this event, the old cosmos with its various antithetical fundamental structures (e.g., circumcision/uncircumcision; flesh/Spirit) dies. The flesh is equated with the old aeon, and the Spirit with the new.[81] Though not drawing on Martyn in the explicit way Russell does, Ridderbos argues something very similar about the aeons and the new creation.[82] It seems that both Ridderbos and Russell consider their salvation-historical interpretation to be a milder variant of the apocalyptic approach of Martyn or Käsemann. This same tendency to conflate the salvation-historical and apocalyptic to some degree can also be seen in those like Douglas Moo and Thomas Schreiner, who blend redemptive-historical and anthropological-ethical aspects of the σάρξ.[83] However, those of the apocalyptic school of Käsemann, Martyn, and their successors are vigorously opposed to the salvation-historical approach and view it antithetically to their own.[84] The fact that the apocalyptic interpreters could take such opposition to the salvation-historical approach suggests strongly that there is nothing intrinsically apocalyptic about this approach. Salvation-historical considerations may be divorced from apocalyptic interpretations of Paul and considered in isolation. Below we will explore a decidedly non-apocalyptic approach to the salvation-historical aspects of the σάρξ-πνεῦμα antithesis.

---

79. Russell, *Flesh/Spirit Conflict*, 225.

80. See also Silva, *Explorations in Exegetical Method*, 183; Schreiner, *Galatians*, 184n32.

81. Russell, *Flesh/Spirit Conflict*, 21, 122–23; citing Martyn, "Apocalyptic Antinomies."

82. Ridderbos, *Paul*, 91–93.

83. Moo, *Galatians*, 31–32; Schreiner, *Galatians*, 76–78, 350–52, 378–80.

84. We have already seen this above with respect to Käsemann. For Martyn, see Martyn, *Galatians*, 343–49; Harink, "Partakers of the Divine Apocalypse," 85–88; Moo, *Galatians*, 31–32.

A Summary of the Argument of the Thesis

In chapter 2, we shall analyze the spectrum of meanings exhibited by the Old Testament "flesh" terms, primarily בָּשָׂר and σάρξ. We shall do so by arranging them into ten categories of usage that begin with the most literal and prosaic and proceed to meanings of increasing theological significance. We shall also note when these uses are carried over into the NT without modification. We shall see that "flesh" is one of the most profound anthropological terms of the Old Testament, capturing in one succinct term man's mortal and moral weakness. This anthropological meaning of "flesh" was set from the time of its first usage in Genesis 6:3, and we shall closely examine this passage in its context to see how the writer establishes this weighty anthropological significance of "flesh."

In chapter 3, we examine two of Paul's innovative uses of σάρξ, both employing the construction κατὰ σάρκα. The first has to do with κατὰ σάρκα relationships, similar to a morally neutral meaning of "flesh" first examined in the OT context in chapter 2. However, even though relationships described as κατὰ σάρκα are also morally neutral, there is always present a contrast with a greater kind of relationship. At times the contrast is explicit, but it is always at least implied. The second use we will examine has to do with κατὰ σάρκα identity and values. Paul stresses in Rom 2:25–29 that the identity conditions of God's people are not determined according to the flesh, but on another basis entirely. Furthermore, Paul stresses in 1–2 Corinthians that God's people are not to live by a "sarkic" value system, according to which "wisdom" they falsely evaluate Christ's messengers, just as they once falsely regarded Christ.

In chapter 4 we begin our analysis of Paul's σάρξ-πνεῦμα antithesis, which will occupy our attention for the remainder of the thesis. The meaning of this antithesis is greatly debated. In this chapter we will clarify four theoretical issues that complicate the matter and affect our understanding of this antithesis: (1) The issue of mirror-reading Paul's letter to the Galatians, and the need and the propriety of appealing to the epistle to the Romans for clarification of the theological issues Paul raises in Galatians; (2) lexical ambiguities of the word σάρξ, in that it can mean drastically different things according to context, which leads to apparently contradictory statements by Paul, a circumstance which is not always clarified by a simple appeal to the lexicons; (3) what is Paul's theological framework for the σάρξ-πνεῦμα antithesis: anthropological, salvation-historical, or both? This is the fundamental issue, and we will argue that *both* theological frameworks are necessary to account for everything Paul says about the σάρξ-πνεῦμα antithesis; (4) what understanding of the relationship between the individual and community underlies Pauline and NT theology in general, and the σάρξ-πνεῦμα antithesis texts in particular?

In chapter 5, we examine carefully the references to the flesh in Romans 6–8, taking careful note of the temporal indicators and contrasts, which establish that Paul clearly does employ a salvation-historical sense of σάρξ. Jewish believers were "in the flesh" and "under the Law" prior to the work of Christ, a circumstance of slavery and futility with regard to sin. Now, all believers are in the Spirit and not under the Law, and so are not enslaved to sin, but to God and righteousness. In a brief excursus we critique N. T. Wright's contrary exegesis of Romans 7–8, in which the Law is still operative for God's covenant people, but now redeemed from sin and death and enabled by Christ's work to fulfill the purpose for which it was intended: to give life. Having established that God's people are no longer "in the flesh" in a salvation-historical sense, we will then argue that, nonetheless, they are clearly still "flesh" in an anthropological sense. Then we will clarify how Paul still predicates σάρξ to God's new covenant people in a somatic and ethical sense. We conclude with a description of a tripartite salvation-historical schema that can be seen in Paul, in which the two comings of Christ separate three temporal periods in which any two adjacent periods may be contrasted with one another in the way σάρξ may or may not be predicated of God's people.

The tripartite salvation-historical schema uncovered in chapter 5 leads naturally into the question of the relationship of the flesh-Spirit antithesis to Paul's eschatology. Thus in chapter 6 we examine the question of whether the flesh-Spirit antithesis is to be identified with the "old age"-"new age" antithesis. This leads us to the related questions of whether we should conceive of our current Christian existence as the "overlap of the ages," and how Paul's concept of "new creation" in 2 Corinthians 5:17 and Galatians 6:15 is to be understood and related to these topoi.

In chapter 7 we shall provide the context for our major σάρξ-πνεῦμα passage of Galatians 5:13–26 by surveying the epistle as a whole. This will require us to sort out some thorny controversial issues regarding the purpose of the epistle, the threat to the gospel from the Judaizers' non-gospel, including the danger of apostasy for the Galatians. This will also require us to clarify the meaning of justification in Galatians. We will also trace the flow of Paul's argument in the epistle, and see how Paul introduces the σάρξ-πνεῦμα antithesis in 3:2–3 and develops it by relating it to a set of parallel antitheses that deepen the contrast. We will conclude with a summary of this nexus of antitheses within which the flesh-Spirit antithesis is embedded.

In chapter 8 we shall exegete Galatians 5:13–26 to surface the meaning of Paul's σάρξ-πνεῦμα antithesis in the climactic passage of the epistle.

In doing so we will see that the passage has both a deliberative function as a part of Paul's argument against submission to Torah, and also an ethical function in which Paul exhorts the Galatian believers in the proper way to live out their freedom in Christ by walking by the Spirit. Here we shall argue that most occurrences of σάρξ in this passage have an anthropological meaning that is still applicable to Christians (qua human beings) prior to the parousia, and therefore is a fitting subject of Paul's ethical warning to the Galatians. One exceptional instance of σάρξ is in 5:24, which we shall argue is properly understood in terms of an old identity that is definitively ended at conversion, synonymous to our "old man" in Rom 6:6, and in antithesis to a "new creation" (Gal 6:15; see also 2 Cor 5:17). Finally, we shall conclude the chapter with a more thorough description of what Paul means by "walking by the Spirit," and how that translates into a practical program of Christian discipleship, transformation, and loving service in the church.

— 2 —

The Old Testament Background to the Theme of "Flesh"

A long history of the concept of the "flesh," expressed in various terms in different languages in the cultural milieu of the Mediterranean world, preceded Paul's writing. Before turning to Paul's works, we will survey the use of "flesh": בָּשָׂר in the Hebrew Bible (HB) or Old Testament, which is rendered as σάρξ and κρέας (*kreas*) in the Septuagint (LXX), the same two terms employed in the New Testament. While we are primarily interested in Paul's distinctive antithetical use of σάρξ in this study, the term's OT antecedents and interrelationship with the other two terms בָּשָׂר and κρέας require us to survey the use of all three words in order to understand the way the concept of "flesh" was employed in Jewish Scripture prior to Paul, as well as the Christian literary tradition that was roughly contemporaneous with Paul. From this vantage point we will then be ready to analyze how Paul draws on Old Testament usage and develops the theme in his own way.

The terms בָּשָׂר, σάρξ, and κρέας may be grouped into ten semantic domains[1] which cover the use of "flesh" in the Old Testament. Let us begin by first examining the most literal meaning, and then move progressively by extension to the more figurative meanings with increasingly theological implications.[2] Many of these meanings are also carried on into Hellenistic and Greco-Roman times, as their usage in the LXX implies. Examples from later texts and the New Testament will also be included here when they have

---

1. A semantic domain or field, as defined by Johnson, *Expository Hermeneutics*, 310: "A definable area of cultural experience (1) covered by a set of related words, or (2) by one word with a range of different uses; the defining features of the field are represented by the diagnostic implications shared in common by the set of words, or the defining features of the field of one word are represented by the sum of the compatible implications."

2. Another Hebrew term for flesh is שְׁאֵר (*šĕ'ēr*), which shall only receive passing attention due to its relative infrequency and its extensive semantic overlap with בָּשָׂר. See BDB, s.v. שְׁאֵר; *HALOT*, s.v. שְׁאֵר.

the same meaning; these examples may even be drawn from Paul when dealing with more prosaic meanings of σάρξ. Innovative uses of "flesh" that appear and develop in the New Testament will be analyzed in subsequent chapters. As we reach the end of this survey, we shall encounter the most theologically rich uses of "flesh" that are used to describe man over against God. At that point, we shall engage in a careful examination of the initial use of "flesh" in this sense in Genesis 6.

Seven Old Testament Meanings of "Flesh" (בָּשָׂר, Σάρξ, and Κρέας): From Flesh to Family

We shall now examine the first seven categories of usage of "flesh," which are fairly straightforward. However, at times there may be some overlap at the boundaries of these categories, and some instances could conceivably fit under more than one category for that reason. This may also occur because of some ambiguity regarding the author's intended meaning in the passage in which the word occurs, or if the author uses a literalistic image in a metaphorical way.

(Meaning 1) "Flesh" as a Reference to Literal Flesh

Both בָּשָׂר and σάρξ refer most literally to the actual flesh of living things, both man and beast. That is, they refer collectively to the muscle, fat, and skin which covers the bones. They can also specify the skin alone, in effect functioning as a synonym for עוֹר (ʿôr), "skin." Both can also refer specifically to the muscle or fat, distinct from the skin. The terms בָּשָׂר and σάρξ can also refer to the flesh of human beings or different kinds of animals, whether alive or dead. An interesting usage of these terms often appears in the OT when the "flesh" is depicted as something consumable.[3]

In their most basic usage, בָּשָׂר and σάρξ refer in general to the soft parts of the body, the muscle, fat, and skin, which covers the bones, without any distinction among these elements. The very first use of בָּשָׂר in the Bible is an example: "So the LORD God caused a deep sleep to fall upon the man,

---

3. With reference to בָּשָׂר, see s.v. בָּשָׂר, in BDB, definition 1; in *HALOT*, definitions 1–2; in Chisholm, "Flesh," 777; Seebass, "Flesh," 672. With reference to σάρξ, see s.v. σάρξ, in BDAG, definition 1; in Friberg et al., *Analytical Lexicon*, definition 1; in LN, 102; in Gingrich, *Shorter Lexicon*, definition 1; R. J. Erickson, "Flesh," 303–6; D. H. Johnson, "Flesh," 374–75; Seebass, "Flesh," 674–75. For discussion of this category of meaning for both בָּשָׂר and σάρξ, see Ryken et al., *Dictionary of Biblical Imagery*, s.v. "Body," 105–6; Thiselton, "Flesh," 679–80.

and while he slept took one of his ribs and closed up its place with flesh" (Gen 2:21, ESV). The LXX here translates בָּשָׂר as σάρξ. Another example of the literal usage of "flesh" is Daniel 1:15 (in the MT and Theodotian's Greek translation; the Old Greek omits the reference to "flesh"): "At the end of ten days it was seen that they were better in appearance and fatter in flesh than all the youths who ate the king's food" (Dan 1:15, ESV).

As we would expect of this most basic significance of "flesh," the usage of σάρξ with this meaning is also attested in the noncanonical Hellenistic Jewish literature of the Second Temple period, and in the New Testament. In Sirach 19:12 (RSV), we read the proverb, "Like an arrow stuck in the flesh of the thigh, so is a word inside a fool." The "ungodly" Antiochus Epiphanes is described in 2 Maccabees 9:9 (RSV) such that his body is "swarmed with worms," and while living in pain "his flesh rotted away." The book of 4 Maccabees depicts, in gruesome detail, the torture and martyrdom of Eleazar and seven brothers for their commitment to the Jewish religion. There are many references to "flesh" in a literal sense as skin, muscle, and fat, usually in the process of being torn, burned, or violently separated from the body. See, for example, 4 Macc 6:6; 9:17, 20; 10:8; and 15:15. In Psalms of Solomon 4:19, the author invokes a curse: "May the flesh of man-pleasers be scattered by wild animals, and the bones of lawbreakers dishonored under the sun" (my translation). In the New Testament, the literal use of σάρξ is seen in Luke 24:39 (ESV): "See my hands and my feet, that it is I myself. Touch me, and see. For a spirit does not have flesh and bones as you see that I have."

בָּשָׂר and σάρξ can be used to describe not only the flesh of human beings, but also of animals.[4] In Genesis 41:2-4, 8, and 19, Pharaoh's visionary dream is described in which he saw seven cows who were "fat of flesh," or "choice of flesh" as it is rendered in the LXX. These were then eaten by seven cows who were "thin of flesh." In Job 41:23 (MT and LXX, 41:15), the folds of Leviathan's flesh stick together. In the New Testament, Paul speaks of the different kinds of flesh possessed by men, beasts, birds, and fish in 1 Corinthians 15:39.

בָּשָׂר and σάρξ can also be used to refer to the skin alone, distinct from the muscle and fat,[5] in effect functioning in these instances as synonyms for, respectively, עוֹר and χρώς (krōs) or δέρμα (derma), "skin" (although δέρμα more frequently refers to the hide of a skinned animal, that may have been tanned and turned into leather[6]). In Genesis 17:11, 14, 24-25, there are

---

4. Wolff, *Anthropology of the Old Testament*, 26, notes that 104 out of 273 occurrences of בָּשָׂר relate to animals.

5. Wolff, *Anthropology of the Old Testament*, 27, explores some of the finer distinctions that can be made between the physical constituents of the flesh.

6. Although BDAG, 3d ed., defines δέρμα merely as "hide," i.e., the skin of an animal

several references to circumcising "the flesh of your foreskin" (בְּשַׂר עָרְלַתְכֶם; bĕśar ʿorlatkem; Gk. τὴν σάρκα τῆς ἀκροβυστίας ὑμῶν, tēn sarka tēs akrobustias humōn). In both the Hebrew and Greek, the words for flesh are part of a pleonastic construction in which "of the foreskin" specifies "the flesh" by apposition.[7] In Leviticus 13:10, the terms בְּשַׂר חַי (bāśār ḥay) and σάρξ ζῶσα (sarx zōsa) are used to refer to "raw flesh" in a swollen, sore area on the skin. The MT continues to use בְּשַׂר חַי with this meaning in the MT of Leviticus 13:14–16, and 18, while the LXX switches to use the phrase χρώς ζῶν (chrōs zōn), "raw skin" (or its contradictory phrase χρώς ὑγιής (chrōs hugiēs), "healthy skin"). In Exodus 4:7, בָּשָׂר and σάρξ refer to Moses' healthy skin, to which the restored skin of his hand is compared. In 2 Kings 5:10 and 14, the terms refer to the skin of Naaman, both "leprous" and healthy. In Leviticus 21:5, the terms are used in a command forbidding the priests from making any cuts in their skin. Similar usage is seen in the poetic literature of the OT. In Job 4:15 (MT), the hair of Eliphaz's skin stood up, implying "goose bumps"; in the LXX version, Eliphaz's skin and hair quivered. In Psalm 102:5 (MT 102:6; LXX 101:6), as a result of the psalmist's suffering, his bone clings to his flesh. Taken absolutely literally, of course, this would suggest that "flesh" should not be understood as "skin." However, it seems unlikely that the author intends to say that his bone clings to his muscle, for that is the normal state of things. Furthermore, in verse 4, the psalmist says his heart has "withered," and that he has forgotten to eat his bread. Accordingly, the NIV rendering of verse 5 seems apt: "I am reduced to skin and bones."[8]

The use of σάρξ to refer specifically to the skin is also seen in the Second Temple literature and the NT. Sirach 38:28 speaks of a smith working the iron at the anvil, enduring the heat of the furnace, as "the breath of the fire melts his flesh" (RSV). Here, "flesh" refers to his skin, which, exposed to the heat of the fire, "melts"—a hyperbole, one hopes. In 4 Maccabees 9:28 and 15:15, "flesh" is used to refer to skin being flayed from the body of martyrs. The skin involved in circumcision is also referred to with the term "flesh." Sirach 44:20 speaks of Abraham and the covenant established "in his flesh." Paul warned the Galatians in 6:13 that the Judaizers sought to circumcise them in order to "boast in your flesh." Walter Russell argues that Paul is claiming the Judaizers intend to boast in the "flesh" of the Galatian

---

that has been detached from the animal and perhaps tanned, its repeated use throughout Leviticus 13 (LXX) demonstrates that it can also be used for the skin of a living person (see, for example, vv. 2–8, 10–13).

7. See Arnold and Choi, *Guide to Biblical Hebrew Syntax*, 24 (2.4.5); Wallace, *Greek Grammar Beyond the Basics*, 95–99.

8. See Wolff, *Anthropology of the Old Testament*, 28.

believers' foreskins, if they succeed in winning them over to their way of life epitomized in circumcision and Torah-observance.⁹

In contrast to the use of בָּשָׂר and σάρξ to refer exclusively to the skin, these terms can also be used to refer specifically to the muscle or fat (taken separately or together), distinct from the עוֹר, χρώς or δέρμα, "skin." In Leviticus 4:11, בָּשָׂר and σάρξ refer specifically to the muscle of the sin offering, which are to be burned up with the skin or hide outside the camp. Here, בָּשָׂר and σάρξ do not refer to the fat (Heb. חֵלֶב, ḥēleb; Gk. στέαρ, stear) of the animal, all of which is removed in 4:8–10 and burned up on the altar. In Job 19:20, בָּשָׂר and σάρξ refer to Job's muscle and fat, which, together with his skin (Heb. עוֹר, Gk. δέρμα), stick to his bone (according to the MT; the LXX uses the terms in the same way, but otherwise greatly changes the meaning of the verse). In Ezekiel's vision of the dry bones, בָּשָׂר and σάρξ in Ezekiel 37:6 and 8 refer to the muscle and fat that God causes to come upon the bones, which are then covered with skin (Heb. עוֹר, Gk. δέρμα) as well. In Job 10:11, the MT states that in the womb God clothed Job with skin (עוֹר) and flesh (בָּשָׂר), so the latter term most likely refers to Job's muscle and fat, distinguished from the skin. Interestingly, the LXX here uses the term κρέας for Job's flesh, a term which is more commonly used to refer to flesh as "meat."¹⁰ However, we do not find comparable examples in which σάρξ specifically denotes muscle and fat and not the skin in the literature of the Second Temple period or the New Testament.

Whether "flesh" serves to denote the body's skin, fat, and muscle, separately or collectively, it represents the soft parts of the body, in distinction from bone. It is the most perishable part of the body, which "rots" (Zech 14:12), "wastes away" or "fades away" (Job 33:21) or is torn by thorns (Judg 8:7), or eaten (see below).¹¹

There are many passages in which בָּשָׂר and σάρξ are used to depict the flesh as something consumable—to be eaten. In some passages this is a strictly literal eating of the flesh, while in others this idea is used in a more metaphorical way as either a depiction of exploitation and injustice, or as a prophetic threat of judgment. At the literal end of the spectrum there are many examples. In Genesis 40:19, Pharaoh's baker is told that Pharaoh will lift up his head off of him, hang him on a tree, and then the birds will eat his flesh off of him. In Leviticus 26:29, the Israelites are warned of the judgments that will come upon them for persistent disobedience, eventually resulting in a siege by their enemies, and a resulting hunger so

---

9. Russell, *Flesh/Spirit Conflict*, 192–93.
10. BDAG, s.v. κρέας. See also category two below.
11. Ryken et al., *Dictionary of Biblical Imagery*, s.v. "Body," 105–6.

great that the starving parents among them would eat the flesh of their sons and the flesh of their daughters. This warning is reiterated in Deuteronomy 28:52-57, and verses 53 and 55 use the term "flesh" the same way (although in verse 53, the LXX employs κρέας instead of σάρξ). Jeremiah 19 warns the Jerusalemites that the threat of this judgment is imminent, as God is "about to" (19:3) bring it upon them, and in 19:9, בָּשָׂר and σάρξ are used in similar fashion. In 1 Samuel 17:44, Goliath boasts that he will give David's flesh to the birds of the sky and the beasts of the field—an empty threat as it turns out. In contrast, in 2 Kings 9:36, a prophecy of Elisha that dogs would eat the flesh of Jezebel is recalled after events proved that this was not an empty threat. Psalm 79:2 [LXX 78:2] laments: "They have given the bodies of your servants to the birds of the heavens for food, the flesh of your faithful to the beasts of the earth" (ESV).

This idea of eating one's flesh can also be employed in a less literal way to speak of an enemy's oppression and exploitation, or as a threat of divine judgment. In Psalm 27:2 [LXX 26:2], David speaks of enemies who came against him to eat his flesh. Here he speaks with poetic metaphor, but a metaphor in which his flesh is consumable nonetheless. In Zechariah 11:9, 16, the prophet speaks the Lord's word of judgment upon his disobedient people. He would be their shepherd no more, but abandon them to their fate. "What is to be destroyed, let it be destroyed. And let those who are left devour the flesh of one another" (Zec 11:9, ESV). The language here is metaphorical, with "those who are left devour the flesh of one another" signifying that the survivors of the judgment would destroy, oppress, or exploit one another. In verse 16, the Lord warns that he is raising up an evil "shepherd"—i.e., an evil ruler—who does not care for them but "devours the flesh of the fat ones, tearing off even their hoofs" (ESV). The prophet depicts an exploitation so severe that even the parts of the "sheep" that are considered undesirable—the hooves—would be torn off. In contrast, Isaiah 49 speaks of a future time of deliverance and consolation for his covenant people, and a time of judgment for their oppressors. The Lord says in Isaiah 49:26, "I will make your oppressors eat their own flesh, and they shall be drunk with their own blood as with wine. Then all flesh shall know that I am the LORD your Savior, and your Redeemer, the Mighty One of Jacob" (ESV). In this metaphorical prophecy of the eschatological deliverance of Israel from its enemies, God promises that Israel's oppressors would destroy themselves through their own efforts to destroy Israel. The language with which this is expressed, that they would "eat their own flesh and be drunk with their own blood as with wine," is of particular interest for its similarity to language employed in John's Gospel that speaks of eating flesh and drinking blood as wine. In Ezekiel 39:17-18, a great eschatological judgment occurs in which the enemies of God and Israel also have their flesh and blood consumed, this time not by themselves, but by birds, who will participate in it as "a great sacrificial feast" (ESV).

Similar uses for σάρξ are seen in the intertestamental literature and New Testament. A literal example is found in Baruch 2:3, which speaks of parents eating the flesh of their children during the Babylonian conquest. In James 5:3, we see a more metaphorical use: "Your gold and silver have corroded, and their corrosion will be evidence against you and will eat your flesh like fire. You have laid up treasure in the last days" (ESV). James speaks in terms of literal flesh, but with a metaphorical intent to speak of eschatological judgment in a manner consistent with the OT. Similarly, in an apocalyptic vision, Revelation 17:16 describes the judgment on the "great prostitute"—that the "ten horns" and the "beast" would make her "desolate and naked, and devour her flesh and burn her up with fire" (ESV). Finally, in an echo of Ezekiel 39:17–18, Revelation 19:18 and 21 (ESV) says that "the flesh of kings, the flesh of captains, the flesh of mighty men, the flesh of horses and their riders, and the flesh of all men, both free and slave, both small and great" of those who oppose the return of Christ are consumed by birds.

The idea of "flesh" as something consumable also provides a suitable point of transition into our next semantic category for "flesh."

(Meaning 2) "Flesh" as a Reference to Meat

A second semantic domain of בָּשָׂר, σάρξ, and κρέας is "meat." When בָּשָׂר is used with this intent in the Old Testament, the translators of the LXX regularly translate with the term κρέας rather than with σάρξ. "Flesh" can be used to denote meat intended for all sorts of purposes, including meat that is to be eaten as a meal, meat that one is forbidden to eat, and meat used for sacrificial purposes—some of which may be eaten and some of which may be burned up on the altar.[12]

We first encounter this kind of usage in Genesis 9, in which God grants to Noah and his descendants to eat animals as they had been granted to eat plants before. So, by implication, they could now eat meat. However, 9:4 gives one stipulation: "But you shall not eat flesh with its life, that is, its blood." Here, as usual, the LXX translates בָּשָׂר as κρέας (as it will be for all other examples unless otherwise clarified). In Exodus 16, the Israelites grumbled about their hunger and longed for the time in Egypt in which they "sat by the pot of flesh and ate bread to the full" (16:3, MT [my translation]). In

---

12. With reference to בָּשָׂר, see s.v. בָּשָׂר, in BDB, definition 1; in *HALOT*, definitions 3–4; Seebass, "Flesh," 672.

verses 8 and 12, the people are told that God would give them flesh to eat in the evening, and bread to eat in the morning, and that they would eat their fill and know that he was Yahweh their God. The psalmist reflects on this event in Psalm 78:27 (LXX 77:27), saying that God "rained flesh on them like dust, winged birds like the sand of the seas." (MT, my translation). Most interestingly, the usual pattern of terms is reversed—here the MT uses שְׁאֵר, while the LXX uses σάρξ. In Numbers 11, the people grumble again with the same complaint, and the same demand for meat (11:4, 13), and God again gives them meat to eat for a month (11:18, 21), but also a plague as a judgment upon their faithless craving (11:33). In Deuteronomy 12, God gives the Israelites permission to slaughter and eat meat in their towns (12:15, 20), but without the blood (12:23), and the proper location for sacrifices must be observed, the flesh of which they could also eat (12:27). In Proverbs 23:20, we are warned not to keep company with drunkards and "gluttonous eaters of flesh" (MT, my translation). In fact, this kind of behavior is often characteristic of a culpable disregard of God, that continues in ignorance of God's fast-approaching wrath until God's judgment finally falls upon them (see Isaiah 22:13 in the surrounding context).

Reference is also made to various kinds of "flesh" or "meat," in a non-sacrificial context, that is not to be eaten for various reasons. An ox that had gored someone to death was to be killed, but its flesh was not to be eaten (Exod 21:28). The meat of an animal that had been killed by wild beasts in the field was not to be eaten, but given to the dogs (Exod 22:31). Leviticus 11 lists a variety of animals that were considered unclean. Their flesh was not to be eaten, and these animals were to be detested and their carcasses were not to be touched (Lev 11:8, 11; cf. also Deut 14:8).

This category of meaning for "flesh" also includes reference to sacrificial meat. When "flesh" is used in reference to meat, it is most frequently pertaining to that of sacrificial animals. It is no surprise that בָּשָׂר is used most frequently in Leviticus.[13] In some cases, this meat is to be burned up (Exod 29:14; Lev 7:17–20; 8:17, 32; 9:11; 16:27; Num 19:5; Judg 6:19–21). In other cases, the sacrificial meat was to be eaten (Lev 6:27 [MT and LXX, 6:20]; 7:15; 8:31; Hos 8:13). There are also instances where sacrificial meat is mentioned, but it is not specified what is to be done with it (Jer 11:15; Ezek 40:43; Hag 2:12).

Finally, there is the sacrificial meat or flesh of the Passover lamb that is sacrificed. In Exodus 12 we see the initial instructions that were given concerning this sacrifice. Before the last great plague on Egypt was carried

---

13. Wolff, *Anthropology of the Old Testament*, 26n4 (cf. p. 233) indicates sixty-one times.

out, the Israelites were commanded to keep the Passover. This entailed the slaughter of a year-old male lamb at twilight on the fourteenth day of the first month of the year. After smearing some of the lamb's blood on the doorposts and lintel of their houses, the Israelites were to roast the lamb and to eat its flesh that night (Exod 12:9). This provided protection against God's deadly judgment which fell upon all the firstborn of Egypt that night. Subsequent to the Passover feast, the judgment on Egypt, and Israel's expulsion from Egypt, God again gave instructions pertaining to the keeping of the Passover for future generations. Here it was stipulated that it would be eaten in one house, and that none of its flesh was to be taken out of that house, and furthermore, "you shall not break any of its bones" (Exod 12:46).[14]

In the Second Temple literature, Wisdom 12:5-6 gives a gruesome reference to sacrificial flesh in describing the practices of the Canaanites prior to the Israelite conquest: "their merciless slaughter of children, and their sacrificial feasting on human flesh and blood. These initiates from the midst of a heathen cult, thou didst will to destroy by the hands of our fathers" (RSV). In this case, σάρξ is employed, not κρέας. In the New Testament, κρέας is the preferred term for referring to "meat" (see, e.g., Rom 14:21; 1 Cor 8:13; 10:25).

(Meaning 3) "Flesh" as a Reference to the Genitals and/or the Sexual Urge

A more euphemistic use of בָּשָׂר and σάρξ is to refer to the genitals, although the LXX is just as likely to use other terms to express this as it is to use σάρξ (e.g., αἰδοῖον [aidoion] in Ezek 23:20; οἱ δίδυμοι [hoi didumoi] in Deut 25:11 LXX; note also σκεῦος [skeuos] in 1 Thess 4:4).[15] Whereas the previous categories understood "flesh" as a human (or animal) substance, this category treats flesh as a part of the body.

In Exodus 28:42, the priests were commanded to wear linen undergarments reaching from their hips to their thighs in order to cover the "flesh of nakedness" (Heb. בְּשַׂר עֶרְוָה), bĕśar 'erwâ). In the LXX the phrase is rendered ἀσχημοσύνην χρωτὸς (aschēmosunēn chrōtos), "shameful nakedness of skin."

---

14. All of this would later be highly relevant to John's later development of the "flesh" theme and his depiction of Jesus Christ as the true Passover Lamb.

15. With reference to בָּשָׂר, see s.v. בָּשָׂר, in BDB, definition 3; in HALOT, definition 5b. With reference to σάρξ, see s.v. σάρξ, in BDAG, definition 2cβ; in Friberg et al., Analytical Lexicon, definition 4; in LN, 292; in Thayer, Greek-English Lexicon, definition 2c; in Gingrich, Shorter Lexicon, definition 8. With reference to αἰδοῖον, see s.v. αἰδοῖον, in LSJ. With reference to οἱ δίδυμοι, see s.v. δίδυμος, in LSJ, definition III.2. With reference to σκεῦος, see s.v. σκεῦος, in LSJ, definition III; in BDAG, definition 3.

In both cases, the phrases work as a whole to refer to the priests' genitals. The Hebrew עֶרְוָה and Greek ἀσχημοσύνη (*aschēmosunē*), by themselves are sufficient to convey this meaning; combining them with the terms בָּשָׂר and χρώς just expresses the idea more thoroughly.

In Leviticus 15, the Israelites were given various regulations pertaining to different bodily emissions from the genitals, male and female, and detailing to what degree these emissions made one unclean. Throughout this chapter, the Hebrew uses בָּשָׂר to refer to the genitals, while the LXX tends to make the statements more general by employing the word σῶμα, "body." In this way, reference is made to the male genitals in 15:2, and the female genitals in 15:19. (However, there are also instances where it is clear that בָּשָׂר intends to convey something like "body," such as 15:7, 13, and 16, and this is accurately reflected in the LXX's use of σῶμα.)

Finally and unforgettably, there are the prophetic denunciations of Judah's spiritual harlotry in Ezekiel 16 and 23, in which Ezekiel describes in scathing tones the nation's unfaithfulness. He shockingly depicts the nation as a prostitute lusting after her paramours who are described as "great of flesh" (Heb., גִּדְלֵי בָשָׂר, *gidlê bāśār*; Gk. μεγαλοσάρκους, *megalosarkous*), in 16:26 and in 23:20 as having "flesh (Heb., בָּשָׂר; Gk. σάρξ) like the flesh of a donkey" and "issue like that of horses" (the LXX changes the latter phrase to make it also a comparison of genitalia using the term αἰδοῖον).[16]

In the New Testament, this sexually-oriented usage of σάρξ continues, but is also broadened to speak of sexual desire and behavior. Here, although continuing to speak generally of human sexuality, it does so less as a body part, and more of an aspect of human beings. A debated example is the reference to "the will of the flesh" in John 1:13, which arguably refers to sexual desire, which typically leads, eventually, to the birth of children.[17] In 2 Peter

---

16 Wolff, *Anthropology of the Old Testament*, 27–28. His translation of the Ezekiel passages is more explicit.

17. Carson, *Gospel According to John*, 126; Morris, *Gospel According to John*, 89; Beasley-Murray, *John*, 13; Lincoln, *Gospel According to Saint John*, 103. Keener, *Gospel of John*, 1:404, argues that it refers to "parental passion," but also that it is probably intended to reflect the "context's contrast between children born of God (1:12) and genetic Israel (1:11), whom some early Christians called Israel 'according to the flesh.'" Similarly, Bultmann, *Gospel of John*, 60n2, argues that the phrase describes the human sphere and may also be indicating sexual desire. Starting to argue in a contrary direction, however, is Michaels, *Gospel of John*, 72–73, who argues that the phrase "refers simply to choice or initiative, not to sexual or any other kind of desire," even though he acknowledges that "the subject is sexual intercourse between a man and a woman"—which seems a rather fine distinction. Also advocating a nonsexual interpretation is Ridderbos, *Gospel of John*, 47, who takes it as a term denoting creaturely humanity in contrast to God. Similarly, see also Köstenberger, *John*, 40; Barrett, *Gospel According to St. John*, 137.

2:10, the author condemns false teachers who "go after the flesh [σάρξ] in the lust of defilement" (my translation), a reference to sexual immorality. Similarly, in Jude 7–8, the author makes two references to sexual immorality. In Jude 7 he cites the example of the people of Sodom and Gomorrah, who "went after strange flesh" (NASB), a euphemism for homosexual behavior. In verse 8, he drew a parallel to contemporary false teachers who, among other things, "defile the flesh," i.e., through sexual immorality.

Other passages in the New Testament and Hellenistic Jewish literature make reference to "the lusts of the flesh" (αἱ ἐπιθυμίαι τῆς σαρκὸς, *hai epithumiai tēs sarkos*) and "the passions of the flesh" (τὰ πάθη τῆς σαρκὸς, *ta pathē tēs sarkos*). For example, we read of "the lust(s) of the flesh" (αἱ ἐπιθυμίαι τῆς σαρκὸς) in Ephesians 2:3; 2 Peter 3:18; and 1 John 2:16; and of "the passions of the flesh" (τὰ πάθη τῆς σαρκὸς) in 4 Maccabees 7:18. However, it is not clear in all of these cases whether sexual lusts or passions are exclusively in view, as opposed to a more generalized reference to bodily appetites and emotions; or perhaps sexual lusts and passions are seen as the epitome of our bodily appetites and passions.

(Meaning 4) "Flesh" as Part of the Body, Used in Merisms to Refer to the Whole Body, Person, or Humanity in General

The fourth category of usage for בָּשָׂר and σάρξ focuses on the flesh as either a body part or substance, but uses the term in tandem with another body part or substance to form a merism whereby a more holistic effect is achieved. In this way the merism may refer to one's body as a whole, to a whole person, or even to humanity in general. As such this is a category of the usage of a particular form, which may have several distinct meanings, some of which will overlap with other categories.[18]

A frequent combination is that of bone and flesh. In Job 2:5, Satan challenges God to "stretch out your hand and touch [Job's] bone and his flesh, and he will curse you to your face" (ESV, altered). It is evident here that "bone and flesh" is a merism representing Job's body as a whole. In Proverbs 14:30, the MT uses בָּשָׂר, although the LXX changes the verse and omits any reference to "flesh." The proverb states, "A tranquil heart gives life to the flesh, but envy makes the bones rot" (ESV). Here "flesh" and "bones" are used in clauses that form an antithetic parallelism, and it seems that the author is referring to the benefits of a tranquil heart to the whole person,

---

18. With reference to בָּשָׂר, see s.v. בָּשָׂר, in *HALOT*, definition 5. With reference to σάρξ, see Seebass, "Flesh," 674–75; Johnson, "Flesh," 375. With reference to both terms, see Ryken et al., *Dictionary of Biblical Imagery*, s.v. "Body," 105–6.

and the contrasting detriments of envy to the whole person. In Proverbs 3:22, the LXX changes the MT greatly and results in the use of σάρξ in a merism with "bones." The author tells his audience to keep his counsel and insight, "so that your soul may live, and grace may be around your neck; and it will be health to your flesh, and safety to your bones" (my translation). With the last two clauses set in synonymous parallelism, the author seems to be treating "flesh" and "bones" as a merism for the body as a whole. On the other hand, it may be the author's intention that they are to be taken with "soul" of the earlier part of the verse, such that the three terms "soul," "flesh," and "bones" refer collectively and holistically to the entire person. We shall see below in category seven that "bone and flesh" is also a frequently-used combination to denote kinship relations.

Another frequently occurring combination is "flesh" and "soul" (or "life")—in Hebrew, בָּשָׂר and נֶפֶשׁ (*nepeš*); and in Greek, σάρξ and ψυχή (*psuchē*). In Job 13:14, Job asks, "Why should I take my flesh in my teeth and put my life [Heb. נֶפֶשׁ, Gk. ψυχή] in my hand?" (ESV). The context favors understanding the merism as holistically as possible to refer to Job's person. In the immediate context Job is noting the risk he takes in trying to make a case for himself before God. In Job 14:22, Job speaks of the man whose hope has been destroyed through prolonged suffering: "Surely his flesh upon him is in pain, and his soul upon him mourns" (my translation). The Hebrew word for "upon" (עַל, *'al*) can be used in an idiomatic fashion with terms like "soul" and "heart" to suggest the oppressive burdensomeness of one's emotions acting upon him.[19] Flesh and soul seem to be in parallelism, such that the two describe the person Job as a whole, despite the use of the personal pronoun "him" modifying the two terms. The psalmist is also fond of using this merism, as is seen in Psalm 63:1 (MT 63:2, LXX 62:2): "O God, you are my God; earnestly I seek you; my soul thirsts for you; my flesh faints for you, as in a dry and weary land where there is no water" (ESV). There are two ways to understand this verse at the micro-level. First, it may be that the two terms "flesh" and "soul" work together to represent the whole person, and parallel the "I" of the first clause. Alternatively, it may be the case that the three clauses are to be read in parallel fashion to describe David's need for God, with David described by all three terms: "I," "my flesh," and "my soul."[20] Regardless of the specific interpretation of the functioning of the parts of

---

19. S.v. עַל, BDB, definition II.1.d.

20. If this is the proper way to understand the verse, it may be more properly regarded as an example of category six usage of σάρξ.

this verse at the micro-level, its gist as a whole at the macro-level is clear in describing David as a whole person who needs God.²¹

Another merism used by the psalmist is "heart" and "flesh." In Psalm 84:2 (MT 84:3, LXX 83:2), he writes, "My soul longs, yes, faints for the courts of the LORD; my heart and my flesh sing for joy to the living God" (ESV). "My heart and my flesh" are set in synthetic parallelism with "my soul," and are probably intended to describe the psalmist holistically. In Ezekiel 44:7 and 9, the prophet records the criticism of God that the Israelites had admitted into his sanctuary foreigners who were "uncircumcised in heart and uncircumcised in flesh" (NASB), and says that this will happen no more. The phrase "uncircumcised in heart and uncircumcised in flesh" most likely denotes the entire person and describes their improper status before God as unfit to enter his sanctuary. In the Old Greek of Daniel 4:33 (but not Theodotian or the MT), Nebuchadnezzar (the implied narrator of the passage) says, "my flesh and my heart were changed" (my translation). Here "heart and flesh" are most probably a merism equivalent to "body and soul" to refer to the whole person, although the possibility cannot absolutely be ruled out that the two terms speak individually of the specific changes that happened to Nebuchadnezzar's body and mind.

Another term used in tandem with "flesh" is "blood." In the Old Testament, there are three main uses for this combination of "flesh" and "blood." The first pertains to the prohibition against eating meat or "flesh" with the blood in it, which has been examined above. The second use is in speaking of sacrifices, which has also been examined above. The third has to do with people being killed, as in warfare or divine judgment. Here, "flesh and blood" do not function so much as a merism to represent holistically a human person; rather, they tend to function as a *fractured* merism, in that these two elements are often depicted as separated as the result of a violent death. As Ryken et al. observe, "An enemy's body, slain on a battlefield, is 'flesh and blood.'"²² In Moses's song, Yahweh swears concerning his adversaries who hate him, "I will make my arrows drunk with blood, and my sword shall devour flesh [Heb. בָּשָׂר, Gk. κρέας]" (Deut 32:42, ESV). This text could just as well be placed in category one as a text in which the flesh is depicted as consumable. This is also true of Ezekiel 39:17–18, as it depicts slain enemies in terms of flesh and blood. Isaiah 49:26 probably satisfies both of these thematic categories as well, since it seems that Yahweh's enemies eating their own flesh and being drunk on their own blood is likely a poetic description of their violent deaths. In Ezekiel 32:5–6, God says concerning the Egyptians,

---

21. Aubrey R. Johnson, *Vitality of the Individual in the Thought of Ancient Israel*, 38.
22. Ryken et al., *Dictionary of Biblical Imagery*, s.v. "Body," 105–6.

"I will strew your flesh upon the mountains and fill the valleys with your carcass. I will drench the land even to the mountains with your flowing blood, and the ravines will be full of you" (ESV). According to Zephaniah 1:17 (LXX), in the day of the Lord, God will deal thusly with his enemies, "he will pour out their blood like dust and their flesh like dung" (my translation). (The MT reads "entrails" instead of "flesh.")[23]

This usage of "flesh and blood" continued beyond the OT in the Hellenistic Jewish literature, but it evolved significantly during this time and the resultant changes are evident in the New Testament. We have already cited Wisdom 12:5 in category two. Note that in this verse, all three ideas of "flesh and blood" as representing (1) human slaughter, (2) sacrifice, and (3) the eating of flesh with the blood are all combined in a reference to Canaanite human sacrifice and ritual feasting on the flesh and blood of children. In 1 Maccabees 7:17, the language of "flesh and blood" (σὰρξ καὶ αἷμα, *sarx kai haima*) representing violent death is applied to the Jewish martyrs during the persecution of Antiochus Epiphanes: "The flesh of your faithful ones and their blood they poured out all around Jerusalem, and there was no one to bury them" (NRSV).[24] However, by this time,[25] a new usage for "flesh and blood" had appeared in Jewish literature, in which it referred to humanity in general, especially in contrast to God. (We will examine the use of "flesh" by itself to denote this in categories eight and nine below.) Sirach 14:18 says, "Like flourishing leaves on a spreading tree which sheds some and puts forth others, so are the generations of flesh and blood: one dies and another is born" (RSV). This verse uses "flesh and blood" to describe the transience and perishing nature of humanity, a circumstance which calls for wisdom to live appropriately (cf. 14:17—15:1). This idea of human transience and weakness is also a prominent theme of Sirach 17, combined with the theme of human sinfulness in the Lord's sight and our need to repent. Both themes are present together in 17:30-32, although "flesh and blood" is used in verse 31 only to speak explicitly of human sinfulness:

---

23. Ryken et al., *Dictionary of Biblical Imagery*, s.v. "Body," 105–6.

24. This statement is presented as a citation of Scripture, and probably is an allusion to Psalm 79:2 [LXX 78:2], which, however, only mentions "flesh," but not in combination with "blood."

25. First Maccabees is dated to sometime after 134 BC, most likely in the range 104-63 BC, according to deSilva, *Introducing the Apocrypha*, 247–8; see also Metzger, *Introduction to the Apocrypha*, 130. The Hebrew original of Sirach—only fragments of which are now extant—is dated to a range of 196-175 BC, and the Greek translation is dated some time after 132 BC; see deSilva, *Introducing the Apocrypha*, 157–58; Metzger, *Introduction to the Apocrypha*, 78–79.

> ³⁰ For not all things are able to be in men,
> for a son of man is not immortal.
> ³¹ What is brighter than the sun? And yet its light fails.
> So flesh and blood devise²⁶ evil.
> ³² He marshals the power²⁷ of the height of heaven;
> but all men are dust²⁸ and ashes.
>
> (Sirach 17:30–32, my translation from the Greek version)

Subsequent to Sirach, "flesh and blood" (Heb. בָּשָׂר וָדָם, *bāśār wādām*), came to be used as a technical term in rabbinic texts to denote, generally, man or human agency in contrast to God or divine agency.²⁹ By the NT period, this use of "flesh and blood" to denote humanity had apparently crowded out its use for denoting human beings as the victims of bloodshed or divine judgment. This can be seen even in those NT passages previously cited as examples of flesh as something consumed or eaten that were also allusions to OT passages which readily make reference to "flesh and blood." For example, Ezekiel 39:17–20 uses "flesh and blood" for this purpose, and is alluded to in Revelation 19:17–20, yet the latter passage only employs the term "flesh." The New Testament's primary use of "flesh and blood" is to speak of humanity in its weakness and transience, as opposed to God or other spiritual realities (e.g., Matt 16:17; 1 Cor 15:50). We will examine this in more detail below.

---

26. The Greek verb here is future tense, which suggests the possibility that the original Hebrew verb was in the imperfect tense, and the translator understood this in a future sense. However, the Hebrew imperfect can also be used in the same way as the English present tense to denote customary, habitual action, as well as gnomic action and this latter use makes the best sense in this context, in my judgment. See Waltke and O'Connor, *Introduction to Biblical Hebrew Syntax*, 504; Arnold and Choi, *Guide to Biblical Hebrew Syntax*, 56–60.

27. Gk. δύναμις (*dunamis*), a term frequently used in the LXX to render the Hebrew terms חַיִל (*ḥayil*; power, wealth, army), גְּבוּרָה (*gĕbûrâ*; strength, mighty deeds), עֹז ('*ōz*; might, strength, ramparts), כֹּחַ (*kōaḥ*; strength, power), צָבָא (*ṣābā'*; army, host). If the original Hebrew read חַיִל, "army" or "host" may have been the intention rather than "power," which seems a better fit contextually. Rather than translate based on this conjecture, I have followed the Greek and noted the possibility here. See s.v. δύναμις, Thayer, *Greek-English Lexicon*; cf. *HALOT*, s.v. צָבָא, כֹּחַ, עֹז, גְּבוּרָה, חַיִל.

28. Gk. γῆ (*gē*), "earth", a term frequently used in the LXX to render the Hebrew עָפָר, ('*āpār*), "dust, soil, earth"—for example, in Gen 2:7; 3:14, 16. Given the strong correlation between these two Hebrew and Greek terms, and between them and the term "man" (see also Sir. 17:1), it seems a virtual certainty that the original author intended the meaning "dust," and I have translated accordingly. See BDAG, s.v. γῆ; *HALOT*, s.v. עָפָר.

29. Davies and Allison, *Commentary on Matthew VIII–XVIII*, 623; Strack and Billerbeck, *Das Evangelium nach Matthäus*, 730; Schweizer, "σάρξ, σαρκικός, σάρκινος," 124; see also Snaith, *Ecclesiasticus*, 75.

Another example of an NT use of "flesh" in a merism to represent a whole is found in 2 Corinthians 7:1: "Therefore, having these promises, beloved, let us cleanse ourselves from all defilement of flesh and spirit, perfecting holiness in the fear of God" (ESV). Here "flesh and spirit" are used to represent the whole person, whom Paul desires to be completely holy and devoid of any defilement before God.

(Meaning 5) "Flesh" as a Reference to the Body as a Whole

Given the above use of "flesh" in merisms to denote the whole body, it is unsurprising that it could also be taken by itself simply to denote the body. In the Old Testament, when בָּשָׂר intends this meaning, it is frequently translated in the LXX by σῶμα, and "body" in the English translations.[30]

In Leviticus we find a few clear examples where this is the case. In Lev 14:9, we read, "And on the seventh day he shall shave off all his hair from his head, his beard, and his eyebrows. He shall shave off all his hair, and then he shall wash his clothes and bathe his body [MT בָּשָׂר, LXX σῶμα] in water, and he shall be clean" (ESV). It seems clear here that "body" is intended. There are instances in Leviticus 15 where this must also be the case, despite the frequent use of בָּשָׂר in that chapter to denote the genitals. For example, in 15:16, we read that a man with a seminal emission "shall bathe *his whole body* (MT אֶת־כָּל־בְּשָׂרוֹ, 'et-kol-bĕśārô; LXX πᾶν τὸ σῶμα αὐτοῦ, *pan to sōma autou*) in water and be unclean until the evening" (ESV, emphasis mine). Several other verses in Leviticus speak of washing the בָּשָׂר or σῶμα: 16:4 (the second instance of בָּשָׂר), 24, 26, 28; 17:16; 22:6; see also Num 19:7–8. Interestingly, the translators of the LXX resisted translating בָּשָׂר as σῶμα in Leviticus 13:2, 3, 4, 11, and 13, where it seems to be the intended meaning. In verses 2, 3, 4, and 11, the MT reads עוֹר־בְּשָׂרוֹ ('ôr-bĕśārô), literally "the skin of his flesh," in which "flesh" seems to be understood as "body." In each of these verses, the LXX opts for δέρματι χρωτὸς αὐτοῦ (*dermati chrōtos autou*), "the skin of his skin"—using two different Greek words for "skin." The intention of "body" is even plainer in verse 13, which reads "if the leprous disease has covered *all his body* [MT אֶת־כָּל־בְּשָׂרוֹ, 'all his flesh']" (ESV, emphasis mine), and yet here the LXX renders it δέρμα τοῦ χρωτὸς αὐτοῦ (*derma tou chrōtos autou*),

---

30. With reference to בָּשָׂר, see s.v. בָּשָׂר, in BDB, definition 2; in *HALOT*, definition 6; Seebass, "Flesh," 672. With reference to σάρξ, see s.v. σάρξ, in BDAG, definition 2; in Friberg et al., *Analytical Lexicon*, definition 2; in LN, 94; in Thayer, *Greek-English Lexicon*, definition 2; in Gingrich, *Shorter Lexicon*, definition 2; Ryken, et al., *Dictionary of Biblical Imagery*, s.v. "Body," 105–6; Erickson, "Flesh," 303–6; Seebass, "Flesh," 674–75. For discussion of this category of meaning for both בָּשָׂר and σάρξ, see Thiselton, "Flesh," 679–80.

"the skin of his skin." It seems far more likely that in these verses "the skin of his body" is intended rather than "the skin of his flesh (understood as skin, muscle, and fat collectively)."

Other places in the Old Testament are not as clear as these passages from the Pentateuch, but probably also intend to speak of the "body" by means of the term בָּשָׂר. Both 1 Kings 21:27 [LXX 20:27] and 2 Kings 6:30 speak of putting sackcloth on one's בָּשָׂר. Interestingly, the LXX opts for σῶμα in the former verse, but σάρξ in the latter. In Ecclesiastes 11:10, the Preacher writes, "Remove vexation from your heart, and put away pain from your body [MT בָּשָׂר, LXX σάρξ], for youth and the dawn of life are vanity" (ESV). In Ezekiel 10:12 (MT), the prophet describes the cherubim and their wheels: "*And their whole body* [Heb. וְכָל־בְּשָׂרָם, *wĕkol-bĕśārām*], and their backs, and their hands, and their wings and the wheels were full of eyes all around" (my translation and emphasis). The LXX omits the italicized phrase. While it is possible that בָּשָׂר could merely refer to the cherubim's "flesh" here, since it is preceded by כָּל, "body" seems to make the best sense, and it is unsurprising that this is the consensus of English translations.

This usage of σάρξ to mean "body" continues into the New Testament. In 2 Corinthians 4:11, Paul writes, "For we who live are always being given over to death for Jesus' sake, so that the life of Jesus also may be manifested in our mortal flesh" (ESV). In this passage, Paul makes a contrast between the powerful resurrection life of Jesus, and our mortal body, which reflects the overall tenor of the passage that our spiritual treasure is in weak, common vessels. In Galatians 2:20, Paul says, ". . . And the life I now live in the flesh I live by faith in the Son of God . . ." (ESV). The life Paul lives in his body, i.e., his present bodily existence, is lived through faith in Christ. Similarly, in Philippians 1:22, Paul ponders whether he will be executed or released, and which would be a preferable outcome. He writes, "If I am to live in the flesh, that means fruitful labor for me. Yet which I shall choose I cannot tell" (ESV). In verse 24, he writes, "But to remain in the flesh is more necessary on your account" (ESV), concluding that there is much work to be done for the sake of the church. He thus concludes he will continue to live "in the flesh," that is, in the body, rather than being executed and going on to be present with the Lord. Peter in 1 Peter 4:1–2 also speaks of "living in the flesh" as "living in the body": "Since therefore Christ suffered in the flesh, arm yourselves with the same way of thinking, for whoever has suffered in the flesh has ceased from sin, so as to live for the rest of the time in the flesh no longer for human passions but for the will of God" (ESV).

(Meaning 6) "Flesh" as a Reference to the Person as a Whole

By means of a slight extension from the idea of "flesh" as a body, we come to the next category of use for "flesh": to refer by means of synecdoche to the person as a whole.[31] This use is pronounced in the poetry and wisdom literature of the Old Testament, and is also seen in the Hellenistic Jewish literature and New Testament.[32]

Psalm 16 [LXX 15] provides for us a prime example:

> [8] I have set YHWH before me continually;
> because (he is)[33] at my right hand,
> I will not be shaken.
>
> [9] Therefore my heart is glad,
> and my glory[34] rejoices,
> and my flesh dwells in security.

---

31. Johnson, *Vitality of the Individual*, 38.

32. With reference to בָּשָׂר, see Seebass, "Flesh," 672. With reference to σάρξ, see s.v. σάρξ, in BDAG, definition 3a; in Friberg et al., *Analytical Lexicon*, definition 3; in LN, 105 (section 9.11); in Thayer, *Greek-English Lexicon*, definition 3; in Gingrich, *Shorter Lexicon*, definition 3; Ryken et al., *Dictionary of Biblical Imagery*, s.v. "Body," 105–6; R. J. Erickson, "Flesh," 304; Johnson, "Flesh," 375; Seebass, "Flesh," under heading 674–75.

33. Not in the MT text, but implied by the context.

34. This is a difficult and controversial word in the text. As it stands in the MT, it reads כְּבוֹדִי. (*kĕbôdî*), "my glory." If this is the correct reading, it could also be understood as "my honor," a reading preferred by BDB (see s.v. כָּבוֹד). Accepting the text as כְּבוֹדִי, "my glory," is the judgment adopted in the NASB and KJV. However, some argue that the text should be emended to כְּבֵדִי (*kĕbēdî*), "my liver," which would then be understood in a non-literal sense parallel to "my heart" in the first clause of the verse. In this view, "my liver" could be understood to mean something like "my soul." This is the reading adopted by the ESV ("my whole being") and RSV ("my soul"). *HALOT* (see s.v. כָּבֵד) and *TWOT* (see s.v. כָּבֵד, subsection 943g, כְּבֵדָה) argue in support of emendation. The LXX translated this portion of the verse as "my tongue," and this is the reading followed by the NIV (1984 and 2011). The כָּבוֹד (*kābôd*) vs. כָּבֵד (*kābēd*) controversy also appears in the MT of Pss 30:13; 57:9; and 108:2. This emendation makes sense contextually in my judgment. My one reservation is that "glory" is from the *plene* spelling כָּבוֹד, rather than the "defective" spelling כָּבֹד. Therefore, to support the conjectural emendation we must add a second speculation that the original reading in the text was the ambiguous כבד, leading to an argument over its correct vocalization, which was then resolved by some scribe adding ו to get כבוד. This is not an implausible scenario, but we must remain tentative. In my translation, I have followed the MT.

> ¹⁰ For you will not abandon my soul to Sheol,
> nor will you give your pious one to see a pit
>
> ¹¹ You cause me to know the path of life;
> with you (is) an abundance of joy;
> at your right hand (are) eternal pleasures
>
> (Ps 16:8–11, MT, my translation)

Here "my flesh" (MT בְּשָׂרִי, LXX σάρξ), should most likely be understood as functionally equivalent to "I." The whole context of the passage speaks of David in a very holistic manner: *I* have set the Lord before me, *I* will not be shaken, *my heart* is glad, *my flesh* dwells in security, you will not abandon *my soul*, nor *your pious one* (i.e., David) to a pit. Even if one accepts the reading "my glory" in verse 9, these features are sufficient to justify the conclusion that David is using "flesh" here to represent himself. If the argument is correct for conjectural emendation of "my glory" to "my liver," such that it functions in a non-literal way analogous to "my heart," the argument for "my flesh" as equivalent to "I" is even stronger. (Note the ESV rendering based on this understanding, "Therefore my heart is glad, and *my whole being* rejoices; my flesh also dwells secure" [my emphasis].) Another example from the Psalms where "flesh" is equivalent to the person may also be found in Psalm 63:1 [MT 63:2, LXX 62:2], which has been discussed above in category four, and is arguably just as suitably placed in this category, since reference is made to David by means of three co-referring terms, "I," "my soul," and "my flesh," in three parallel clauses describing his need for God. Johnson notes of this passage that "the parallelism with נֶפֶשׁ is occasionally so marked that the use of the term for 'flesh' almost approaches the common use of the former term as a periphrasis for the personal pronoun."[35]

The author of Proverbs uses "flesh" in a similar manner to stand for the whole person. Speaking of his fatherly words of wisdom to his son, he writes in 4:22, "For they are life to those who find them, and healing to all his flesh" (my translation). The specific intention for "flesh" here is not clear, but given the surrounding context it is probably referring to the person as a whole, with "flesh" as the appropriate complement to "healing." Note the synonymous parallelism between the clauses, such that "life" parallels "healing," and "those who find them" parallels "his flesh." This lends credence to the idea that "flesh" here stands for whole persons. Whatever the exact intention

---

35. Johnson, *Vitality of the Individual*, 38.

of the author, it is clear that the usage is not literal, but metaphorical.[36] In Proverbs 5:11, the author warns of the consequences of adultery: "and at your end you groan, when your flesh [Heb. בָּשָׂר, "flesh"] and body [Heb. שְׁאֵר, "flesh"] fail" (my translation). In 5:1–14, 22–23, the author describes many of the consequences of adultery that affect many different aspects of the person, including his social standing, reputation, financial ruin, failing health, and even death. It is hard to identify precisely what the referent of "flesh" here is, and it is used in a phrase that includes both Hebrew words for "flesh," בָּשָׂר and שְׁאֵר, while the LXX renders it σάρκες σώματός σου (*sarkes sōmatos sou*), "the flesh of your body." It may be that this verse intends a purely physical sense for "flesh," but the overall context is holistic, detailing the manifold consequences of adultery to the whole person. It does not seem that a strictly literal sense of this verse, perhaps as a warning that one will get a venereal disease from adultery, captures the fullness of the author's warning against adultery's consequences.

The Preacher of Ecclesiastes also seems to speak of "the flesh" in reference to the person as a whole when he writes in 5:6 (MT and LXX 5:5), "Do not permit your mouth to cause your flesh to sin" (my translation from the MT). Here "your flesh" seems to be functionally equivalent to "you." Similarly, in 12:12, he writes, "Of making many books there is no end, and much study is a weariness of the flesh" (ESV). Here the Preacher most likely describes a weariness of the whole person, not just of his body. This idea of weariness first appears in 1:8, where it is coupled with the idea of dissatisfaction. Along with the familiar theme of vanity, these themes pervade the entire book, in which they are portrayed as the inevitable result of all attempts to find meaning and satisfaction under the sun through the pursuit of pleasure, work, striving, and even human wisdom and study, apart from God. The Preacher is not merely tacking on to the end of the book a freestanding admonition about the wearying effect of study on the body. He is actually recapitulating the theme of the vanity, frustration, sorrow, and weariness that plagues even the most worthy of human pursuits under the sun—the quest for knowledge and wisdom. We can see an inclusio of these themes in chapter 1 and chapter 12 if we compare 1:2–3, 8, and 13–18 with 12:8–12. Since this weariness of the whole person comes from a striving for things "under the sun," the Preacher periodically counsels the only remedy: a God-centered and God-fearing perspective in which man views all aspects of his life under the sun, not as the fruits of his own striving, but as gifts of God which he is to receive with contentment. Having recapitulated the themes of vanity in 12:8–12, he

---

36. Although Wolff, *Anthropology of the Old Testament*, 28, categorizes this reference as an instance of "flesh" used as "body," he acknowledges that "the parallelism is moving [בָּשָׂר] in the direction of the personal pronoun."

presents the remedy for our weariness one last time as his conclusion: "Fear God and keep his commandments."

This usage of σάρξ is seen as well in the Apocrypha's wisdom literature. Jesus ben Sira laments the circumstances of a man who has "an evil wife" in Sirach 25, and in verse 26 advises, "If she does not go as you direct, separate her from yourself [Gk. ἀπὸ τῶν σαρκῶν (apo tōn sarkōn), from your flesh] (RSV)." In Sirach 31:1, he writes, "Wakefulness over wealth wastes away one's flesh, and anxiety about it removes sleep" (RSV). As was the case with Proverbs 4:22, the specific intention for "flesh" here is not clear, but given the surrounding context of 30:21—31:6, it is probably referring to the person as a whole. In 30:21-24, he counsels against self-affliction, sorrow, and anxiety. Anxiety is picked up again in 31:1, and the description of its result as one's "flesh wasting away" is perhaps chosen as an appropriate complement to the metaphor of "severe illness" in 31:2. In verse 5, the author speaks of being led astray, and in verse 6 of being ruined and destroyed, all due to the pursuit of money. These features of the surrounding text suggest that the author intends a metaphorical sense for his warning of the manifold dangers posed by excessive concern for wealth. These dangers affect many different aspects of the person, not just one's physical health.

In the New Testament, we see this use of flesh (σάρξ) to stand for the whole person continued as well. In Acts 2:26, Peter quotes a text we examined above, Psalm 16:9 [LXX 15:9] thus: δὲ καὶ ἡ σάρχ μου κατασκηνώσει ἐπ' ἐλπίδι (de kai hē sarx mou kataskēnōsei ep elpidi), "and my flesh also will dwell in hope" (my translation). Luke takes this verbatim from the LXX, which is even more clear than the MT that "flesh" here cannot be taken in a literal sense of referring to one's body. Given also the fact that the quotation is quite lengthy, with Acts 2:25-28 quoting Psalm 16:8-11, the author has reproduced the original context in all of its holistic emphasis to communicate that to his audience. This seems to make it obvious that the overall sense of the statement in 2:26 is "*I* will live in hope."

Another text that seems to be equally obvious in identifying σάρξ with a whole person is 2 Corinthians 7:5, where Paul writes: "For even when we came into Macedonia our flesh had no rest, but we were afflicted on every side: conflicts without, fears within" (NASB). Here "flesh" probably denotes the entire person, since many of the afflictions of 7:4-9 and 13 are emotional rather than physical. Paul's deep anxiety as he awaited Titus's return to Macedonia and the report upon the outcome of the Corinthian situation can also be seen in 1:16-17, 23; 2:1-13. By writing "our flesh had no rest," Paul is saying that "*we* had no rest" because of personal conflicts and the emotional anxiety produced by them.

(Meaning 7) "Flesh" as a Reference to One's Family, Relatives, or Kin

By extension from the previous category, we derive an even more euphemistic use of בָּשָׂר and σάρξ, "flesh" to denote one's family, relatives, and kin, which can be extended to include fellow tribe-members, fellow countrymen, or those sharing a common ethnicity. This use continued beyond the Old Testament, into later Hellenistic Jewish literature, and into the New Testament.[37]

The phrase "bone and flesh," modified by a possessive pronoun and then predicated of a person—e.g., "he is our bone and flesh"—expresses a kinship relation of varying degrees of closeness.[38] In Genesis 29:14, Laban says to his nephew Jacob, "Surely you are my bone and my flesh!" (RSV). In 2 Samuel 19:13 (MT and LXX 19:14), David says to his half-Ishmaelite nephew Amasa,[39] "Are you not my bone and my flesh?" (ESV), a rhetorical question that functions as an assertion. In Judges 9:2, Abimelech says to his extended family members from his mother's family, "I am your bone and your flesh" (ESV). In 2 Samuel 19:12 (MT and LXX 19:13), David says to his fellow members of the tribe of Judah, "You are my brothers; you are my bone and flesh" (ESV). In 2 Samuel 5:1 (cf. 1 Chr 11:1), all the tribes of Israel say to David, "we are your bone and your flesh" (NASB).

The first time the phrase is used is to speak of the marriage relation between Adam and Eve in Genesis 2:23, where Adam says of Eve, "This at last is bone of my bone and flesh of my flesh" (my translation). The first marriage relation is conceived of as a type of kinship relation (or "flesh-and-blood" relation), and in fact as the precursor to all kinship relations. As the marital union is that which generates all kinship relations, it supersedes them in importance. The male-female union is the only relation to be

---

37. With reference to בָּשָׂר, see s.v. בָּשָׂר, in BDB, definition 4; in Chisholm, "Flesh," 778; Seebass, "Flesh," 672. With reference to σάρξ, see s.v. σάρξ, in BDAG, definition 2a, the section "Married Couples form μία σάρξ," and definition 4; in Friberg et al., *Analytical Lexicon*, definition 5; in Thayer, *Greek-English Lexicon*, definition 2b; in Gingrich, *Shorter Lexicon*, definition 4; in LN, 112; Erickson, "Flesh," 304–6; Seebass, "Flesh," 675. With reference to both terms, see Ryken et al., *Dictionary of Biblical Imagery*, s.v. "Body," 105–6.

38. See Wolff, *Anthropology of the Old Testament*, 29, for a discussion of the different degrees of kinship relations. However, his use of the term "blood relations" confuses the discussion, particularly when he applies the term even at the tribal level, for this would make his statement that Leviticus 18:6 prohibits all sexual intercourse with blood relations to be plainly false, especially given the Jewish preference (and that of Middle Eastern peoples generally) for endogamous marriages. See Matthews, "Family Relationships," 291–99, esp. 294, 297–98.

39. Cf. 2 Sam 17:25; 1 Chr 2:13–17.

described as "one flesh," and is considered to be legitimate only as a marital union that is binding and indissoluble.⁴⁰ Therefore, the narrator of Genesis comments, henceforth the marriage relationship instituted between a man and a woman would trump all previous kinship relations in importance as the man and the woman would become united as "one flesh": "Therefore a man shall leave his father and his mother and hold fast to his wife, and they shall become one flesh" (ESV). Hence "one flesh" (Heb. בָּשָׂר אֶחָד, *bāśār 'eḥād*; Gk. μία σάρξ, *mia sarx*) will become one of the most powerful of terms for describing that most intimate, unified, and enduring of human relationships. It will also have a strong impact on the view of marriage expressed in the New Testament.

Another way to denote a kinship relation in the Old Testament is simply by the use of the term "flesh" with a possessive pronoun. In Genesis 37:27, Joseph's brothers reason that they ought not to harm him, for after all, "he is our brother, our flesh" (my translation). In Nehemiah 5:5, the people say, "our flesh is as the flesh of our brothers, our children as their children" (ESV), that is, our children are like the children of our fellow Jews (who are enslaving our children). An interesting variant on this use of "flesh" is seen in the phrase "the flesh of one's flesh" in Leviticus to denote a close relative, with whom "one-flesh" relations are prohibited. In Hebrew, this phrase uses two different Hebrew words for flesh, בָּשָׂר and שְׁאֵר. In Leviticus 18:6, the term is שְׁאֵר בְּשָׂרוֹ (*šĕ'ēr bĕśārô*), "the flesh of his flesh," which is rendered in the LXX as οἰκεῖα σαρκὸς αὐτοῦ (*oikeia sarkos autou*), "[the] house of his flesh." The same phrase is used in Leviticus 25:49.⁴¹

An ambiguous use of "flesh" for kinship terms is found in Isaiah 58:7 (MT), when God describes the kind of "fast" he expects of his people: "Is it not to share your bread with the hungry and bring the homeless poor into your house; when you see the naked, to cover him, and not to hide yourself from your own flesh?" (ESV). The overall context of the chapter has to do with God's expectation that his people would do justly towards their fellow man, or neighbor, or fellow Israelite. But this verse's use of flesh seems to refer more closely to one's family members, a judgment supported by the fact that simple references to one's "flesh" typically denote a closer relation than one's "bone and flesh." Accordingly, while the Hebrew of the text simply says "and . . . from your flesh" (וּמִבְּשָׂרְךָ, *ûmibbĕśārĕkā*), most of the English translations heighten the possessive aspect of the term by rendering it as "from *your own* flesh," or something similar (e.g., KJV, RSV, ESV, NASB, NIV).

---

40. Chisholm, "Flesh," 778, citing Wenham, *Genesis 1–15*, 70–71.

41. See p. 46n38 above for reservations regarding the discussion of Wolff, *Anthropology of the Old Testament*, 29, on this passage.

Although it does not use σάρξ here, the LXX reflects the same understanding of the MT as the English translations. It renders the Hebrew as τῶν οἰκείων τοῦ σπέρματός σου (*tōn oikeiōn tou spermatos sou*), which can be roughly translated as "the household members of your seed," a phrase which BDAG translates in dynamic fashion as "your blood relatives."[42]

In the Hellenistic Jewish literature, the use of "flesh" (σάρξ) to express a kinship relation continues. Echoing Leviticus 18, Sirach 23:16–17 condemns one who commits incest: "Two sorts of men multiply sins, and a third incurs wrath. The soul heated like a burning fire will not be quenched until it is consumed; a man who commits fornication with his near of kin [Gk., ἐν σώματι σαρκὸς αὐτοῦ (*en sōmati sarkos autou*), lit., 'with the body of his flesh'] will never cease until the fire burns him up. ¹⁷ To a fornicator all bread tastes sweet; he will never cease until he dies" (RSV).[43]

In the New Testament, the use of "flesh" (σάρξ) to denote kinship relations continues, although we do not see this expressed by the phrase "one's bone and flesh." The most noteworthy aspect of this use of flesh is the continued influence of Genesis 2:24, which is quoted four times: in Mark 10:7–8; in the parallel Matthew 19:5–6; in Ephesians 5:31; and in 1 Corinthians 6:16. Interestingly, in the latter passage, Paul is not speaking of a man and his wife, but of a man and a prostitute: "Or do you not know that he who is joined to a prostitute becomes one body with her? For, as it is written, 'The two will become one flesh'" (ESV). Paul denies that there is any such thing as casual sexual relations that have no consequences for one's body, spirit, and spiritual union and relationship with Christ. It is shocking to think of the "members of Christ" being made members of, or one body with, a prostitute. We shall see below that it is often the case with Paul that there is a deep connection to the idea of "body" in his use of σάρξ, and that is also true in this occurrence. The prevalence of the term "body" (σῶμα) throughout the context of 1 Corinthians 6:13–20 bears this out.

There are other instances in the New Testament where "flesh" expresses kinship relations besides quotations of Genesis 2:24. For example, in Hebrews 12:9, the author speaks of "the fathers of our flesh," i.e., our earthly fathers, in contrast to "the Father of spirits," i.e., God. In Romans 11:14, Paul speaks of his fellow Israelites as "my flesh" (μου τὴν σάρκα, *mou tēn sarka*).

---

42. S.v. οἰκεῖος, definition a. In contrast to these judgments, Wolff, *Anthropology of the Old Testament*, 29, asserts that "your flesh" in the MT of Isa 58:7 refers not only to family members but to "our fellow-men, who are in general related to us in kind."

43. The Greek commences v. 17 with the second sentence: "The soul heated . . ."

Two Theologically Weighty Categories: "Flesh" as Man, Mankind, or Humanity

It is a small conceptual step from the idea of "flesh" expressing kinship terms that can extend to one's countrymen, to the use of "flesh" as a reference to man, all mankind, humanity in general, or even living things in general (category eight). It is then a small step beyond that to use "flesh" to refer to man and contrast him with God (category nine). These two categories of "flesh" are both filled with profound theological significance. From a logical and systematic viewpoint, it makes sense to examine category eight first, and then category nine. However, other considerations make it preferable to deviate from this systematic approach. Therefore, let us examine Genesis 6, the biblical passage that introduces both of these uses in such a way that they mutually define and clarify one another, with the clear intention of integrating concepts from the overall context of Genesis from the creation accounts through the flood narrative. How this text defines man as flesh and in contrast to God then becomes programmatic for the rest of the Bible. Following this analysis, we will then list other prominent examples of category eight (man as flesh without an explicit contrast to God), followed by examples of category nine (in which man is explicitly contrasted with God).

Man is Flesh, Not God, and All Flesh Have Corrupted Their Way—Genesis 6:3 and 12 in Context

The first reference to man as "flesh" (בָּשָׂר), in Genesis 6:3, is stated very simply: "he is flesh." However, this simple statement occurs in a passage that is notoriously fraught with interpretive difficulties, namely, 6:1–4. This precedes the first occurrence of the important phrase "all flesh" (כָּל־בָּשָׂר, kol-bāśār) in 6:12, a phrase used a total of seven times in the flood narrative of Genesis 6–8. Because these are the first instances of these significant uses of "flesh" and "all flesh," which continue throughout the Old and New Testaments, including Paul's epistles, we will take an extended look at them in context.

This passage is the first of two paragraphs (6:1–4 and 6:5–8) that conclude the *toledoth* of Adam (5:1—6:8). They serve as a bridge between that *toledoth* and the *toledoth* of Noah, and a rationale for the flood it describes. Let us first situate them in the early chapters of Genesis.

Previously, God had created man from the dust of the ground and breathed into his nostrils the breath of life to make him a living being (Gen 2:7). He had commanded man as male and female to be fruitful and multiply and fill the earth (1:26–28). But before man had begun to multiply at all, he had already violated the command not to eat of the tree of the knowledge of good and evil lest he die (2:17). Accordingly, God told the man he would return to the ground and to the dust (3:19). Now the man could not be permitted to eat of the tree of life, and live forever (3:22), and so was banished from the garden. The implications of eating the tree of the knowledge of good and evil are manifested in Genesis 4 through Cain's act of murder and the continued moral and spiritual degeneration of his descendants' culture. Despite the many references to murder in Genesis 4, there is no mention of dying. It is not until the *toledoth* of Adam, beginning in Genesis 5, that the reality of the sentence of death is emphasized with the phrase "and he died" repeated eight times in the genealogy of Adam and his descendants through Seth (vv. 5, 8, 11, 14, 17, 20, 27, 31); after this, the verb "die" is not used again until 7:22. As the *toledoth* moves toward its conclusion, it first introduces Noah (5:28–32) as one who would bring rest from the curse and painful toil that afflicted men's work (which anticipates 8:21–22).

References to Noah in 5:32 and 6:8 bracket the final two paragraphs of the *toledoth*, which then leads into the *toledoth* of Noah and the flood narrative. These two paragraphs serve as a link between the two *toledoth* and provide background information on what was happening in the land in the days of Noah that served as the consummate provocation for the judgment of the flood. The two paragraphs record two different instances of human evil and God's response to each. Both the evil and the divine reaction are intensified as we move from 6:1–4 to 6:5–8. The first paragraph may be translated as follows:

> [1] And it came to pass when man began to multiply on the face of the ground, and daughters were born to them, [2] then the sons of the gods saw the daughters of man, that they were attractive, and so they took for themselves wives from all which they chose. [3] And so God said, "My spirit will not be strong in man forever, for he is flesh. His days shall be one hundred and twenty years." [4] The Nephilim were in the land in those days, and afterwards, when the sons of the gods went in to the daughters of man, and they bore children to them. These were the mighty men from of old, men of renown. (Gen 6:1–4, my translation)

It is beyond the scope of this chapter to examine the various positions that have been taken on the many issues of controversy in this difficult passage. It will have to suffice for us to give a brief exegesis and justification of a few of the interpretive choices made. For the first time we read that man is multiplying on the face of the land. The word for "ground" is used here, most likely to underscore man's mortality, perhaps as a subtle reminder of his source of origin (2:7), and his eventual destiny to return to the ground because of God's judgment in the garden (3:19); at the same time, it also serves to foreshadow the mortal fate that is soon to come upon him. Man is multiplying, as God had originally commanded (1:28), but all is not well.

Next we read of the sons of הָאֱלֹהִים (hā'ĕlōhîm). In my judgment, this refers, not to fallen angelic beings, nor to the line of Seth, but to Mesopotamian kings who claimed divine or semi-divine status as sons of gods.[44] As such, the translation above takes הָאֱלֹהִים as a true Hebrew plural referring to false gods, hence "the sons of the gods."[45] Furthermore, these "divine kings," these so-called "sons of the gods," are linked to the kings of the Mesopotamian city-states by historical-cultural parallels, as well as to the descendants of Cain in 4:17–24 by their city-building activities. This link between the Mesopotamian kings, Cain's descendants, and the "sons of the gods" is further strengthened when we consider their interaction with "the daughters of man."

"The daughters of man" are simply women. The "sons of the gods" saw that they were attractive (lit., "good") and "took for themselves wives from all which they chose." The verse, with its use of *saw*, *good*, and *took*, recalls Genesis 3:6. The language in 6:2 suggests multiple interrelated sins: in addition to the sin of polytheistic idolatry,[46] there are the sins of polygamy and of taking these women as wives by force, which further suggests tyranny, oppression, and violence. The evidence for polygamy comes from the practice of the Cainite Lamech, who "took for himself" two wives (4:17–24). It is further seen in the practice of polygamy among the kings of the ancient Near East. Finally, we have the language of our text, which says that they took wives "from all which they chose."[47] From a thematic point of view, this fits with the polemic for monogamy and against polygamy that runs through Genesis (seen in 1:26–31; 2:18–24; 4:17–24; and in the depiction of problems caused by polygamy in Genesis 16, 21, and 29–30).[48]

Furthermore, the language suggests that these women were taken away by force (or the implicit threat thereof)[49] to become their wives: they

44. Kline, "Divine Kingship"; Birney, "Exegetical Study"; Walton, *Genesis*, 290–98.

45. Kline, "Divine Kingship," 192. Wenham, *Genesis 1–15*, 135, 139–40, adopts this translation, but interprets them as angelic beings.

46. Implicit in the exegesis given above regarding the בְּנֵי־הָאֱלֹהִים (běnê-hā'ĕlōhîm).

47. Kline, "Divine Kingship," 195–96; Birney, "Exegetical Study," 47–49; Walton, *Genesis*, 277–78.

48. Birney, "Exegetical Study," 49.

49. Note that the sin in view here is not forcible rape, but the taking of the woman to become a wife as an act of power that may be accompanied by force. See Hamilton,

saw that the women were *good*, and *took* them as *wives*.⁵⁰ This language is echoed in two other narratives in Genesis where this happened, and a third in which it nearly happened (Genesis 12, 20, and 26). Note the linguistic and conceptual parallels:

Table 1: Linguistic and Conceptual Parallels of Genesis 12, 20, and 26 with Genesis 6:2

Genesis 12:

v. 11- "You are a woman beautiful of appearance (i.e., face)"

v. 12- "When the Egyptians *see* you . . ."

v. 14- ". . . the Egyptians *saw* that she was very beautiful."

v. 15- "[they] *saw* her . . . she *was taken* . . ."

v. 17- " . . . Sarai, *the wife of Abraham*."

v. 18- " . . . she was *your wife* . . . "

v. 19- " . . . I *took her for my wife* . . . . Here is *your wife, take her* . . . "

Genesis 20:

v. 2- " . . . Sarah *his wife* . . . Abimelech . . . *took* Sarah."

v. 3- " . . . the woman you have *taken* . . . "

Genesis 26:

v. 7- " . . . she was *attractive* [*good*] of appearance [i.e., face] . . . "

The evidence for tyranny, oppression, and violence is seen in the violence of Cain and Lamech (Gen 4:8-15, 23-24); in Abraham's and Isaac's fear of violence from the kings in Gen 12:11-13; 20:10-11; and 26:7-9; in the suggestion of violence in the term "mighty men" (6:4); and the

---

Genesis, Chapters 1–17, 265; Gordon J. Wenham, *Genesis 1–15*, 140–41. Wenham argues, erroneously in my view, that no force is implied at all, but rather consent of the woman and her family. Though it may be granted that consent was occasionally present, this is an absolutely irrelevant consideration when living under the power of a tyrant.

50. Relating this to the culture of the ancient Near East, it may also refer to the practice of compelling women to join the king's harem, see Wenham, *Genesis 1–15*, 140; Kline, "Divine Kingship," 196. Alternatively, it may reflect the practice of the *droit du seigneur* or "right of the first night," attributed in the Epic of Gilgamesh to that ruler: "He will couple with the wife-to-be, he first of all, the bridegroom after" *Epic of Gilgamesh*, 2.159–60 (George, *Epic of Gilgamesh*, 15), a possibility entertained by Walton, *Genesis*, 293–94.

statement in 6:11 and 13 that "the land was full of violence," although that probably represents a progression to conditions more severe than those found in 6:1–4.

Bypassing for the moment verse 3, it seems these "sons of the gods" were indeed "mighty men," "men of renown"[51] (v. 4). As such, it seems most likely that the "sons of the gods" were also the "Nephilim" who were in the land "in those days, and also afterwards." The term applies as well to their offspring, who would be their dynastic successors. The term "Nephilim" (literally, "the fallen ones") is not a proper name, but seems to be a pejorative Hebrew epithet given to this group retrospectively—a one-word polemic[52] against those who are purported to be mighty, but who fall in judgment. The use of the definite article with Nephilim does not necessarily make this a "specific or well-known group"[53] *to those who were living in those days*. Rather, it means that they were a specific or well-known group *to the original audience of the text*, arguably due to hindsight. Knowing the fate of this group, any of the descendants of Noah could have applied this term "Nephilim" to them, such that the author and original audience of Genesis would understand the reference. It is arguably the case that the term is a non-rigid designator[54] that can rightly be applied to any group that fits the concept, as opposed to being a proper name. It is therefore unlikely that there is any connection, other than thematic, between these Nephilim and other Nephilim mentioned in Scripture, e.g., in Numbers 13:33.[55] The significance of their name is most likely that, as Ronald Hendel points out, no matter where Nephilim appear in Scripture, they do the same thing: they fall; they die—their reputation or pretensions to might notwithstanding.[56]

Genesis 6:3 gives us Yahweh's evaluation of these circumstances and the hint of judgment. Let us make a few more brief observations of the rest of the passage that forms the overall context for Genesis 6:3 before

---

51. Heb. אַנְשֵׁי הַשֵּׁם, (*'anšê haššēm*), literally, "the men of the name." However, the phrase seems intended to specify a particular group of men (i.e., the renowned men of might), but not a specific name. The article attached to שֵׁם is required by the construct-absolute construction so that the whole construct can be definite. The sense of the construction in the context would be "the men of name," i.e., the men of reputation or fame. Hamilton, *Genesis 1–17*, 270–71, points out the link with the builders of the tower of Babel, who sought "to make a name" for themselves (11:4), as well as the contrast with God's promise to make Abram's name great in 12:2.

52. Similar to the way the Hebrew term בֹּשֶׁת (*bōšet*) functions as a pejorative replacement for the term בַּעַל; (*baʿal*); cf. s.v. בֹּשֶׁת, *HALOT*.

53. *Pace*, Mathews, *Genesis 1–11:26*, 338.

54. See Kripke, *Naming and Necessity*, 24, 47–49.

55. *Veritate*, Mathews, *Genesis 1–11:26*, 336–37.

56. Hendel, "Of Demigods and the Deluge," 21–22.

addressing that text directly. The next paragraph, 6:5–8, parallels and intensifies the previous one. Whereas before men multiplied in the land and the "sons of the gods" saw that the women were good (vv. 1–2), in verse 5 Yahweh saw that the wickedness of man in general was great in the land. We note that "great" or "much" is רַב (*rab*), the feminine adjective from the same root as רָבַב (*rābab*), "to multiply." The LXX, accordingly, renders the phrase, "the wickedness of man was multiplied," using the Greek verb πληθύνω (*plēthunō*). The thought of man was evil continually. God had commanded man to multiply and fill the land, but by the early verses of the flood narrative, we see that man had multiplied his wickedness in the land (6:5), and filled the land with violence (6:11). In verse 7, the implied judgment of 6:3 has now become an explicit declaration of total judgment.

Now let us take a closer look at Genesis 6:3: "And so God said, 'My spirit will not be strong in man forever, for he is flesh. His days shall be one hundred and twenty years'" (my translation). Here "my spirit" (רוּחִי, *rûḥî*) does not refer so much to the Holy Spirit[57], but to the spirit or breath (רוּחַ, *rûaḥ*) of life that God breathed into man to make him a living being. The narrative in which this is related uses a synonym for "breath" in 2:7—נְשָׁמָה (*nĕšāmâ*). These terms רוח and נְשָׁמָה are used in synonymous parallelism in Isaiah 42:5.[58] Accordingly, it is unsurprising that we see throughout the flood account references to "all flesh" having the רוּחַ of life dying in the flood (6:17; or similar descriptions in 7:15 of the animals excepted from this judgment that are taken aboard the ark), and finally in 7:22, we read that "all in whose nostrils was the breath [נְשָׁמָה] of the spirit [רוּחַ] of life died" (NASB), bringing these terms together with the verb "die," which has been absent from the text since 5:31. Johnson underscores man's dependence on God's רוּחַ when he states, "Yahweh, . . . being 'רוּחַ and not flesh,' is the author and sustainer of 'the רוּחַ of all flesh.'"[59]

This gives us some assistance in facing our next exegetical problem. The author says of the spirit that it will not יָדוֹן (*yādôn*) in (or with) man forever. This verb is very difficult. This is its only appearance in the MT, and it has long been debated by translators and commentators. None of

---

57. Although from the vantage point of a broader biblical and theological perspective, we would certainly affirm that the Holy Spirit is the active agent of the Godhead that gives life and makes one alive (Gen 1:2; John 3:6; 6:63; 2 Cor 3:6). However, it is not the Holy Spirit that is in living things *qua* living things. It is the spirit of life given by God. See also Ps 104:29–30, in which arguably the first instance of רוּחַ is the spirit of life in a living thing, and the second is the Holy Spirit of God who gives life. A similar usage of רוּחַ is seen in the Preacher's speculations in Eccl 3:19–21. See also Mathews, *Genesis 1–11:26*, 321.

58. Johnson, *Vitality of the Individual*, 29.

59. Johnson, *Vitality of the Individual*, 32–33.

the options reflected in the ancient or modern translations receive more than tepid support.⁶⁰ Accordingly, the suggestion of Walton and Hendel may point the way forward. Walton argues יָדוֹן is the qal imperfect of an unknown root דנן (*dnn*) meaning "to be or become strong." This is also the argument of Hendel, who cites the Akkadian cognate verb *danānu*, its appearance in Ugaritic texts, and most significantly, the existence of the Hebrew root in the name of the Israelite town *Dannāh* (in Joshua 15:49), located in the Judean hill country. The town's name means "stronghold"

---

60. Cf. BDB, s.v. דִּין, in which four common options are discussed, with even the best of them assessed with reservations. For convenience sake, we will follow BDB's enumeration as we discuss the options.

(1) "Abide, live, stay, remain" follows the LXX's καταμείνῃ (*katameinē*), and the Vulgate's *permanebit*. This is the basis of the renderings given in the RSV, NRSV, ESV, NET, and HCSB, and is supported by Wenham, Hamilton, Mathews, Westermann, Cassuto, and Sarna. The main reason it is endorsed is its contextual fit in Gen 6:3; secondly because of its use in the ancient versions (not a significant factor for Mathews); while the philology is debated, as acknowledged by Hamilton, Mathews, and Sarna. Originally, Cassuto (1961, in *Genesis*) argued that philologically the word must be derived from the stem דָּנַן (*dānan*), which in turn is derived from the Akkadian *danānu*, but he rejected this as a bad contextual fit for Gen 6:3. Subsequently, Cassuto (1973, in "Sons of God and the Daughters of Man") argued for philological support for the reading "abide," citing cognates in Akkadian, Aramaic, Arabic, and late Hebrew, and these arguments have been cited by Wenham, Westermann, and more tentatively, Hamilton, who acknowledges that he goes along with the LXX reading "simply out of preference, but admit[s] the inconclusiveness of this position" (267). See Wenham, *Genesis 1–15*, 142; Hamilton, *Genesis 1–17*, 266–67; Mathews, *Genesis 1–11:26*, 333; Westermann, *Genesis 1–11*, 375; Cassuto, *Genesis, Part One*, 295–96; Cassuto, "Sons of God and the Daughters of Man," 17–28; Sarna, *Genesis*, 46.

(2) "To rule," from דִּין (to judge, to govern), resulting in "My spirit will not rule in man." This is the position advocated by BDB, although supported only by Zech 3:7.

(3) "To be humbled," which would result in "My spirit will not be humbled in man." This reading may be supported philologically by appealing to an Aramaic derivation, but such a reading could have no basis in Hebrew, according to BDB.

(4) "To strive with or contend with," which "is hardly justified" (BDB). This is nonetheless the basis for the renderings in NASB, ASV, KJV, and NIV (1984 and 2011). Waltke, *Genesis*, 117, makes a bizarre, doubly-wrong argument on behalf of this view. He asserts that the Greek translator guessed at the meaning "contend," yet the LXX actually reads καταμείνῃ ("abide"). He also refers to *HALOT* in support of this view: "the most recent authoritative lexicon prefers this meaning." However, *HALOT* (1:217) actually prefers "to stay" or something similar due to the context; nor is its preference expressed very authoritatively, as it is both marked with a question mark notation in the lefthand margin of the entry, and prefaced with the sigla "unexpl." (i.e., unexplained, unexplainable).

Skinner, *Genesis*, 143–44, feigns no hypothesis but does discuss the options in footnote 3. According to von Rad (*Genesis*, 14), the word *yādōn* is derived from a word *dûn*, "to be mighty, to rule." Contrary to Hamilton's statement (*Genesis 1–17*, 266n16), von Rad does not derive this from the Akkadian *danânu*. See also Walton, *Genesis*, 295; and Hendel, "Demigods and the Deluge," 15n10.

or "fortress." Hendel argues that the form יָדוֹן can be taken as a stative verb meaning "to be strong."⁶¹ Since the verb is a negated imperfect stative verb, it should probably be interpreted as being future oriented, hence the translation: "My spirit will not be strong in man forever." Brueggemann is probably on the right track in explaining what this means, "The judgment is that God will not endlessly and forever permit his life-giving spirit to enliven those who disorder his world. The breath of life (Gen. 2:7; Ps. 104:29–30) remains his to give and to recall."⁶²

Given the judgment of God that has already condemned man to death; given the degenerating trajectory of man; given the use of the word עֹלָם (*ʿōlām*) for the first time since 3:22, when God drove man away from the tree of life and expressed his will that man not live forever, we are already pointed towards understanding this as a statement of judgment, which will be confirmed in the remainder of the verse, and in the flood narrative, where we have already seen that there is a strong connection with the spirit and life.

A rationale follows: "for he is flesh." However, it will be easier to define what this means after considering the other elements in the narrative, so let us proceed to examine God's verdict: "His days shall be one hundred and twenty years." There is much debate about what exactly is meant by this phrase. There are two basic views: (1) God has decided that he is going to reduce human life spans to 120 years. Alternatively, (2) God has decided that he is going to judge man (by means of the flood) in 120 years. Both of these views are initially plausible. Let us examine them in turn.

The first interpretation, that God is limiting human life spans to 120 years, has three points in its favor. First, it fits the Sumerian cultural context. We see in the *Epic of Gilgamesh*, for example, a quest for immortality, which the gods prevent man from obtaining. We also see in the Sumerian King List a gradual diminishment of long (very long!) life spans after a great flood. Second, on this interpretation the statement follows naturally as an explanation of "my spirit will not be strong in man forever," that is, because God will only allow him to live 120 years. Third, we do see a general reduction in human life spans following the flood, that eventually gets down to something like 120 years. The patriarchs often exceeded that amount, but Walton suggests the possibility that they were exceptionally blessed with the *ruach* of God as his chosen ones. Also, Moses, the central figure of the Pentateuch, lived to exactly 120 years.⁶³

---

61. Walton, *Genesis*, 295; Hendel, "Demigods and the Deluge," 15n10.
62. Brueggemann, *Genesis*, 72; a view also endorsed by Waltke, *Genesis*, 117.
63. Walton, *Genesis*, 296.

By way of rejoinder, there are two potential problems for this view. The first is that it raises the even thornier problem of how we are supposed to understand these extraordinary life spans in the early portions of the Bible in the first place. It seems that our confidence in this first interpretation is proportional to the degree of confidence that we have truly understood what the author intended here. To the degree one takes these life spans literally, then to that degree this view will present no problem. On the other hand, if one suspects that some kind of symbolism or hyperbole is being used here with the life spans, especially if we have lost the relevant knowledge of the cultural background by which we can properly understand them,[64] then one will be equally at a loss to make sense of the idea that God shortened man's life spans to 120 years. After all, if I do not know what the Bible means by the extraordinary life spans, then I do not know what it means in shortening them, either. These considerations are not just a matter of a tension between the biblical text and our common observations of recorded history and human experience; it is a tension within the Bible as well. To the degree that one accepts Mosaic authorship in the Pentateuch (or at least Mosaic influence that accurately preserves his voice), and accepts the same for Psalm 90, then one will be confronted with this tension. For in Psalm 90 Moses speaks of our life span as seventy years, or maybe eighty "by reason of strength," but this seems to be considered an outlier.

The second problem with this interpretation applies whether one regards the life spans literally or not. Commonly, proponents of this view note that the post-flood generations continued to live long life spans. They explain this difficulty by positing that God gradually carried out this verdict, gradually reducing human life spans over many generations. But this raises a severe difficulty: how does God's execution of the verdict in this manner, delayed so that it only falls on those who live several generations later, constitute a meaningful judgment or penalty on the wicked generation that provoked the judgment in the first place? Let us see if the second interpretation fares any better.

This view, that God has decided to judge man in 120 years, also is very plausible. Whereas the first view arguably makes sense of what preceded 6:3, the second view makes sense of the coherence between 6:3 and what follows it. Specifically, God says, "My *spirit* will not be strong in *man* forever, for he is *flesh.*" Additionally, the *land* was mentioned in 6:1, and in 6:4 the author mentions that the Nephilim or *mighty men* (הַגִּבֹּרִים, [*hagibbōrîm*], from גִּבֹּר [*gibbōr*] or גִּבּוֹר [*gibbôr*]) were "in the *land.*" All five of these things—spirit, man, flesh, land, and mighty men—are referred

---

64. Waltke, *Genesis*, 111–2; Gordon J. Wenham, *Genesis 1–15*, 133–4, 145–6.

to several times in the flood narrative as objects of that judgment, the first four explicitly and the fifth obliquely:

Table 2: Five Elements of the Flood Narrative

"man"	6:4, 5, 6, 7; 7:21, 23
"breath/spirit (רוּחַ) of life"	6:17; 7:15 (exceptions to be saved), 22 (coupled with "breath")
"all flesh"	6:12, 13, 17, 19 (exceptions to be saved); 7:15–16 (exceptions to be saved), 7:21; 8:17 (bring them out); 9:1 (never again), 9:15–17 (covenant with)
"(in the) land"	6:5, 6, 11, 12, 13, 17; 7:3, 4, 6, 10, 12, 14, 17, 18, 19, 21, 23, 24; 8:1, 3, 7, 9, 11, 13, 14, 17, 19, 22; 9:1, 2, 7, 10, 11, 13, 14, 16, 17, 19
"the mighty men (הַגִּבֹּרִים, from גִּבֹּר or גִּבּוֹר)"	in 7:18, 19, 20, 24, the waters of the flood *prevail* (Hebrew verb גָּבַר [gābar], to be strong or mighty, to increase, to prevail), an oblique and contrasting reference to the הַגִּבֹּרִים, who fall and die, while the waters prevail exceedingly (גָּבְרוּ מְאֹד מְאֹד [gābrû m'ĕōd m'ĕōd]), or "prevail mightily" as the ESV renders it in 7:20.

We see that five things mentioned in 6:1–4 which either provoked God or are involved in the implied future judgment of 6:3 are mentioned in the flood narrative. "Man" and "all flesh" having the "breath" of life which are in the "land" become the objects of that judgment in the flood narrative, and the final culmination of that judgment occurs in 7:21–23, which is bracketed in 7:18–20 and 7:24 by reference to the mightily prevailing waters by which this judgment is accomplished. It seems that all of the forward-looking references of 6:3 are satisfied in the flood account.

In my judgment, these considerations should carry more weight than those that are in favor of the first interpretation, and so I am more inclined to favor the second interpretation.[65] God has determined to judge man in 120 years. Two caveats should be mentioned at this point. First, the possibility that this number is symbolic cannot be overlooked; regardless, it suggests a much shorter period of time in comparison to the life spans reported for the antediluvians. Secondly, God's determination to judge man is not incompatible with his grace and mercy. From a broader canonical perspective, in the Old Testament, God does announce his intent to judge, and yet it is conditional on whether or not man repents. We see this clearly in Jonah

---

65. This is also the conclusion of Hamilton, *Genesis 1–17*, 269, but for other reasons.

3:4–10. It may be possible to understand 6:3 in the same way. However, if 6:5–8 is viewed as a historical progression from 6:1–4 and not just a parallel description of it, then 6:5–8 represents an increase in man's sinfulness both in intensity and in extent, as it seems to describe the evil of man generally, as opposed to that of the "sons of the gods" in the previous paragraph. Far from repenting, man has become even more sinful. He is now ripe for judgment. God is bitterly grieved. Certainly by this point, the judgment is no longer contingent; there is no question of averting the judgment. Now God's grace and mercy can only act *through* the judgment. When we narrow our perspective to look specifically for parallels from Genesis, we see in 3:14–24 and 4:8–16 grace and mercy combined with the judgments on Adam and Eve, and on Cain. We see as well that "Noah found favor in the eyes of the LORD" (6:8, NASB). Man would be blotted out, but Noah would be saved, and would be the means through which a remnant of man and beast would be preserved. The closest parallel to Noah in this regard is Lot (Gen 19:29), and their actions after their deliverance seem to be set in a formal parallel (cf. 9:18–28 and 19:30–38).

Genesis 6:3 may be understood as communicating three basic ideas: (1) God's spirit of life will not remain strong in man forever (but will be withdrawn), (2) for man is flesh, and (3) God will judge man in 120 years. Clause (1) is God's decision to withdraw his spirit of life from man, clause (2) gives the rationale for (1), and clause (3) specifies the timing in which the judgment of (1) is to be carried out. We have clarified the relation of the three clauses, and the meaning of clauses (1) and (3). Now let us examine more closely the meaning of clause (2), which is of central concern to us: "man is flesh."

The first step in surfacing the meaning of this statement is to look at what we have seen of man and flesh so far in Genesis. Although man is created by God in his own image, he is formed from the dust of the ground and it is only the breath (נְשָׁמָה) or spirit (רוּחַ) of life from God that makes him a living being. Although man is not yet described as flesh (but only having flesh in 2:21), it seems fit to say that it is an apt description of him, given this utter dependence upon God's רוּחַ for his life. From the beginning, the idea of man's weakness, his perishability, and his potential mortality are present. The threat and potential of death are openly expressed in 2:17, and stated as a determinative reality for man in 3:19. In 3:22–24, man is kept from the tree of life, forbidden from living forever, and driven out from the garden—the first separation of man from God and life. That mortality is first seen in the murder of Abel, and then in the routine death of Adam and his descendants in chapter 5. Yet, up to this point, the author still has not called man "flesh." He withholds this predication until 6:3.

God's statement in 6:3 suggests a stark contrast between himself and man who is flesh (hence a category-nine usage of "flesh"); but it is only when we broaden our perspective to the whole of the Old Testament that the contrast becomes most explicit. Whereas at times נֶפֶשׁ is applied to God in about three percent of its instances, בָּשָׂר is never applied to God.[66] It becomes clear that בָּשָׂר "is what God is not, and what humankind is."[67] The following context also makes it clear that God's spirit of life is to be removed from mankind, from "all flesh," and the result is that they all perish and die (6:17; 7:21–22). God withholds the term "flesh" until 6:3, when the narrative is introduced that will demonstrate dramatically the universal mortality of "all flesh," a purpose achieved by 7:22, which concludes with another word that has been absent since 5:31—"died."

Truly man as flesh is weak and mortal, ever dependent on God for continued existence and life. If he were to withdraw his spirit, "all flesh would perish together, and man would return to dust" (Job 34:15, ESV). However, to focus exclusively on the physical weakness and mortality of man as flesh in Genesis 6 is to overlook or minimize the moral weakness and corruptibility of mankind, which is even more significant. In fact, it was the moral weakness that resulted in man's potential mortality becoming an actuality. The author of Genesis could have described man as "flesh" even before the fall, in that even then man already had the potential for sin, disobedience, and corruptibility. As Hamilton says,

> To be sure, the OT in general, and the opening chapters of Genesis in particular, do not teach that simply being flesh is sinful, as if the two were synonymous. After all, the man used this same word to describe his partner in 2:23, and together they became "one flesh" (2:25). But *bāśār* does seem to be a general term to describe the limitation and fallibility of mankind. And it is this fallibility that makes possible any kind of trespass.[68]

We have seen that the author withheld the predication "flesh" to man until 6:3, where he could demonstrate the fullness of man's physical weakness and mortality in the judgment of the flood. In a parallel fashion, the author delayed referring to man as flesh until this point when he could demonstrate the depth of man's moral weakness and corruptibility. This he does powerfully in 6:5–7, 11–12.

---

66. Wolff, *Anthropology of the Old Testament*, 26.

67. The view of Lys, "L'arrière-plan et les connotations," 178; cited in Hamilton, *Genesis 1–17*, 269n24.

68. Hamilton, *Genesis 1–17*, 268–69.

> ⁵ Then the LORD saw that the wickedness of man was great on the earth, and that every intent of the thoughts of his heart was only evil continually. ⁶ The LORD was sorry that He had made man on the earth, and He was grieved in His heart. ⁷ The LORD said, "I will blot out man whom I have created from the face of the land, from man to animals to creeping things and to birds of the sky; for I am sorry that I have made them . . ."
>
> ¹¹ Now the earth was corrupt in the sight of God, and the earth was filled with violence. ¹² God looked on the earth, and behold, it was corrupt; for all flesh had corrupted their way upon the earth. (Gen 6:5–7, 11–12 NASB)

Here in 6:12 we see the first use of the phrase "all flesh" (Heb. כָּל־בָּשָׂר; Gk. πᾶσα σάρξ, *pasa sarx*), which shall appear throughout Scripture. It is used here to emphasize the extensiveness of man's sinfulness and corruption, and complements the description of the intensity of man's sin in verses 5–7. Although 6:12 helps us to understand what is meant by "he is flesh" in 6:3, unlike that verse, there is no explicit contrast with God. However, the use of "all flesh" in 6:12–13, 17, 19; 7:15–16, 21–22, shows conclusively that the phrase "all flesh" can incorporate animals as well as man under this concept of God's frail creatures who perish apart from God's spirit of life.

Mathews emphasizes the importance of holding together both the mortal, physical weakness and the moral weakness of man as "flesh" to understand the implications of this depiction of man in Genesis 6–7:

> The essential sense of *bāśār* is human helplessness or weakness, whether it is the inherent frailty of corporeal life (e.g., 7:21) or the endemic moral flaws of humanity (e.g., 6:12). If "mortal" [i.e., the NIV reading] is its proper nuance in our verse, we ask how this can be reason for God's reproof (v. 3). Alternatively, moral depravity would fit better contextually, giving reason for the judgment. Yet this ambiguity created by *bāśār* actually bridges the cause-effect sense of both meanings. It is humanity's mortality that is foremost in mind in this passage since the cessation of God's life-giving is tied to the life and death of mankind (cf. 2:7 with 7:22), but the moral failing of human life cannot be dismissed altogether, for standing behind mortality is sinful corruption (3:17–19, 22–24).[69]

---

69. Mathews, *Genesis 1–11:26*, 334.

(Meaning 8) "Flesh" as a Reference to Man, Mankind, Humanity, or Living Things in General

A few more significant examples will suffice to reveal the breadth and significance of this use of flesh.[70] We have already seen the inaugural use of "all flesh" in Genesis 6:12 and the ensuing uses in that passage. Deuteronomy 5:26 says, "For who is there of all flesh, that has heard the voice of the living God speaking out of the midst of fire as we have, and has still lived?" (ESV), employing "flesh" to refer to all humanity (except Israel). In OT poetry, it is often used in a universalistic sense of "all humanity" to describe a future expectation that all people would come to God (Ps 65:2, ESV [MT 65:3, LXX 64:3]: "O you who hear prayer, to you shall all flesh come."), or an exhortation to let all people praise God (Ps 145:21, ESV [LXX 144:21]: "My mouth will speak the praise of the LORD, and let all flesh bless his holy name forever and ever").

In the prophetic literature, it is commonly employed to speak of eschatological judgment, such as in Isaiah 66:16: "For by fire will the LORD enter into judgment, and by his sword, with all flesh; and those slain by the LORD shall be many" (ESV). Similarly, in Jeremiah 25:31 (LXX 32:31), the prophet writes: "The clamor will resound to the ends of the earth, for the LORD has an indictment against the nations; he is entering into judgment with all flesh, and the wicked he will put to the sword, declares the LORD" (ESV). Likewise, Ezekiel 21:4-5: "Because I will cut off from you both righteous and wicked, therefore my sword shall be drawn from its sheath against all flesh from south to north. ⁵ And all flesh shall know that I am the LORD. I have drawn my sword from its sheath; it shall not be sheathed again" (ESV).

Alternatively, the prophets also used "all flesh" in expressions of eschatological hope and expectation for redeemed humanity. One of the most poignant of such expressions is found in Joel 2:28 [MT and LXX 3:1]: "And it shall come to pass afterward, that I will pour out my Spirit on all flesh; your sons and your daughters shall prophesy, your old men shall dream dreams, and your young men shall see visions" (ESV)—which seems to be a prophetic counterpoint to Genesis 6:3. And in Isaiah 40:5, the prophet writes: "And the glory of the LORD shall be revealed, and all flesh shall see it together, for the mouth of the LORD has spoken" (ESV);

---

70. With reference to בָּשָׂר, see s.v. בָּשָׂר, in BDB, definition 6; in *HALOT*, definition 9; in Chisholm, "Flesh," 777; Seebass, "Flesh," 672. With reference to σάρξ, see s.v. σάρξ, in BDAG, definitions 3a and 4; in Friberg et al., *Analytical Lexicon*, definitions 5–6; in LN, 105–6; in Thayer, *Greek-English Lexicon*, definition 3; in Gingrich, *Shorter Lexicon*, definitions 4–5; Ryken et al., *Dictionary of Biblical Imagery*, s.v. "Body," 105–6; Erickson, "Flesh," 304–6; Johnson, "Flesh," 375; Seebass, "Flesh," 674–75.

this is a passage that continues with more references to flesh that must be placed in category nine.

Beyond the Old Testament, this reference to mankind by use of the phrase "all flesh" continued in books like Sirach. In Sirach 1:9–10 (LXX; RSV 1:7–8), the author writes: "The Lord himself created her [i.e., wisdom] and saw and counted her [or numbered her] and poured her out upon all his works, [10] with all flesh according to his gift, and he supplied her to those who love him" (my translation). "All flesh" is most likely referring to all human beings. Note the increasing specificity of the passage: reference to all his works, then to all human beings (arguably), then to those who love God.

In the New Testament we see this usage continued as well. In a passage very reminiscent of the OT prophets, Jesus says, "And if the Lord had not cut short the days, no human being would be saved [lit., all flesh would not be saved]" (Mark 13:20, ESV; cf. // Matt 24:22). On the other hand, Luke 3:6 quotes Isaiah 40:5 thus: "and all flesh shall see the salvation of God" (my translation). Then in Acts 2:17, Luke quotes Joel 2:28 (MT and LXX 3:1): "And in the last days it shall be, God declares, that I will pour out my Spirit on all flesh, and your sons and your daughters shall prophesy, and your young men shall see visions, and your old men shall dream dreams."

Finally, Paul says that "all flesh" will neither be justified (Rom 3:20) nor boast (1 Cor 1:29) before God.

(Meaning 9) "Flesh" as a Reference to Man, Humanity, or Human Nature in Contrast to God

"Flesh" is used in its most pointed theological sense when it is used of man in contrast to God. We have already seen this in Genesis 6:3. There are many other OT passages in which the weakness and transience of man as flesh is contrasted with the strength and eternity of God (or of his Spirit or word).[71] Here are some of the most prominent examples.

In 2 Chronicles 32:8 the author writes of the King of Assyria, "with him is an arm of flesh, but with us is Yahweh our God, to help us and to fight our battles" (my translation). In Psalm 56:4 (MT 56:5, LXX 55:5), David writes: "In God, whose word I praise, in God I trust; I shall not be afraid. What can

---

71. With reference to בָּשָׂר, see s.v. בָּשָׂר, in BDB, definition 5; in *HALOT*, definition 8b; in Chisholm, "Flesh," 777; Seebass, "Flesh," 672–74. With reference to σάρξ, see s.v. σάρξ, in BDAG, definitions 2a and b; in Friberg et al., *Analytical Lexicon*, definitions 5–6; in LN, 105–6, 322–23; in Thayer, *Greek-English Lexicon*, definitions 3–4; in Gingrich, *Shorter Lexicon*, definitions 4–5; in Erickson, "Flesh," 305–6; Seebass, "Flesh," 674–75. With reference to both terms, see Ryken et al., *Dictionary of Biblical Imagery*, s.v. "Body," 105–6; Thiselton, "Flesh," 678–79.

flesh do to me?" (ESV). Here flesh refers to man in general, as is clear from the parallel in verse 11. However, David is concerned with specific enemies in verses 1–2, 5–7, but he shall not be afraid because they are merely flesh and he trusts in God. In Psalm 78:39 (LXX 77:39), the fact that man is only flesh is one reason God is so compassionate towards us: "He remembered that they were but flesh, a wind that passes and comes not again" (ESV). Here Asaph, in referring to the Israelites, notes that they were but flesh, in an implicit contrast between their weak, transient, and fickle nature compared to God's strong, enduring, and faithful nature. Interestingly, here their flesh is *likened* to רוּחַ / πνεῦμα, here clearly intended as "wind."

There are several noteworthy instances of this usage in the prophets. Isaiah 31:3 says "The Egyptians are man, and not God, and their horses are flesh, and not spirit. When the LORD stretches out his hand, the helper will stumble, and he who is helped will fall, and they will all perish together" (ESV). (However, "spirit" is missing in the LXX.) In the preceding category we noted Isaiah 40:5. That passage continues in verses 6–8 with more references to man as flesh, but now in direct contrast to God: "A voice says, 'Cry!' And I said, 'What shall I cry?' All flesh is grass, and all its beauty is like the flower of the field. ⁷ The grass withers, the flower fades when the breath of the LORD blows on it; surely the people are grass. ⁸ The grass withers, the flower fades, but the word of our God will stand forever" (ESV). In Jeremiah 17:5–6, the prophet warns: "Cursed is the man who trusts in man and makes flesh his strength, whose heart turns away from the LORD. ⁶ He is like a shrub in the desert, and shall not see any good come. He shall dwell in the parched places of the wilderness, in an uninhabited salt land" (ESV). In this passage, Jeremiah's contrast between God and the man who makes flesh his strength is imputed. On the other hand, in an echo of wisdom literature (e.g., Psalm 1), Jeremiah has a strong contrast between this foolish man in verse 6 and the faithful man who is likened to a strong tree in verses 7–8.

In the Hellenistic Jewish literature, this use of "flesh" continues, but begins to undergo some development. As a representative example of the manner of usage inherited from the Old Testament, consider Sirach 28:5, which, speaking of an unforgiving person, says: "If he himself, being flesh, maintains wrath, who will make expiation for his sins?" (RSV). The context suggests that "flesh" is not just a reference to being human, but an implicit contrast to God. The author counsels that we are all sinners in need of God's mercy, and therefore we should seek God's mercy while at the same time being merciful and forgiving to others; for how can we ask God to pardon our sins when we are unwilling to pardon others?

However, in the Hellenistic era, the phrase "flesh and blood" begins to be used to communicate this meaning, whereas in the Hebrew OT this had always been done with the word "flesh" alone. In Sirach 14:17–18 we see both types, as ben Sira writes: "All living beings [lit., all flesh] become old like a garment, for the decree from of old is, 'You must surely die!' [18] Like flourishing leaves on a spreading tree which sheds some and puts forth others, so are the generations of flesh and blood: one dies and another is born" (RSV). The first instance of flesh uses the "all flesh" form characteristic of category eight, but has a meaning which implies a contrast to God, since they wear out like an old garment and are confronted by the ancient decree from the eternal God that they must die. "All flesh" refers to humanity, as the context is talking of the wisdom of acting with the knowledge of the brevity of life. The second reference to man as "flesh and blood" refers to human beings who are mortal and perishing, one generation after another. Sirach 17:31 in a similar way refers to human beings who are weak, sinful, mortal, and perishing: "What is brighter than the sun? Yet its light fails. So flesh and blood devise evil" (RSV).

By the first century, the use of "flesh and blood" to express this meaning of flesh seems to have crowded out the older expression that merely used "flesh" to refer to human beings in contrast to God or other spiritual realities (except for direct quotes of the OT). There are several examples of this in the New Testament. Jesus says to Simon Peter: "Flesh and blood has not revealed this to you, but my Father who is in heaven" (Matt 16:17, ESV). After Paul's conversion in response to the revelation of the gospel to him by Jesus Christ (Gal 1:11), he "did not immediately consult with flesh and blood" (v. 16, ESV). Our struggle is not with "flesh and blood, but against the rulers, against the powers, against the world forces of this darkness, and against the spiritual forces of wickedness in the heavenly places" (Eph 6:10, ESV). In 1 Corinthians 15:50, Paul writes, "I tell you this, brothers: flesh and blood cannot inherit the kingdom of God, nor does the perishable inherit the imperishable" (ESV). Paul refers to the weak, perishable nature of humanity, and contrasts it powerfully with the imperishable kingdom of God.

Besides instances of the "flesh and blood" phrase, the New Testament also has instances where it uses "flesh" to speak of human beings in contrast to God. Of course, the clearest examples are where the New Testament quotes the Old Testament. So, for instance, Peter quotes Isaiah 40:6-8 in 1 Peter 1:23-25, and in verses 24-25 we read: "All flesh is like grass and all its glory like the flower of grass. The grass withers, and the flower falls, but the word of the Lord remains forever" (ESV). Here Peter employs Isaiah to contrast our perishable humanity with the imperishable and enduring word of God, which was preached to the believers and by which they were born again.

A final intriguing example comes from Mark 14:38 (// Matt 26:41), in which Jesus warns Peter, "Watch and pray that you may not enter into temptation. The spirit indeed is willing, but the flesh is weak" (ESV). This last statement has the ring of a proverb or traditional saying. There is a contrast here between the spirit and the flesh that is superficially similar to Paul's, but this instance lacks the redemptive-historical contrast which characterizes Paul's usage.[72] "The spirit" spoken of here is unlikely to be the Holy Spirit understood as the characteristic mark of the believer under the New Covenant, as in Paul. Rather, Jesus is more likely speaking either of (1) the human spirit, or (2) the spirit of God in the OT sense in which it is God's spirit that makes one alive or makes one strong. If (1) is intended, it would be akin to Paul's description of the pious Israelite under the Law, who can say "I have the desire to do what is right, but not the ability to carry it out" (Rom 7:18, ESV). This matches what Jesus says about the flesh; however, it does *not* match what Jesus says about the spirit here. Paul is describing a situation of futility, in which the "inner man" of the faithful Israelite was powerless to do what he ought. So it would make no sense for Jesus to direct the disciples to look to the resources of their own inner spirit. This makes interpretation (2) much more likely, especially since we see that Jesus has directed them to pray—the disciples need strength from God's spirit of life and power that is so often described in the Old Testament. In this case, the "flesh" referred to by Jesus would be the disciples' very selves described in their totality, the accumulated resources of which are woefully inadequate for the time of testing or temptation that is rapidly approaching.

A Final Category

(Meaning 10) "A Heart of Flesh"

One last example shows a sense of flesh that is uniquely positive, in contrast to the other uses that have any moral and spiritual significance. Ezekiel contrasts a heart of stone with a heart of flesh. In Ezekiel 11:19 he writes: "And I will give them one heart, and a new spirit I will put within them. I will remove the heart of stone from their flesh and give them a heart of flesh" (ESV). Then in 36:26, he writes: "And I will give you a new heart, and a new spirit I will put within you. And I will remove the heart of stone from your flesh and give you a heart of flesh" (ESV). God promises a future time for Israel in which he will remove a heart that is hard and dead to God and replace it with one that is soft, sensitive, and alive to him, and this description is accompanied with mention of "a new spirit" that God will put within.

---

72. France, *Gospel of Mark*, 587.

Conclusion

The Old Testament provided a rich heritage that helped form the lexical and theological environment in which Paul and other New Testament writers expounded the gospel of Jesus Christ. In telling the story of Jesus and its continuing significance in the life of believers, these writers drew on the OT theme of flesh. They did so with consistency and faithfulness to their OT inheritance, but also with the innovative developments necessary to describe appropriately the utter newness of the work of Jesus and the consequent life in the Spirit. It is to these new uses of "flesh" developed by Paul that we must now direct our attention.

— 3 —

Kata Sarka and *En Sarki* Relations, Identity, and Values in Paul

We have seen how the Old Testament uses the word "flesh" (the Hebrew בָּשָׂר, and the Greek σάρξ and κρέας in the LXX) with a range of meaning from the mundane to the profound. Beginning with its most literal sense of the skin, muscle and fat which covers the bones, the biblical writers employed such devices as merism, synecdoche, metaphor, and euphemism in order to employ "flesh" to refer to meat, parts of the body (such as the genitals), the body as a whole, the person as a whole, kinship relations, and, most expansively, as people at large, all mankind, humanity, or human nature. In its most theologically pregnant sense, "flesh" speaks of humanity as weak, transitory, corruptible, and perishable in both a physical sense and a moral sense, all in stark contrast to God in his power, eternity, incorruptibility, and faithfulness.

We have also seen that these uses for the most part continued into the New Testament, albeit sometimes with modification. For example, the NT began to speak more often of "flesh and blood" to denote mere human beings in contrast to God, and generally eschewed the OT use of that phrase to denote violent death. Similarly, while the NT continued to use the term "flesh" to denote kinship relations, it dropped the use of "bone and flesh" to express this.

Besides the many continuities between the OT and NT uses of "flesh," there are also some new developments in the way σάρξ is used in the New Testament, particularly by Paul, and this shall be the focus from this point forward. Paul's usage is more prolific in quantity and more distinctive in quality than that of any other NT author. Paul uses σάρξ ninety-one times in his thirteen letters, accounting for almost two thirds of the 147 occurrences in the NT. If we distinguish between the undisputed Pauline letters[1] and the disputed Pauline letters,[2] the undisputed letters account for seventy-two occurrences, and the disputed ones, nineteen. While in many instances his uses are typical of what we see in the Old Testament, there are also some striking differences, as we shall see in this chapter when we consider two of the ways Paul employs the constructions κατὰ σάρκα and ἐν σαρκί. Paul's third and most arresting innovation, his development of the σάρξ-πνεῦμα antithesis, will be the focus of the remaining chapters. This will culminate in the exegesis of Galatians 5:13-26, one of the central σάρξ-πνεῦμα texts, and an exploration of what it means to walk by the Spirit. For ease of reference and comparison we will continue the enumeration of the categories from the previous chapter.

(Meaning 11) Natural, Earthly Relationships: Κατὰ Σάρκα Plus the Language of Descent, Kinship, or Other Relation

The first new category of usage for σάρξ is very similar to what we saw in category seven in chapter 2, in that both indicate natural, earthly relationships, including kinship relations or natural descent from one's ancestors. However, the use of constructions formed with κατὰ σάρκα and the language of descent or kinship is quite distinct in the New Testament. Like the use of "flesh" in the Old Testament to describe such relations, the use of κατὰ σάρκα to indicate natural descent or kinship is morally neutral. However, when this idea is expressed with κατὰ σάρκα, it at least implies and at times explicitly states a comparison in which the κατὰ σάρκα relationship is always inferior to the alternative.

Jesus, Seed of David Κατὰ Σάρκα

This is even true when this construction is used to refer to Jesus' natural human descent. Paul writes of Jesus in his greeting to the Romans: "concerning his Son, who was born[3] of the seed of David according to the flesh,

---

1. I.e., Romans, 1-2 Corinthians, Galatians, Philippians, 1 Thessalonians, and Philemon.

2. I.e., Ephesians, Colossians, 2 Thessalonians, 1-2 Timothy, and Titus.

3. Greek τοῦ γενομένου (*tou genomenou*), from γίνομαι (*ginomai*), "to become, to happen, to come to be, to be." The translation "to be born" is debated because it is a rare rendering of γίνομαι, and because γεννάω (*gennaō*) is the usual verb for "I beget, I give birth to," or in the aorist passive, ἐγεννήθην (*egennēthēn*), "I was born." While I am sympathetic with Douglas Moo's reservations about rendering this participle as "who was born" and his preference for something like "who came," in my judgment

who was designated[4] [the] Son of God in power[5] according to the Spirit of holiness by [the] resurrection from the dead, Jesus Christ our Lord" (Rom 1:3-4, my translation). To speak of "being born of the seed of David according to the flesh [κατὰ σάρκα]" certainly bears no negative connotation, moral or otherwise, and in fact would constitute a ground of boasting for any Jew in the first century. However, it pales in comparison to being "declared Son of God in power according to the Spirit of holiness [κατὰ πνεῦμα ἁγιωσύνης, kata pneuma hagiōsunēs] by the resurrection from the dead"—a vastly superior designation.[6]

Abraham, Forefather of the Jews Κατὰ Σάρκα

In Romans 4:1, Paul speaks of Abraham, the ancestor of the Jews κατὰ σάρκα: "What then shall we say that Abraham, our forefather according to the flesh, has found?" (NASB).[7] Paul then proceeds to set up a contrast be-

---

the following prepositional phrase ἐκ σπέρματος Δαυίδ (ek spermatos Dauid) and the parallel example of Gal 4:4 in which γενόμενον (genomenon) seems to mean "born" gives that rendering a slight edge in plausibility in Rom 1:3. See Moo, *Romans*, 45-47, 46nn33-34; BDAG, s.v. γίνομαι, definition 1. See also the comments on the meaning of γίνομαι in Rom 1:3-4 and Gal 4:4 in Fee, *Pauline Christology*, 212n15, 242-43.

4. Greek τοῦ ὁρισθέντος (tou horisthentos), from ὁρίζω (horizō), "to set limits to or mark out a boundary, to determine, to fix, to define, to appoint," and with regard to persons, "to appoint, to designate, to declare," although the meaning "declare" is a post-first-century usage according to Lagrange, *Saint Paul*, cited in Moo, *Romans*, 47-48, 47nn38-39. See also BDAG, s.v. ὁρίζω.

5. The prepositional phrase ἐν δυνάμει (en dunamei) is taken to be functioning adjectivally to modify υἱοῦ θεοῦ (hiou theou), rather than adverbially to modify ὁρισθέντος. Accordingly, the full content of Jesus' post-resurrection designation is "Son of God in power." Jesus was of course "his Son" (i.e., God's Son, v. 3) prior to his resurrection, but now, because of his atoning death and resurrection, Jesus attains a new exalted status as "Son of God in power," or the status of "Lord" (cf. Phil 2:6-11). See Moo, *Romans*, 48-49; see also Jobes, "Jerusalem, Our Mother," 314-15, 315n31.

6. See also Dunn, *Theology of Paul*, 65; Fee, *Pauline Christology*, 241.

7. An alternate translation of 4:1 is advocated by Hays, "'Have We Found Abraham,'" 76-98; cf. also Cranford, "Abraham in Romans 4," 73-76. The proposed translation (as reflected in the title of Hays's article) is: "What then shall we say? Have we found that Abraham is our forefather according to the flesh?" This is problematic for several reasons. First, it leaves the infinitive εὑρηκέναι (heurēkenai) without an expressed subject, since the accusative Ἀβραάμ (Abraam) is taken to be the direct object of the infinitive instead of its subject. The subject of εὑρηκέναι must be assumed to be the "we" carried over from the ἐροῦμεν (eroumen) of what has (by the insertion of a question mark) become the preceding rhetorical question. But none of Hays's examples of τί ἐροῦμεν (ti eroumen) in Romans leaves an infinitive without an expressed subject such that one must be borrowed from the preceding sentence (noted by Tobin, "What Shall We Say," 443n14). Secondly, the traditional understanding of the verse is a setup to establish the premise that

tween Abraham's fatherhood[8] κατὰ σάρκα and another type of fatherhood, which, however, is not described with a κατὰ-construction in antithetic parallel fashion. Paul uses leading questions to guide his audience to the conclusion that Abraham found justification (being counted righteous by God) through faith, not works (vv. 2–5); and, furthermore, that this justification came prior to Abraham's circumcision (vv. 9–11a). Paul argues that this was so that Abraham "may be the father of all who believe while uncircumcised, so that righteousness may be credited to them, and the father of circumcision to those who are not merely circumcised but who also follow in the footsteps of the faith which our father Abraham had while uncircumcised" (vv. 11b–12, my translation). So here we see that Paul has set up a clear contrast between Abraham's fatherhood κατὰ σάρκα and what we might call "Abraham's fatherhood κατὰ πίστιν (kata pistin)," with the latter being incomparably superior than the former. For it is not having Abraham as one's father κατὰ σάρκα that brings justification and the inheritance of God's promises, but having Abraham as one's father "κατὰ πίστιν" (vv. 13–16, 22–25). As Moo points out, there is a hint of the pejorative sense in Paul's characterization of Abraham's paternity κατὰ σάρκα, for it is limited in a twofold sense in comparison to Abraham's fatherhood over all who

---

Abraham found grace or justification (or being considered righteous by God) by faith, which is entirely intelligible in the context of the preceding passage and the argument that follows, and makes a great deal of sense as a summative retrospective evaluation of Abraham's life; after all, in the argument that ensues, Paul draws on Gen 15:6, mentions the circumcision of Genesis 17, and may be lifting the εὗρον χάριν (heuron charin) language of Gen 18:3 LXX as an entirely appropriate way to frame the question. This is not to say that this is the final point of Paul's argument here, but it is a key premise, and the traditional translation coheres with Paul's argument. Thirdly, the proposed retranslation has Paul asking a rhetorical question that expects a negative answer, in effect a denial that Abraham is the Jews' forefather according to the flesh. This is extremely problematic, for Jews and Judaizers would certainly respond with a resounding "Yes!" (consider Matt 3:9; Luke 1:55, 73; John 8:33–40, 53; Acts 7:2; and see also Tobin, "What Shall We Say," 445, for an example from Josephus) and Paul's argument would not even get off the ground. Paul would more likely begin his argument with what is agreed upon and is evidently scriptural, and then lead his audience to accept his conclusion as the implication of these agreed-upon facts. Therefore, it arguably makes more sense to exegete this passage as Paul *conceding* the fact that Abraham was the forefather of the Jews according to the flesh, but then arguing from Scripture to deny the *significance* of that in comparison to being the forefather of all who believe, whether Jew or gentile. Cf. also the criticisms in Dunn, *Romans 1–8*, 199; Moo, *Romans*, 259n13.

8. I.e., "forefatherhood." Out of respect for the English language and to show mercy to the reader's ears, let us refrain from employing this awkward neologism. However, this is the precise meaning intended by Abraham's "fatherhood" in this paragraph. In the original historical context, the terms προπάτωρ (propatōr) and πατήρ (patēr) could be used interchangeably to speak of one's forefather (cf. Matt 3:9; John 8:39; Rom 4:12, 16; Moo, *Romans*, 259n12).

believe. First, it is limited in extent to the Jews, whereas Abraham's spiritual paternity is expansive to include all who believe. Secondly, it is limited in the salvation-historical sense that it is a "narrow, 'old era' perspective" in comparison to the "new era" perspective, in which Abraham is the father of all who believe, whether Jew or gentile.[9]

Romans 9:1–8 has three instances of this kind of relationship expressed with σάρξ, although only two of them with the construction κατὰ σάρκα.

The Jews, Paul's Brothers Κατὰ Σάρκα and Abraham's Children Τῆς Σαρκὸς

In Romans 9:3, Paul refers to unbelieving Jews as his brothers and his kinsmen according to the flesh. In this case, there is no direct contrast set up between this kind of κατὰ σάρκα relationship and a greater spiritual brotherhood in Christ. However, a survey of Paul's letters gives evidence that such a contrast was deeply embedded in Paul's mindset. Paul uses the term "brother" or "brothers" 133 times[10] in his letters to refer to literal biological brothers, to spiritual brothers in Christ, as a form of direct address to brothers in Christ, and here in Romans 9:3 to refer to unbelieving Jews. In the fifty-nine cases[11] where Paul refers to brothers in Christ, and in the seventy-one instances[12] where Paul addresses Christian brothers,[13] the context makes this clear even though he merely uses the unelaborated terms "brother" or "brothers." It is only in Romans 9:3 that Paul refers to unbelieving Jews as "brothers," and here the term does not stand alone, but is coupled with the appositional phrase "my kinsmen according to the flesh." In all of Paul's letters, he only refers to "kinsmen" here and in Romans 16:7, 11, and 21. The three references in Romans 16 are to kinsmen (*simpliciter*, not κατὰ σάρκα) and these are Paul's fellow Christians. It is clear that the usage of "brothers" for fellow Christians is consistent and customary, without

---

9. Moo, *Romans*, 259–60; cf. also Dunn, *Theology of Paul*, 65.

10. Specifically, 113 times in the undisputed Pauline epistles, twenty times in the disputed ones.

11. I.e., forty-six times in the undisputed epistles, thirteen times in the disputed ones.

12. I.e., sixty-four times in the undisputed epistles, seven times in the disputed 2 Thessalonians.

13. The use of ἀδελφός (*adelphos*) in the vocative case to address his audience is pervasive in the Pauline corpus. However, a noteworthy exception to this is found in Ephesians, Colossians, and the Pastoral Epistles, which lack any occurrences of ἀδελφός in the vocative—a datum that raises some questions for this supporter of Pauline authorship, questions which nonetheless must be left for others to debate.

needing any qualifying terms or adjectival phrases to clarify Paul's intent. We do not see the same for Paul's brother Israelites in the merely ethnic sense. Admittedly, this point is mitigated by the possibility that there was rarely an appropriate occasion in Paul's letters to refer to his fellow Jews in that way; and the evidence of Acts is that Paul did address unbelieving Jews as brothers in oral proclamation and conversation according to Jewish convention (Acts 13:15–16, 26, 38; 22:1; 23:1, 5–6; 28:17).

The strongest evidence for this subtle, implicit contrast between the κατὰ σάρκα brother/kinsmen and Christian brotherhood is seen in two passages that are found on either side of the text in question. The first is the glorious description Paul gives of spiritual sonship in Romans 8:12–17:

> [12] So then, brothers, we are debtors, not to the flesh, to live according to the flesh. [13] For if you live according to the flesh you will die, but if by the Spirit you put to death the deeds of the body, you will live. [14] For all who are led by the Spirit of God are sons of God. [15] For you did not receive the spirit of slavery to fall back into fear, but you have received the Spirit of adoption as sons, by whom we cry, "Abba! Father!" [16] The Spirit himself bears witness with our spirit that we are children of God, [17] and if children, then heirs—heirs of God and fellow heirs with Christ, provided we suffer with him in order that we may also be glorified with him. (ESV)

Then in Romans 9:6–8, mere natural descent from Israel or Abraham as "children of the flesh" (τὰ τέκνα τῆς σαρκός, *ta tekna tēs sarkos*) is discounted in favor of those who are "children of the promise."

> [6] But it is not as though the word of God has failed. For not all who are descended from Israel belong to Israel, [7] and not all are children of Abraham because they are his offspring, but "Through Isaac shall your offspring be named." [8] This means that it is not the children of the flesh who are the children of God, but the children of the promise are counted as offspring. (ESV)

Thus we see in Romans 9:1–8 two instances in which the Israelites are conceived of as Paul's brothers and kinsmen κατὰ σάρκα, and as τὰ τέκνα τῆς σαρκός, and both conceptions, though morally neutral, are contrasted unfavorably with an alternate status: brothers and kinsmen κατὰ σάρκα subtly contrasted by implication and the broader context with being spiritual brothers and fellow adopted children of God; and τὰ τέκνα τῆς σαρκός explicitly contrasted with "the children of promise."

The Israelites, from Whom Is the Christ Κατὰ Σάρκα

The third instance of a κατὰ σάρκα relationship in Romans 9:1–8 refers to that which obtains between Christ and the Israelites. This instance occurs in 9:5, a verse that occasions much debate over whether Christ is referred to as θεός (*theos*). Here is the passage in context, with the debated portions untranslated:

> ³ For I could wish that I myself were accursed from Christ for the sake of my brothers, my kinsmen according to the flesh, ⁴ who are Israelites, whose [ὧν, *hōn*] are the adoption, and the glory, and the covenants, and the giving of the law, and the worship [i.e., service in the Temple], and the promises, ⁵ whose [ὧν] are the fathers, and from whom [καὶ ἐξ ὧν, *kai ex hōn*] is the Christ according to the flesh, ὁ ὢν ἐπὶ πάντων θεὸς εὐλογητὸς εἰς τοὺς αἰῶνας [*ho ōn epi pantōn theos eulogētos eis tous aiōnas*], ἀμήν.

It seems clear that Christ is "over all" (ἐπὶ πάντων). However, many are reluctant to understand Paul to be using the epithet θεός with reference to Christ, preferring instead an interjected doxology to θεός, understood as referring to the Father.[14] A number of considerations, however, support the conclusion that θεός here is referring to Christ. First of all, it is not surprising that Paul would use this title only sparingly for Christ since it is typically

---

14. See the list of exegetes who hold this position in Harris, *Jesus as God*, 152nn18–19. See Metzger, *Textual Commentary*, 459–62, for an account of the UBS committee's reasoning concerning the editorial punctuation for this verse; the committee's punctuation supports Christ being referred to as θεός. Note that Fee, *Pauline Christology*, 272–77, advocates rendering the verse: "the Messiah as to his earthly life. May God who is over all things be blessed forever." On p. 272, he admits that if it were not for the *content* of what was said, the *grammar* would make the translation attributing the title θεός to Jesus preferable. The ultimate basis of his objection is that Paul would not use θεός as an epithet for Jesus, but would reserve it strictly for the Father. However, there is also Titus 2:13 (which, however, Fee notes but also argues against as an example of θεός referring to Jesus, pp. 274n86, 440–46). Fee's exegeses of these passages are less natural in our judgment (as he himself seems nearly to concede). Furthermore, while Fee is right that Paul consistently uses θεός for the Father and κύριος (*kurios*) for Jesus, this need not be taken as an ironclad consistency. For one thing, Paul calls the Holy Spirit κύριος (most likely to be understood in the manner of the LXX's substitution for YHWH) in 2 Cor 3:16–18 (see Fee, *God's Empowering Presence*, 310–19); secondly, in Phil 2:6, Paul says Jesus existed in "the form of God," and had "equality with God," and in 2:9–11 that he was given "the name above every name"—i.e., κύριος (most likely reflecting the LXX's rendering of YHWH in Isa 45:21–25) (see Fee, *Pauline Christology*, 373, 376–81, 396–410); finally, if the preceding is correct, this would make Paul consistent with other NT writers who also generally reserved the epithet θεός to the Father, but occasionally applied it to the Son and the Spirit (e.g., Acts 5:3–4; 20:28; John 1:1, 18; 20:28; Heb 1:8).

reserved as a designation for the Father, and careless usage of it could lead to linguistic confusion or to a mistaken identification of Jesus with the Father.[15] Secondly, Paul does not reserve θεός exclusively as a reference to the Father, for he uses it for various gods, false gods, and even Satan.[16] How much more likely it is that he would use it on a few occasions for Christ, who is even here described as "over all," which is a uniquely exalted status true only of God. In a similar fashion Paul regularly puts Jesus in the place of God by applying divine titles to him, uniquely divine roles, and applying OT texts that speak of Yahweh to Jesus—most notably in 1 Corinthians 8:4-6, where Jesus is worked into the Shema as the "Lord" mentioned in that text, one with "God"; and in Philippians 2:5-11, where Jesus exists "in the form of God," has "equality with God," and receives the worship of all creation that Yahweh receives in Isaiah 45:23-24.[17] Thirdly, to understand θεός as a reference to the Father as a new subject in the sentence requires one to take the participle ὤν in ὁ ὢν ἐπὶ πάντων θεὸς εὐλογητός as superfluous or otiose, rather than having the function of continuing to predicate something of ὁ Χριστός (*ho Christos*), a ready antecedent that agrees with the participle.[18] Fourthly, if the final part of 9:5 were a doxology to God the Father, it would be asyndetic, unlinked to any preceding subject, but Paul always links his doxologies to a preceding subject.[19] Fifthly, in independent doxologies in the LXX, the word εὐλογητός always precedes the name of the one to whom glory is ascribed— i.e., God—whereas here εὐλογητὸς comes after θεός.[20]

For these and other reasons, Murray Harris argues that θεός (as well as ὁ ὢν ἐπὶ πάντων and εὐλογητός) refers back to ὁ Χριστός. To be more precise, ὁ Χριστός is ὁ ὢν ἐπὶ πάντων, a phrase followed by the appositional θεὸς εὐλογητὸς εἰς τοὺς αἰῶνας, ἀμήν, which acts as a descriptive doxology to Jesus. The resulting translation is "the Christ according to the flesh, who is above all [(,) *or* (as)] God blessed forever, amen."[21]

---

15. Harris, *Jesus as God*, 169–70.

16. 1 Cor 8:4–5; Phil 3:19; 2 Cor 4:4; see also Harris, *Jesus as God*, 167–68.

17. Harris, *Jesus as God*, 168; Bauckham, *God Crucified*, 25–40, 51–53.

18. Harris, *Jesus as God*, 157–59; Metzger, *Textual Commentary*, 460–61.

19. Harris, *Jesus as God*, 160–61, 164–65, 171; Metzger, *Textual Commentary*, 461.

20. Harris, *Jesus as God*, 160–63, 171; Metzger, *Textual Commentary*, 461. An exception to this trend is Ps 67:19–20 (LXX; ET 68:18–19), where we find two consecutive sentences in which the first ends with a doxology and the second immediately begins with one: "... κύριος ὁ θεὸς εὐλογητός 20 εὐλογητὸς κύριος ..." ("... the Lord God be blessed. Blessed be the Lord ..."). See the discussion in Harris, *Jesus as God*, 161–2.

21. Harris, *Jesus as God*, 165–66. An extensive list of commentators who take θεός as a reference to Christ can be found in Harris, *Jesus as God*, 154n22.

Since κατὰ σάρκα is typically used by Paul, even in morally neutral circumstances, in some type of antithesis or at least implied contrast with a superior state of affairs or relationship, we may wonder if there is a similar dynamic at work in Romans 9:5. Harris offers three considerations that suggest that ὁ ὢν ἐπὶ πάντων θεὸς εὐλογητὸς εἰς τοὺς αἰῶνας expresses an informal contrast to τὸ κατὰ σάρκα. First, if τὸ κατὰ σάρκα did not anticipate some contrast with a greater aspect of Christ's person that did not originate with the Jews, then the phrase would become superfluous, along with the rest of the sentence. Paul could have finished his listing of Jewish privileges and ended his sentence with ὁ Χριστός. Secondly, ending his list of Jewish privileges with a reference to ὁ Χριστός would be a suitable climax to that list, but to state about the Christ who descended from Israel according to the flesh that he was over all as God blessed forever serves to dramatically heighten both the privilege of the Jews and the tragic disappointment of their failure to benefit from it. Third, Paul seems to be setting up a manifold contrast consisting of: (1) the contrast between (a) Jesus' Jewish descent and (b) his universal supremacy above all (ἐπὶ πάντων); (2) between (a) Jesus' humanity (τὸ κατὰ σάρκα as a reference to humanity and functionally equivalent to ἄνθρωπος [anthrōpos]) and (b) his deity (θεὸς); and possibly (3) between (a) his implied earthly origin and (b) his eternal existence and reign (ὁ ὤν, εἰς τοὺς αἰῶνας).[22]

Our Masters Κατὰ Σάρκα and Ἐν Σαρκί

Natural relationships other than kinship are also described with σάρξ in the New Testament. Paul uses σάρξ to describe the master-slave relationship. Two instances come from the disputed Pauline letters of Ephesians and Colossians, and one instance from the undisputed letter to Philemon. Although the master-slave relationship is not a kinship relation, it is an earthly one, and so Paul[23] refers to slaves' earthly masters as "masters according to the flesh [κατὰ σάρκα]" in Ephesians 6:5 and Colossians 3:22. In both cases there is a slight contrast between the master κατὰ σάρκα and the Master in heaven, i.e., God or Christ (Eph 6:5–9; Col 3:22—4:1), as well an appeal to work diligently and sincerely as for the Lord. A similar use of σάρξ occurs in Philemon 16, though with some noteworthy deviations. Paul urges Philemon to accept Onesimus back, suggesting that the purpose for which Onesimus was taken away from Philemon was so that he could have him back "no longer as a slave but more than a slave, as a

22. Harris, *Jesus as God*, 155–56, 159n47, 167.
23. Or, if you prefer, "Paul."

beloved brother—especially to me, but how much more to you, both in the flesh [ἐν σαρκί] and in the Lord [ἐν κυρίῳ (*en kuriō*)]." Perhaps it is the case that Philemon and Onesimus had a shared ethnicity, that they may be considered brothers "in the flesh." It is notable that Paul deviates from the use of κατὰ σάρκα. It is probably the case that Paul used ἐν σαρκί because it corresponds more closely to ἐν κυρίῳ. And here of course we do have a contrast between being brothers in the flesh and the greater relationship of being brothers in the Lord.

(Meaning 12) Life Κατὰ Σάρκα or Ἐν σαρκί: Superficial Appearances and Conventional Wisdom Contrasted with Spiritual Realities

This contrastive use of σάρξ and πνεῦμα is heightened when Paul speaks of the outward side of life, of that which is merely physical or external, of superficial appearances, and of superficial conventional wisdom, as opposed to more substantial spiritual realities. The most common construction employed is still κατὰ σάρκα, but ἐν σαρκί is also used. This can occur in contexts in which Paul speaks pointedly about who are the true covenant people of God, and what are the identity conditions for God's people. This contrast is also used with reference to the proper attitudes, values, and behaviors that should characterize the people of God. As such, the contrast between what is κατὰ σάρκα and κατὰ πνεῦμα is not merely implicit in these cases, but explicit, for the consequences, for our life or even our eternal destiny, of being κατὰ σάρκα are grave.

Circumcision Ἐν Σαρκί, Israel Κατὰ Σάρκα

Paul frequently disparages the relevance of Jewish national identity along with its epitome in circumcision and Torah. These are irrelevant to one's status before God as his covenant people or as a mode of life that pleases God. They are neither necessary nor sufficient to make somebody a member of God's covenant people or to live rightly in his sight.[24]

We see this clearly in Romans 2:25–29. In this passage, Paul is denying the relevance of circumcision, but he is not yet challenging the Law (that will come later in 3:19–31; 4:13–16; and 7:1—8:4). In Paul's reasoning, if a Jew does not keep the Law, his circumcision is then reckoned as uncircumcision; and conversely, if a gentile were to keep the Law, his

---

24. Barclay, *Obeying the Truth*, 208.

uncircumcision is reckoned as circumcision (Rom 2:25–26). Paul explains in verses 28–29: "For he is not a Jew who is one outwardly, nor circumcision that which is outward in the flesh [ἐν σαρκὶ], but he is a Jew who is one inwardly, and circumcision is of the heart by the Spirit, not by the letter; his praise is not from men but from God" (my translation). We can see from Romans 4:9–12 that Paul believed that Abraham's physical circumcision was to signify a covenant that was based on God's response to an inward reality of righteousness by faith. This Pauline reading of Genesis 15 and 17 is supported by exhortations in the Old Testament for Israel to be circumcised in heart, not just in flesh (Deut 10:16; Jer 4:4); and by warnings of God's eschatological judgment upon Israelites who are circumcised in flesh but not in heart (Jer 9:25–26). Furthermore, Moses looked forward to a time in which God would circumcise the hearts of the Israelites in Deuteronomy 30:6, but the context here is not explicitly eschatological, and seems to be a general and gnomic description of God's treatment of the Israelites with blessings and curses in accordance with their love and obedience to him; nonetheless, this passage should most likely be taken as anticipating a distinctive eschatological fulfillment. This is what we see in prophetic promises of a new covenant in which God would put his law within their hearts (Jer 31:31–34), and grant to them a new heart and a new Spirit (i.e., God's Spirit) who would be in his people and enable them to walk in his statutes (Ezek 11:19–20; 36:26–27). These are most likely the Scriptural antecedents to what Paul has written in Romans 2:28–29. What is not immediately clear in these OT antecedents is that this eschatological, new covenant work of the Spirit would redefine who God's true covenant people are, which is what occasioned all of the controversy surrounding Paul's understanding of the gospel and his gentile mission, and hence required his justification of the same in his epistles.[25]

For Paul, physical circumcision demarcated Israel κατὰ σάρκα under the Old Covenant, but spiritual circumcision demarcates God's new covenant people. Accordingly, a contrast can now be made between an Israel κατὰ σάρκα, an identity of no ultimate significance, and an Israel τοῦ θεοῦ (*tou theou*), who are the people of God, and for whom circumcision or uncircumcision is utterly irrelevant (1 Cor 10:18; Gal 6:15–16). Moyer Hubbard relates Romans 2:28–29 to Galatians 6:15–16, and hence to Paul's "new creation" motif. Both of these passages reflect Jeremiah 9:22–25, and Hubbard's analysis shows that Paul understood a cause-and-effect relationship to obtain between Jeremiah 9:22–23 and 9:24–25: improper boasting

---

25. Schreiner, *Paul*, 81; Hubbard, *New Creation*, 113–20, 220–21. See also Dunn, *Theology of Paul*, 65, 69; Ridderbos, *Paul*, 135–37; Moo, *Romans*, 174–75.

is caused by an uncircumcised heart. One key aspect of Paul's new creation motif that is seen in Romans 2:28–29 is the internal-external antithesis, with an emphasis on the *interiority* of the Spirit's work in God's new covenant people. This inner dynamic of the Christian life, in which the Spirit renews the inner man and works itself out through love, trumps the external issue of circumcision or uncircumcision (Rom 6:4; 7:6; 12:2; 1 Cor 5:6–8; 2 Cor 3:3–6; 4:16; 5:17; Gal 5:2–6; 6:15).[26]

Wisdom Κατὰ Σάρκα, among Men of Flesh in 1 Corinthians

Paul also speaks of values that are κατὰ σάρκα and antithetical to the Christian life and the Spirit of God. In 1–2 Corinthians, Paul is engaged in a struggle with his Corinthian congregation, the values of whom are κατὰ σάρκα, focused on outward appearance, superficial matters, and sophistic rhetorical values that are antithetical to a Christian mindset regarding people, discipleship, and preaching. The major source of opposition to Paul in Corinth came from sophistic cultural values. The people of Corinth prized the rhetorical style of the sophists, and imposed these expectations on Christian teachers. The sophists boasted of their own superiority because of their rhetorical training, and magnified the sense of inferiority and inadequacy of those who lacked such training.[27] The sophists also cultivated a zealous devotion among their admirers that in effect turned them into exclusive followers and disciples of individual sophists. In Paul's eyes, this bordered on idolatry.[28] The sophists also employed manipulative rhetorical techniques and eloquence that far overshadowed the substance of their content in order to persuade audiences. For Paul, this was a compromise of the gospel.[29] When Paul came to Corinth, he deliberately adopted an anti-sophistic stance and refused to conform to sophistic standards of oratory or lifestyle.[30] This was not understood by the Corinthian believers, and they began to identify themselves as zealous followers of particular Christian teachers in the manner of the disciples of sophists. They devoted themselves particularly to Paul, or Peter, or most notably to Apollos, and divided themselves into factions around their favored orator (1 Cor 1:10–12).[31]

26. Hubbard, *New Creation*, 136n23, 152, 197, 220–21, 227–31, 236.
27. Winter, *Philo and Paul*, 182–94.
28. Winter, *Philo and Paul*, 184–86.
29. Winter, *Philo and Paul*, 186–88.
30. Winter, *Philo and Paul*, 145–48, 151–70.
31. Winter, *Philo and Paul*, 170–78; Hubbard, *New Creation*, 140–45; Schreiner,

Paul rebukes this tendency and directly confronts the Corinthian believers' conformity to this sophistic mindset that is not pleasing to God or in conformity with his values (1 Cor 1:13–25). Paul himself had refused to conform to sophistic standards of rhetorical technique in his preaching, and did nothing to conceal what would be considered by those of this mindset to be the "foolishness" of the cross (vv. 17–18). Paul then contrasts the gospel message, which is God's power to save despite its apparent foolishness, with the "wisdom" that rejects it. That "wisdom" is exposed as something that is transient, foolish, and opposed by God: it is the characteristic of those who are perishing; it has been rendered foolish; it will be destroyed and set aside; and it does not lead one to the knowledge of God for it cannot accept a crucified Messiah. But if the "foolish and weak" crucified Messiah is actually the wisdom and power of God, what is the implication for the "wise man," the scribe, and the debater of this age? They are shown to be foolish and brought to naught (vv. 18–25).

The three terms used in 1:20—"the wise man" (σοφός, *sophos*), "the scribe" (γραμματεύς, *grammateus*), and "the debater of this age" (συζητητὴς τοῦ αἰῶνος τούτου), *suzētētēs tou aiōnos toutou*)—show how pervasive this "wisdom of the world" was which perceived the cross as foolishness to Jews and Greeks. The term σοφός was a general term that could be applied to sophists, but also to their students who had been trained in rhetoric and oratory as a part of their education. Those of this sophistic educational background now constituted part of the ruling elite of Corinthian society.[32] The γραμματεύς was a Jewish scribe. There was a large Jewish presence in Corinth, and they had rejected Paul's gospel and opposed his ministry, and eventually attempted (unsuccessfully) to secure a judgment against Paul from Gallio the proconsul of Achaia (Acts 18).[33] The συζητητής was explicitly a reference to the sophists and their values, which Paul goes on to criticize in 1:26–31.[34]

In his greeting to the Corinthians, Paul has already affirmed the enrichment of their speech and knowledge in Christ such that they are not lacking anything (1:4–7). The implication is that the lack of rhetorical skill according to sophistic values is irrelevant for the Corinthian Christians; their perceived inadequacy comes from a false value system.[35] Now in 1:26–31, he continues

---

Paul, 23–25. See also Litfin, *St. Paul's Theology of Proclamation*.

32. Thiselton, *First Corinthians*, 182–83; Winter, *After Paul Left Corinth*, 68; Winter, *Philo and Paul*, 189.

33. McRay, *Archaeology and the New Testament*, 319; Witherington, *New Testament History*, 268–73.

34. Winter, *Philo and Paul*, 187–89.

35. Winter, *Philo and Paul*, 182–84.

his direct challenge to their exaltation of sophistic values by indicating that God did not choose them in accordance with such values:

> [26] For consider your call, brothers, that (there were) not many wise according to the flesh, not many powerful, not many noble [i.e., of noble birth, well-born]; [27] but God chose the foolish things of the world, so that he may put to shame the wise (things), and God has chosen the weak things of the world to put to shame the strong (things), [28] and the base things [i.e., ignoble, low, insignificant, not of noble birth] of the world and the despised God has chosen, the things that are not, so that he may nullify the things that are, [29] so that no flesh may boast [lit., that πᾶσα σάρξ may not boast] before God. [30] But because of him you are in Christ Jesus, who became for us wisdom from God, and righteousness and sanctification, and redemption, [31] so that, as it is written, "Let him who boasts, boast in the Lord." (1 Cor 1:26-31 my translation)

Paul invites his readers to think back upon the circumstances from which God called them to faith. Very few of them were from the ranks of the educated, influential, or well-connected. The three terms in verse 26, "wise" (σοφοί, *sophoi*), powerful (δυνατοί, *dunatoi*), and noble (εὐγενεῖς, *eugeneis*), spoke of the Corinthian believers' social status and the honor they were perceived to possess in the eyes of Corinthian society. Very few measured up. There were some office-holders and members of the elite among the Corinthian congregation, which seemed to be a fair cross section of the city; but the *prima facie* meaning of 1:26 would indicate that this was a distinct minority, with the relative proportion of the poor being much larger than the well-off and influential.[36]

---

36. Thiselton, *First Corinthians*, 178-83. Thiselton traces the scholarly debate over the Corinthian believers' social status on pp. 181-83. For a contrary view, see Meggitt, *Paul, Poverty, and Survival*, who insistently argues from the general fact of widespread poverty in the Roman Empire and its urban centers to a universal negative conclusion regarding the conditions of all members of a very particular subset of that population: "*Paul and the Pauline churches shared in this general experience of deprivation and subsistence. Neither the apostle* nor any members *of the congregations he addresses in his epistles escaped from the harsh existence that typified life in the Roman Empire for the non-élite*" (75, italics Meggitt's, emphasis mine). Logically, of course, this sweeping conclusion does not follow. Admittedly scholars on both sides of this controversy are trying to draw probabilistic conclusions from fragmentary evidence, but it does not seem truth-conducive to argue against the grain of what little evidence we do have regarding the particular situation in Paul's churches and to explain away that evidence. In his argument against Winter and other proponents of the "new consensus" on this issue, Meggitt dismisses a fair number of indicators that suggest there were some in Paul's churches who were exceptions to the general poverty that was endemic to the

But all three of the terms in v. 26, σοφοί, δυνατοί, and εὐγενεῖς, are condemned by Paul by the adjectival phrase κατὰ σάρκα attached to σοφοί. The value system underlying this "wisdom" is merely κατὰ σάρκα, and furthermore, it is thoroughly linked to the sophistic value system. The terms σοφοί, δυνατοί and εὐγενεῖς were all used of those instructed by the sophists. Additionally, the sophists themselves are the σοφοί who came from families of the δυνατοί and εὐγενεῖς. These designations reveal the social class of the sophists, and of those educated by them and who emulated them. These terms were commonly used by first-century authors to describe the ruling class of cities in the eastern Roman Empire. For example, an extant account of a first-century sophistic debate parallels elements of 1 Corinthians 1:26-30. The debate contained much boasting about status, wealth, and success. The sophists cited their fame, their honors, and the offices they had attained. They engaged in a demeaning comparison with their opponents and applied a contrasting set of antonyms to their opponents to shame them: dishonorable, without reputation, lowly and undistinguished, and so forth.[37]

The influential sophists paraded their exclusive and expensive education as proof of their wisdom. But Paul turns this value system upside down in vv. 27-31. He used a set of antonyms to indicate that God had

---

Roman Empire (pp. 97-153). His arguments against the "explicit evidence" (p. 102) of 1 Cor 1:26 seem particularly tendentious. On the one hand, he claims that the face-value reading of the text (that "not many" were of high social rank, thus implying that a few were) may be misleading, because the terms are so imprecise and equivocal, and so elusive in meaning that it may be that actually none of the Corinthian believers are exceptional, in which case, the "not many" turns out to be a curious way to indicate "none" (pp. 102-5). On the other hand, he insists that Paul's descriptions of the general character of those whom God called in 1:27-28 apply "to *all* of the Corinthian community, *all* of the called," which certainly goes beyond and even against the evidence we have (p. 106, italics Meggitt's). It seems clear that Meggitt holds inconvenient evidence to a greater burden of proof, while for considerations that favor his hypothesis, mere possibility is treated as sufficient demonstration. Buried in the midst of the special pleading, Meggitt grudgingly concedes, "By itself Paul's words in 1 Cor. 1:26 can tell us nothing concrete about the social constituency of the congregation he addresses *except that a small number were more fortunate than the others*. How much more fortunate it is impossible to determine. It may be that *the few wise, powerful, and well-born* were a small group of literate, *ingenui*, artisans—who amongst the urban poor would have appeared relatively more privileged but whose lives would still have been dominated by fears over subsistence" (pp. 105-6, italics mine). This concession sounds much closer to the position I have suggested than it does to Meggitt's original claim.

37. Winter, *Philo and Paul*, 189-93. The first-century debate account is cited without further identification on pp. 192-93. Some of the sophistic reasoning is exemplified in Philo, *Det.* 33-34, cited by Winter, *Philo and Paul*, 192n65. See also Thiselton, *First Corinthians*, 182-83.

chosen the very ones the sophists and other like-minded members of the elite disparaged.³⁸

> God, however, has put to shame οἱ σοφοί by choosing those whom they themselves describe as τὰ μωρὰ τοῦ κοσμοῦ [ta mōra tou kosmou] (verse 27b); τὰ ἰσχυρά [ta ischura] by choosing those described as τὰ ἀσθενῆ [ta asthenē] (verse 27c); and τὰ ὄντα [ta onta] by choosing τὰ ἀγενῆ τοῦ κοσμοῦ, καὶ τὰ ἐξουθενημένα, τὰ μὴ ὄντα [ta agenē tou kosmou kai ta exouthenēmena, ta mē onta].³⁹

God has humbled all men, rebuking in particular those of this sophistic mindset who are merely wise κατὰ σάρκα, so that no one may boast before him. Their "wisdom" was actually foolishness, for it did not lead to the knowledge of God. God had called a few from the elite class, but God rendered status insignificant. Upon all of them, God, through the "foolishness" of the cross of Christ, had conferred a lasting status of wisdom, righteousness, holiness, and redemption. This rendered the social status of all of the Corinthian believers superfluous. Since it was God's work that had given this new status, and not their own merit, all arrogance and boasting is nullified, except for boasting in what the Lord has done. We have already noted the influence of Jeremiah 9:22-25 on Paul's motif of boasting, and Paul's view that improper boasting was the result of an uncircumcised heart.⁴⁰

Accordingly, here "wise according to the flesh" refers to that which is wise, esteemed, and honored according to a merely human value system that is antithetical to God's values. There is not a direct antithesis with πνεῦμα here, though it is certainly implied by the contrasting estimations of what is "wise" and "foolish" in the light of the Corinthian value system on the one hand, and what God has done through Christ crucified, on the other. This antithesis is made explicit as Paul continues into chapter 2, in which he describes his ethos of preaching, which magnified Christ crucified rather than himself, and depended on the Spirit's power, rather than on "persuasive words of wisdom" (2:1-5). Paul goes on to speak of a hidden wisdom of God, which the "mature" (τέλειος, teleios) are able to receive. Ultimately, it is only the Spirit who may unveil this wisdom; it is not something that man can discover otherwise (2:6-11). This is the Spirit and the wisdom that Paul has received, and that he speaks in his preaching, but it is not received or welcomed by the natural man (the ψυχικὸς ἄνθρωπος,

---

38. Winter, *Philo and Paul*, 191, 193.

39. Winter, *Philo and Paul*, 193.

40. Winter, *Philo and Paul*, 193-94; Thiselton, *First Corinthians*, 178-82; Hubbard, *New Creation*, 214-15.

psuchikos anthrōpos) for this wisdom is spiritually discerned. The spiritual man (the πνευματικός, *pneumatikos*) discerns all things, but is himself not discerned by anybody (2:12–15).

In 3:1–4, Paul writes that he had hoped to speak to the Corinthians as πνευματικοί (*pneumatikoi*), but found them to be "as men of flesh" (σάρκινος, *sarkinos*), mere infants in Christ. They were not the mature (τέλειος, 2:6) who could receive the spiritual wisdom that was contrary to the rulers of this age (see 2:6–8); rather, they could only take "milk," not "solid food" (v. 2). This is because they were "fleshly" (σαρκικός), as evidenced by the continued "strife" (ἔρις, *eris*) among them (3:3; cf. 1:11). Accordingly, Paul repeats the accusation by asking rhetorically, "Are you not σαρκικοί, and walking according to man [κατὰ ἄνθρωπον, *kata anthrōpon*]?" (v. 3). Then, citing again their earlier mentioned devotion to individual teachers in the manner of the disciples of sophists (3:4; cf. 1:10–12), he asks again, "Are you not (mere) men?" (3:4).

Two adjectival forms derived from σάρξ appear in this passage, σάρκινος and σαρκικός. It was once argued that a distinction could be made between these words, with σάρκινος describing a constitution or nature of flesh, and σαρκικός characterizing a fleshly disposition or ethical stance.[41] Although Fee still maintains this distinction,[42] it seems the terms are largely synonymous, with both capable of expressing both meanings.[43] Certainly it seems that Paul used them synonymously in 1 Corinthians 3:1, 3, perhaps using the two different terms for stylistic reasons to avoid redundancy. Note that σάρκινος is contrasted with πνευματικός, equated with being "infants in Christ," unable to take solid food, but only milk, while the Corinthians' σαρκικός mindset is evidenced by the jealousy, strife, and divisive factions among them (1:10–13; 3:3–8), such that they are "walking according to man" [κατὰ ἄνθρωπον] and as "(mere) men." "Walking κατὰ ἄνθρωπον" is probably to be taken in the sense of "behaving in a merely human manner." Winter relates these descriptions specifically to the Corinthian believers' sophistic attitudes and cultural values.[44]

Although it is difficult to pin down the exact meaning of σάρκινος and σαρκικός with precision, noting the relationships the terms bear to other phrases in the context offers some clarification. Thiselton adds further clarification by noting the relationships to some other relevant terms in the wider

---

41. See Thiselton, *First Corinthians*, 288n335 for a listing.

42. Fee, *First Corinthians*, 121, n 1, 123–4; also cited in Thiselton, *First Corinthians*, NIGTC, 288 n 336.

43. BDAG, s.v. σάρκινος; s.v. σαρκικός; Thiselton, *First Corinthians*, NIGTC, 288.

44. Thiselton, *First Corinthians*, NIGTC, 288, 292–5; Winter, *Philo and Paul*, 170–75.

context, πνευματικός ("spiritual," or "spiritual man," 2:13, 15; 3:1) and ψυχικός ("natural, worldly, pertaining to this life," or a person so characterized—the natural man; 2:14). All three of the other terms are in contrast to πνευματικός, but they can be put on a spectrum of increasing contrast. First, there is ψυχικός, which "is virtually *neutral*. It means *unspiritual* . . . in the neutral sense of **an entirely human** (unrenewed) nature, without further subtext (cf. AV/KJV, *natural*)." Second, there is σάρκινος, which means "*unspiritual* in a *descriptive* sense: in 3:1 such a person shows no sign of the presence and power of the Spirit of God, but appears to be motivated **by human, natural drives** alone (cf. REB, *on the natural plane*; NJB, *people living by their natural inclination*)." And finally, there is σαρκικός, which, "in 3:3 means **unspiritual** (first translation) in an *evaluative* sense, which carries with it *theological appraisal*: such a person in this context is **unspiritual** in every sense conveyed by σάρξ (*flesh*)." Thiselton, following Bultmann and J. A. T. Robinson, argues "that this included *human self-sufficiency, life in pursuit of its own ends*, or *being* **centered on the self** (second translation)."⁴⁵

Regarding People and Regarding Christ Κατὰ Σάρκα

Finally, let us examine one last example of κατὰ σάρκα: "so that from now on, we regard [οἴδαμεν, *oidamen*] no one according to the flesh. Even though we once regarded [ἐγνώκαμεν, *egnōkamen*] Christ according to the flesh, now we regard [γινώσκομεν, *ginōskomen*] (him that way) no longer" (2 Cor 5:16, my translation⁴⁶). Paul does not regard anybody according to conventional or merely human standards that focus on mere appearances.

---

45. Thiselton, *First Corinthians*, 292–93. Emphasis is Thiselton's, with the bold print employed by Thiselton to indicate the renderings he adopted in his translation of the passage. Cf. also the analyses of Garland, *1 Corinthians*, 105–10; and Winter, *Philo and Paul*, 172–73.

46. With Bultmann, *Theology of the New Testament*, 1:237–39, I take the κατὰ σάρκα phrases to function adverbially in modifying the "regard" verbs οἴδαμεν and ἐγνώκαμεν. However, his conclusion is unwarranted that this meaning is equivalent to taking these phrases as adjectival and modifying Christ; "Christ after the flesh" is *not* equivalent to "Christ regarded in the manner of the flesh," nor is it the case that such a Christ can only be perceived in such a manner. It is not necessary that "Christ as a phenomenon in the world" must be perceived in the "worldly" (or "fleshly") manner of seeing. Though Paul did not "see" the historical Jesus, it seems that he would agree, since, by analogy, if it is possible to regard a person "not according to the flesh," as per 5:16a, it would be possible to regard Jesus the same way. Surely John made a distinction between those who saw the historical Jesus and perceived him in a fleshly way, and those who saw and perceived him in a non-fleshly way (cf. John 1:14; 6:60–64; 8:15; 9:35–41; 11:40; 12:35–45; 15:22–24; 19:31–37; 20:8; 21:4, 7; and Bauckham, *Jesus Among the Eyewitnesses*, 384–409). But that is a subject for another time.

From 4:18 on, this theme of mere appearances and visible things versus more substantial spiritual and eternal realities is present. This worldly and fleshly way of thinking is what prevented people from recognizing Christ. Moyer Hubbard argues that Paul's dismissal of κατὰ σάρκα standards of evaluating people recalls Paul's earlier criticisms towards the cultural values that upheld sophistic views of rhetoric in 1 Corinthians 1–3, esp. 1:10–31. Accordingly, 5:16a is most likely a not-so-subtle exhortation "to the Corinthians to put behind them their worldly, sarkic [sic] judgments—especially of their apostle—and to reject once and for all those who boast ἐν προσώπῳ [en prosōpō] and not ἐν καρδίᾳ [en kardia] (5.12)."[47] Just as Paul had once viewed Christ according to the flesh, by merely human standards based on his Jewish messianic ideas that were incompatible with the crucifixion, so too the Corinthian believers had misunderstood Paul and his preaching; because of their merely human standards based on sophistic cultural values, they did not understand the significance of the cross for Paul's manner of preaching, or for their own discipleship.[48]

---

47. Hubbard, *New Creation*, 175–76.
48. Hubbard, *New Creation*, 176–77.

— 4 —
Preliminary Theoretical Issues Regarding Paul's *Sarx-Pneuma* Antithesis

The κατὰ σάρκα mindset which we examined in the previous chapter, along with Paul's condemnation of it, is a deeply rooted manifestation of a core sense of σάρξ that is highly distinctive of Paul's thought compared to other biblical writers, and a matter of central concern to the apostle. It is here that we encounter the σάρξ-πνεῦμα antithesis at its most fundamental level. We will be examining Paul's development of this antithesis over the next five chapters, beginning in this chapter with an introduction to the antithesis and then a clarification of four preliminary theoretical issues that affect our conception of it.

(Meaning 13) Paul's Σάρξ-Πνεῦμα Antithesis: Anthropological-Ethical and/or Salvation-Historical

Unfortunately, the exact nature and significance of this σάρξ-πνεῦμα antithesis is greatly debated among scholars. Some commentators see an anthropological antithesis within man's nature in which a man's σάρξ is at war with the πνεῦμα (understood as either the Holy Spirit or the person's own spirit) over the ethical conduct of his life. Others see a salvation-historical antithesis between the age of σάρξ with its emphasis on Torah on the one hand, and the new era of the πνεῦμα inaugurated by Christ's work. On this view, σάρξ and πνεῦμα therefore represent two antithetical modes of existence that characterize these two eras which are sharply and definitively separated by the cross. Consequently, the old mode of life is to be rejected as inappropriate to the Christian life.

Four Complicating Factors

A combination of factors have contributed to the complexity of Paul's σάρξ-πνεῦμα antithesis. The first factor is the familiar problem of the uncertainty involved in mirror-reading Paul's letters.[1] The second factor is the lexical ambiguity of the term σάρξ. The third factor is the uncertainty regarding the theological framework(s) within which σάρξ must be understood: is it anthropological, salvation-historical, both, or neither? A fourth factor is the difficulty of locating the σάρξ-πνεῦμα antithesis or conflict in relation to communities and individuals: is it an intercommunity conflict, an intra-community and interpersonal conflict, an intra-individual conflict, or perhaps a conflict that can occur at multiple levels? We shall now briefly examine these issues in turn.

(Complication 1) The Problem with Mirror-reading

The problem with mirror-reading arises because of our lack of background knowledge concerning the problems that gave occasion for Paul to write his epistles. This is particularly so in the Galatian church(es) and the letter to the Galatians, which features a prominent σάρξ-πνεῦμα antithesis. Much of the circumstances behind the letter are debated, and even if some of the standard reconstructions are accepted, the paucity of our understanding here poses problems in understanding Paul's use of σάρξ. Regarding the basic background issues, although by no means certain, it seems more plausible than not to accept the view that the recipients were in South Galatia, where Paul had established churches on his first missionary journey in Acts 13–14.[2] This view is usually correlated with an early date shortly before the Jerusalem council meeting of Acts 15, c. 48 or 49. This judgment makes the best sense of the facts that (1) they deal with the same controversy over the circumcision of gentile converts, (2) the Jerusalem council rendered a verdict in agreement with Paul's view of the matter, (3) and yet Paul did not mention this fact, and (4) Galatians reads as though it were written in the midst of the controversy with the outcome of the conflict uncertain.[3] Finally, the traditional interpretation that Paul had only one

---

1. Barclay, "Mirror-Reading a Polemical Letter"; Silva, *Interpreting Galatians*, 103–8; Schreiner, *Galatians*, 31–35.

2. For arguments supporting the South Galatian theory over the North Galatian theory, see Bruce, *Galatians*, 43–56; Bruce, "Galatian Problems: 2."; Longenecker, *Galatians*, lxiii–lxxxvii; Hemer, *Book of Acts*, 277–307; Hemer, "Acts and Galatians Reconsidered"; Schreiner, *Galatians*, 22–31.

3. See previous note; also, Bruce, "Galatians Problems: 4." For an exhaustive

group of opponents in Galatia, the Judaizers[4], is far superior to theories of additional opponents, such as anachronistic conjectures about the presence of gnostics, or speculations about the presence of libertines, which is opposed by the evidence of the letter that the Galatians were tempted by the opposite problem of Torah observance.[5]

Even granting agreement on these background issues, it is still difficult to define precisely the meaning of the σάρξ-πνεῦμα antithesis in Galatians from the text of the letter itself. We know that Paul taught personally in the Galatian churches, and must assume that this teaching was more systematic and most probably gave them sufficient theological background so that they could understand what exactly he meant in the letter by his σάρξ-πνεῦμα antithesis. Nonetheless, interpreters today do not have that benefit. In order to compensate, it is necessary for us to draw extensively on Paul's other letters. Romans is particularly helpful in this regard, since it is acknowledged by most scholars that there is a special relationship between these two letters due to the similarity of themes and theological concerns. Furthermore, since Paul had never visited Rome before writing Romans, the letter is by far the most systematic and full in presenting his theology and his gospel, for Paul could not depend on previous oral teaching to fill in explanatory gaps in the letter. Therefore, Romans serves as a most reliable commentary on Galatians.[6] At the same time, we must avoid uncritically reading Romans into Galatians and beware of superficial similarities. We shall attempt to walk this line carefully below.

It must be frankly acknowledged that this interpretive strategy presupposes a basic coherence and consistency in Paul's theology across his

---

treatment, see Hoehner, "Chronology of the Apostolic Age," 153–224, 239–44. For a view accepting the South Galatians as recipients but favoring a later date, see Silva, *Interpreting Galatians*, 129–39.

4. I am sympathetic to the view of Barclay, *Obeying the Truth*, 36n1, that "agitators" is a more apt epithet in some ways than "Judaizers," since the literal historical referent of the latter term (participial forms of the verb Ἰουδαΐζω [*Ioudaizō*]) was to *gentiles* who adopted Jewish ways, not to Jews who encouraged them to do so. However, the convention of referring to the latter as "Judaizers" is now so well-entrenched that to buck the trend would only result in terminological confusion. Moreover, the term "agitators" is not very descriptive regarding what the opponents were agitating *for*, so with no other candidate term, "Judaizers" will have to suffice.

5 Barclay, *Obeying the Truth*, 36–74, 218; Russell, *Flesh/Spirit Conflict*, 11–31; Russell, "Who Were Paul's Opponents,"; Schreiner, *Galatians*, 39–52. For an example of a scholar who sees additional opponents, see Jewett, *Paul's Anthropological Terms*, 95–108, who sees Paul engaged in a battle on two fronts against Judaizers and libertinists.

6. Hubbard, *New Creation*, 221, and see 221n146. See also Martyn, "Romans as One of the Earliest Interpretations of Galatians," in *Theological Issues in the Letters of Paul*, 37–45.

letters, particularly Galatians and Romans. Therefore, it stands against the theories of those such as Drane and Hübner that Paul's theology underwent significant development such that its major components were inconsistent from time t_1 to t_2.[7] Even more does it stand against the theories of radical inconsistency which claim that Paul's theology was inconsistent and incoherent at a given time t.[8] Rather than digress at this point to criticize these theories in detail,[9] let us attempt to justify the assumptions that form our starting point for interpreting the text over against their assumptions. Given the circumstances concerning Paul as a writer and ourselves as his interpreters far distant from him in history and culture, certain assumptions are appropriate. We assume that Paul is in a position superior to us with regard to understanding his own teaching and circumstances; we are largely dependent upon him for our understanding of these matters. If we reject his testimony, we are also rejecting the main basis to claim to know anything of Paul's teaching and circumstances. Secondly, the fact of the disadvantage of our position (vis-à-vis Paul's) grounds our assumption that perceived inconsistencies should be considered to be a result of our own lack of information and understanding rather than conclusive proof of incoherence on Paul's part.[10] That is to say, interpreters in such a position should presume that the writer merits the benefit of the doubt that he is coherent and consistent—though of course this presumption is defeasible. The benefit of the doubt may be forfeited if the specific evidence of his writings conclusively establishes the writer's inconsistency. However, this is a burden of proof issue—does Paul have to be proven consistent, or proven inconsistent? Arguably the latter, and if a coherent and consistent reading of Paul is even possible, it ought to be adopted over readings that imply incoherence.[11] Given that most interpreters of Paul do not follow

---

7. Drane, *Paul*; Hübner, *Law in Paul's Thought*.

8. E.g., Räisänen, *Paul and the Law*.

9. For discussion and criticism, see Westerholm, *Perspectives Old and New*, 164–77; Silva, *Interpreting Galatians*, 143–50; Dunn, *Theology of Paul*, 13–19, 19n55, 23; Schreiner, *Paul*, 37–38, 107n2; Wright, *Climax of the Covenant*, 2–13. See as well Beker, *Paul the Apostle*, 11–16, who advocates that we balance the coherence of Paul's thought with the contingency of its expression in his letters to the churches in ways that were relevant to their particular situations. An updated version of his coherence-contingency interpretive model is presented in Beker, "Recasting Pauline Theology."

10. See Dunn, "Works of the Law," 523; Achtemeier, "Finding the Way," 26–27.

11. Because of the modality of truth, a noncontradictory reading does not have to be known to be *actually true*; a noncontradictory reading that is merely *possibly true* is sufficient to refute the charge of inconsistency and contradiction, for contradictions are *not possibly true* and cannot be merely *possibly true* statements that just happen to be *actually false*.

the theorists of Pauline inconsistency, but are agreed that Paul is coherent, and argue among themselves which coherent theory actually corresponds to his view, we conclude that there are multiple coherent, possibly true theologies of Paul. Therefore, we will not be detained by theories of inconsistency any longer and shall join those attempting to adjudicate which of them is most likely to be actually true.

(Complication 2) Lexical Ambiguities with the Word Σάρξ

The second factor hindering our understanding of Paul's σάρξ-πνεῦμα antithesis is a set of lexical issues with the word σάρξ itself. We have already seen the wide range of meanings that the term "flesh" is capable of expressing in the Old Testament. Nonetheless, it is not terribly difficult to determine what meaning is intended. However, this is not the case in the Pauline corpus. Not only does Paul introduce some innovations in the use of the term σάρξ, he does so in ways that seem to equivocate. Perhaps Paul did so because it was rhetorically appropriate in the context of the Judaizer controversy, but this benefit may have come at the cost of terminological precision. Far be it from this writer to criticize the diction of the Apostle Paul (or the Holy Spirit), for it is most likely that by various means the author was able to make his intent clear for those to whom he wrote: the first-century Galatian churches—not the twenty-first-century church at large. Paul's ambiguous uses of σάρξ were likely to be much clearer to his original audience of Galatian believers who had sat under his teaching in person; but modern interpreters who have been denied such a benefit are left to grapple with such apparent contradictions as:

> "you are not in the flesh but in the Spirit." (Rom 8:9, NASB)

> "make no provision for the flesh in regard to its lusts." (Rom 13:14, NASB)

> "if I am to live on in the flesh . . . yet to remain on in the flesh is more necessary for your sake." (Phil 1:22, 24, NASB)

> "And I, brethren, could not speak to you as to spiritual men, but as to men of flesh . . . you are still fleshly . . . are you not fleshly, and are you not walking like mere men?" (1 Cor 3:1–3, NASB)

> "brothers, . . . flesh and blood cannot inherit the kingdom of God, nor does the perishable inherit the imperishable . . . we

[will] be changed. For this perishable must put on the imperishable." (1 Cor 15:50–53, NASB, altered)

"do not turn your freedom into an opportunity for the flesh . . . But I say, walk by the Spirit, and you will not carry out the desire of the flesh . . . Now those who belong to Christ Jesus have crucified the flesh with its passions and desires." (Gal 5:13, 16, 24, NASB)

Some of these apparent contradictions are easy to resolve. For example, it is certainly the case that Philippians 1:22 and 24 uses a purely somatic sense of σάρξ, and so is not difficult to understand coherently with Romans 8:9, where something other than a somatic sense is clearly intended. However, it is not so easy to place Romans 8:9 side-by-side with Romans 13:14 or 1 Corinthians 3:1–3; and in one and the same passage of Galatians 5:13–26 we see the flesh both as threatening to take advantage of opportunities to carry out its desire, and opposing the Spirit, *and* also the same flesh and its desires *crucified*. In wrestling with such difficulties, we may take some consolation in the fact that Peter, though living much closer in time, space, and culture than we, and *speaking by the Holy Spirit*, said of Paul's letters that they contained some things that are hard to understand (2 Pet 3:15–16).[12]

Nor do the lexicons give much help in clarifying the distinctive Pauline meaning of σάρξ. Walter Russell has noted how the treatment of the distinctively Pauline antithetical sense of σάρξ in the major lexicons has been heavily colored by the perceived theological function of the term in Paul. Rather than providing a definition of σάρξ, a brief description of Paul's theology of σάρξ is given. To a certain extent this may be unavoidable in a lexicon for theological writings like the New Testament. However, it can be problematic if the theology of σάρξ is too complex to be illuminated by mere lexicography—after all, individual words are not containers of theology. That is to say, Paul finds σάρξ a fitting word to use in expressing his theology because it already has a certain range of lexical meaning—which the lexicons are suited to reveal to us—not because the word σάρξ comes pre-loaded with that theology. This situation can be exacerbated to the point of misdirection if the lexicons' understanding of Paul's theology of σάρξ is mistaken or inadequate in some way. It is Russell's contention that this is in fact the case with regard to the lexical treatment of σάρξ in Paul.[13]

---

12. The point is not materially affected even if it turns out that 2 Peter is pseudonymous.

13. Russell, *Flesh-Spirit Conflict*, 8–11. Russell cites the treatment of σάρξ in BDAG, LSJ, and LN.

(Complication 3) Paul's Theological
Framework for the Word Σάρξ

This raises the third difficult issue that must be resolved in order to understand Paul's σάρξ-πνεῦμα antithesis, namely: what is Paul's theological framework for his use of σάρξ? This is really the core issue, and is greatly debated among Pauline scholars. Russell has described the anthropological framework for σάρξ assumed by many scholars in describing Paul's σάρξ-πνεῦμα antithesis.[14] He argues that this framework is inadequate and must be replaced by a salvation-historical framework. Russell seems to be correct that the anthropological framework for σάρξ is not *sufficient* to account for much of Paul's argumentation in Judaistic contexts such as in Romans and Galatians where he associates σάρξ with the Law, circumcision, and Jewish identity, and denies the normative relevance of these for Christian identity and Christian living. At these points there is evidently a salvation-historical contrast at work between the condition of God's people under the Law and the condition after the work of Christ that has culminated in the Holy Spirit's advent to dwell in God's people. However, Russell errs in dispensing with the anthropological framework.[15] We have already seen in our analysis of Genesis 6:3 and 12 that "flesh" was a paradigmatic anthropological term for the Old Testament, and it is antecedently unlikely that Paul would jettison it; we should expect that any claim to the contrary should bear the burden of proof. There are also clear examples that Paul did use σάρξ in continuity with the anthropological meanings he inherited from the Old Testament, such as in Galatians 2:16; Romans 3:20; and 1 Corinthians 1:29. Furthermore, Paul emphatically describes man as weak, perishing, corrupt, and sinful in ways that match the depiction of man's mortal weakness and moral corruption that we saw in Genesis 6:1–8 in chapter 2. Paul does not use the actual term σάρξ in his well-known indictment of man in Romans, but we can see that his depiction of man's weakness, sinfulness, and mortality is conceptually equivalent to that of the Old Testament in Romans 1:18—2:12; 3:9–18; and especially 5:12–21 with its echoes of the early chapters of Genesis. Of course, Paul does connect σάρξ with man's weakness, sin,

---

14. Russell, *Flesh-Spirit Conflict*, 1–11. Fee advocates a similar view in *God's Empowering Presence*, 816–22.

15. Schreiner, *Paul*, 143n6; Fee, *God's Empowering Presence*, 817–19; Dunn, Review of *The Flesh-Spirit Conflict*, 281. Russell seems to be at pains to minimize the anthropological aspect of σάρξ and to insist on its bodily aspect, *Flesh-Spirit Conflict*, 2–3, 11, 221. This seems unduly narrow. The body is certainly an important aspect in Paul's use of the σάρξ, but the anthropological sense of σάρξ can accommodate a bodily emphasis without denying other anthropological aspects of the σάρξ which cannot be reduced to the mere bodily sense.

and death in 6:19; 7:5, 18, 25; 8:6, 13; Galatians 5:19–21; and 6:8.[16] We will look more closely at these passages below. We note as a final consideration that it is not necessary for Paul to dispense with an anthropological sense of σάρξ to accommodate a salvation-historical contrast.

On the contrary, it makes more sense to say that Paul inherited and retained the OT paradigmatic meaning of σάρξ as an anthropological term with ethical implications, and superimposed upon it a horizontal, salvation-historical framework. The OT anthropological framework of flesh defines man apart from God as perishing and weak in a mortal sense and a moral sense. Ridderbos stresses that it is just this anthropological background that makes σάρξ suitable for Paul's adaptation of it for his salvation-historical framework.[17] Paul is *enabled* to add to this anthropological and ethical conception of "flesh" a salvation-historical contrast because he stands on the other side of Calvary and Pentecost and can see the distinctive and qualitative difference that is made by the finished work of Christ and the continuing work of the Holy Spirit who dwells in God's people. Paul is *required* to make this salvation-historical contrast because the Judaizers are advocating an anachronistic identity, and mode of life and discipleship for the people of God rooted in Torah rather than the Holy Spirit. Both the anthropological and salvation-historical theological frameworks are jointly necessary and sufficient to explicate Paul's σάρξ-πνεῦμα antithesis.

We would preempt those who reply to this proposal that it is gratuitous to appeal to two salvation-historical frameworks by suggesting that such a response needs to be justified by more than a mere preference for simplicity or elegance in one's theological constructs. Rather, a proposed theological construct is justified insofar as (1) it has some grounding or basis for believing that it is the case, and (2) it can explain or make sense of the biblical data. We believe that each of the two theological constructs we are proposing are solidly grounded in events of world-changing significance in history: specifically, the anthropological sense of σάρξ is grounded in the creation and fall of man, while its salvation-historical sense is grounded in the work of Christ and the Spirit. We shall attempt in subsequent chapters to substantiate the claim that our dual proposal successfully explains the biblical data and makes intelligible Scriptural passages that otherwise remain opaque.

---

16. Note also Ridderbos, *Paul*, 93.
17. Ridderbos, *Paul*, 103–4.

(Complication 4) Locating the Σάρξ-Πνεῦμα Conflict with Respect to Communities and Individuals

Another complicating aspect of Paul's use of σάρξ and the σάρξ-πνεῦμα antithesis is the degree to which it pertains to an individual, or to the community of God's people in a more corporate sense. It has been common in biblical scholarship in recent decades to move away from the individual in favor of a more corporate emphasis. In many ways this is warranted, for a strong case can be made that Jews from the OT era to the first century, as well as Greco-Romans in the time of early Christianity were comparatively more community-oriented and less individualistically-oriented than many people today, particularly from Western countries. The cultural difference and distance between the original and modern audiences needs to be acknowledged and compensated for if the Bible is to be heard correctly. Furthermore, an attentive reading of Paul's letters reveals a strong emphasis on addressing entire church communities with appeals to unity and harmonious and edifying relationships in the churches in which the members love, care for, and serve one another. Unfortunately, however, it has become fashionable to go beyond advocating an increased corporate *emphasis* to advocate instead a thoroughgoing collectivism coupled with anti-individualism. Many New Testament scholars set individual and community in an antithetical binary opposition and argue that Mediterranean peoples were collectivist in orientation and not at all individualist.[18]

Russell follows this general trend in New Testament scholarship in favor of the community over the individual. He rightly denies that "flesh" speaks of a "sinful nature" or "part" of the individual person that is in an internal conflict with the Spirit as a "new nature." Rather, he describes the flesh-spirit conflict as a contrast between antithetical salvation-historical eras, antithetical identities for the people of God, and of antithetical modes of existence and mindsets, with the poles of the antitheses separated by Christ's work in objective fact (Paul's indicative account of the Galatians' identity and status before God). However, this must be appropriated subjectively by the Galatian Christians by choosing to belong to the community of the Spirit rather than the community of the flesh that depends on nomistic observance for deliverance from sin's power (Paul's imperative). In this analysis, the flesh-spirit conflict only takes place at the level of the community, as the Galatian Christians grapple with the issue of their

---

18. Note the balanced assessment of Silva, *Interpreting Galatians*, 108–12, who expresses appreciation for but advocates caution toward some of the claims made from a social-science perspective. Silva's intuition will be provided some theoretical justification below.

community identity, whether to be identified with the community of the flesh or that of the Spirit. It is a contrast between two kinds of community. The flesh-spirit conflict does not appear at the individual level—with the possible exception that the individual Christian could possibly grapple with the question whether to defect to the flesh community; but insofar as the individual eschews circumcision and remains identified with a like-minded community, then he is walking in the Spirit, and the flesh-spirit conflict does not have much bearing on his individual existence. Or perhaps it is more correct to say that its significance has become almost entirely an indicative description of his mode of discipleship, but its imperatival implications have almost vanished.[19]

To his credit, Russell argues for an emphasis on the community but not an exclusion of individual concerns.[20] However, when he turns to social-science analysis for the background of the conflict in Galatians, he unfortunately relies, to a large extent and in an uncritical manner, on the work of Bruce Malina[21] and Jerome Neyrey[22] who do exhibit a radical anti-individualism in their scholarship, combined with a particular methodology of using models that is controversial in social-science research, as we will see below. Taking the Malina-Neyrey account of the completely collectivist and anti-individualist mindset of the Galatians as a given, coupled with an appreciation for Paul's concern for relationships in the community, results in the individual nearly disappearing from view in Russell's discussion of the flesh-spirit conflict, as we will observe below.[23]

There is no need for this. One can accommodate the social or group aspects of flesh without denying the flesh or flesh-Spirit conflict as it pertains to the level of the individual. The term "flesh," like the thing itself, is exceedingly supple and capable of expansion and contraction as circumstances require.

---

19. Russell, *Flesh-Spirit Conflict*, 1–11, 31–32, 61–62, 138, 143–47, 150–62, 166–67, 202, 209–10.

20. Russell follows Fee, "Freedom and the Life of Obedience," whom he quotes at length in *Flesh-Spirit Conflict*, 144.

21. Specifically, Malina, *New Testament World*; Malina, *Christian Origins and Cultural Anthropology*; both cited in Russell, *Flesh-Spirit Conflict*, 112n4, 114n16, 115n22. Cf. Malina, *New Testament World*, 61–67.

22. Specifically, Neyrey, "Reading Paul in Social Science Perspective"; Neyrey, "Bewitched in Galatia: Paul and Cultural Anthropology," 72–100; cited in Russell, *Flesh-Spirit Conflict*, 112nn1, 4.

23. See Russell, *Flesh-Spirit Conflict*, 87–98, 102, regarding the Malina-Neyrey model; also, see 144–48, 150–67, regarding the diminished individual. For a more recent presentation of the Malina-Neyrey model applied to Paul, see Malina and Neyrey, *Portraits of Paul*, esp. 1–18, 153–201.

If we are going to rightly interpret Paul's flesh-spirit conflict in Galatians, we must remove distorting lenses fashioned in an alien cultural context that can obscure the circumstances of the first-century Galatians. One set of distorting lenses can be fashioned by an unreflective cultural individualism characteristic of modern Western society. But the ideological bias of a modern academic subculture can do the job just as well, and arguably this has in fact happened. Malina and Neyrey have been justly criticized for flaws that are characteristic of sociology, cultural anthropology, and the social sciences in general.[24] One of the ideological biases of these disciplines in general is a thoroughgoing reductionist stance toward the individual as an acting subject or agent whose ideas and purposes can form internal motivations for acting in ways that can affect his community. In contrast, in much social-science scholarship, the individual is a passive object largely determined by impersonal social forces; for the most part, the arrow of causality runs from the social to the individual, and not in the other direction. This bias has been subjected to significant internal critique by anthropologist Anthony P. Cohen, most pointedly in *Self-Consciousness: An Alternative Anthropology of Identity*.[25] As a result, we see that the theoretical foundation in the social-sciences for Malina and Neyrey's view of a pervasive collectivism and a non-existent individualism in the New Testament world is rather dubious.

Malina and Neyrey have also been specifically criticized for the model of the New Testament world they have constructed on this foundation. Critics have noted the overgeneralized portrait drawn of Mediterranean people, with insufficient temporal and ethno-cultural distinctions observed, such that fourth-century BC Greeks, fourth-century AD Romans, and first-century Jews are homogenized into a uniform body of collectivists.[26] Similar distinctions are lacking between the mindset of Galilean peasant villagers and the inhabitants of Greco-Roman cities.[27] We shall see that this is because all are homogenized to fit a standardized model imposed from above, rather than based on evidence derived from below pertaining to specific

24. Esler, Review of *Portraits of Paul*. In general, Esler is very much in favor of social-science criticism and a community emphasis in interpreting the New Testament, so his critique of Malina-Neyrey's exaggerated collectivism and anti-individualism, though a gentle one, should be given some weight.

25. Cohen, *Self-Consciousness*. Cohen is also cited by Esler in his review of Malina-Neyrey, *Portraits of Paul*, 114. Burnett also critiques the underlying theoretical foundation for Malina and Neyrey's sociological model of community in the New Testament world. He appeals in part to Cohen as well. See Burnett, *Paul and the Salvation of the Individual*, 6–10, 23–29.

26. Grimshaw, Review of *Portraits of Paul*.

27. Bruce, Review of *The New Testament World*.

people groups in particular spatio-temporal-cultural settings. Malina and Neyrey also ignore indications of individualism found in Greek sources, Latin sources, in various philosophical movements, in Gnosticism, and in Christianity itself. After all, many became converts to Christianity in defiance of their community background. The countercultural ethos that pervades Paul's teaching is also neglected.[28]

In short, a less wooden, more dynamic conception of the relationship between community and individual is necessary to rightly understand the New Testament in general and Paul's flesh-spirit conflict in particular. In some ways, primacy should go to the individual. The individual is definable in a way the community is not. Furthermore, the individual is ontologically prior to all communities, with the exception of the family that gave him birth. But even the exception of this most natural community proves the rule: for the mere event of conception does not a community make, although it does make a new individual. Something more is needed to turn a bare biological act and its actors into a community. From a Christian perspective, there does seem to be an immanent teleology or purpose to sexuality and the family; there is some normative element that *ought* to be present to make the family what it ought to be as the most basic and natural community that generates and nurtures new individuals. One key element is a settled complex of *mental states of the individuals* in the family: a commitment of the will to the family, a sense of mutual belonging to one another, and of interpersonal identity. Lacking that, the community of the family will sadly disintegrate, to the detriment of its individual members.

So even this most basic of communities, which is most clearly definable and grounded in a natural state of affairs, depends for one of its necessary grounds of existence on its individual members, particularly on a settled disposition of their mental states toward that community. If this is true of the family as the paradigm community par excellence, then we should expect it to be true of, or at least analogous to, all communities. In some way, all communities exist in part in the hearts and minds of its individual members.

In fact, the strain of social science research advocated by Cohen has proposed just such an understanding of individuals and their respective

---

28. See the thorough critique by Burnett, *Paul and the Salvation of the Individual*, 30–43, for background discussion, and 43–57 for an evaluation of Malina, other researchers, and the evidence pertaining to the first-century Hellenistic world. On the related issue of how biblical scholars appropriate social-science analysis of the honor-shame value orientation, see Herzfeld, "Honour and Shame"; Chance, "Anthropology of Honor and Shame." Chance (p. 143) notes the influence on biblical scholars of Peristiany and Pitt-Rivers, *Honour and Shame*. For example, consider Russell, *Flesh/Spirit Conflict*, 94–98; Malina, *New Testament World*, 26–57.

communities. In his *The Symbolic Construction of Community*, Cohen describes the symbolic dimension as a necessary component of a community which is often missing from other analyses of community in the anthropological literature.[29] The symbolic dimension of a community is basically a sense of meaning, identity, belonging, and purpose that exist in the minds of its individual members. To the degree that sense is shared by the members, the greater unity and cohesion there is in the group, and a symbolic boundary is formed which defines who is a part of the community and who is not.[30] Cohen concludes that, in part, "the reality of community lies in its members' perception of the vitality of its culture. People construct community symbolically, making it a resource and repository of meaning, and a referent of their identity."[31] In short, Cohen's method clearly depicts a dynamic relationship between a community and its individual members, with a two-way flow of influence and causality between the two, in which a crucial element of the community is in the subjective perception of its members, who in turn receive from the community a sense of belonging and intersubjective identity. In comparison with the overly simplistic Malina-Neyrey model, Cohen's approach offers a far more fruitful conception of the individual-community relation for illuminating the social-science aspects of the types of community we find in the Bible and in early Christianity.[32]

---

29. Cohen, *Symbolic Construction*.

30. Cohen, *Symbolic Construction*, 11–21, 97–98; see also Hamilton, "Editor's Foreword."

31. Cohen, *Symbolic Construction*, 118.

32. I carefully refrained from referring to Cohen's approach as a "model," for the use of models is itself a subject of controversy in social-science research. The controversy is whether models are appropriate as a priori descriptions of social behavior or community structure, akin to generalized "social laws"; or whether they should only be used as a posteriori summaries or simplifications of the results of empirical research of a local, particular sort, which can then be used to compare to circumstances elsewhere. See Hamilton, "Editor's Foreword," 9; Cohen, *Symbolic Construction*, 20–23. This debate also occurs among social-science interpreters of the NT. For example, David G. Horrell criticizes Philip Esler and especially Bruce Malina on this issue, and characterizes Malina as committed to an inappropriate use of "models" in the sense of generalizable social laws that enable social scientists to understand, predict, and control. Horrell explicitly contrasts these assumptions with the approach of Cohen. Furthermore, he subjects Malina's approach to NT exegesis to withering criticism. See Horrell, "Models and Methods," 83–93, esp. 86nn8–9, 89, and 92n24; and Horrell, "Social Sciences," 3–28; see 10–14, 17–20 for a discussion of Malina's approach. In my judgment, this debate reveals a profound need for a deeper grounding in analytic philosophy for social-science theorists in general and in particular for those applying such methods to biblical studies, for they regularly traipse all over the terrain of epistemology and philosophical anthropology (to say nothing of metaphysics), yet seem to have only the most superficial awareness of the topography. This is evident in the attachment that social-science theorists

Although he does not interact with Cohen, Ben C. Dunson applies a similar understanding of community and individual to Paul's writing. In a "state of the question" article[33] Dunson relates this issue to many of the debates in Pauline scholarship.[34] He contends that the very act of pitting individual and community against each other in antithesis is wrongheaded and unhelpful, and distorts the reading of Paul. Accordingly, he argues against the excessively collectivist, anti-individualist trend in Pauline scholarship, while carefully maintaining support for the community emphasis in the New Testament as well. In this way he avoids overreacting against the community focus, as he charges Burnett with doing occasionally.[35] In my judgment, Dunson is entirely correct that we need to reinstate the individual to his rightful place in the Christian community in Pauline scholarship, and this is particularly true if we are going to understand the flesh-spirit conflict, and what it means to walk by the Spirit according to Paul.

Conclusion

This chapter we have attempted to draw attention to four theoretical issues that affect one's interpretation of Paul's σάρξ-πνεῦμα antithesis. Regarding these issues, we have argued: (1) that it is appropriate to appeal to Paul's epistle to the Romans to guide the exegete in interpreting the letter to the Galatians, which necessarily requires a certain degree of mirror-reading, a precarious endeavor which benefits from guidance from Paul's most systematic letter. (2) Furthermore, we cautioned that appeal to the lexicons will not resolve the meaning of the σάρξ and πνεῦμα in Paul's letters, and to the degree that the lexical treatment has been colored by

---

have to prescriptive models which presume that human beings, their communities, and their behavior can be subsumed under "scientific" or social-scientific "laws." In contrast to this vision, philosopher Roderick Chisholm argued forcefully in a 1964 lecture defending libertarian freedom that one of its inescapable implications is that there is not and *cannot* be a science of man. This argument (representative of many that could be cited) raises an external conceptual problem for the basic presuppositions of a major stream of social-science research with which few of its practitioners are engaging. See Chisholm, "Human Freedom and the Self," 46–56.

33. Dunson, "Individual and Community in Pauline Scholarship."

34. E.g., the New Perspective vs. Reformation view debate; Paul's new creation motif as cosmological or anthropological; the debate over faith and πίστις Χριστοῦ (*pistis Christou*) as subjective-genitive or objective-genitive; the apocalyptic Paul debate; the individual-corporate election debate, and even the anti-Imperial political Paul debate.

35. See also Dunson, "Individual and Community in Paul's Letter to the Romans," 1–14. See pp. 13–14 for the mild critique of Burnett. For a similar view to Dunson, cf. Bowers, "Fulfilling the Gospel," 187–88.

an inadequate theological view of these terms, it could obscure their true significance in Paul's thought. (3) Then we argued a crucial point: that the OT anthropological framework for σάρξ is a given that remains basic to Paul's thought, and that his post-Pentecost perspective allows him to make the salvation-historical contrast that he needs to make to deal with the Judaizing controversy in Galatians. In short, both the anthropological and salvation-historical theological frameworks are jointly necessary and sufficient to explicate Paul's σάρξ-πνεῦμα antithesis. (4) Finally, we argued that the σάρξ-πνεῦμα antithesis has relevance both at the level of the community and at the level of the individual such that to exclude either dimension is to distort our understanding of the conflict.

— 5 —

Paul's Supplementary Salvation-Historical Framework of *Sarx*: Romans 6–8

Now that we have clarified some of the theoretical issues that color one's understanding of Paul's flesh-Spirit antithesis, let us turn directly to Paul's own writings, beginning with Romans 6–8.

A Brief Assay of Paul's Salvation-Historical Usage of Σάρξ

Romans 6–8: Christians Are Not "in the Flesh" in a Salvation-Historical Sense

Above we mentioned Romans 5:12–23 as an example of Paul's description of man in accord with that of the Old Testament. Additionally, this passage grounds Romans 6–8 in the widest possible salvation-historical context,[1] commencing with the rupture between God and man that affected all by bringing spiritual death to the whole human race, as a result of which all sinned.[2] The giving of the Law to Israel is placed within this wider context, preparing us for Romans 6–8, which clarifies the people of God's relationship to the Law now that Christ and the Spirit have come. Romans 6–8 gives us the clearest sense of the salvation-historical framework that structures Paul's understanding of the outworking of the gospel. The overall flow of this passage is helpfully summarized by Paul himself in Rom 7:4–6[3]:

1. Hubbard, *New Creation*, 93; Moo, *Romans*, 314–15, 319, 340.

2. The controversial ἐφ' ᾧ (*eph hō*) of 5:12 is to be understood in a consequential sense, *not* a causal sense: "death spread to all men *on the basis of which* all sinned" (or in less stilted renderings, "with the result that" or "so that"). See Fitzmyer, "Consecutive Meaning of ΕΦ' Ω"; Schreiner, *Romans*, 274; Schreiner, *Paul*, 146–48.

3. Hubbard, *New Creation*, 107; Fee, *God's Empowering Presence*, 503–8; Russell, "Insights," 520–21; Dunn, *Romans 1–8*, 358; Moo, *Romans*, 414, 418–22. Moo makes explicit the connection between 7:4 and 6:1–23; less so the connection between 7:5

> ⁴ Therefore, my brothers, you also were made to die to the Law through the body of Christ, so that you might belong to another, to him who was raised from the dead, in order that we might bear fruit for God. ⁵ For when we were in the flesh, the sinful passions, which were [aroused] through the Law, were at work in our members [i.e., of our bodies] to bear fruit for death. ⁶ But now we have been released from the Law, having died to that by which we were bound, so that we serve in the newness of the Spirit and not in the oldness of the letter. (Rom 7:4-6, my translation)

The verses correspond in order with these three chapters (7:4 to 6:1-23; 7:5 to 7:7-25; and 7:6 to 8:1-17). Notice also the correlation between the tenses and time frames. Romans 7:4 and 6:1-23 describe past events and their present results, in which the recipients died to the Law (and sin) and were united to Christ, and now are alive to God and serve him rather than sin. Romans 7:5 and 7:7-25 describe life prior to this, when "we *were* in the flesh," during which time sinful passions were aroused by the Law and at work in the members of the body to bear fruit for death. Romans 7:6 states, "but *now we have been released from the Law*, having died to that by which we were bound, so that we serve in the newness of the Spirit and not in the oldness of the letter," upon which 8:1-17 elaborates. Romans 7:4-6 clearly establishes the contrast between the former time when the people of God *were* under the Torah, and the present time in which they are not. Furthermore, this is confirmed in 8:1-4, 9, which refers to several conditions from 7:14-25 and indicates that they have now been nullified by Christ's work and the Spirit's indwelling. In 8:2 the Spirit (who was absent throughout 7:14-25), has set free the one who had been in bondage (7:14), and had been a prisoner (7:23), and had needed to be set free (7:24). Similarly, "the law of the Spirit of life in Christ Jesus"⁴ has set those free who had been subject to the law of sin and death throughout 7:21-25. Before, the person was unable to do the good things commanded by the Law, and unable to refrain from doing the evil things proscribed by the Law (7:15-21), and the Law "could not do" anything to help him (8:3); but now by sending Christ, God has accomplished judgment upon sin in the flesh, so that the righteous requirements of the Law may be fulfilled in those who walk according to Spirit (8:3). Verse 9 makes it definitive that those who have Christ and the Spirit are not in the flesh. There is no way that the circumstance of being "in

---

and 7:7-25, and between 7:6 and 8:1-17. See also Moo, *Encountering Romans*, 120-23.

4. Jesus Christ is also absent from 7:5-25, if one grants that verse 25 represents Paul exclaiming premature praise to God in anticipation of the deliverance to be described in 8:1-17.

the flesh" (in the sense discussed in these chapters) can coincide with being "in Christ" or "in the Spirit."[5] There is a clear salvation-historical movement from the time of Torah, which is associated with σάρξ, to the new time of the Spirit in which the Torah is no longer operative. It was in the former time in which God's people were "under Law" that they were also "in the flesh" in a salvation-historical sense (cf. Rom 6:14; 7:4-6).

N. T. Wright's Interpretation of Romans 7-8

It should be obvious from what has been said thus far that we do not follow N. T. Wright's exegesis of Romans 7-8 from *Climax of the Covenant*. Let us digress a moment to address his reading. Wright argues that "righteousness via faith in Christ is the climax of a covenant still in force."[6] More specifically, that covenant is the Torah, which is still in force for the people of God. The Torah is "the covenant document," and the forensic language of righteousness and justification are all covenant terms; in fact, in Wright's understanding δικαιοσύνη (*dikaiosunē*; "righteousness") just means "covenant membership" when applied to humans, and "covenant faithfulness" when applied to God.[7] This is not the meaning of "righteousness" in Paul, and Wright has been appropriately criticized on that account.[8] While a strong case can be made that "covenant faithfulness" is an expression of God's righteousness, that does not entail a reduction of the latter to the former. If indeed God's righteousness is the basis of his covenant faithfulness, then the two must be related and yet cannot be identical.[9] In contrast to our sketch of

---

5. Therefore, we find untenable Dunn's interpretation (*Theology of Paul*, 469-582) of Romans 6-8 in which God's new covenant people are described as simultaneously "in the flesh" and "in the Spirit," explained in terms of the eschatological tension of living in "the overlap of the ages" (a subject to be explored at length next chapter). Furthermore, Dunn claims that Paul was "thinking . . . in terms" of "ideal types" in describing "the flesh person" and "the Spirit person," which types real persons match in varying degrees, and Paul is giving an "implied exhortation" to align as much as possible with the ideal "Spirit person." This is an exegetically inadequate treatment of the passage at hand. Dunn is correct to observe eschatological tension and some continuity of "flesh" for God's new covenant people, but in our judgment, this requires a different theological explanation, which we will seek to provide.

6. The characterization of Wright's argument given by Capes et al., *Rediscovering Paul*, 176-77.

7. Wright, *Climax of the Covenant*, 194, 203, 241; Wright, *What St. Paul Really Said*, 95-111, 124-25.

8. See the criticism of Bird, *Saving Righteousness of God*, 100-103.

9. See the arguments to this effect in Schreiner, *Paul*, 197-203; Bird, *Saving Righteousness of God*, 10-17, 35-39, 74-75.

Romans 7:4–6 above and our more detailed analysis of Romans 6–8 below, Wright argues that Torah is still operative, and that in fact it is the Torah that is the referent of νόμος (*nomos*) throughout Romans 7–8.[10] In Wright's reading, when Paul "sees another law at work in his members" (Rom 7:23), it is the very same Torah that his mind affirms, only now it has been "taken over and used by sin operating through the foothold which is the flesh."[11] As a result of its encounter with the flesh and its sinfulness, the Law is "bifurcated," just as the person is, such that simultaneously the Law is affirmed in the mind, but at work for sin and death in the body.[12] Similarly, in Romans 8:2 Wright sees in "the law of the Spirit of life in Christ Jesus" a reference to Torah in a third phase, in which the Torah is now able to give life because (8:3) Jesus has nullified the Torah's opponents—flesh and sin—which had frustrated the Torah's purpose before.[13] Perhaps it is Wright's view that Torah is operative throughout the times depicted in Romans 7–8 that leads him to depict the conflict of Romans 7:13–25—which occurs under the Law between the flesh and the inner man—as the same as the flesh-Spirit conflict of Romans 8:5–11.[14] We will show in our own analysis below that these conflicts are not at all the same. This should be immediately obvious though, from the fact that Romans 7:13–25 does not even feature the Spirit, and describes a situation before the "now" of Romans 8:1 introduces the new situation brought into effect by Christ's work.

At the heart of Wright's error, however, is his insistence that every instance of νόμος is a reference to Torah. This has profound exegetical implications for Romans 7–8, and so we would like to make some extended criticism on this point. While it may be true that some Pauline scholars suffer from a justification-reflex that is triggered by any occurrence of δικαιόω (*dikaioō*) or its cognates, it seems to be the case that Wright suffers from an analogous Torah-reflex whenever νόμος is in the immediate vicinity. All instances of νόμος are references to the Torah, and never references to other kinds of laws or principles that are at work. In Wright's exposition, every instance of νόμος is a reference to Torah, albeit in different phases of salvation history (or different phases of a narrative sequence model Wright proposes and imposes on the text—about which more below). So when Paul writes in 7:22 that he concurs with the Law of God (i.e., Torah) in his inner man, but in 7:23 that he sees "a different law" at work in his body "waging

---

10. Wright, *Climax of the Covenant*, 199, 204, 208–211.
11. Wright, *Climax of the Covenant*, 198.
12. Wright, *Climax of the Covenant*, 197–99.
13. Wright, *Climax of the Covenant*, 204, 207–9.
14. Wright, *Climax of the Covenant*, 200–201, 213.

war" against the "Torah" which Paul concurs with in his mind; and when a third law (of the Spirit of life in Christ) comes and sets "you" free from the second law of sin and death—Wright insists[15] that we do not have three laws interacting with the person, but one law—Torah—considered in three phases. However, on the face of it, this exegesis is not right, and goes against what the text actually says.[16] Wright proposes that the Torah is actually the protagonist or hero of Paul's narrative in Romans 7–8, and that the narrative is about the redemption of *Torah*, as opposed to the redemption of people who could not be redeemed by Torah.

This is shown to be false by the fact that Romans 3:21 says that the righteousness of God comes *apart* from the Law. However, Wright attempts to evade the implication of 3:20–22 by redefining the terms used in these verses, viz., "works (of the Law)," "faith in Christ," and "righteousness." According to Wright, "the Law" and the "works of the Law" refer specifically to "those practices which mark Israel out from among the nations"[17]—i.e., circumcision, the Sabbath, and the food laws. These became for the Jews a source of racial or national boasting, and a sense of religious privilege before God. Israel therefore sinned in misusing the Torah to exclude gentiles and "confine grace to one race."[18] God intended Torah to play a paradoxical role; despite the Jews' misuse of it, God intended the

---

15. Often with gratuitous swipes at his exegetical rivals, such as the remark that those who suggest any other view of νόμος in 7:21 and 23 than Wright's have escaped "the deep rush of Paul's argument" to "paddle off into a shallow and irrelevant backwater," *Climax of the Covenant*, 199. It seems that where Wright's exegetical arguments are at their thinnest, his invective is at its thickest.

Consider as well his reiteration on p. 209 that νόμος in 8:2 is also a reference to Torah, followed by this criticism of Räisänen: "Räisänen's opposition to the idea [in *Paul and the Law*, p. 52–53] seems to relate more to his determination that Paul shall be read as declaring the law abolished than to actual exegesis." A *tu quoque* criticism would be appropriate given Wright's determination to find Torah in every instance of νόμος. However, if one were to consult Räisänen one would see, beside the obvious axe to grind and an inordinate fondness for exclamation marks, an actual exegetical argument on this particular point that is not so easily brushed aside.

In defense of the same point (on p. 210) Wright offers this blanket criticism of opponents: "In short, the only reasons I can see for continuing to deny that both uses of νόμος in 8.2 refer to the Torah have to do with *a priori* assumptions about what Paul could and could not have said—either because we know him to be 'consistent' within a tight pre-given theological structure, or because we wish to prove him 'inconsistent' within an equally tight and arbitrary scheme." It is amazing that Wright could say this apparently without a hint of self-awareness that he himself is doing a very similar thing by arbitrarily imposing a narratival-structural model on the text, as we shall see below.

16. See also Schreiner, *Law and Its Fulfillment*, 33–36.
17. Wright, "Romans and the Theology," 37.
18. Wright, *Climax of the Covenant*, 240.

Torah to be kept by faith, so that the gentiles could be brought into the covenant family and Israel could be transformed into a worldwide multi-ethnic family. However, this "faith" mentioned in 3:20-22 is not the faith of believers toward Christ (πίστις Ἰησοῦ [pistis Iēsou] taken as an objective genitive), but the faithfulness of Christ (πίστις Ἰησοῦ taken as a subjective genitive). Christ's faithful obedience on the cross brings an end to Jewish national privilege and opens "covenant membership" (i.e., "righteousness" in Wright's terms) to the gentiles (Rom 3:21-22; cf. also Gal 2:21). Now Christ is the end of the use of "works of Torah" for the purpose of exclusion from the covenant, but Torah remains in force as God's Law, as the covenant document, which was itself vindicated when Christ was crucified and brought the covenant's purpose to fruition.[19]

Having already cited criticisms of Wright's redefinition of righteousness, let us note some problems with his understanding of "works of the Law." It is obvious from the way Paul uses "the Law," "the things of the Law," and "the work of the Law" in Romans 2, that these terms cannot refer to ethnic boundary markers. Rather, they refer to any and all things that the Law demands, including the observation of the Law's prohibitions. Paul's uses in that chapter include commandments from the Decalogue (2:21-22). Furthermore, 2:14-15 would be nonsensical on Wright's interpretation, for it is impossible by definition for gentiles to observe Jewish identity markers, instinctively or otherwise, nor does it seem that any intelligible sense can be made of the notion of having circumcision written on the heart. Nor do verses 25-27 seem to make much sense on this view. Therefore, Wright's attempt to evade the force of 3:21 is unconvincing in our judgment.[20]

If we return to the text at hand in Romans 8, we see our proposed reading of 3:21 is corroborated: so far from being the focus of the story, "law" drops out of view completely after 8:7, as the text goes on to talk about the life in the Spirit for those who have been redeemed (and even in 8:7, it is not clear that this "law" is referring to Torah). Wright tells a coherent story about a law that is redeemed and enabled to carry out its

---

19. Wright, *Climax of the Covenant*, 240-42; Wright, "Romans and the Theology," 37-39; Wright, *What St. Paul Really Said*, 105-7, 127-29; Gathercole, *Where Is Boasting?*, 218-22; Westerholm, *Perspectives Old and New*, 178-83.

20. Note the criticism of Dunn's similar view about "works of the Law" in Moo, *Romans*, 213-5. Note also Gathercole, *Where Is Boasting?*, 224-25, for additional argumentation that the righteousness of God is manifested apart from the Law, and that therefore *all* are justified by faith. Accordingly, Paul is not just describing how gentiles are added to the covenant people. Jews and gentiles are justified by faith apart from Torah. For the πίστις Χριστοῦ (*pistis Christou*) debate, see Bird and Sprinkle, *Faith of Jesus Christ*.

originally intended function. But this is *not* the story Paul is telling or appealing to in Romans.[21]

The source of Wright's exegetical mistake seems to be his decision to adopt the actantial narrative analysis model proposed by Richard Hays which posits three normal sequences in a narrative, in which six actants (i.e., agents or actors) play certain functional roles. The rationale is that there is a story that underlies Paul's argumentation, and Wright seeks to uncover its narrative structure by applying this model to Romans 8:3-4 and its surrounding context.[22] Wright is certainly correct that Paul's argument presupposes a story, and that uncovering its narrative structure would therefore illuminate Paul's argument. The problem is that Wright applies Hays's analytical model in such a heavy-handed fashion.[23] Wright himself acknowledges: "it may be true that we can ultimately get out of such an analysis what we put into it."[24] This is exactly what is to be feared. If we just take some model and impose it upon the text, the risk of eisegesis is great. This is exactly what Wright does. It is evident he is superimposing a model on the text from the top down and smothering the text as a result. This is not a model that emerges from the bottom up to summarize what is found in the text (or across Pauline texts).

It can be demonstrated that this is in fact what Wright does by considering the following statement: "The normal dictates of the model are that the Subject of the initial sequence [i.e., the Torah] should become the Receiver of the topical sequence, since the point of the topical sequence is to enable the (initial) Subject to accomplish his (previously impossible) task: this suggests that the law is the Receiver, though this is not explicit in 8.3b. We thus have"—and at this point Wright produces a diagram in which the Law is implied (indicated by parenthesis) to be the beneficiary of the act of God in Christ in 8:3.[25] It is not surprising then that Wright concludes: "The point of the action, as becomes clear in 8.4, which forms the *final sequence*

---

21. Wright, *Climax of the Covenant*, 208-11. See also Moule, "Jesus, Judaism, and Paul," 47-48, where he affirms (against his former position on the matter, in Moule, "'Justification' in its Relation") that you cannot force νόμος to be translated as Torah in every instance, but must often render it as "principle" to conform to the way that Paul used the term in a variety of senses. See also the criticism of Wright and others regarding νόμος in 7:22—8:3 in Moo, *Romans*, 462-65, 473-80.

22. Wright, *Climax of the Covenant*, 204-8. Hays originally presents his model in Hays, *Faith of Jesus Christ*.

23. This is strangely reminiscent of the way Bruce Malina imposed sociological models on the NT text, as discussed above.

24. Wright, *Climax of the Covenant*, 206.

25. Wright, *Climax of the Covenant*, 207.

[Wright's italics], is that *the law might be set free* [my italics]."²⁶ It is clear from the foregoing that Wright, on the basis of a prescriptive model of the kind of narrative structure he thinks Paul should exhibit, has filled in what must therefore be an omission, an empty space on the model narrative structure, such that in Wright's telling the Torah becomes the beneficiary of the narrative action. We now see how Wright has derived the story that he is telling. But that is N. T. Wright's story; it most emphatically is *not* the story that Paul is telling in Romans 7–8.

Paul's Development of the Theme of Σάρξ in Romans 6–8

In contrast to Wright, we have argued that the Torah was formerly in authority over God's people in the past, but no longer, for they have been released from the Law to serve by means of the Spirit. We arrived at this conclusion on the basis of 7:4–6 and the correspondence of those verses with chapters 6–8, including the correlation of the tenses and time frames that definitively put the time of flesh and Torah before the work of Christ, and the period of the Spirit from that time forward. We saw a clear salvation-historical movement from the time of Torah, which is associated with σάρξ, to the new time of the Spirit in which the Torah is no longer operative. God's people are no longer "under Law" or "in the flesh" in a salvation-historical sense (Rom 6:14; 7:4–6; 8:1–4, 9). Now let us make our own analysis of Romans 6–8 and see how Paul develops the theme of σάρξ in his salvation-historical framework, and how that relates to the anthropological sense of σάρξ.

Although Paul has inherited the anthropological framework of σάρξ from the Old Testament, in which the term captures what it means to be merely human, mortal, and sinful, we see that he is now imposing a new salvation-historical framework in which being "in the flesh" is functionally equivalent to being "under the Law." We will not do a full exegesis of Romans 6–8, but will attempt to trace the broad outline of Paul's argument, noting his uses of σάρξ in a salvation-historical sense. In Romans 6, Paul teaches that in virtue of the Roman believers' being united with Jesus in his death, they died to sin and live to God. They are no longer to be slaves of sin, but slaves to God and his righteousness. Being free of the Law frees them from sin's mastery, and allows them to serve God and righteousness.²⁷

In Romans 7, Paul directly addresses the problem with the Law. He first gives an analogy from marriage that illustrates how a death can free

---

26. Wright, *Climax of the Covenant*, 208.

27. Σάρξ in 6:19 is not an instance of a salvation-historical meaning. We shall address it below.

one from a binding jurisdiction, which is what Jesus' death did for Jewish believers with respect to the Law (7:1–6). He then clarifies that the Law itself is not evil (7:7–12) nor the direct cause of "death" for those under its jurisdiction (7:13–25). Beyond these generalities, the precise exegesis of these two paragraphs is debated, but a strong case can be made that in both paragraphs Paul speaks in the first person in a representative sense. In Paul's rhetorical strategy, the "I" is not referring directly to himself, as in ordinary language. Rather, Paul puts himself in the place of the typical believing Israelite and describes the experience and effects of the coming of the Law to Israel at Sinai in 7:7–12. Although the Law gave the benefit of defining sin for the believer, it also exacted a horrible cost—it aroused and provoked sin, in effect reviving it or bringing it to life, with the result that it deceived and brought death to the believer. Although Paul is not referring directly to himself, to the literal "I," the passage is certainly applicable to him, as it would be to all Jews, because the giving of the Law had abiding effects on all Israel from the time of Mount Sinai until the present (i.e., the present of Paul and the Romans). Then in 7:13–25, Paul describes the experience of the typical believing Israelite living under the Law. This was an experience of being in bondage to sin, of frustration and futility in which the inner man concurred with the Law, but was unable to do what the Law prescribed because of his captivity to the law of sin at work in his body. Again, Paul is not the exclusive or direct referent of this "I," but would be included in it as it pertained to his former experience as a non-Christian Jew living under the Law.[28]

Of course, this general interpretation is but one of many contending explanations for Paul's intention in Romans 7.[29] Arguably, this best accounts for the data, respects the clear temporal indicators of Paul's salvation-historical schema, and best handles the objections of competing interpreters. The objections to this understanding of Romans 7:7–25 are by no means insuperable. The first objection is that Paul should be understood to be referring to himself since throughout the passage he uses first-person verbs and even unnecessarily uses the first-person pronoun ἐγώ (*egō*; 7:9–10, 14, 25) and the emphatic form ἐμοί (*emoi*; 7:8, 13, 18, 20, 21). However, the idea that the "I" here is to be taken as totally autobiographical founders on 7:9, for how could Paul have ever lived apart from the Law?[30] Only a representational view of the "I" could match this circumstance.

---

28. Moo, *Romans*, 440–67; Schreiner, *Romans*, 379–90; Russell, "Insights," 522–24; Lambrecht, *The Wretched "I*," 48, 84–85, 90. See also Wilder, *Perspectives on Our Struggle with Sin*.

29. A general survey and critique of the various interpretations of Rom 7:7–25 is found in Moo, *Romans*, 423–31; for the paragraph 7:13–25, see 442–51.

30. Fitzmyer, *Romans*, 464; Chester, "Retrospective View of Romans 7," 72–73.

Two candidates present themselves. Either Paul is representing himself as Adam,[31] or as an Israelite encountering the Law at Sinai. However, Adam is not in view in the passage at all. There is a superficial similarity that is accounted for by the fact that Adam is a paradigmatic example of one under temptation in Genesis 2–3. Contextually, if this passage had occurred in Romans 5:12–23, it could possibly refer to Adam. But by this point in Romans, Paul has moved on to talk about the Law that was given at Mount Sinai that affected Jews up to Paul's time.[32]

Furthermore, the narrative sequence of Romans 7:8b–10 corresponds with the distinction that Paul makes between sin and transgression, and transgression's relationship with the Law in Romans 4:15 and 5:13–14, 20. Moo describes the theological pattern that is shared by these passages:

> The "coming to life [again]" of the previously "inert" sin (v. 8b) is a vivid portrayal of what Paul describes more prosaically in 1 Cor 15:56b: "the power of sin is the law." And the "death" of the ἐγώ at the coming of the commandment corresponds closely with Paul's understanding of the Mosaic law as an instrument which imprisons under sin (Rom 7:6; Gal 3:22, 23), enables wrongdoing to be "charged" to each individual's account as trespass (Rom 5:13; cf. Gal 3:19) producing wrath (Rom 4:15) and death (2 Cor 3:7). Even the life of the ἐγώ before the coming of the commandment (v. 8b) can be compared with Paul's description of the situation of people before Sinai whose sins were not

---

31. A reference to Adam is seen in 7:9 by Dunn, *Romans 1–8*, 387–9; Dunn, *Theology of Paul*, 90–91, 94–100, 151; Stuhlmacher, *Paul's Letter to the Romans*, 110–12; and Käsemann, *Commentary on Romans*, 192–8.

32. Moo, "Israel and Paul," 123–29; Lambrecht, *Wretched "I,"* 84; Russell, "Insights," 521; Fitzmyer calls the "Adamic" interpretation of this passage "eisegetical" (*Romans*, 464). Kim, *Paul and the New Perspective*, 70n234, 154 (and n102), seeks to blend the views of Moo and Dunn, arguing for an allusion to Adam and to Israel's experience, such that the passage teaches "the inability of the Adamic humanity as a whole and Israel in particular to keep the law." Chester argues a similar blended position in "Retrospective View of Romans 7," 72–73. We doubt that Paul intends an allusion to Adam here, since he dealt with the salvation-historical import of Adam in Romans 5:12–21. The implications from that passage can then be taken as a theological given applicable to all segments of (unjustified) humanity without needing to be specified. Therefore, of course, the Adam narrative provides the necessary background for the Israel narrative, and so some relationship between them must obtain. In our judgment, that consideration combined with the fact that the Adam narrative is the paradigm narrative of temptation, misleads interpreters to see it as the intentional focus of Romans 7. While Israel's Adamic status is certainly more theologically relevant than other facts about Israel, such as, say, bipedalism, to see it in Romans 7 still seems to us like a redundancy that is not really exegetically justified by the text itself, which specifically has in view Israel's plight under the Law.

"reckoned" as they were after the possession of the law (Rom 5:13). These indisputable similarities between the narrative of Rom 7:8–10 and Paul's theology of the Mosaic law lead to the conclusion that Paul in this passage depicts the effect of the giving of the law on Israel. "When the commandment came" can then be taken naturally as a reference to the promulgation of the Sinaitic revelation.[33]

Paul is using "I" as a rhetorical device, but also retains some autobiographical reference.[34] He identifies himself in a corporate sense with his people Israel. The first person singular is used similarly in Jeremiah 10:19–22; Micah 7:7–10; Lamentations 1:9–22; 2:20–22, and Psalms of Solomon 1:1—2:6 to represent Jerusalem or Israel, yet at the same time to identify the writer with experiences of the people corporately.[35] Paul describes the experience of Israel at Sinai, "but uses the first person because he himself, as a Jew, has been affected by that experience."[36]

We have given reasons above to be cautious about some of the sociological theory that underlies much of what may be described as an overemphasis on a corporate focus to the exclusion or negation of the individual in New Testament studies. Those caveats understood, we can still give much credence to the argument of Russell that this representational, corporate use of "I" would not be strange to the ears of Paul's contemporaries, whether Jewish or Greek.[37] We would certainly not dispute that the first-century Jews had a stronger sense of community identity than modern Westerners. Furthermore, the remembered historical events of the exodus and the giving of the Law at Sinai, as well as the rule of life by Torah which distinguished Jews from gentiles, often at the cost of antagonism and persecution (such as that suffered under Antiochus Epiphanes) would have certainly been powerful symbolic constituents of a perceived sense of communal identity in the minds of the Jews in a way that fits Cohen's approach that insists on recognizing the essential symbolic aspects of community.

Based on the sociological factors, Russell argues that it would not have been Paul's idiosyncratic experience with the Law that would have interested his audience, but his experience to the extent that it is representative.

33. Moo, "Israel and Paul," 127.

34. Moo cites Kümmel, *Römer 7 und die Bekehrung des Paulus* (Leipzig: Hinrichs, 1929) who demonstrates Paul's use of "I" as a rhetorical device, but insists against Kümmel that not all personal reference can be removed in Romans 7. See Moo, "Israel and Paul," 127–29; Moo, *Romans*, 427, 444.

35. Moo, "Israel and Paul," 128–29; Russell, "Insights," 522.

36. Moo, "Israel and Paul," 129.

37. Russell, "Insights," 522. See also Di Vito, "Old Testament Anthropology."

We would add as well that this is what Paul's argument requires if it is to be effective; his audience must feel some resonance with Paul's experience. Russell concludes that Paul's experience must be

> representative of his group identity if it is to be meaningful to his recipients. Therefore, the most likely group identification that Paul would have in light of those he is addressing in Romans 7 ("those who know the Law" in 7:1) is that of an Israelite who also knows the Law and has lived under its authority. Therefore Paul's "I" in Rom 7:7–25 is most likely representative of both his experience and that of all pious Israelites.[38]

This is not to say that Paul is addressing Jewish Christians here exclusively or even for the most part, for Paul's audience was probably predominantly composed of gentiles (see 1:5–7, 13), though a minority of them were probably from a Jewish background.[39] It is not improbable that those gentile Christians who had previously been proselytes to Judaism or even God-fearers could engage sympathetically with the Jewish experience of bondage to sin, and the inability to do the Law despite mental agreement with it.

A second objection raised against the interpretation of "I" as representing believing, pious Israelites (including Paul) under the Law is the use of present tense verbs in Romans 7:14–25. It is argued that this is evidence against the passage being a depiction of a situation in the past, and for it as an account of Paul's present experience.[40] In response, Moo, Schreiner, and Russell all argue that this offers little support for the view that "I" is a Christian. Rather, the present tense depicts more vividly the condition of the one enslaved to sin. This is a struggle that believing Israelites had felt since the time of Sinai. Furthermore, the present tense is appropriate in this paragraph since the struggle is one Paul himself (and his audience) had experienced personally and individually, in contrast to the giving of the Law at Sinai depicted in verses 7–11.[41]

A third difficulty is the sequence of Paul's lament for deliverance from his wretched state (7:24), followed by the thanksgiving to Jesus (7:25a), followed by a reiteration of Paul's servitude to sin (7:25b). Thus, it is argued, Paul depicts his present circumstance as one in which a follower in Christ remains a servant of sin vis-à-vis his flesh.[42] Schreiner rebuts this

---

38. Russell, "Insights," 522–23.

39. Moo, *Romans*, 9–13.

40. E.g., Dunn, *Theology of Paul*, 474.

41. Moo, "Israel and Paul," 129; Moo, *Romans*, 448; Schreiner, *Romans*, 386–87; Russell, "Insights," 521.

42. E.g., Dunn, *Theology of Paul*, 474.

facile objection: "That Paul interjected the solution to the problem in verses 24–25a before articulating the conclusion is hardly surprising, for he did not always write in the neat and tidy way we might expect. He could not restrain himself from exclaiming over the victory believers have in Christ."[43] Paul's description of the wretched state of the slave of sin, whose inner man is imprisoned by the law of sin in his body, immediately provokes the lament for deliverance, which in turn immediately evokes Paul's gratitude to God (through Jesus). Now it is barely possible that Paul could be thankful for the deliverance from "this body of death" at the future parousia, but that would give Paul's lament the following absurd sense: "Who will set me free (at the parousia) from this body of death?" Now we no longer have a lament over real felt circumstances that were present to Paul and the Israelites (previously under the Law, in my interpretation); rather, we have a real question of a matter of fact asked in heightened emotional tones, even though Paul and his audience already had the answer to that question. To call this highly improbable would be a generous description of this interpretation's tenability. It is more likely that Paul is emotionally provoked by recalling the past bodily servitude to sin, and therefore gives thanks for deliverance from that state, yet conceiving it as something that Jesus has already accomplished in the past; and this is confirmed explicitly when we get to 8:2. Nonetheless, Paul's jubilant exclamation is premature in his argument, so he must go back and summarize his "description of the dividedness between law and flesh that he and his fellow believing Israelites had experienced."[44]

Other objections are also easily handled by this interpretation. The faithful Jews of the Old Testament era did rejoice and delight in God's Law, but were unable to keep it, because they lacked the Holy Spirit. This clearly fits the passage, which does not depict all non-Christians, but rather those believing Israelites who lived under the Law, outside of and before Christ. Furthermore, the reference to the inner man need not refer to Christians.[45]

Finally, the opposing but popular view that 7:21–25 describes a Christian in the new covenant era suffers fatal problems. Romans 6:6–7, 11–14, 16–22; 7:4–6; and 8:2 clearly describe the new covenant Christian in ways that prohibit the description of 7:14–25 from being applied to him.[46] Furthermore, the tenses of the verbs in these passages put the time of the Law and slavery to sin in the past; now, rather than being slaves of sin, we are

---

43. Schreiner, *Romans*, 386.

44. Russell, "Apostle Paul's View," 221.

45. Schreiner, *Romans*, 387–89; Fee, *God's Empowering Presence*, 511, 513–14; Russell, "Apostle Paul's View," 221.

46. Schreiner, *Romans*, 387.

freed from Torah and sin to live in the Spirit, by which we may fulfill the righteous intent of the Law. The other view ignores all of these temporal markers and collapses the salvation-historical description of two antithetical eras which Paul keeps distinct by means of those temporal markers and by the antithetical characteristics of those eras.[47] The proponent of the other view, moreover, has to bring Torah (albeit redefined without exegetical justification) into the new covenant era, contrary to numerous Pauline texts, including 6:14; 7:4–6; and 8:1–3.[48] Romans 8:1–3 is not as explicit as the other two passages, but when one notes how tightly the link is drawn between the Torah and the law of sin and death in Romans 6–8, the inference is unavoidable: God's people are set free from Torah and are not bound by it. Finally, Schreiner points out that Paul would never describe believers as "under sin" (7:14). "Paul consistently uses negative ὑπό (*hypo*) phrases to denote unbelievers and the old era in salvation history; nowhere does it refer to new covenant believers." Examples can be seen in Rom 3:9, 19–20; 1 Cor 9:20; Gal 3:10, 23, 25; 4:2–5, 21; and 5:18.[49] These appear to be insuperable objections.

Accordingly, we may conclude that Paul clearly presents a salvation-historical framework in Romans, and in that framework, the σάρξ does not refer to human nature per se, or to a part or faculty of human nature, such as the "sin nature" as the NIV 1984 rendered σάρξ. This imports ontological language into the text that Paul did not intend.[50] On the contrary, σάρξ refers to human existence in all its weakness and propensity to sin and death apart from the life and empowerment of God's Spirit. This is the defining

---

47. Dunn does so explicitly in *Theology of Paul*, 472–77. However, Dunn does not fully conflate the two antithetical eras, but overlaps them. For Dunn, "the overlap of the ages" schema is the "exegetical solution" that enables one to circumvent Paul's temporal indicators and make 7:7–25 descriptive of the eschatological tension Christians experience presently in the "now and the not yet." We shall examine the "overlap of the ages" schema more closely next chapter.

48. Russell, "Insights," 523. See also Dorsey, "Law of Moses and the Christian," for an incisive critique of the idea that the Mosaic Law or any part thereof has any legally binding jurisdiction in the NT era, as well as a helpful depiction of the positive role that it does have. This article underscores the wrongheadedness of the implications of the popular interpretation of Rom 7:14–25. We should also note that Dunn is in qualified agreement with this implication (cf. *Theology of Paul*, 631–32, and n26), but his treatment is more sophisticated, and the continuing relevance of the Law as a regulatory function (*not* a life-giving function) in the life of a Christian is strongly qualified in a Christomorphic way (an apt description taken from Dunn's citation of Hays in *Theology of Paul*, 668n189). See *Theology of Paul*, 150–54, and the lengthy discussion in 625–69.

49. Schreiner, *Romans*, 389.

50. Moo, *Romans*, 418n51; Schreiner, *Paul*, 143; Russell, *Flesh/Spirit Conflict*, 9–11, 203; Fee, *God's Empowering Presence*, 819, 822.

characteristic of life before and outside of Christ. In Judaistic contexts, Paul makes it clear that Jewish identity, circumcision, and Torah-observance are merely σάρξ as well. Trusting or boasting in such things leads to death, not life. Life in the σάρξ under the Old Covenant was characterized by frustration and bondage to the sin that so easily took advantage of the Law and subjugated the body, regardless of one's intent. The Law was powerless to overcome sin. But now the work of Christ and the Spirit has set God's people free from the Law and from the domination of sin. God's people can no longer be characterized in a salvation-historical sense as "in the σάρξ," but rather as "in the Spirit."[51] They are given new life by the Spirit and indwelt and empowered by him.

This new circumstance illuminates for us the enigmatic passage, Romans 7:17-18:

> So now, no longer am I the one doing it, but sin which *dwells* [οἰκοῦσα, *oikousa*] in me. For I know that *nothing good dwells* [οἰκεῖ, *oikei*] in me, that is, in my flesh, for the willing is present in me, but the doing of the good is not. (Rom 7:17-18, NASB, emphasis mine)

In Romans 8:9-11, however, Paul writes,

> However, you are not in the flesh but in the Spirit, if indeed *the Spirit of God dwells* [οἰκεῖ] in you. But if anyone does not have the Spirit of Christ, he does not belong to Him. [10] If Christ is in you, though the body is dead because of sin, yet the [S]pirit is [life]* because of righteousness. [11] But if the *Spirit of Him who raised Jesus* from the dead *dwells* [οἰκεῖ] in you, He who raised Christ Jesus from the dead will also give life to your mortal bodies through His Spirit who dwells [ἐνοικοῦντος, *enoikountos*] in you. (Rom 8:9-11, NASB [*altered[52]], my emphasis)

By comparing these two passages, we see that the enigmatic statement from Romans 7:17-18 that *nothing good* dwells in him or in his flesh speaks to the *absence of the Holy Spirit and his life and power*, which is then characteristic of being "in the flesh." Formerly, in the time of the Law, believers did not have the Spirit dwelling in them and empowering them to serve God and righteousness.

---

51. Fee, in *God's Empowering Presence*, puts it aptly: "'flesh' is not a Christian alternative; to live in the flesh is to live outside Christ altogether" (554).

52. Moo, *Romans*, 492; Schreiner, *Romans*, 414-15; Cranfield, *Epistle to the Romans*, 1:372, 389-90; Fee, *God's Empowering Presence*, 542-43, 548-52.

There is one final relevant point about Paul's discussion of the salvation-historical flesh-Spirit antithesis in Romans 8 that must be noted. Seyoon Kim has argued that Paul's claim in Romans 8:3-4 (i.e., that the work of Christ and the Spirit has resulted in the righteous requirement [δικαίωμα, *dikaiōma*] of the Law being fulfilled in those who are in Christ[53]) is an allusion to Ezekiel 36:26-27 (and the parallel Ezekiel 11:19-20), in which God promised his people that very thing: that he would put his Spirit into them and enable them to walk in his statutes or ordinances (LXX ἐν τοῖς δικαιώμασίν μου [*en tois dikaiōmasin mou*], Ezek 36:27; cf. 11:20). These texts, combined with Jeremiah 31:31-34, were key portions of Scripture which enabled Paul to interpret both the Jesus traditions and his own Damascus Road experience as fulfillments of the scriptural promises of a New Covenant and the indwelling Spirit who would enable the fulfilling of the δικαιώματά (*dikaiōmata*) of God's Law.[54] Similarly, Paul also alludes to these same Ezekiel texts in Romans 8:9, 14, when he identifies the New Covenant people of God as all and only those whom the Spirit of God or of Christ indwells. Furthermore, in Romans 8:11, Paul most likely alludes to Ezekiel 37:4-14 when he speaks of the Spirit who will give life to the mortal bodies of those whom he currently indwells. Paul's dependence on these texts is noteworthy, and he also meditates on them to profound effect in 2 Corinthians 3, in his contrast and comparison of the Old and New Covenants, and of Moses and Paul himself as ministers of those respective covenants.[55]

What is fascinating for our study is the likelihood that these texts also played a crucial role for Paul in the development of his flesh-Spirit antithesis,[56] and yet Paul, in Romans 8, seems to have carefully avoided quoting the key "flesh" portions of the Ezekiel texts in Ezek 11:19 and 36:26 (which we saw in chapter 2, category ten):

> And I will give them another heart, and will put a new spirit in them; and I will extract the heart of stone [τὴν καρδίαν τὴν

---

53. For a discussion of the crucial difference between believers *doing* or *keeping* the Law in Rom 8:4 and Gal 5:14, and its righteous requirement *being fulfilled* in them, cf. the different perspectives of Moo, *Romans*, 481-85; Moo, *Galatians*, 345-48; and Schreiner, *Paul*, 325-29. For its relation to OT prophetic texts, see Moo, *Romans*, 484n66.

54. Kim, *Paul and the New Perspective*, 157-63. Wenham, *Paul*, 232, supplements the discussion of eschatological salvation by including the crucial component of the relational knowledge of God, which is promised in Jer 31:31-34 and reflected upon by Paul in 2 Corinthians 3 (see esp. vv. 3-6, 12-18) as the driver of the transformation that results in the fulfillment of the Law's δικαιώματά addressed by Kim.

55. Kim, *Paul and the New Perspective*, 158, 160. Cf. also Balla, "2 Corinthians," 755-56, 758-59.

56. Kim, *Paul and the New Perspective*, 161-63.

λιθίνην, *tēn kardian tēn lithinēn*] from their flesh, and will give them a heart of flesh [καρδίαν σαρκίνην, *kardian sarkinēn*]. (Ezek 11:19 LXX; cf. also 36:26)

The most likely reason for this is that Paul has typically characterized the flesh-Spirit antithesis in such a way that σάρξ always bears negative connotations in salvation-historical theological argumentation, especially those which occur in the Judaizing controversy or in relevantly similar circumstances, so that for Paul to quote the Ezekiel passage directly would be contrary to this trend and perhaps confusing to his audience. Moreover, the term σάρξ was also used by Judaizers and non-Christian Jews to boast of their circumcision as God's covenant with them in their flesh, following the LXX of Genesis 17:13.[57] On Paul's part there is clearly a heightened negativity towards "the flesh" in his salvation-historical arguments that is congruent with the more intensely heated rhetoric and the sharper-edged words he employed in the Judaizing controversy. This is seen in epistles that were written before Romans (i.e., Galatians, e.g., 1:6-9; 5:12; 6:12-13) and also after Romans (i.e., Philippians, e.g., 3:2-9, 18-19[58]).

Moo's nuanced discussion of Paul's purposes in writing the epistle to the Romans shows the plausibility that these considerations were relevant for this letter as well. Paul continued to deal with the tensions inherent in

---

57. Jewett, *Paul's Anthropological Terms*, 96-98; Barclay, *Obeying the Truth*, 179-80; Russell, *Flesh/Spirit Conflict*, 120.

58. In Phil 3:2-9, Paul clearly has the Judaizers in view. The identity of Paul's target in verses 18-19 is more debated, but we understand the references to "enemies of the cross of Christ," those "whose god is their belly," and those "whose glory is in their shame," to be additional references to the Judaizers expressed with heightened rhetoric, and the last two phrases to be speaking specifically of the insistence on the observation of food laws and circumcision. For a similar perspective, see Witherington, *Paul's Letter to the Philippians*, 192, 215-16; Hawthorne, *Philippians*; and Williams, *Enemies of the Cross*, 222-27. For an additional survey of the discussion, see O'Brien, *Philippians*, 450-58; Fee, *Philippians*, 366-75; Hansen, *Letter to the Philippians*, 263-67. Commentators such as Fee and Hansen who do not accept this identification cite the fact that Paul does not actually view the observance of Jewish food laws as idolatrous, or circumcision as shameful. In our judgment, this objection overlooks the key distinction between Paul's view (expressed in sober terms) of the *intrinsic* worth of these observances as benign adiaphora, on the one hand, and on the other, his judgment (expressed in the polemical rhetoric of controversy) that the Judaizers' insistence on these observances as necessary conditions for being part of God's covenant people is a "false gospel" and anathema (Gal 1:6-9). It is this twofold distinction of Paul's views and modes of expression that make sense of the fact that Paul can consistently describe circumcision (in itself) as irrelevant (Gal 5:6), and also describe it (considered as the centerpiece of the Judaizers' false gospel) as "mutilation" (Phil 3:2). Fee himself notes this distinction with respect to circumcision (Fee, *Philippians*, 297n51) but fails to see the relevance of this consideration for identifying the opponents of 3:18-19.

the incorporation of gentiles with Jews in the one new covenant people of God. This was the underlying issue that needed resolution, which called for reflective theological exegesis of the OT Scriptures, necessitated deliberation and debate among the apostles at the Jerusalem council of 49, provoked the Judaizing controversy between opposing factions on the issue, and left residual cultural tensions in mixed Christian communities. This issue therefore impinged on several background factors to the letter to the Romans: Paul's recent and continuing battles with Judaizers; his hopes for the support of the Roman church for Paul's mission to Spain; his hopes for Roman participation in the collection for the Jewish saints in Jerusalem; his desire to promote unity, love, and acceptance between Jewish and gentile believers in Rome; and the need to explain, clarify, and defend his understanding of God's program of salvation in the gospel.[59] Moo is most likely correct in stating that the last factor was both the most important one and that it was also the cumulative result of the other factors: all these other factors "forced Paul to write a letter in which he carefully rehearsed his understanding of the gospel, especially as it related to the *salvation-historical questions* of Jew and gentile and the continuity of the plan of salvation."[60] Moo has picked up on the key element of salvation-history that informs the letter to the Romans, and we argue that Paul wants to make a key salvation-historical contrast by means of the flesh-Spirit antithesis, in which "flesh" characterizes an inferior past status. Therefore, to use Ezekiel's language without modification to speak of the new and living heart in terms of "flesh" would be counter to his argumentative agenda.

Nonetheless, it is clear that Paul sees an analogy between his own flesh-Spirit antithesis and the stony heart-fleshly heart of Ezekiel. As Ezekiel's "heart of stone" relates to the "heart of flesh," so also does Paul's "flesh" relate to "the Spirit." Thus, in the different circumstances regarding the Corinthian church, he writes of the Corinthian believers in 2 Corinthians 3:2–3: "You yourselves are our letter, written in our hearts, known and read by all men; being manifested that you are a letter of Christ, delivered by us, written not with ink but with the Spirit of the living God, not on tablets of stone but on tablets that are hearts of flesh" (my translation).

Kim retraces the likely path of Paul's reflection on his Damascus Road experience, guided by Ezekiel 36–37, that surfaced for him the fundamental problem with the Law and the flesh from which he developed his Law-Spirit and flesh-Spirit antitheses:

---

59. Moo, *Romans*, 16–22.
60. Moo, *Romans*, 20–21 (emphasis mine).

Having experienced on the Damascus road how his turning to the Lord, the Spirit, resulted in the removal of the "veil" and the "heart of stone" (2 Cor. 3:16–18; 4:6), he could now see this fundamental problem of the law. So he realized that there was an inherent correspondence between the fact that the Mosaic law was written on the stone tablets and the fact that those who are under the law have the "stony hearts" or "hardened minds" (2 Cor. 3:3, 7, 14). He probably realized also that because of the structural weakness of the law, the people of Israel had been "stiff-necked," blinded and hardened ever since they received the law at Sinai . . . When the law is responded to by those who have the "stony hearts" or "hardened minds," the consequences are only condemnation and death (2 Cor. 3:6, 7, 9). Just as there is a correspondence between the law written on stone tablets and the "stony hearts" of the Jews, so there is also a correspondence between the Spirit and the "flesh hearts" of the Christians (2 Cor. 3:3). The Spirit touches the "hearts of flesh" . . . and so brings about righteousness and life (2 Cor. 3:6, 9).[61]

Yet Christians Are Still "Flesh" in the Anthropological Sense until the Parousia

Paul in 2 Corinthians 3 describes the fundamental transformation that the Spirit has made in the hearts of believers, bringing them from death to life. In Romans 8:1–14, he makes a very similar point, but being careful to use the word σάρξ in a very different way. Romans 6–8 makes it clear that in a salvation-historical sense, Christians are not "in the flesh." However, Paul still applies the term σάρξ to Christians in manifold ways, and some account must be given of this. Of course, in many places it is obvious that σάρξ is serving as a synonym for σῶμα (e.g., Phil 1:22, 24). However, this somatic use of σάρξ gains more theological significance when we recognize that Paul never uses σάρξ in this way to speak of conditions resulting from the parousia. After the parousia, σάρξ is not an appropriate term for the redeemed human body, or of human existence in general. Paul then uses σῶμα exclusively to speak of Christians' bodies after Christ's return. This is often coupled with modifiers to distinguish it from the type of somatic existence Christians experience prior to the parousia. A fascinating example of this is seen in 1 Corinthians 15:35–57, in which Paul compares the current body Christians have with the new one they will receive when Christ

---

61. Kim, *Paul and the New Perspective*, 162.

returns. In 15:39, Paul speaks of the σάρξ of men, noting that different kinds of creatures have different kinds of flesh. Then in 15:50, Paul says that σάρξ καὶ αἷμα (*sarx kai haima*) cannot inherit the kingdom of God, but must be transformed. The kind of transformation Paul has in mind from the old body to the new body can be described as follows from 15:40–53:

Table 3: The Current Body vs. The Resurrection Body

The Current Body	The Resurrection Body
σώματα ἐπίγεια (*sōmata epigeia*), natural bodies (v. 40)	σώματα ἐπουράνια (*sōmata epourania*), heavenly bodies
φθορά (*phthora*), corruption, i.e., perishable (v. 42)	ἀφθαρσία (*aphtharsia*), incorruption, i.e., imperishable
ἀτιμία (*atimia*), dishonor (v. 43)	δόξα (*doxa*), glory
ἀσθένεια (*astheneia*), weakness	δύναμις, power
ψυχικός, natural (vv. 44, 46)	πνευματικός, spiritual
χοϊκός (*choikos*), earthy (v. 48)	ἐπουράνιος (*epouranios*), heavenly

In all likelihood it is proper for us to take these five adjectives from the left column as Paul's conception of man as "flesh" in his bodily existence: perishable, dishonorable, weak, natural, and earthy. It is clear that this description applies to Christians as redeemed and waiting for the Lord's return, at which time they will be transformed from one mode of bodily existence to another (15:51). Given the basic anthropological sense of σάρξ, and taking into account Paul's use of it to apply to Christians who are "in the Spirit" in the salvation-historical sense, and his avoidance of the term in even a somatic sense after the parousia,[62] one is led to the conclusion that there is still some significant theological sense in which the Christian may be spoken of in terms of σάρξ.

We can see this as well if we return to Romans 6–8. In Romans 6:19, Paul says that he speaks "in human terms because of the weakness of your flesh" (NASB). We note that Paul is explaining his mode of speaking to them now, as Christians under the New Covenant. This is clearly not a salvation-historical use of "flesh" that refers to their past mode of existence. It clearly predicates σάρξ to them now. It is also noteworthy that it predicates to their flesh weakness (ἀσθένεια), one of the characteristic terms Paul used to describe our state in 1 Corinthians 15:43. It seems clear in this verse that the

---

62. Ridderbos, *Paul*, 116, 548–49, 551.

"weakness of the flesh" refers not so much to a bodily weakness, but to an intellectual difficulty or perhaps insensitivity in understanding spiritual things. Accordingly, this verse is an instance in which σάρξ is used in a basic anthropological sense to describe the general weakness that characterizes human existence, even in a redeemed state under the New Covenant.

Then in Romans 8 we see further references to σάρξ which refer to Christians who are "in the Spirit" in a salvation-historical sense. Romans 8:1–9 details the deliverance from the wretched state Paul had described in Romans 7:14–25. Verses 8–9 make it clear that the believer in Christ is "in the Spirit," not "in the flesh" in a salvation-historical sense. The believer has the Holy Spirit dwelling in him, which is affirmed in two ways in verse 9, first by a reference to "the Spirit of God," and then by reference to the "Spirit of Christ." This sets up a series of statements (8:10–13) on the implications of that fact, which commences with a reference to "Christ in you." Since Christ (through the Spirit) is in you, although the body is dead because of sin, the Spirit is life because of righteousness (v. 10). These two last enigmatic clauses most likely have the following significance: although our bodies are still in need of redemption, being subject to the death that lies ahead, the Spirit of God (who is resident in our bodies even now) is the source of life—the implication most likely being that the Spirit will give life to our bodies in the resurrection (cf. v. 11); furthermore, the reason the body is currently dead is because of sin, while the reason the Spirit will give life to us at the resurrection is the righteousness that is ours in Christ (cf. v. 1, and the first clause of v. 10).[63] This idea is recapitulated in 8:11.[64]

A second implication is introduced with verses 12–13. Strictly speaking, this is an indicative statement, but it implicitly exhorts the reader to live in accordance with the lifestyle that is described. As Schreiner summarizes the logic of the inference of verses 12–13 from verses 5–11: "believers are in the Spirit and not in the flesh, therefore they are not debtors to live according to the flesh."[65] Paul continues with the clarification that those who continue to live κατὰ σάρκα will die—and this death is to be taken in the fullest sense of eschatological and eternal judgment—but those who by the Spirit put to death the deeds of the body will live (i.e., eternally; v. 13). Here we encounter a sharp paradox where the indicative meets the imperative. God has saved believers through faith in Christ, a fact which at the same time enables as well as necessitates that believers walk in holiness through the power of the

---

63. Moo, *Romans*, 491–92; Schreiner, *Romans*, 414–15; Fee, *God's Empowering Presence*, 548–52.

64. Schreiner, *Romans*, 415.

65. Schreiner, *Romans*, 419.

Holy Spirit.[66] Romans 8:12–13 implies that even though we are no longer "in the flesh," and no longer "belong" to it, we are still in contact with it and subject to its influence, such that Paul can reasonably warn and exhort us against surrendering to its influence. Moo provides a helpful analogy: "Like freed slaves who might, out of habit, obey their old masters even after being released—'legally' and 'positionally'—from them, so we Christians can still listen to and heed the voice of that old master of ours, the flesh."[67]

Finally, we see one last exhortation to believers in 13:14 to "make no provision for the σάρξ for its lusts." Here we have an ethical command pertaining to believers, who are "in the Spirit" in a salvation-historical sense, and yet they are enjoined regarding the lusts of the σάρξ. Here the lusts of the flesh cannot refer merely to bodily appetites, for jealousy and strife are among the sins proscribed to the believers (v. 13).

Preliminary Conclusion: Paul's Tripartite Salvation-Historical Temporal Schema

Paul's ambiguous use of the term σάρξ makes it a challenge to interpret him consistently. A few things are evident. First, we can say that in a salvation-historical sense we are not "in the flesh" but "in the Spirit." However, in an anthropological sense we remain "flesh," and we live this life "in the flesh" in a somatic sense. Yet, even when Paul uses "flesh" with this somatic sense, it cannot be a pure synonym for "body" in an unqualified sense. Rather, "flesh" would substitute for a phrase like "mortal body" or "weak body." This is apparent, since our body is never described with the word "flesh" beyond the parousia, so it seems that for our earthly lives as Christians, even though we are aided by the Spirit, our human and bodily life still exhibits some of the mortal and moral weakness of an incomplete redemption. That redemption has begun, and because of the Spirit within us we are no longer enslaved to sin, but nonetheless that redemption is not completed yet. We long for (ἀπεκδέχομαι, *apekdechomai*), hope for (ἐλπίζω, *elpizō*), and groan inwardly (στενάζω, *stenazō*), for the consummation of our salvation (Rom 8:23–25), which is the redemption of our bodies. Referring to the return of Christ and our future resurrection, Paul speaks of this same groaning in 2 Corinthians 5:2, 4, and the same longing in Philippians 3:20 and 1 Corinthians 1:7. (What Paul means in Galatians 5:5 by "we eagerly await the hope of righteousness" is less clear, but we shall revisit this below.) Meanwhile, in this intervening time

---

66. Moo, *Romans*, 494–96; Schreiner, *Romans*, 420; Fee, *God's Empowering Presence*, 556–59.

67. Moo, *Romans*, 494.

between our conversion and the parousia, this time of *weakness* (ἀσθένεια, see Rom 6:19; 1 Cor 15:43), the Spirit helps us and prays for us (Rom 8:26).

Secondly, from the data of the texts we have examined so far, especially Romans, we can see that three specific salvation-historical times are distinguished by Paul. For brevity's sake, let us abbreviate "salvation-historical" as "SH." Let us give each of these SH times a label[68] and a description. For the time being, we should avoid using any label that makes reference to "ages," because our preliminary conclusions regarding this tripartite temporal schema are derived solely from observations of the different characteristics that may be discerned regarding these three SH periods; we have yet to examine Paul's use of "age" language to see what relationship obtains between his eschatological view of the "ages" and the SH periods we have discerned. We shall discuss that relationship more in the following chapter. For now, we merely summarize the tripartite SH temporal structure that results from the previous argumentation.

(1) "The SH-Yesterday"

The first SH time is characterized by the flesh, but not the Spirit. Of course, man is "flesh" in the OT anthropological sense. Furthermore, Paul describes people in this SH time as "in the flesh," because they are solely flesh, apart from the Spirit's indwelling and empowering presence, in contrast to the Christian experience. In an objective historical sense, this would be the time before Jesus Christ's salvific work of death and resurrection, and the Spirit's advent. For the Jews it would be the time associated with Torah, according to Paul.[69] Believers living during this time in history experienced conflict between "the inner man" and "the flesh," as described in Romans 7:5, 14–25. Living in the SH-Yesterday in the individual subjective sense would apply to any individual outside of Christ or prior to conversion and inclusion in Christ. However, the individual who continues to be in the flesh, to live in

---

68. It is hoped that the following labels are at least analytically adequate, even if they may leave something to be desired aesthetically.

69. Westerholm, *Perspectives Old and New*, 429–37; Schreiner, *Law and Its Fulfillment*, 39–40, 127–9, 132–3. It is extremely unlikely that the basis for Paul's view was an antecedent Jewish belief about the abrogation of the Torah in the Messianic age, but is more likely to be the result of his own reflective evaluation of the implication of salvation through faith in the death of Christ. For further discussion, see Westerholm, *Perspectives Old and New*, 438–9; Schreiner, *Law and Its Fulfillment*, 157; Sanders, *Paul and Palestinian Judaism*, 479–81; Davies, *Torah in the Messianic Age*, 78–94; against the interpretations of the rabbinic evidences given by Schoeps, *Paul*, 168–83, and the views of Schweitzer, *Mysticism of Paul*, 187–92.

the SH-Yesterday after Christ comes, or after Christ is presented to him, has a more sharply antithetical relationship with God. Here the flesh-Spirit antithesis is heightened (Rom 8:5–9).[70]

(2) "The SH-Now"

The second time distinguished by Paul is after the work of Christ and the Spirit, and subjectively for each individual, after conversion when they are placed "in Christ." Such persons are not "in the flesh," but are "in the Spirit" in a salvation-historical sense, for the Spirit indwells them and empowers them. However, anthropologically, these people are still "flesh," exhibiting the weaknesses typical of humanity, such that they need the Spirit's help and intercession.[71] Furthermore, it is appropriate for Paul to exhort them not to submit to its desires. Paul can also use σάρξ as a near-synonym for σῶμα, but this brings in additional theological connotations of weakness and mortality. Biblical passages that are descriptive of the SH-Now include Romans 6; 7:4, 6; and 8:1–17, 23–27—and, I will argue below, Galatians 5:16–18, 22–25. This time is brought to an end by the parousia of Christ, which demarcates the commencement of the third period.

(3) "The SH-*Soon!*"[72]

This is the time of the redemption of our bodies, in which we are given a σῶμα πνευματικόν (*sōma pneumatikon*), and the σάρξ makes no more appearance.

---

70. Note that the flesh-Spirit antithesis of Romans 8:5–9 is more antagonistic than what is depicted in Romans 7:14–25 (which, technically speaking, is not a flesh-Spirit antithesis passage, because the Spirit is absent; instead, we have a text in which the flesh dominates and subjugates the inner man, who affirms God's Law but is unable to do it). It is likely the case that the Romans 8 antithesis is more antagonistic in that Christ and the Spirit have come but have been rejected, and the person in the flesh continues to insist on trusting in his flesh/Torah (given that the Jews are most likely in view here). The works of this flesh-mindset are listed in Galatians 5:19–21.

71. See also the helpful and concise description of "the present" as a time of conflict in Wenham, *Paul*, 232. We will address the relationship of the present or SH-Now to the two ages in the next chapter.

72. For consistency's sake, "SH-Tomorrow" would have been fitting, except that its pedestrian quality lacks the tone of anticipation necessary to capture Paul's longing for the parousia and the consummation of our salvation. It is hoped as well that the term "SH-*Soon!*" captures the sense of imminency and urgency with which the future return of Christ is to impact our present life, according to Paul.

This is the full consummation of our salvation that we are waiting for (Rom 8:18–25; 1 Cor 15:21–28, 35–57; Phil 3:20–21[73]).

However, it is important to note that in Paul's letters, he does not usually deal with all three parts of this schema at once. Rather, he usually seems to be contrasting only two of the three parts at any given time: either the SH-Now with the SH-Yesterday, or the SH-Now with the SH-*Soon!* Both of these comparisons would be starkly antithetical as if one were comparing night to day. Comparing the unenabled person "in the flesh" living in the SH-Yesterday with the person "in the Spirit" living in the SH-Now is the difference between a corpse and a person full of life. Likewise, the difference between our life in the SH-Now and our life in the SH-*Soon!* is as stark as the difference between shameful weakness and glorious power.

Our consideration of the salvation-historical framework of σάρξ has led us to postulate a tripartite salvation-historical temporal structure in Paul's thought. However, this is not the only way to synthesize the data of Paul's epistles. We have already alluded several times to an alternate view which characterizes Pauline eschatology in terms of "the overlap of the ages." We now turn to a comparison of these two schemata to ascertain whether they are equivalent, or if, alternatively, one is more exegetically adequate and better able to integrate what Paul has to say about the flesh and the eschatological ages.

---

73. Galatians 5:5 may also be an example, since it uses two words commonly found in passages dealing with our eschatological expectation: ἀπεκδέχομαι ("I wait eagerly") and ἐλπίς (*elpis*; "hope"). We will consider this below.

— 6 —
Paul's *Sarx-Pneuma* Antithesis and the Schema of Overlapping Ages

Now that we have established Paul's salvation-historical flesh-Spirit antithesis and have seen that it results in a tripartite temporal schema, we must make a clarification regarding the relationship between this schema and Pauline eschatology.

A Final Clarification: Should We Construe the Salvation-Historical Flesh-Spirit Antithesis as Two Overlapping Ages?

Inaugurated Eschatology, the Ages, and the Flesh-Spirit Antithesis

One more issue must be clarified if we are to properly understand Paul's σάρξ-πνεῦμα antithesis. The question is to what extent this antithesis should be identified with the "present age"-"age to come" antithesis, and whether we should understand the time of the SH-Now as a time period of the "overlap of the ages." One aspect of Pauline theology in particular and NT theology in general is an eschatological understanding that makes sense of the fact that Jesus' work has inaugurated aspects of the long-anticipated Messianic kingdom, but not its fullness; the old age of things persists as we await the final consummation of Jesus' kingdom. It is important to clarify that we do not question a single element mentioned in the previous statement. Phrases like "the now and the not yet" are attempts to capture this eschatological tension which is undeniably present in the New Testament. However, caution is in order lest such phrases begin to substitute for careful thought and exegesis. It seems that just such a thing has occurred with the very common description of the Christian life as lived in "the overlap of the ages," which has become ubiquitous among

NT scholars. This description has become untethered from the text of the New Testament and drifts freely over the theological landscape to alight wherever convenient antitheses may be found.

One area where the alleged "overlap of the ages" is frequently invoked is in discussions of Paul's flesh-Spirit antithesis. Yet if one looks at the relevant flesh-Spirit conflict passages, one searches in vain for "age"-talk, let alone of two overlapping ages. It is not until one consults the commentators that one encounters such language.[1] Another conspicuous aspect of the "overlap of the ages" construct is how often it is assumed, asserted, or illustrated,[2] yet how rarely its proponents attempt to argue for the concept exegetically (much less demonstrate it). Furthermore, we shall maintain below that these exceptional attempts typically are based on the dubious identification or substitution of various theological terms. This leads us to a position that is at odds with a rather large consensus of Pauline scholarship. Nonetheless, we remain unconvinced by that consensus view, and believe that it ought to be questioned, rethought, and then either defended more vigorously than it typically is, or jettisoned in favor of a more adequate synthesis.

1. For contemporary expositions see, e.g., Barclay, *Obeying the Truth*, 205-6; Moo, *Romans*, 26-27, 49-50, 373-75, 489-90; Moo's succinct expression of this view and his understanding of its relation to the flesh-Spirit conflict can be found in Moo, *Encountering Romans*, 42-43; Fee, *God's Empowering Presence*, 430-33, 751, 817, 820-22; Ridderbos, *Paul*, 66; Russell, *Flesh/Spirit Conflict*, 121-22, 215, also citing and quoting at length George Ladd, Heinrich Schlier, J. Louis Martyn, and Robert Jewett. See also Ladd, *Theology of the New Testament*, 65-67, 409-11, 595-97; Dunn, *Theology of Paul*, 41, 461-98. Several scholars contributed to the development of this interpretation of Paul. Vos, *Pauline Eschatology*, 37-39, was an early proponent (first edition published in 1930) of the view that the age to come began with the resurrection, but at a heavenly, higher plane than this age, such that what resulted was "the overlap of the ages." Cullman was quite influential in the promotion of this general concept in his argument and diagram illustrating that the coming of Christ no longer coincides with the midpoint or division between the ages, but that it precedes it, in *Christ and Time* (the English translation of *Christus und die Zeit* published in 1946), 81-93 (see esp. the diagram on p. 83). However, the characteristic terms that have become attached to this view, e.g., "the overlap of the ages," came later. Cullmann spoke in terms of the "mid-point of time" and "a new division of time." Conzelmann, *Theology of St. Luke* (the English translation of *Die Mitte der Zeit*, 1953), 150, in a description of Luke's salvation-historical structure, describes the period between Jesus' first and second comings as "the last age." Despite their differences, Cullmann viewed this analysis as a supplement to his own which developed the idea of "the already and not yet" (cf. Cullmann, "Introductory Chapter to the Third Edition," in *Christ and Time*, xxii-xxiii). For a Jewish perspective, see Schoeps, *Paul*, 97-104. See also the combination of temporal and spatial aspects (similar to and influenced by Vos) in Lincoln, *Paradise Now and Not Yet*, 170-77.

2. E.g., Ladd, *Theology of the New Testament*, 66-67; Vos, *Pauline Eschatology*, 38; Cullmann, *Christ and Time*, 83; Dunn, *Theology of Paul*, 464-65, 475 (we have already critiqued some of Dunn's argumentation based on his view of Romans 7:7-25); Hagner, *New Testament*, 75; Arnold, *Power and Magic*, 154.

It is arguably the case that Paul's use of the term αἰών (*aiōn*) and his tripartite salvation-historical schema (analyzed above in terms of SH-Yesterday, SH-Now, and SH-*Soon!*) just do not map on to each other exactly.[3] Paul did not write any systematic presentation of his overall eschatology in the NT, so it is unsurprising that he did not give any label to the different times of salvation history which he nonetheless clearly distinguished (as we discerned above). What we have labeled the "SH-yesterday" and the "SH-now" are clearly contrasting salvation-historical periods, but are not spoken of by Paul as contrasting "aeons." Hence, to speak of "overlapping ages" may not be the best way to characterize Paul's conception. It seems the "present age" includes both the SH-Yesterday and the SH-Now, while "the age to come" seems to be identical with the SH-*Soon!* This claim can be defended by analyzing the σάρξ-texts and the αἰών-texts.

A listing of the relevant σάρξ-texts (i.e., those that have a salvation-historical emphasis with temporal import) and the relevant αἰών-texts (i.e., ignoring constructions meaning "forever") generates two parallel lines that hardly intersect; admittedly, in a few instances they appear to come close, but never in a way that establishes the connection between the "overlap of the ages" and the flesh-Spirit antithesis). The principal αἰών-texts are Romans 12:2; 1 Corinthians 1:20; 2:6–8; 3:18; 10:11; 2 Corinthians 4:4; Galatians 1:4; Ephesians 1:22; 2:2, 7; 3:9, 11; Colossians 1:26; 1 Timothy 6:17; 2 Timothy 4:10; and Titus 2:12.[4] However, we grant Lincoln's point that an αἰών can be considered as a spatio-temporal complex, and thus κόσμος can function interchangeably with αἰών.[5] Something of this sort appears to occur in 1 Corinthians 1:20; 2:12 (cf. "age" in 2:6-8); 3:18-19, 22; and Galatians 6:14. Of these, only in 1 Corinthians 1–3; Ephesians 2:1–7; and Galatians 6:14 is σάρξ found in the context, and we shall address these below.

---

3. Perhaps by way of analogy, we may think of the use of the term "Russia" during the Cold War era to mean "the Soviet Union"—though the two terms were certainly related, they were not truly synonymous or co-referring terms.

4. Since I am trying to *disprove* that *any* Pauline passage defines the flesh-Spirit antithesis as an antithesis of the two ages, my argument here is indifferent as to the disputed authorship of some of the letters. If none of the thirteen epistles attributed to Paul have such a link, it is irrelevant to the overall argument if some of those epistles are considered Deutero-Pauline; the conclusion is unaffected. However, it would be noteworthy if a distinction were found between the disputed and undisputed Pauline letters on this issue. If the former showed evidence of the link I am trying to disprove, while the latter did not, then as long as the authenticity of the disputed letters remained even a possibility, then so would the hypothesis I am seeking to falsify. For the sake of the completeness of the argument, therefore, it is best here to argue that there is no link between these two antitheses in *any* of the thirteen allegedly Pauline letters.

5. Lincoln, *Paradise Now and Not Yet*, 171–72.

1 Corinthians 10:11

Before we move on to consider the major σάρξ-passages, let us briefly address 1 Corinthians 10:11, which many commentators assert provides a framework for Paul's thought regarding the relationship between the past and future ages. Here is our text: "Now these things happened to them as an example, but it was written for our instruction, upon whom the ends [τὰ τέλη, *ta telē*] of the ages have come [κατήντηκεν, *katentēken*]" (1 Cor 10:11, my translation). It is here that many interpreters of Paul, particularly those of an apocalyptic bent,[6] see warrant for an "overlap" or "meeting point" of the past and future ages. Their interpretation is heavily influenced by a general perspective on Paul's theology that it is apocalyptic, and ought to be read as fundamentally structured around the two ages. We will revisit this apocalyptic view of Paul below. For now, let us consider the specifically exegetical argument from 1 Corinthians 10:11 offered by these commentators. The crux of their exegetical argument is the verb καταντάω (*katantaō*), indicated in brackets in the verse above. This verb, according to BDAG, has a range of meaning that includes: to come to, arrive at, or reach a geographical destination; to attain or reach a goal or a desired condition; or to meet. However, a related verb, ἀντάω (*antaō*), means to come opposite to, or to meet.[7] Accordingly, Johannes Weiss[8] and Jean Héring read 1 Corinthians 10:11 to mean that the two ages had come together or met. Héring speculates that ἀντάω in the active form may have the middle meaning of "to meet one another," and so concludes:

> The Apostle means, therefore, according to our view: 'The two ages meet one another at their extremities at the point where we Christians stand. We are at the point of intersection of the two worlds.' This idea is in perfect harmony with that other, current in the New Testament, that the Christians live on the one hand in the last days of the former age, and on the other, in the Kingdom of Christ, which is an anticipation of the future age.[9]

---

6. Examples of such interpreters of Paul include Ernst Käsemann, J. Christiaan Beker, and J. Louis Martyn. For wider background discussion, see Aune, "Apocalypticism"; Kreitzer, "Eschatology." For a brief representative apocalyptic "overlapping age" interpretation of Paul's eschatology, see Soards, *Apostle Paul*, 20–21, 37–41, 80–81, 180. For a negative assessment of this interpretation of Paul, see Matlock, *Unveiling the Apocalyptic Paul*.

7. BDAG, s.v. καταντάω. See also LSJ, s.v. ἀντάω.

8. Weiss, *Der este Korintherbrief*, 254, cited in Thiselton, *First Corinthians*, 743.

9. Héring, *First Corinthians*, 89.

In an astonishing feat of argumentative acrobatics, Ladd presents a similar interpretation before rejecting it, while simultaneously asserting that it's true nonetheless:

> It is possible that this unique expression [i.e., "the ends of the ages"] is used precisely to designate the fact that the two ages—this age and the Age to Come—overlap, that the first part of the Age to Come reaches back into the last part of the old age, so that the period between the resurrection and the parousia is a period "between the times," or better, a period that belongs to two times. *Telē* "designates the ends of the two lines, in one case the end, in the other case, the beginning" of the two ages. *This view is very attractive and actually corresponds to Paul's thought.* However, since the context is concerned with the relationship of Old Testament history to Christians, it is better to understand *telē* in its teleological rather than its temporal sense . . . The phrase designates the time introduced by Christ as the time in which the ages of history have found their fulfillment. However, the nature of this fulfillment consists in the fact that Messiah has come and begun his reign, the resurrection has begun, the eschatological gift of the Spirit has been poured out. The amazing fact is that these eschatological events have occurred before the Day of the Lord, before the dawn of the Age to Come, in the midst of the present evil age. *It is correct to say of Paul's thought as a whole, even if not of 1 Corinthians 10:11,* "In a surprising way visible only to faith the end of the old aeon and the dawn of the new has come upon the community."[10] [emphasis mine]

We agree with the actual interpretation Ladd advocates for 1 Corinthians 10:11, but it is bracketed by two gratuitous statements (in our italics) that are utterly unsupported by the text in question. The statements are audacious assertions that have not been paid for with any evidence whatsoever. The effect of the entire paragraph is to leave the undiscerning or sympathetic reader with the impression that 1 Corinthians 10:11 says what Ladd acknowledges that it does not. Rhetorically, this is a very effective argument, but ought to be rejected by any discriminating auditor.

Weiss and Héring's interpretation is followed forthrightly by Thiselton because of its fit with Paul's "now and the not yet" eschatology, and because of its suitability for responding to two theologies Thiselton believes to have been present at Corinth: a theology of presumption and a contrasting theology of

---

10. Ladd, *Theology of the New Testament*, 409–10, quoting first Weiss, *Der este Korintherbrief*, 254; then Michel, "καταντάω, ὑπαντάω, ὑπάντησις," 625; emphasis mine.

despair.¹¹ Fitzmyer comes to the same conclusion on the basis of the meaning of καταντάω and Paul's apocalyptic eschatology.¹² Marion Soards not only adopts this conclusion, but makes this interpretation of 1 Corinthians 10:11 "the key," not only to 1 Corinthians, but also to Paul's thought in general—by which, of course, he means Paul's apocalyptic thought.¹³

Now we would caution that inferring a "key" to Paul's letter—and, *a fortiori*, his thought in general—from 1 Cor 10:11 is a rather precarious undertaking. For one thing, the phrase in question is a mere prepositional clause to describe the "us" which is the subject of Paul's exhortation to avoid Israel's mistakes, which is the point of the overall passage. Paul could have dropped the prepositional clause and still communicated that main point, and we do not know how much emphasis he intended in that adjectival clause. Of course, this does not rule out the possibility that the phrase is a hint, a "tip off," a revealing "tell" of Paul's apocalyptic mindset, but it nonetheless seems we should be hesitant to put so much weight on what is not the main point of the passage, or even the verse. However, it must be noted that apocalyptic interpreters of Paul also appeal to other verses to support this interpretation, passages such as 2 Corinthians 5:17 and Galatians 6:15—which are themselves debated, and which we are on the cusp of debating at this very moment. We seem to search in vain for even one firm basis for this conception.

When we take an exegetical look at 1 Corinthians 10:11, we concede that the meaning of καταντάω *may* possibly accommodate their view—and they themselves frequently state the matter in terms just as weak. Certainly the plural αἰώνων (*aiōnōn*) makes their view possible. We would also grant the plurality of the word τέλη could support their view.¹⁴ Unfortunately, though, the meaning of τέλη is the rock upon which this interpretation runs aground and sinks; and it is on this rock that opponents of this exegesis take their stand. This interpretation stretches the meaning of τέλος (*telos*) intolerably, which means "end" or "goal," but never "beginning."¹⁵ It seems

11. Thiselton, *First Corinthians*, 743–44; Thiselton, *First Corinthians*, 153–54. See also, more tentatively and in acknowledgment of the debate on this point, Wenham, *Paul*, 69.

12. Fitzmyer, *First Corinthians*, 387–88.

13. Soards, *Apostle Paul*, 20–21, 37–41, 80–81, 180; Soards, *1 Corinthians*, 12–15, 203–4, 207.

14. Though, as Dunn acknowledges, the plural here is puzzling (*Theology of Paul*, 41n72).

15. This is the prime criticism of Barrett, *First Corinthians*, 227–28; Conzelmann, *1 Corinthians*, 168; and Garland, *1 Corinthians*, 465. Garland actually accepts Soards's view of the overlap of the ages, but does not believe this can be the meaning of this verse. See also BDAG, s.v. τέλος. Other commentators deny the "overlap" or "meeting"

that what is in play here is the common fallacy of making time analogous to space. It is a fallacy to treat temporal "ends" in the same way that we treat spatial "ends." With spatial ends, either end may be an *archē* or a *telos*, depending on one's perspective. Not so with temporal ends, in which case, because of the irreversible direction of time's arrow, there is just an *archē* and a *telos*, period.[16] This makes sense of the fact that if on December 31 you utter, "The ends of the years have come upon us!," people would be stupefied to know what you were talking about, but they certainly would not conclude that one of the "ends" was January 1. Similarly, whatever Paul means by his statement, it seems unlikely in the extreme that he means that the *telos* of the old era is upon us and the *archē* of the new is also upon us. Accordingly, this αἰών-text does not support an understanding of the flesh-Spirit salvation-historical antithesis as an "overlap of the ages."[17]

The Inaugurated Kingdom, the Last Days, and the Age to Come

Actually, in Héring's attempt to defend that mistaken view quoted above, he may have overlooked a truer formulation found in his own words: "Christians live . . . in the last days of the former age."[18] It is not clearly stated in Paul, but there is a clear sense in other New Testament writings that what Jesus inaugurated with his kingdom in his first coming is not the new age, but *the last days of the old age*. This is clearest in Hebrews 1:1-2, and in Jesus's promise that he is with believers "until the end of the age" in Matthew 28:20, which makes sense if we conceive of "the age" as the continuing "old age" and the "new age" to be the age of consummation beginning at Jesus'

---

of the ages interpretations, in some cases without specifying precisely the meaning of εἰς οὓς τὰ τέλη τῶν αἰώνων κατήντηκεν: (*eis hous ta telē tōn aiōnōn katentēken*): see Witherington, *Conflict and Community in Corinth*, 223; and Orr and Walker, *1 Corinthians*, 246–47, where Orr and Walker list three potential interpretations without any mention of the view we are critiquing. Ciampa and Rosner, *First Corinthians*, 465–66, seem to skirt the controversy in their treatment of the clause.

16. This argument assumes the A-theory of time against the B-theory. See Craig, *Tensed Theory of Time*; Craig, *Tenseless Theory of Time*; and DeWeese, *God and the Nature of Time*, 1–89.

17. On this occasion we are more interested in establishing what 1 Cor 10:11 *does not* mean than what it does, but it seems that the various possible readings suggested by Barrett, *First Corinthians*, 227–28, and Garland, *First Corinthians*, 465, remain live options. Also, see Ladd, *Theology of the New Testament*, 410n48: "The precise phrase *ta telē tōn aiōnōn* occurs in Test. Levi 14:1 in one ms., designating merely the last days of history."

18. Héring, *First Corinthians*, 89.

return. Other references to "the last days" that clearly indicate present realities support this reading (in the disputed Pauline 2 Timothy 3:1, but also the similar 2 Peter 3:3; also Acts 2:17 and James 5:3).[19]

This also matches the OT eschatological expectation, which was typically expressed in terms of "in the last day(s)"[20] (e.g., Isa 2:2; Jer 23:20; Ezek 38:16; Hos 3:5; Mic 4:1). Jeremiah 31:27-34 does not precisely match the linguistic pattern, but its repeated "Behold, days are coming" (vv. 27, 31), "In those days" (v. 29), and "after those days" (v. 34), coupled with the content of the passage, makes a compelling case for a conceptual equivalence with the "last days" of other passages. Similarly, the "after this" and "in those days" of Joel 2:28-29 is clearly to be understood the same way, according to Luke who renders the first phrase "in the last days" in Peter's quote of the passage in Acts 2:17-21.[21]

At this stage, we note that many proponents of the "overlap of the ages" make an argument to the effect of the one given above, and then go beyond that argument by substituting or identifying one of its inaugurated eschatological elements with "the new age" or "the age to come." However, this substitution is never demonstrated from the NT (we will argue below that it cannot be, for it would depend on an identification that is not made in the NT). For example, Ladd exposits the Gospels as describing how Jesus' ministry inaugurates the kingdom of God, which is now present as a mystery, and will only be brought to consummation at the second coming of Christ.[22] However, he goes beyond the NT and the evidence of his arguments when he claims, "inheriting eternal life and entrance into the Kingdom of God are synonymous with entering into the Age to Come" (p. 62), and cites the substitutions among these concepts in Mark 10:17-30 (note vv. 17, 23, and 30).[23] The reason this argument is inadequate is that "eternal

---

19. 1 John 2:18's reference to "the last hour" may be a stylistic variant expressing the same truth, but John does not clearly relate "the last hour" to the first coming of Jesus, but rather to the present appearance of "many antichrists."

20. The OT did not use eschatological "age" talk in the same way as the NT to refer to "this age" or "the age to come." The occurrences of עוֹלָם ('ôlām) and αἰών and their cognates are typically used in constructions meaning "forever" (or, negatively, "never"), "days of old," "eternal, everlasting" or "permanent, lasting." (Based on our own survey of hundreds of occurrences.)

21. For the textual issue regarding this phrase in 2:17, see Bock, *Acts*, 137–38; Metzger, *Textual Commentary*, 256.

22. *Theology of the New Testament*, 60–67. Note as well that Ladd's final diagram shows no "overlap of the ages," and "the age to come" (which is *not* identified with the kingdom of God) commences with the second coming of Christ, all of which is correct in our view.

23. See also Ladd, *Presence of the Future*, 196.

life" and "the kingdom of God" are widely recognized as having inaugural and consummative aspects, but the debated point is whether this is true of "the age to come." It is most likely the case that in the interaction with the rich young ruler, with his background knowledge of the Jewish theological heritage, and the pericope's setting in the earthly ministry of Jesus, that the aspects of eternal life and kingdom of God assumed to be under discussion are the *future consummative ones, not the inaugural ones established by Jesus' first coming*.[24] Hence their substitution for (or, at least, synonymous parallelism with) "the age to come" in this passage cannot establish that this latter concept has inaugural aspects.[25]

A parallel phenomenon occurs in arguments about Paul's eschatology. For example, Beker states, "The inclusive view of the age to come as an already operative reality is especially clear in Rom 14:17," a text which only mentions the kingdom of God, and nothing about "the age to come." Nowhere is it established that these are to be identified.[26] Similarly, Lincoln notes that "in contexts where ὁ μέλλων αἰών [*ho mellōn aiōn*] could conceivably have been employed the apostle prefers ἡ βασιλεία τοῦ θεοῦ [*hē basileia tou theou*] (cf. 1 Thess. 2:12; 2 Thess. 1:5; Gal. 5:21; 1 Cor. 6:9, 10; 15:50; Eph. 5:5)."[27] However, while there is admittedly some overlap between these terms, no reason is given that these are to be identified. We can see a distinction between them in the verses cited: while Paul frequently speaks of Christians "inheriting" the kingdom of God, he never speaks of "inheriting" "the coming age" or "the age to come." Similarly, Ladd identifies being "in Christ" with being "in the new age," and cites 2 Corinthians 5:17, apparently assuming "new creation" is to be taken as synonymous with "new age," an issue requiring further discussion below.[28]

Let us proceed now to look at the σάρξ-texts.

The Σάρξ-Texts and the Αἰών-Texts

The major σάρξ-passages are (with their broad contexts): Romans 6–8; Galatians 5–6; Philippians 3; 1 Corithians 1:10—3:4; Ephesians 2:1–7. In the first three passages, which have significant salvation-historical instances of

---

24. Noted by Ladd, *Presence of the Future*, 115–16.

25. Hagner does something similar in the midst of an otherwise fine exposition of the inaugurated and future kingdom in *New Testament*, 68–80, when he identifies the kingdom with "the new age" on p. 75, yet without any argument at all.

26. Beker, *Paul the Apostle*, 146.

27. Lincoln, *Paradise Now and Not Yet*, 170.

28. Ladd, *Theology of the New Testament*, 596.

σάρξ or of parallel antitheses of Law vs. grace, faith, or promise, the term αἰών is totally lacking, although there is a significant occurrence of κόσμος in Galatians 6:14, which shall be addressed at length below. Only in the latter two passages listed above does the term αἰών appear at all. In 1 Corinthians 1:10—3:4, it is obvious that the κατὰ σάρκα values and behavior that Paul criticizes are those of the present αἰών or κόσμος, yet nowhere does Paul describe something like an "αἰών of the σάρξ" in terms of salvation-history. Strictly speaking, this is more of an ethical rather than a salvation-historical use of σάρξ.[29] The values of this αἰών are characterized as "sarkic," but the σάρξ-πνεῦμα antithesis is not defined as a clash between two succeeding yet overlapping αἰῶνες (*aiōnes*). Similarly, in Ephesians 2:1–7, the gentile believers formerly walked according to the αἰών of this κόσμος, while the Jewish believers formerly lived in the lusts of the σάρξ and indulged the desires of the σάρξ and the mind. Certainly there is a parallel here between the characteristics of the two unregenerate groups, but we do not have here a salvation-historical σάρξ-πνεῦμα antithesis defined in terms of aeons. Then in Ephesians 2:7 we are told of the riches of God's kindness in Christ that we will experience in the "ages to come"—with the plural "ages" perhaps a stylistic variant, so that the phrase is functionally equivalent to "the age to come," or as a general conception of a cumulative abundance of the time, extending forever into the future during which we will experience God's goodness.[30] This gives us a clue to the relationship between Paul's use of σάρξ and his understanding of the αἰῶνες. Most likely the use of σάρξ in the 1 Corinthians and Ephesians passages is basically an anthropological one rather than a salvation-historical one. As for the ages, we all live in the present evil αἰών, and the αἰών to come is an age of *consummation, not merely inauguration*. Therefore, while the salvation-historical sense of σάρξ, or being "in the σάρξ," is no longer applicable to believers because they are "in the Spirit," the anthropological sense of σάρξ, with all of its weaknesses and limitations, is still operative until the end of this αἰών.

---

29. See above for our discussion on this passage, pp. 79–85.

30. O'Brien, *Ephesians*, 173, favors the latter interpretation, and dismisses any connection to the two-age scheme.

"New Creation" in Paul, and the Age to Come

> So if anyone is in Christ, [he is] a new creation. Old things passed away; new things have come. (2 Cor 5:17, my translation)

> But may it never be for me to boast except in the cross of our Lord Jesus Christ, through whom the world has been crucified to me, and I to the world. For neither is circumcision anything, nor uncircumcision, but a new creation. (Gal 6:14–15, my translation)

Paul is quite clear: there is one age present that everybody is in: the present evil age. It is not the case that some people are in the old age and some are in the new. The present evil age is an objective fact. Yet many scholars import the idea of "the new age" or "the age to come" into our present circumstance of being "in the Spirit" by interpreting "new creation" in 2 Corinthians 5:17 and Galatians 6:15 as "*the* new creation," which is equated with "the age to come." A similar equation is made between the old "age" and the κόσμος in Galatians 6:14 and other places. Moyer Hubbard argues persuasively and at length against both of these propositions.[31] In both passages, "new creation" (καινὴ κτίσις, *kainē ktisis*) lacks the article, contrary to our expectation if Paul was speaking of "*the* new creation" (i.e., the new heaven and earth).[32] Furthermore, a careful reading of these verses in context shows that Paul is not using the "new creation" language from the Old Testament to make *cosmological* statements, but statements that are both *anthropological and pneumatological* that speak of the conversion of the individual—that is, "*a* new creation."[33] Furthermore, Hubbard argues convincingly that even κόσμος in Galatians 6:14 is not cosmological (!), but *anthropological*, referring to Paul's former manner of life in Judaism in which circumcision held such a central value.[34] Hubbard concludes regarding attempts to equate καινὴ κτίσις with *the* new creation, and "the new age":

> no one doubts that "new creation" describes a positive, even exuberant, *present* reality, yet Paul often speaks of the present age (ὁ αἰὼν οὗτος, ὁ νῦν καιρός, οὗτος κόσμος [*ho aiōn houtos, ho nun kairos, houtos kosmos*]) and *nowhere* does he describe it in anything other than negative terms. According to Paul, "this present age" has its own god (2 Cor. 4.4), its own (false) wisdom

---

31. See Hubbard, *New Creation*, esp. pp. 133–233, which comprise two chapters devoted to the careful exegesis of 2 Cor 5:17 and Gal 6:14 in context.
32. Hubbard, *New Creation*, 214–18, 222–24.
33. See Hubbard, *New Creation*, 170–87 on 2 Cor 5:17; 209–29 on Gal 6:14–15.
34. Hubbard, *New Creation*, 215–18, 222–30.

(1 Cor. 1.20; 2.6; 3.18), its own rulers (1 Cor. 2.8), and its own ephemeral perspectives (Rom. 12.2). It is, in fact, "the present *evil* age" (Gal. 1.4). To be sure, believers experience deliverance (ἐχέληται ἡμᾶς ἐκ τοῦ αἰῶνος τοῦ ἐνεστῶτος [*exelētai hēmas ek tou aiōnos tou enestōtos*], Gal. 1.4), though all agree that the force of the verb ἐξαιρέω [*exaireō*] here is not "to take out of" this age, but "to deliver from within" this age. Paul makes this point quite explicit in Romans 12.2: "Do not be conformed *to this age*, but be transformed by the making anew (ἀνακαίνωσις [*anakainōsis*]) of your mind" (cf. 2 Cor. 4.16). From Paul's perspective, the newness of Christian experience was the Spirit's work *within* (Rom. 5.5; 7.6; 8.1-17; 1 Cor. 6.19; 2 Cor. 1.22; 3.6, 18; 5.5; Gal. 3.2-4; 4.6, 29; 5.25), so it is less accurate to speak of the believer entering the new age *than it is to speak of the new age entering the believer.*[35]

Hubbard's characterization of "the new age entering the believer" is a vast improvement as a pithy description of our New Covenant circumstances as we await the return of Christ. Nonetheless, caution remains in order, for while "new creation" is used to speak of the Spirit resident in man, an inaugurated reality of the new age, it seems that the actual terminology of "the age to come" is reserved to speak of the full *consummation* of Christ's kingdom. The new creation reality of the Holy Spirit in us enables us to look forward to the new age with certain expectation and to know that this present evil age is certain to pass away—soon! If the Holy Spirit is the eschatological marker of the new age, perhaps it is best to think of him as the *downpayment* or *pledge* (to use Pauline language, ἀρραβών [*arrabōn*], from 2 Corinthians 1:22, and—if you can accept it—Ephesians 1:13-14), which is given *proleptically* in advance of the new age in all its fullness.[36]

Disputing "New Creation" in 2 Corinthians 5:17

However, there has been some significant criticism of Hubbard's argument, most notably by Gregory K. Beale, Douglas J. Moo, and T. Ryan Jackson, which we must address. Beale and Moo argue for a cosmological interpretation of 2 Corinthians 5:17 and Galatians 6:15, yet in our judgment their

---

35. Hubbard, *New Creation*, 224, emphasis Hubbard's.

36. It is interesting that Moo is also uncomfortable characterizing present Christian life as "between" the ages. However, in contrast to the position advocated here, Moo's criticism of this characterization is that it does not sufficiently emphasize "the decisive past transfer of the believer into the new age." Moo has mistakenly identified being "in the Spirit" with being in "the age to come." See Moo, *Romans*, 489-90.

arguments do not even come close to overturning Hubbard's argument for the anthropological view. Let us address their arguments by focusing specifically on Beale, with a few additional comments about Moo. A careful reading of Beale's case for a cosmological interpretation of "the new creation," "the new age," or "the new world" in these Pauline texts[37] shows the extent to which his argument depends on (1) mere assertion; (2) restating Paul's teaching in terms more amenable to his position, but without sufficient justification in the text or context; and (3) gratuitous repetition of those terms as if to wear down the reader by means of attrition. For example, in his exegesis of 2 Corinthians 5:17, he first discusses the context of the preceding verses. Commenting on verses 14–15, Beale says: "Verse 14 affirms that believers are identified with Christ's death, so that they are considered to have died to *the old world* and to their part in *the old world*." The italics are mine, not Beale's, and they mark concepts that are Beale's, not Paul's. In a similar fashion, Beale interprets verse 16 to mean that we are to evaluate things by Christ's *word* "and not by the *unregenerate word of the world*," and in "a radically different way from that of the *old, unregenerate world* of humanity." Verse 17 provides the rationale: "The point is that to live for Christ and not for ourselves is to evaluate differently from people in *the old creation* precisely because *we live in the new creation*." Once again, the italics are mine, and the concepts are from Beale, with no exegetical justification in Paul's text whatsoever. The exposition of verse 17 is particularly egregious, for Paul just does *not* say that the one in Christ "*lives in the* new creation"; rather, Paul says he *is a* new creation[38]—of course, the verb ἐστίν (*estin*) must be understood for it is not explicitly stated here, but an implied εἰμί (*eimi*) verb is not at all uncommon; there is certainly nothing in the text that implies the English "*lives in the* new creation." All of these examples come from one paragraph that is unfortunately quite representative of the argumentation throughout Beale's treatment. He continues with a series of paragraphs in which he argues against the straw man that Paul is saying the Corinthians are only experiencing something "*like* the eschatological prophecies of new creation" in Isaiah 43:18–19 as opposed to the real thing—a position that I am not sure anybody actually advocates.[39] Of course, the pertinent question is, How does Paul think prophecies such as Isaiah 43:18–19 apply to the Corinthian believers?

---

37. Beale, *New Testament Theology*, see 298–314 for his treatment of 2 Cor 5:17 and Gal 6:15.

38. Beale, *New Testament Theology*, 299.

39. Beale, *New Testament Theology*, 299–300.

Moo exhibits similar tendencies in his treatment of both letters, with frequent references to "epochal significances," "epochal turning points," "transfers from the old age to the new," and free substitutions of "creation," "age," and "world," whether of the old or new version.[40] For 2 Corinthians 5:17, he advocates the following translations:

> Therefore, if anyone is in Christ, the new creation has come: The old has gone, the new is here! [the rendering of the then-current TNIV, retained in the later NIV 2011, and similar to the NJB and HCSB]

> "If anyone is in Christ, the new creation has come *to that person.*" [Moo's translation and italics]

> "if anyone is in Christ, that person belongs to the new creation." [Moo's translation][41]

Moo justifies the first translation on the basis that Paul can change the subject from protasis to apodosis in a conditional sentence.[42] However, in the example he cites of 1 Corinthians 10:27, the context makes it explicit that such a change is necessary, but this is not the case in 2 Corinthians 5:17. In his own translations, Moo is suggesting that we fill out the elliptical 2 Corinthians 5:17 by adding a lot of new and specific information, whereas the simplest route to a complete thought is to take "a new creation" as a predicate nominative for the "anyone" who is in Christ.

Let us take the opportunity to clarify our own position. Obviously, new creation is something that has been inaugurated by the work of Christ. We could say that it is a subset of the work of redemption, which began immediately after the fall. New creation is the phase of redemption beginning with the finished work of Christ. However, just as redemption is a broader concept than new creation, so also new creation is a broader concept than the new heavens and new earth. The new heavens and the new earth is the *culmination* of God's work of new creation. Therefore, the two are not identical, and careless substitutions are to be avoided. Furthermore, it is essential to note that the work of new creation proceeds in reverse order from that of creation—starting from the transformation of the hearts and minds of individuals, extending to their embodied lives, to fellow believers, to unbelievers, to nations, to the whole earth, and finally to the renovation/recreation

---

40. Moo, "Creation and New Creation," 47–49 contains some representative examples.
41. Moo, "Creation and New Creation," 51–52.
42. Moo, "Creation and New Creation," 52n40.

of a new heavens and earth.⁴³ Accordingly, it would seem one can speak of different aspects of "new creation" which may be in view when alluding to the fulfillment of new creation prophecies.

Precisely what aspect of new creation is in view in a given instance must be established by careful exegesis. Margaret Thrall and Murray Harris both come to the same conclusion as Hubbard that "a new creation" in 2 Corinthians 5:17 must refer to an anthropological reality, for which each presents a strong exegetical argument.⁴⁴ (Harris maintains this interpretation for 2 Corinthians 5:17, even though he generally holds to an "overlapping ages" view of Pauline eschatology. He just denies that this view can be supported from this text, but must be derived from 1 Corinthians 10:11 and Galatians 1:4.)⁴⁵ The elements of verse 17 point so decisively towards an anthropological view that even Beale is forced to explain the verse in such a way in spite of himself. When he addresses how the Corinthian believers fulfill Isaianic prophecies of new creation, he inevitably is forced to describe it in terms of inaugural or beginning fulfillment⁴⁶—which just happens to occur at the anthropological level. Beale gives the game completely away when he asks: "how can [Paul's] understanding of the way new creation has begun be squared hermeneutically with what Isaiah has in mind? Isaiah had in mind a new physical heaven and earth, *and Paul had in mind a new spiritual condition of individual believers.*"⁴⁷ Of course, this just is the anthropological view. Whenever Beale stops talking in generalities⁴⁸ about "*the* new creation" or consciously defending his interpretation, and gets down to talking about what the concept means in its

---

43. Cullmann, *Christ and Time*, 115–18, makes a similar observation regarding the dynamic progress of redemption, which first goes through a narrowing, selecting a nation, a remnant, and only one man who is the Servant of Yahweh, Son of Man, the Christ. Then this dynamic reverses to continual broadening and greater inclusivity, from the first disciples and apostles, to the people of the saints in the church, composed of representatives of all mankind, and ultimately to a redeemed creation and the new heavens and earth.

44. Thrall, *Second Corinthians*, 1:420–28; Harris, *Second Corinthians*, 432–34; see also p. 360. The anthropological view of new creation is also argued by Hoegen-Rohls, "Κτίσις and καινὴ κτίσις in Paul's Letters," 117–19. Thrall (*Second Corinthians*, 1:423) also gives a positive appraisal of the anthropological view of Gal 6:15, and seems to favor it over the cosmological view, but she does not firmly and conclusively commit herself.

45. Harris, *Second Corinthians*, 434.

46. Beale, *New Testament Theology*, 300–301.

47. Beale, *New Testament Theology*, 301, italics mine.

48. I.e., the linguistic currency of the "lumper."

context,[49] he inevitably comes up with something very close to Hubbard's anthropological-soteriological view.

Jackson argues for a mediating position, accepting Hubbard's anthropological view, but insisting that Paul also intends a cosmological sense of new creation in 2 Corinthians 5:17. He correctly criticizes Hubbard's application of a distinction between Deutero-Isaiah (with an emphasis on soteriology and redemption) and Trito-Isaiah (with an emphasis on cosmology and creation) to the interpretation of Paul's text, for Paul himself would not have made that distinction. However, Hubbard's distinction is unnecessary for his thesis, for, as Jackson rightly observes, one cannot sharply distinguish creation and redemption in Isaiah.[50] This means that Paul is dealing with complex theological concepts that are composed of multiple aspects. Therefore, this permits the selective use of a concept focusing on a specific aspect of it on a given occasion. Accordingly, Jackson's criticism that Hubbard sets up a false dichotomy[51] is groundless. To be selective on a given occasion is not necessarily to be exclusive in the sense of negating other considerations. Paul can speak selectively of the anthropological aspect of new creation without implicitly denying the reality of the cosmological. Scholars can likewise attempt to follow Paul's argument on a given occasion without considering things that Paul does not mention. By assuming that one must always be all-inclusive in dealing with new creation in all of its thematic aspects and implications or be guilty of being exclusionary, Jackson seems to be laboring under his own false dichotomy. Similarly, even when acknowledging the need for the individualistic interpretation of new creation, Jackson must always include the objection that it cannot be limited to the individual.[52] There seems to be some sort of implicit straw man conception at work that any reference to the individual implies an *atomistic* understanding. This need not be the case.

Jackson's exegetical arguments are more subtle and nuanced than those of Beale and Moo, for he recognizes the necessity of an anthropological, soteriological interpretation that makes reference to individual conversion to make sense of the passage, and that this is impossible on a strictly cosmological view.[53] Nonetheless, in our judgment, his attempts to demonstrate cosmological aspects of new creation in 2 Corinthians 5:17 are strained. For example, he appeals to Paul's general eschatology as a modified apocalyptic

---

49. I.e., trading in the coin of the "splitter."
50. Jackson, *New Creation in Paul's Letters*, 120–22, and n3.
51. Jackson, *New Creation in Paul's Letters*, 4.
52. Jackson, *New Creation*, 137–38.
53. Jackson, *New Creation*, 133.

overlap-of-the-ages, which is itself questionable, as the background of the new creation issue. Then he claims that Paul uses new creation to express that eschatological view—which is clearly a question-begging move.[54]

Jackson also has a tendency to exaggerate the weight of the most minimal of considerations that could conceivably support his view. In one instance, he criticizes Hubbard for rejecting the cosmological view because in the context of 2 Corinthians 5:17, Paul is not focused on an "external problem." Jackson's rejoinder is that Paul in fact does have an external problem: the attacks on his apostolic authority, which ultimately spring from an old-age epistemology that has not been transformed to that of the new age that was inaugurated by Jesus.[55] It seems that *everything* is part of the spatiotemporal nexus that is the cosmos or the age, or can be linked to it in some way, and therefore *anything* counts as support for the cosmological view. Arguably, though, a more discriminating standard will help us to clarify precisely what Paul does say in a given passage, and to avoid reading things into the text based on our presuppositions about Paul's wider outlook. Besides, if the problem Paul was facing concerned epistemologies and value systems, it seems to direct the discussion towards the individual and to render much of the rest of the cosmos and age to be extraneous. Jackson's generous evidential standard is also seen when he concludes from the mere use of tensed language to describe the death of Christ and a converted value system in verses 14–15 that Paul was using this language "to locate himself on God's calendar of the ages."[56]

Finally, we note with some bewilderment Jackson's claim that in defending his apostolic authority in 2 Corinthians, Paul makes "his conception of new creation as the eschatological turn of the ages" the "organizational matrix and linchpin of his defense."[57] We find that to be an amazing feat, given that Paul does not say anything remotely resembling this in the context. Jackson appropriately cites in support J. L. Martyn, and not Paul, for it is easy to find frequent statements to this effect in Martyn, but not in Paul. In fact, we maintain that Paul does not say anything like this anywhere: not in 1 Corinthians 10:11, not in 2 Corinthians 5:17, and as we shall now see, not in Galatians 6:14–15.

---

54. Jackson, *New Creation*, 128–29.
55. Jackson, *New Creation*, 129.
56. Jackson, *New Creation*, 132.
57. Jackson, *New Creation*, 129.

Disputing "New Creation" in Galatians 6:14–15

Beale's treatment of Gal 6:14–15 is similar to that of 2 Corinthians 5:17. He constantly vacillates on whether Paul is speaking of the old or new creation (or world) in whole or in part. Typically Beale first makes a grandiose general statement that Paul is speaking of the whole, followed by a more specific statement that the previously mentioned realities obtain only in part. That is to say, Beale first gives an entire universe with his right hand and immediately takes it all back except for an anthropologically-shaped remainder with his left. In each case, we would like to press Beale for specificity: is Paul speaking of new creation realities in whole or in part? And if in part, which part? It is obviously the case in every one of Beale's clarifications, that it is at the anthropological level that new creation realities obtain for the believer by means of the Spirit. Whenever Beale gets specific, he affirms something very close to Hubbard's soterio-anthropological view. However, this is always accompanied by assertions that a holistic, cosmological concept of "new creation" or "world" is also in view, even though it is superfluous and extraneous to the specific passage in question.[58]

For example, in speaking of the "crucified world" of 6:14, Beale says:

> Paul believes that the entire old world, not merely a part of it, has been struck a fatal blow. Of course, the beginning phase of the destruction is primarily focused on the spiritual aspects and their associated national (physical) signs of separation. Paul, however, likely held the view that the culmination of this beginning process would be some kind of radical destruction of the physical cosmos as well, since elsewhere he sees a reestablishment of a physically transformed earth, including physically renovated resurrection bodies (see, e.g., Rom. 8:18–25; 1 Cor. 15:20–58).[59]

Similarly, in speaking of "new creation" in 6:15, Beale asserts that this "is a holistic reference to the entire new cosmos, part of which has begun to be inaugurated through Christ's resurrection and the spiritual resurrection of saints. Even a partial destruction or reconstitution of the elements in either of these worlds is an ontological reality, not a figurative one." In addition to exemplifying the flaws indicated above, Beale misunderstands 6:14–15 to be describing a destructive process that has only *begun* to be *inaugurated* (!) for the whole cosmos, which will culminate in the establishment of a totally

---

58. Beale, *New Testament Theology*, 312–13.
59. Beale, *New Testament Theology*, 312.

new cosmos.⁶⁰ However, it is clear from the perfect tense verb ἐσταύρωται (*estaurōtai*) that for Paul, this "crucifixion" is a completely accomplished fact. This makes it more likely that Paul is actually speaking in 6:14–15 of his previous identity and way of life that was completely done away with by his conversion, such that circumcision is no longer relevant; what matters now is life by the Spirit as "a new creation."

In the midst of his exposition, Beale makes one explicit attempt to make a specific three-point argument against the anthropological view of Hubbard. His argument is aimed specifically at Hubbard's interpretation of 2 Corinthians 5:17, but he asserts that the same problems afflict Hubbard's treatment of Galatians 6:15. The first criticism is that "the two categories of 'soterio-anthropological' and 'soterio-cosmological' are not mutually exclusive and easily overlap," which Hubbard fails to realize. The second criticism is based on the allusions to Isaiah 43:18–19 and 65:17 in 2 Corinthians 5:17; and the third criticism is based on the fact that Christ's resurrection is mentioned in 5:15.⁶¹ The last two are relevant only if the first argument succeeds, so let us focus on that one. First of all, we can grant that it is true: the anthropological and cosmological aspects of new creation are not mutually exclusive or dichotomous, and either or both concepts may be in view in passages where "new creation" is discussed. Second, however, we are not sure Hubbard is guilty of the charge. To speak of emphasis does not imply the exclusion of what is not emphasized. And to say that Paul intended a soterio-anthropological meaning in a given passage does not necessarily imply the claim that Paul believed there was no connection to soterio-cosmological realities, only that those are not in view in the passage.⁶²

The pertinent question is not whether "soterio-anthropological" and "soterio-cosmological" categories are mutually exclusive, or are separable; the real question is whether they are *distinguishable*. And if they are distinguishable, it seems that no reason can prevent a selective focus on one or the other aspect as a given topic of discussion. Then the pertinent deciding factor comes down to, "What did Paul actually say in the context?" What else Paul may have believed about other aspects of new creation and its connection to the new heavens and earth or a half-dozen other biblical topics then becomes secondary at best, and perhaps, not in view at all in the given context.

---

60. Beale, *New Testament Theology*, 312–13.

61. Beale, *New Testament Theology*, 302–3, n3. Note that this is a criticism also leveled at Hubbard by Jackson, *New Creation*, 3–4, 88–89, 133, 173.

62. See Hubbard, *New Creation*, 52–53, 216, 218. Jackson concedes as much in *New Creation*, 88n33.

Once this point is granted, then criticisms two and three really fall by the wayside, because the issue is clearly, to what use does Paul put these allusions in 2 Corinthians and Galatians, and about what aspect(s) of new creation is Paul talking? When you put the question so sharply, it is clear that Paul is addressing that aspect of the inaugurated new creation that just is those redeemed believers as new creations in Christ—that is, the soterio-anthropological level—and what implication that has for their lives in Christ now. And in fact, we have seen that every time Beale is forced to get specific on what is meant by Paul in the two passages in question, the answer is given in soterio-anthropological terms. The insistence that some cosmological import must also be implied is then justified by some connection to something else that is actually extraneous to the context.

Moo's exegesis of Galatians 6:15 is, if possible, perhaps even more problematic than Beale's.[63] We are truly sympathetic, for surely Galatians is one of the more difficult letters in the New Testament.[64] Nonetheless it must be said in all charity that Moo constructs a rather torturous argument, in which he ties together disparate points of data from the text with the slenderest of logical threads. Let us try to see where he goes awry in his exposition of 6:15. Speaking of the changed circumstances wrought by the cross-work of Christ and the presence of the Spirit, Moo notes that Paul had emphasized in 5:5–6 that what matters now is faith, the Spirit, and love (rather than circumcision and the Law).[65] Since 6:12–18 gives a concluding summary of the letter's key themes, and since 6:15 is parallel to 5:6, we would expect to find a reference to these three priorities of faith, Spirit, and love in 6:12–18—but we do not. Since such a reference is missing, we are justified in expanding the reference of 6:16's "rule" (i.e., new creation is what matters, not circumcision, from verse 15) to include faith, the Spirit, and love, because these are the set of values bound up with the new creation, which is in contrast to the "old age" (1:4) or "the world" (6:14), i.e., "the spatio-temporal state of affairs condemned at the cross," which "has its own set of values—flesh, the law, death."[66]

Moo's gratuitous identification of the "age" of 1:4 with "the world" of 6:14 facilitates a move away from Paul's very particularistic, personal focus in 6:14–15, to a vague, expansive reference to an abstract spatio-temporal state of affairs and its value system. At this point the stage is set for an

---

63. Moo's BECNT commentary on Galatians became available to me in the later stage of my thesis, so my interaction with it was minimal here. Nonetheless, his treatment of this passage in Moo, *Galatians*, 395–98 is not substantially different from that in Moo, "Creation and New Creation," which is critiqued here.

64. A judgment shared by Witherington, *Grace in Galatia*, 1–2.

65. Moo, "Creation and New Creation," 48–49.

66. Moo, "Creation and New Creation," 49.

unlimited expansion of the reference to all sorts of values that are extraneous to the context, as we will see below. Moo's exegesis is not completely wrong. Surely "new creation" does involve the Spirit, and faith working through love, and is indifferent to circumcision (5:5-6). However, when Moo discusses the "crucified world" and "new creation" of 6:14-15, his exegesis is torn between (1) his conception that these terms must be identified with, respectively, the old age and the new age, and (2) the constraints of the context of the passage. The vital interpretive decision must be made: in 6:14-15, is Paul talking in abstract terms about contrasting value systems of "the world"—a "spatio-temporal state of affairs"—or is he talking about contrasting value systems in the minds of individuals which govern their lives and affect their relationships with others—specifically, (1) in Paul's mind which had formerly governed his life, and (2) now, entering the Galatians' minds, attempting to place them back in slavery? Is, "the world" which the cross "crucified" to Paul, and vice versa, the world considered abstractly, or was it "Paul's world" as defined by the value system that he previously lived by? In our judgment, the latter makes the best sense of the passage, while the former struggles merely to attain intelligibility, to say nothing of exegetical justification. However, Moo is equivocal about whether Paul refers to the crucifixion of his own personal value system, or to that of the world or old age considered abstractly. He affirms both, while emphasizing the latter, and giving no explanation of the relationship between the two.[67]

However, in Moo's view, more is entailed by Paul's reference to "the new creation." We can understand the basis of this claim when we recall that Moo's conception of 6:14-15 permits a rather expansive reference to all sorts of values that may be extraneous to the context. The "new creation" is the antithesis to "the world" of 6:15, which in turn is a close equivalent to what Moo calls the "old age" in 1:4—which, note, Paul himself actually calls "the present evil age."[68] Between the old and the new there is a conflict of values, and as we have seen, "new creation" brings with it a whole new set of values which are expressed in 5:5-6 and 6:15. On this basis, Moo then argues that 3:28 should be linked as well to these verses, and provides for us an additional set of values of the new creation and its community: "There is neither Jew nor gentile, neither slave nor free, neither male nor female, for you are all one in Christ." Moo argues that this verse should be linked

---

67. Moo, "Creation and New Creation," 49.

68. Moo, "Creation and New Creation," 48. The treatment of "the present evil age" and "the (old) world [cosmos]" as co-referring terms which are in antithesis to "the new creation" is also prominent in Martyn, *Galatians*; see, e.g., 97–105, 564–65. Martyn considers Paul's reference to "the present evil age" in 1:4 a "distinctively apocalyptic expression" (p. 97).

to 5:5–6 and 6:15 because it has a similar "neither . . . nor" structure and a "Christological focus."[69] However, that seems a pretty thin reed to support all the weight Moo puts on it. The parallelism with 3:28 is not as strong as between 5:5–6 and 6:15, and 3:28 seems quite distant from the context of chapters 5–6. Nonetheless, Moo seems confident that this perceived connection between these three passages gives him all the necessary exegetical justification to proceed to "immanentize the eschaton"[70]:

> These texts together assert that the coming of Christ introduces a whole new state of affairs in the world. No longer do distinctions of ethnicity, social class, and gender that are determinative for this world matter. All "simply human" factors become meaningless in the face of God's world-transforming work in his Son Jesus Christ.[71]

Moo continues to elaborate on "this new state of affairs in the world" effected by the cross, which he sees as fundamental to Paul's argument in Galatians. Central to this new state of affairs is the new Christian community, and thus, "'new creation' in Galatians undoubtedly has some reference to the Christian community as a place where the usual worldly barriers between people are broken down," and then Moo cites 3:28, the wording of which "suggests this relationship between the new community and new creation." It is at this point that Moo begins to raise some good questions about 3:28: "it is puzzling at first glance why, granted the letter's argument, Paul does not content himself with referring to how Christ brings together Jew and gentile. Why add the apparently extraneous pairs 'slave and free' and 'male and female'?"[72] These are pertinent questions indeed, as is the question of why these "extraneous pairs" are mentioned at 3:28, and nowhere else in the letter.[73] Perhaps if Moo had discerned the reason for this he would have seen that his interpretation is

---

69. Moo, "Creation and New Creation," 48.

70. A phrase made famous in the 1950s and 1960s by the political philosopher Eric Voegelin, the aptness of which here is demonstrated in the following quote.

71. Moo, "Creation and New Creation," 48. In his appeal to Gal 3:28 and the implication that Christ's cross eliminated distinctions of ethnicity, class, and gender, Moo is following Martyn, "Apocalyptic Antinomies," 410–24 (see pp. 414–16 regarding Gal 3:27–28); Martyn, *Galatians* (see pp. 37–47, 373–83, 563–74 for Martyn's treatment of Gal 3:28 in conjunction with the "old age/cosmos" vs. "the new creation" antithesis). The criticisms below concerning Moo's appeal to Gal 3:28 are even more applicable to Martyn, who even claims that 3:28 speaks of the abolition of all distinctions, even religious ones (*Galatians*, 37n67, 38).

72. Moo, "Creation and New Creation," 50.

73. Others have noted this "intrusion," e.g., Hansen, *Galatians*, 110–11; Hansen, *Abraham in Galatians*, 136–37; Betz, *Galatians*, 184. These authors speculate on a baptismal liturgy as the basis of 3:28.

mistaken. All of Moo's speculations which he entertains as possible answers to this question miss the point and the context of 3:28, in our judgment, and we will not rehearse them here.[74]

In our view, Paul is not intending here to comment directly on social relations within the church. While Paul clearly has a deep concern for social relationships in all of his churches, there is no evidence from the letter that the Galatian churches are divided along the demographic lines mentioned in 3:28. Rather, Paul addresses the church as if it were a rather unified entity, a gentile church that is being pressured from the outside to Judaize. Paul is attempting to defend this church as a whole against this pressure by establishing that they are already a part of God's covenant people.[75] Accordingly, Paul makes the statement of 3:28, with its three pairs of Jew or Greek, slave or free man, and male or female, when he does because it is a part of a series of arguments in chapters 3 and 4 that have to do with believers in Jesus Christ being reckoned as sons of Abraham who inherit the promises to Abraham. In the Old Testament, the inheritance was something that was only received by *sons* of the family, not daughters, not slaves, and not those outside of the tribe, unless there were some exceptional circumstances (see Gen 15:2–4; 21:10; Deut 21:15–17; Num 27:1–11; 36:1–13).[76] However, in 3:28, Paul clarifies that this inheritance from Abraham is not limited to Jews, or to sons (as opposed to either daughters or to slaves of the household). This is because all—without distinction—who are believers in Jesus Christ are *reckoned as sons of Abraham* and therefore heirs to the promise he received. In short, Galatians 3:28 functions entirely to facilitate Paul's argument that believers in Jesus Christ are the true sons and heirs of Abraham, even though the Jewish background of inheritance customs and laws would ordinarily prevent that. Paul is not intending here to convey to us the value system of the "new community/age/world" or "the new creation."[77]

Contrary to Moo's assertions[78] against Hubbard, internal transformation is a major theme of Galatians, which is one of Paul's most personal

---

74. Moo, "Creation and New Creation," 50.

75. *Pace* Russell, *Flesh/Spirit Conflict*, 104; Bruce, *Galatians*, 187–91; Longenecker, *Galatians*, 156–9; Witherington, *Grace in Galatia*, 278–81; Hansen, *Galatians*, 25; and David Wenham, *Paul*, 61, 235–7, 247, 284–5. The following has obvious implications for the complementarian-egalitarian debate, but we will let that issue remain dormant.

76. Matthews, "Family Relationships," 295–6 (see section 4. Inheritance and Sexual Relations); Branch, "Zelophehad, Daughters of."

77. This view is arguably superior to the competing view because it makes these verses a natural fit in the context rather than an intrusive quote from a hypothesized baptismal liturgy that includes the extraneous pairs.

78. Moo, "Creation and New Creation," 51.

letters, with an emphasis on his own conversion. This is clear from the personal mode of Paul's argumentation in 1:6, 10—2:21; 4:10–20; and 6:14–15, 17. The emphasis on internal transformation is evident in Paul's conversion narratives in 1:11–16, 23–24, and 2:19–20; as well as Paul's statements in 4:12, 19; 5:6, 16, 22–25. In contrast to the letter's evident anthropological focus, Moo makes it into something very abstract—the concept of the radically new state of affairs Christ introduced into the *cosmos* or world order. Moo is right to affirm that the Law was problematic because it was obsolete in a salvation-historical sense. However, he mistakenly denies that Paul argues that the Law was inadequate to transform those who lived by it. Paul made both arguments against the Law, and he argued the latter case as a means of demonstrating the former, particularly in Galatians 3:10–14 and 5:2–4, 13–25. Furthermore, we shall see that Paul's command to "walk by the Spirit" in 5:25 entails a life of transformation. In conclusion, Hubbard's view of new creation in Galatians 6:15 as "the new age entering the believer" by means of the Spirit is more true to the biblical text than Moo's understanding of it as the believer entering the new age.

Now we are ready to begin our search for the elusive meaning of Paul's σάρξ-πνεῦμα antithesis in the epistle to the Galatians.

— 7 —

The *Sarx*, the *Pneuma*, the Gospel, and the Letter to the Galatians

We are getting nearer to our goal of uncovering Paul's distinctive use of σάρξ by exegeting in some detail one of his central σάρξ-πνεῦμα antithesis passages, Galatians 5:13–26. We will attempt to relate what we have discovered about Paul's salvation-historical and ethical uses of σάρξ to this enigmatic passage and to clarify exactly what Paul intended when he called the Galatian converts to walk by the Spirit that they may not fulfill the desire of the σάρξ, and what its significance is to us today.

However, we must first analyze the purpose of Galatians, its major thematic concerns, and the flow of its argument in order to situate our passage in its epistolary context.[1] As we proceed we will take note of and clarify anything that impinges on Galatians 5:13–26 or Paul's antithetical use of σάρξ. Unfortunately, this is not as straightforward a task as one may initially think, for the letter to the Galatians as a whole is the setting for a host of controversies in New Testament scholarship, and these will provide an occasional diversion in our sketch of the letter's argument.

The Purpose of Galatians and the Gospel

The purpose of Paul's letter to the Galatians is to persuade the Galatian gentile Christians not to abandon the true gospel he preached to them in favor of the non-gospel of the Judaizers, who advocated Torah observance and circumcision as the means of completing their faith in Christ and securing their justification before God. At issue primarily was the gospel of justification by grace through faith in Jesus which establishes one's identity

---

1. In the following account of the argumentative structure of Galatians I am deeply indebted in particular to Russell, *Flesh/Spirit Conflict*, 53–62; also Matera, "Culmination of Paul's Argument"; and to a lesser extent Schreiner, *Galatians*, 58.

in the people of God apart from the Law.² A secondary concern was to reassure the Galatians that the Spirit provided sufficient ethical guidance and moral restraint apart from the Law, and to encourage them to conform to the pattern of behavior in which the Spirit would lead them.³ After a brief greeting (1:1–5),⁴ Paul skips over the customary thanksgiving⁵ and states his purpose bluntly in 1:6–10.

Immediately we can see from the introduction that Paul is deeply concerned with the gospel, and is opposed to the non-gospel advocated by the Judaizers.⁶ It is important to clarify that for Paul, the gospel is not just the message of justification by grace through faith in the atoning work of Jesus on the cross and the resurrection. Of course, these elements are the core, the sine qua non of the gospel, but not the totality of it. Paul conceives of the gospel as God's program to bless all the families of the earth, which was preached to Abraham (Gal 3:8, citing Gen 12:3), and was subsequently realized in Christ so that now salvation and blessing can be preached to all (Rom 1:1–5, 16–17), and which program will be fulfilled at Christ's return. It clearly has a historical dimension. For individuals it also has dimensions of past, present, and future. Justification and conversion conferred on the individual a new status of righteousness⁷ before God, and henceforth he looks

---

2. Bruce, *Galatians*, 27–29; Moo, *Galatians*, 19.

3. Russell, *Flesh/Spirit Conflict*, 42–44, Barclay, *Obeying the Truth*, 73; Hansen, *Galatians*, 24–28; Kruse, *Paul, the Law, and Justification*, 64; Ziesler, *Galatians*, xiv–xv.

4. It should be evident from the preceding mentions of 1:4 that we do not see the same "apocalyptic" significance in that verse as Martyn, *Galatians*, 97–105, 564–65, and those who have followed him on this point, e.g., Witherington, *Grace in Galatia*, 76–77; Moo, *Galatians*, 72–73; Russell, *Flesh/Spirit Conflict*, 21. Betz, *Galatians*, 42, rightly notes that this verse does not say that the new aeon has already begun. Rather, it speaks of "the present reality of salvation" in virtue of Christ's coming and "the gift of the Spirit [which has] granted freedom to the believers in Christ . . . Paul, therefore, speaks of the liberation 'out of' the evil aeon and not of the change of the aeons themselves."

5. Dunn, *Galatians*, 38–39; Ziesler, *Galatians*, xvi, 5.

6. Dunn, *Galatians*, 39–42; Bruce, *Galatians*, 80–82.

7. The meaning of justification has become controversial in the wake of the New Perspective on Paul (NPP), which arose in consequence of the revised understanding of Judaism advocated by E. P. Sanders in *Paul and Palestinian Judaism* (1977). Accepting Sanders's "new perspective" on Judaism has implications for the understanding of Paul, but just what those implications are is debated by Sanders and others who follow his view of Judaism. Accordingly, NPP advocates such as Wright and Dunn argued for various revised understandings of Paul, which have been contested by scholars holding to a more traditional view. The literature on the resulting controversy over the NPP in its various aspects is voluminous and continues to grow; more extensive bibliography can be found in the works cited below. For a sample of the debate, particularly as it pertains to justification, see the interchange between Piper, *Future of Justification*, and Wright, *Justification*. A broader historical perspective, though clearly defending the

forward to the return of Christ and the resurrection of his body, but for the present he is also given the Holy Spirit and deliverance from sin's mastery. Accordingly, the gospel also has an ethical component and a pattern of life for the believer. It also has a corporate element in that it constitutes a new covenant people of God that is open to all people impartially, whether Jew or gentile. When somebody responds in faith to the gospel, he is placed in a new set of relationships with brothers and sisters in Christ. Because of this multifaceted nature of the gospel, it is important to clarify in what way a false gospel distorts the truth of the gospel. Such distortions are not always false *teachings* contrary to justification through faith in Jesus apart from works. Distortions of the gospel may also occur through implicit rather than explicit denials of the gospel message. Finally, they may also occur apart from any kind of doctrinal teaching at all, as a result of a *lifestyle* that is antithetical to the gospel of Christ. Whenever Paul raises the subject, we will attempt to clarify precisely how this non-gospel distorts the truth.

A second aspect to consider regarding the false gospel is the different people groups who are related to it. This includes those who are distorting the gospel and propagating a false one in its stead, and those who are affected by the false gospel. The first such group is the Judaizers, whom Paul clearly regards as non-believers, as we can see from the anathema he has pronounced on them in verse 8. Later he will refer to them as "false brethren" (2:4), and will describe them as not free but slaves, born according to the flesh but not the Spirit, and not heirs of Abraham (4:21-31); and as workers of deeds that disqualify them from inheriting the kingdom of God (5:19-21). Their gospel

---

traditional view against the NPP, can be found in Westerholm, *Perspectives Old and New*; and Carson et al., *Justification and Variegated Nomism*. Other representative NPP statements can be found in Dunn, *New Perspective on Paul*, esp. 193-211, 367-80; and Wright, *What St. Paul Really Said*, 113-33.

Regardless of other controversies between the NPP and traditional views (to say nothing of those attempting to take a *via media*), there is a great deal of agreement that justification includes the idea that the believer has a righteous status before God as a result. Wright acknowledges that justification does have a forensic aspect that confers a righteous status on the justified person, a verdict of the last day but anticipated already in the present when one believes in Jesus (*What St. Paul Really Said*, 131). Bird (in *Saving Righteousness of God*, 183-93) has traced how Wright's statements on justification have evolved over the years, such that later statements (see, e.g., Wright, "Shape of Justification") clarify that he indeed affirms that justification confers a status of righteousness on an individual, and that justification includes soteriological as well as ecclesiological aspects (see Bird, *Saving Righteousness of God*, 185-86). See also Schreiner, *Paul*, 194, 205; Witherington, *Grace in Galatia*, 173-75; Kim, *Paul and the New Perspective*, 66-70; Kim, *Origin of Paul's Gospel*, 283, 285-88; and Bird, *Saving Righteousness of God*, 4, 8-9, 17-18, 70-87, 136-41, 145-46, 151-54, 174-76, 181-82 for arguments that justification, regardless of what other implications it may have, does entail a "righteous status" before God.

is thoroughly in error, for they advocate circumcision and Torah-keeping as the means to justification before God, as well as the proper mode of life for God's people.[8] Certainly for them, the effect of following this false gospel is to be shut out of the kingdom of God.

The Danger of Apostasy for the Galatians

The Judaizers' Non-Gospel and Its Consequences

A second group is the Galatian gentile Christians to whom Paul writes. How would they be affected by the Judaizers' non-gospel? Paul puts the matter forcefully in 1:6: "I am astonished that you are so quickly turning away from him who called you by the grace of Christ for a different gospel." Paul's language here is shocking and blunt. His accusation that they were "turning away" (μετατίθεσθε, *metatithesthe*) had negative associations in Greek and Jewish usage. Among Greeks, "*ho metathemenos* means a turncoat who leaves one philosophical school for another."[9] Jews would recall that it was the term (along with the cognate noun μετάθησις [*metathēsis*]) used in 2 Macc 7:24 and 11:24 to describe the apostasy of Jews during Antiochus IV's program of forced Hellenization and suppression of Judaism.[10] Reinforcing this impression of imminent apostasy is Paul's use of "so quickly," which recalls the description of the Israelite apostasy in the episode of the golden calf (cf. Exod 32:8; Deut 9:16).[11] We may assume Paul's language is by design, given that he has omitted the conventional thanksgiving section of his letter. Paul is describing what the Galatians are doing in terms that they most likely would not recognize—it is most improbable that they consider themselves to be deserting the God who had called them by the grace of Christ, for they apparently do not understand the inner logic and implications of the Judaizers' non-gospel, and how these are antithetical to the true gospel that had saved them.[12] Paul's rhetoric is to shock them so he can begin to awaken them to the deep contradiction between these gospels.

This raises some difficult questions regarding the Galatians' future and the danger of apostasy. Are the Galatians actually departing the faith,

---

8. Russell, *Flesh/Spirit Conflict*, 42–44; Westerholm, *Perspectives Old and New*, 368–73; Barclay, *Obeying the Truth*, 45–46, 60–65, 73–74.

9. BDAG, s.v. μετατίθημι 2b, cited in Dunn, *Galatians*, 39.

10. Dunn, *Galatians*, 39–40.

11. Dunn, *Galatians*, 40.

12. Gundry Volf, *Paul and Perseverance*, 205–7; Dunn, *Galatians*, BNTC, 40; Hansen, *Galatians*, 36–37.

turning away from God, or apostatizing? What are the consequences for them if they fail to heed Paul's warning? Can they really lose their salvation by submitting to circumcision? Any attempt to answer these difficult questions must account for four propositions which the evidence of the letter suggests is true of the Galatians: (1) They are genuine Christians by any NT standard, without a hint of anything hypothetical or false about their profession. There is never any suggestion in the letter that Paul did not think the Galatians were genuine believers in Christ. Despite Paul's perplexity at them, they are brothers (1:11; 3:15; 4:12) who have received the Holy Spirit (3:2–5, 14; 4:6); by their faith they had been set free from the slavery of their idolatry (4:7–8; 5:1), and are now sons and heirs of Abraham and of God (3:6–9, 26–29; 4:4–7). While they are being tempted to accept a non-gospel with a false view of justification, it is clear that they themselves are already justified (2:16; 3:6–8, 11).[13] (2) However, they are contemplating submitting

13. There is a question about the timing of justification in Paul's theology. Justification has commonly been understood as an immediate consequence of genuine faith in Jesus, a view derived from passages like Rom 5:1; 8:1 (with the "no condemnation" understood as a clear implication of justification); and 8:30. See Grudem, *Systematic Theology*, 722–23, 727 (and n5); Erickson, *Christian Theology*, 966–68; Grenz, *Theology for the Community*, 434–36. (Although Grenz may have been more flexible with his language than some theologians are comfortable with, a patient reading of these pages shows him to be in substantial agreement with the traditional Reformation view of justification.) We may also add a few other passages for consideration: Rom 4:5–11, 22–25, which immediately precedes 5:1, and strongly suggests that justification follows faith as an immediate consequence; and Rom 5:19.

Presently it is common for exegetes to argue that justification is more properly located at the final judgment, although with the verdict announced beforehand for believers. Sometimes this is described as justification having dual present-future aspects. E.g., Ladd, *Theology of the New Testament*, 482–84, argues for this eschatological view of justification on the basis of his conception of the "overlap of the ages" in which "the Age to Come has reached back into the present evil age to bring its soteric blessings to human beings" (p. 484). See also Gundry Volf, *Paul and Perseverance*, 206. Schreiner, *New Testament Theology*, 351–52, defines justification thus: "Justification in Paul means that one is vindicated in the divine tribunal at the final judgment." However, he acknowledges that the verdict has been announced beforehand. It seems the main exegetical support for the future aspect of justification is Rom 2:13 (see p. 352), which is frequently cited by commentators (e.g., Ladd, *Theology of the New Testament*, 483; Morris, *Apostolic Preaching of the Cross*, 283; McGrath, "Justification," 518–22; Bird, *Saving Righteousness of God*, 155–78; Wright, "Letter to the Romans," 440–42). However, Moo (himself a proponent of this dual view of justification as present and future) denies that Rom 2:13 teaches this view (see Moo, *Romans*, 147–48). Moo argues that Paul is contesting the Jewish view of the *standard* of justification, but is not claiming that the justification of Christians occurs at the final judgment; furthermore, he argues that this conception is contrary to the way Paul generally speaks of both justification and the final judgment (pp. 147–48, and n21), a consideration that we believe cuts against the view of future justification in general. Schreiner (*New Testament Theology*, 351) also cites 1 Thess 1:10 and 5:9 for support for eschatological justification, but he

to Torah and circumcision—the false gospel of the Judaizers, which entails a different means of justification before God and a different mode of life (4:9–21; 5:3). (3) Such a move would constitute deserting God, falling from grace, and being severed from Christ—i.e., apostasy, and would result in the loss of salvation (5:1–4). However, (4) it seems the Galatians were not repudiating Christ explicitly, but implicitly, for they did not perceive that Torah was antithetical to the gospel of Christ. After all, the Judaizers could, and very likely did, make a very plausible scriptural argument from Genesis 17 for the permanence of the rite of circumcision for entry into God's covenant people.[14] Accordingly, these four propositions result in Galatians being arguably the most sobering warning passage in the entire New Testament—and perhaps the least appreciated as such. This is because it posits that genuine Christians may nonetheless lose their salvation for denying the gospel *merely by implication*, without realizing the significance of their actions, which seems to lower the threshold for irrevocable apostasy to a precarious degree. We will see if there is any other factor present in the epistle that mitigates this sobering picture.

It seems that there is a correspondence between the two-part appeal of the Judaizers and the implications that Paul threatens if the Galatians accept

---

himself acknowledges that these verses do not refer to their subjects as justification; we consider his concession to be more weighty than his affirmation. Similarly, he appeals to Rom 5:9 (p. 352), but this is a strange argumentative move, since the verse is damaging to his position, for it presents a definitively present sense of justification, and makes a firm distinction between that and salvation from God's (eschatological) wrath in that the former is the basis of the latter.

Generally, we find such problems to be typical in arguments for future justification. This is not to say that the position is devoid of any support. We grant that the Jewish background belief conceives of justification at the final judgment; and that the final judgment is the ultimate forensic setting, and that the future glorification and revelation of the sons of God (cf. Rom 8:19–39) constitutes something akin to a vindication. But it seems that the future justification view raises more problems than it solves, and that much of its purported exegetical basis evaporates upon closer examination. Accordingly, we are not surprised when some of its advocates present the case for it with a clearly detectable undertone of doubt and ambivalence (e.g., Moo, *Galatians*, 61n83). Therefore, on balance, we find the traditional view of justification at the time of conversion to be better warranted than the future justification view, and the arguments in support of it to be more compelling (see Fung, *Galatians*, 225–26, 232–35.; Hill, *Greek Words and Hebrew Meanings*, 141–62). We are in near-agreement with Moo (*Galatians*, 60–61): in Galatians, the basis of justification is the main point at issue, and in most instances, the time of justification is undefined (we prefer this characterization to "timeless," as Moo puts it), while 3:6 describes justification as present (i.e., immediately consequent upon faith). However, departing from Moo, we hold that the apparent future justification of 2:17 and 5:4 come from the Jewish/Judaizer view with which Paul is contending. We shall address Gal 5:5 below.

14. Schreiner, *Galatians*, 49–51.

the Judaizers' "gospel." First, the Judaizers identified living apart from the Law with being a "sinner," such that the epithet was routinely applied to gentiles (e.g., 2:15).[15] Accordingly, the necessary and sufficient means of justification before God included both faith in Christ and living in accordance with the Law (implicit in Paul's statements in 5:2-4; 6:12). However, Paul argues that this "gospel" fails on both counts: (1) living by the Law fails to justify a person before God. This is because it is antithetical to faith in Christ—the only means of justification—for it denies Christ's sufficiency (2:16, 21; 5:4). Furthermore, attempting to live by the Law subjects one to the covenant curses which inevitably follow upon his failure to do all the works required by the Law. Thus, this attempt at justification results in condemnation (3:10-14). This leads us to the second consequence: (2) the failure to live relatively "sinlessly" under the Law, i.e., in accordance with its righteous ethical requirements, especially those pertaining to love of neighbor. For to live under the Law is to live according to the flesh, which results in the unrighteous deeds of the flesh, including sinful striving and attempts to subject and devour one another, and precludes an inheritance in God's kingdom (1:13-14; 2:4-5; 3:21; 5:13-21, 26). Accordingly, if the Galatians submitted to the Judaizers' gospel of circumcision and Torah, they would forfeit eternal salvation, as well as the deliverance from sin's power through the flesh which is available only by means of the Spirit. Gundry Volf rightly keeps these conjoined concerns together, in contrast to other scholars who would separate them and argue for one to the exclusion of the other.[16]

The Sobering Warning of Galatians 5:2-4

Some exegetes attempt to argue that eternal salvation was not at stake for the Galatian believers. For example, Russell argues that what was at stake was their growth in maturity with respect to practical righteousness and present deliverance from sin's power. He argues this on the basis of Galatians 3:1-3, and the use of the verb ἐπιτελεῖσθε (*epiteleisthe*): "are you

---

15. For a discussion of Paul's use of "sinner" in 2:15 against the background of its Jewish use to refer to gentiles, see Cummins, *Paul and the Crucified Christ*, 190-3; Dunn, *Galatians*, 132-3; Dunn, "Echoes of Intra-Jewish Polemic," 459-477; Kok, "The Truth of the Gospel," 102-5; Barclay, *Obeying the Truth*, 77-78 n 7; also the literature cited in the foregoing. We follow Cummins (p. 192) in the view that Paul used the term more ironically than sympathetically.

16. Gundry Volf, *Paul and Perseverance*, 207-14, similarly describes the consequences in terms of the loss of present benefits from Christ (salvation as freedom from slavery), and the loss of eschatological salvation.

being made complete?" (v. 3).[17] Furthermore, both Russell and Richard Longenecker attempt to lessen the force of Paul's statements in 5:2-4 such that they only have implications for the present life of faith and not eternal salvation. In 5:2, Paul states that if the Galatians accept circumcision, Christ will be of no help to them at all (οὐδὲν ὠφελήσει, *ouden ōphelēsei*). Longenecker argues that the basic point is that righteousness, whether forensic or ethical, must be based either on Torah or faith in Christ, and so this language is appropriate in discussing either sense of righteousness. He concludes, "For Gentiles to revert to the prescriptions of the Jewish law as a necessary form of Christian lifestyle is, in effect, to make Christianity legalistic rather than Christocentric, and so not to have Christ's guidance in one's life."[18] Verse 3 reinforces this warning. Not only would Christ be of no help, but a heavy legal burden would be placed on them. In contrast, Schreiner asserts that the benefit in question is a *saving* benefit.[19] His argument is thin here, but the presence of the word οὐδέν supports his contention that the warning must apply to their eternal salvation, in that Christ will not benefit them *at all*.[20] This seems to preclude any kind of benefit from Christ's work, either with respect to salvation or practical righteous living in the present. Neither aspect ought to be denied.

Paul continues with an even more severe warning in 5:4: "You have been *severed from* [κατηργήθητε ἀπό, *katērgēthēte apo*] Christ, you who *are seeking to be justified* [δικαιοῦσθε, *dikaiousthe*[21]] by the Law; you have *fallen away*

17. Russell, *Flesh/Spirit Conflict*, 60, 81-83nn67, 69, 72. So also Cosgrove, *Cross and the Spirit*, 2, 31-33, 38, who emphasizes 3:1-5 as the interpretive key to what Galatians is really about (i.e., life in the Spirit); yet in order to make his case, Cosgrove must insist on "excluding" or "disqualifying" (his terms, p. 32) both the "apostolic autobiography" of 1:11—2:21 and the "apostolic exhortation" of 4:31—6:10) as irrelevant to interpreting the problem in Galatia. He justifies this by an argument that the data points from those passages leave the problem underdetermined. It seems to us that in his efforts to avoid presumptuous curve-fitting, Cosgrove's methodology results in cherry-picking, for it seems unjustified in treating these extensive passages so dismissively in attempting to understand the Galatian problem. Furthermore, we do not think that Paul intended his readers to "consider 3:1ff. apart from what precedes it," as Cosgrove advocates (p. 32), for it is tightly linked to the preceding passage of 2:15-21, as we shall argue below. See also the criticisms of Cosgrove in Schreiner, *Galatians*, 177, 184n33.

18. Longenecker, *Galatians*, 226.

19. Schreiner, *Galatians*, 312-13.

20. BDAG, s.v. οὐδείς, 2.b.γ. See also Bruce, *Galatians*, 229; Fung, *Galatians*, 221-22; Hansen, *Galatians*, 155-56; Gundry Volf, *Paul and Perseverance*, 208-10, who stresses the present consequences to the Galatians, but notes that οὐδέν indicates the extensiveness of the forfeiture of Christ's benefits, including that of eternal salvation. Schreiner, *Galatians*, 313n5, has misunderstood Gundry Volf on this point. Note as well Dunn's translation: "Christ will be of no benefit to you whatsoever," *Galatians*, 265.

21. Here δικαιόω is understood in a conative sense, as with most translations (e.g.,

[ἐξεπέσατε, *exepesate*] from grace" (my translation and emphases). All three italicized portions must be severely qualified to deny any implication for the Galatians' salvation. The phrase κατηργήθητε ἀπὸ could be translated "released from," as it is in the two other occurrences in Paul: Romans 7:2 and 6, where Paul speaks of those who have been released from the Law by the death of Christ, as a result of which sin and the Law would no longer be master of, or rule over (κυριεύω, *kurieuō*) them (Rom 6:14; 7:1). Russell argues, therefore, that Galatians 5:4 is a reverse parallel, in which believers are unnecessarily putting themselves back under the mastery of the Law and sin, and "releasing" themselves from Christ's liberating lordship. Russell concludes that this parallel supports the idea that the issue is one of present-day deliverance from sin's rule, not eternal salvation.[22] However, the phrase κατηργήθητε ἀπὸ cannot avoid conveying the concept of "separation," even though it is softened considerably by the rendering "released from." Moreover, even in its use in the illustration in Romans 7:2 and 6, it describes *a permanent termination of a relationship* between the woman and the command of the Law that bound her to her husband. Accordingly, other possibilities of translation would be "severed from,"[23] "alienated from,"[24] "estranged from"[25] or "to have nothing more to do with [the other entity]."[26] This does not sound as if submitting to Torah via circumcision ends only one aspect of the Galatians' relationship with Christ, but severs it completely. This impression is only compounded when the other highlighted phrases are taken into consideration.

The second phrase that must be noted is "you have fallen away from grace" at the end of the sentence, which parallels "you have been severed from Christ" at the beginning of the sentence. These two verbs occupy the

---

NASB, ESV, NIV, 1984 and 2011) and interpreters, e.g., Moo, *Galatians*, 325; Schreiner, *Galatians*, 314–15; Dunn, *Galatians*, 267; Burton, *Galatians*, 276.

22. Russell, *Flesh/Spirit Conflict*, 83n72. Similarly, Burton, *Galatians*, 276, suggests as possible renderings of καταργέω ἀπὸ (*katargeō apo*), "to be without effect from," "to be unaffected by," or "to be without effective relation to," and notes that its use in Gal 5:4 is a case of "rhetorical inversion." However, Burton's considered translation of the phrase is: "Ye have severed your relation to Christ," and he argues that Paul characterizes the Galatians' turn to the Law as a "repudiation of Christ" (p. 275).

23. Schreiner, *Galatians*, 314; Moo, *Galatians*, 326. Gundry Volf, *Paul and Perseverance*, 211–12, argues that this phrase indicates "a severance of the Galatians' relation to Christ," regardless of the fact that Paul has chosen the verb καταργέω, with its nuance of "inactivity," in part for its rhetorical effect on the Galatians who were concerned with conduct and attracted to works. Note Fung's translation, "completely severed," *Galatians*, 221.

24. Moo, *Galatians*, 319, 326; Hansen, *Galatians*, 156; see also Longenecker, *Galatians*, 228.

25. Bruce, *Galatians*, 228, 231; BDAG s.v. καταργέω, 4; Dunn, *Galatians*, 267–68.

26. BDAG s.v. καταργέω, 4.

preeminent positions of emphasis at the beginning and end of the sentence, balanced on either side of the antithetical verb phrase "being justified by the law." This phrase helps us to understand, by antithesis, what is meant by "falling away from grace." It is clear from the passage overall that "to fall from grace" is in contrast to "standing firm" in freedom (v. 1), and equivalent to falling back into bondage as a debtor under the Law (v. 3), which is the antithesis of living by grace through faith (vv. 5-6) in Christ. In turning to the Law, divine grace is not being withdrawn from them, but the Galatians are abandoning grace.[27] Certainly this speaks powerfully of the implications of the Law for the Galatians' present life. However, the implications for their eternal standing with God also cannot be denied: for if they have been alienated from Christ and have abandoned his grace, what hope can they have for eternal salvation? For, as Bruce noted, Galatians 5:4 is a reversal of Romans 5:2,[28] which depicts grace as the sphere of Christian existence and the basis of salvation.[29] As Burton argued (in a time when the term "legalism" provoked less controversy), "Grace . . . excludes, and is excluded by, the principle of legalism . . . Logically viewed, the one conception excludes the other; experientially the one experience destroys the other."[30] Although Paul does not use the same language as Romans 4:4-5, there seems to be present here a similar underlying conception: that one has a mutually exclusive choice to relate to God either as a wage-earner or as a gift-receiver, but not both.[31]

The third phrase from Galatians 5:4 that requires discussion uses the verb δικαιόω, commonly translated "to justify." It is unquestionably the case that δικαιόω usually has a forensic meaning in Paul's usage: "to justify" or "to declare righteous." This seems to hold for most instances in Galatians as well. Longenecker, however, argues that δικαιόω can mean "I make righteous," and that is the basis for his rendering δικαιοῦσθε as "you who are trying to be made righteous" in Galatians 5:4.[32] This interpretation leads us directly into the controversy over the possible meanings of δικαιόω. The controversy is usually argued on two bases: (1) the lexical potential of δικαιόω to mean "to make righteous," and (2) the evidence from actual usage in extant Hellenistic literature. Unfortunately for Longenecker's interpretation, the argument

27. Burton, *Galatians*, 277.

28. Bruce, *Galatians*, 231, cited in Gundry Volf, *Paul and Perseverance*, 212; see also Fung, *Galatians*, 223.

29. Gundry Volf, *Paul and Perseverance*, 212-3.

30. Burton, *Galatians*, 277.

31. See also Moo, *Galatians*, 326-7; Kim, *Paul and the New Perspective*, 63-64.

32. Longenecker, *Galatians*, 228. Ziesler, *Galatians*, 75, also inclines to the view that Paul is talking about practical living as God's people, rather than the means of entry into God's people in Gal 5:4.

for this meaning for δικαιόω is weak on both counts. Even its proponents acknowledge that they are arguing for a possible, exceptional meaning of the term with only few possible (arguably dubious) examples of such usage, against a preponderance of evidence that δικαιόω is forensic in meaning and is used as such.[33] Joseph A. Fitzmyer argued:

> Does the verb *dikaioun* mean "to declare upright" or "to make upright"? One might expect that *dikaioun*, being a verb belonging to the *-oō* class, would have a causative or factitive meaning, "to make someone *dikaios*" (as *dēloun*, "make clear"; *douloun*, "enslave"; *nekroun*, "mortify"; *anakainoun*, "renew"). But in the LXX, *dikaioun* seems normally to have a declarative meaning.[34]

Fitzmyer recognizes that the norm of the usage contradicts the argument he sets up based on the word's morphology and formation from the -όω suffix, and so aborts that argument rather than following to its conclusion. This is just as well, for the argument from morphology does not hold up to scrutiny, either. Let us trace the meaning and usage of δικαιόω from older Greek literature, to the LXX, to the NT. Despite the causative form, it is never used in classical Greek to mean "to make right." Rather, with impersonal objects, it denoted "to hold or deem a thing to be right or suitable." With personal objects, it denoted "to do or treat one right or justly," which, in some circumstances, could mean "to condemn, punish, or pass sentence upon."[35] However, when δικαιόω (and other δίκαιος [*dikaios*] words) was used

---

33. For example, Ziesler, *Meaning of Righteousness in Paul*, presents a very nuanced treatment of the verb. An introduction to the controversy between Protestants and Catholics is found in pp. 1–7. The meaning and usage of OT antecedents and their LXX renderings is discussed in pp. 18–22, 47–48, and 52–58; and discussion of rabbinic and Hellenistic occurrences is found in pp. 83–84, 86–87, and 112–13. Non-Pauline NT usage is discussed in pp. 128–30. Pauline usage is discussed in pp. 155–58 (Pastorals and Corinthian letters); 172–74, 179–80 (Galatians); and 189–90, 192–95, 197, 200–201, 205 (Romans). Ziesler consistently finds that δικαιόω (with the Hebrew antecedents to its LXX occurrences) is used in a forensic sense (i.e., "to justify") or demonstrative sense (i.e., "to vindicate"). However, he also appeals to exceptions to the norm, such as where an ethical sense (i.e., "be righteous") cannot be excluded, or a causative sense (i.e., "make righteous") is present or perhaps preferable to the forensic/demonstrative sense. As an example of the latter he cites Isa 53:11 (p. 19). Yet even in this example, it is not at all clear that "to make righteous" is a better rendering of δικαιόω than "to justify." Similarly, cf. *TDNT*, s.v. δικαιόω (subentry under δίκη) p. 211, yet it is acknowledged that the forensic or legal aspect is predominant in the NT and Paul (214–19).

34. Fitzmyer, *Romans*, 118.

35. Hill, *Greek Words and Hebrew Meanings*, 101; Cranfield, *Epistle to the Romans*, 2:94. Moulton and Howard, *Grammar of New Testament Greek*, 2:397, indicate that -όω verbs derived from adjectives of a moral meaning do not have a causative (i.e., to make X) but a factitive meaning (i.e., to regard as or treat as X), and offer ἀξιόω (*axioō*) as a

in the LXX, its range of meaning was altered to represent possible meanings of the Hebrew צָדַק (ṣādaq), and reflected this new biblical Greek usage more than its secular Greek meanings. As a result, δικαιόω is most often used to render the Hiphil הִצְדִּיק (hiṣdîq), which has a forensic significance: "to justify, declare righteous, or acquit."[36] Now it is true that there are exceptions in secular and biblical Greek from this forensic usage, but a survey of these exceptions demonstrate that they prove the rule, or are inapplicable in Paul's uses of δικαιόω, which follow the LXX forensic usage.[37] After a lengthy discussion of NT and Pauline usage, Hill concludes that for Paul

> the verb is primarily and predominantly a forensic term, a word of the law-court, describing a relation to, or a status before God, the judge of all men. It is not a case of God "making righteous" a person who is not so: he "puts in the right" the person who is in the relationship of faith (i.e., trust, surrender and identification) with Christ, in whose life and death the righteousness of God in covenant-faithfulness to man has been manifested.[38]

Similarly, Cranfield concludes that Paul uses δικαιόω to mean "to acquit, to confer a righteous status on," and in his letters the term "does not in itself contain any reference to moral transformation."[39]

Accordingly, the argument cannot be sustained that Paul in Galatians 5:4 intends to say the Galatians seek to be *made* righteous in a merely practical or ethical sense by keeping Torah. Even granting that one concern of Paul and the Galatians involved the practical righteousness of daily life (a concern which can also be seen in the context of Galatians 5 such that "to make righteous" would be a good fit), it is hard to imagine that the original readers would have heard it that way, given its ubiquitous forensic usage, even in the rest of this epistle (2:16–17; 3:8, 11, 24). Hence, it is inescapably the case that Paul is warning the Galatians that accepting the Judaizers' gospel threatens their grace-based relationship with Jesus Christ, and hence their justification before God, and thus their eternal salvation. Submitting to circumcision and Torah represents a whole new further example.

---

36. Hill, *Greek Words and Hebrew Meanings*, 104–9; Cranfield, *Epistle to the Romans*, 2:94.

37. Note the extensive discussion of these exceptions and range of meanings found in secular, the LXX, Apocrypha, Pseudepigrapha, DSS, rabbinic literature, and other NT texts in Hill, *Greek Words and Hebrew Meanings*, 102–39; and more briefly, Cranfield, *Epistle to the Romans*, 2:94–95. See especially the treatment of the post-Pauline *Corp. Herm.* 13.9 (Hill, 102; Cranfield, 94n1).

38. Hill, *Greek Words and Hebrew Meanings*, 160.

39. Cranfield, *Epistle to the Romans*, ICC, 2:95.

basis of relationship to God, and a different gospel that is contradictory to justification by faith in Christ. Although it is a concern, it is not *just* their present deliverance from the power of sin that is at stake.⁴⁰

Paul's Confidence, Rooted in God's Faithfulness, for the Galatians

This brings us back to the question of the possibility of apostasy occurring to genuine Christians at such a low threshold—i.e., of denying the gospel by implication, the unperceived inner logic of accepting Torah and circumcision. The evidence from the epistle to the Galatians seems to be that *if* they accept circumcision according to the Judaizers' gospel, then the Galatians will be committing apostasy and forfeiting their salvation. However, Paul seems convinced that the condition for their apostasy will not obtain. He has written to them to prevent them from going through with circumcision, and he has been persuaded in the Lord that they will heed his warning (5:10) and therefore, that all that they have suffered (or experienced)⁴¹ will not have been in vain (3:4). Gundry Volf argues that Paul trusts in God's faithfulness to prevent the Galatians from committing this error, and that most likely Paul views his own epistle as God's means to that end.⁴²

Paul's Argument in Galatians

Paul's Historical Argument (1:11—2:21)

We have analyzed the threat of the Judaizing gospel, the nature of its ramifications for the Galatian Christians, and Paul's purpose for his epistle to dissuade the Galatians from accepting that non-gospel. Now let us survey the rest of

---

40 Gundry Volf reaches a similar conclusion on the basis of her exegesis of 5:2–4 (*Paul and Perseverance*, 208–14). Cf. also Kruse, *Paul, the Law, and Justification*, 102–3; Hansen, *Galatians*, 155; Witherington, *Grace in Galatia*, 368–69; Schreiner, *Galatians*, 315; Moo, *Galatians*, 325.

41. There is some debate whether ἐπάθετε (*epathete*; from πάσχω, *paschō*) here has its ordinary meaning in the NT, "to suffer," or instead, the meaning "to experience." Moo (*Galatians*, 185–86), Schreiner (*Galatians*, 185), and Bruce (*Galatians*, 150) provide persuasive arguments for "to suffer" from the otherwise uniform usage of the NT, and the adequacy of this meaning's contextual fit. For plausible, but less persuasive, arguments for "to experience," cf. Betz, *Galatians*, 134; Witherington, *Grace in Galatia*, 214–5; Longenecker, *Galatians*, 104; and Kruse, *Paul, the Law, and Justification*, 74.

42. Gundry Volf, *Paul and Perseverance*, 214–16. So also Schreiner, *Galatians*, 318–20, 323–25.

the letter as the context for our flesh-Spirit passage of 5:13–26. After Paul states his purpose in the introduction, he then proceeds directly to his argument in support of this purpose (1:11—6:10). The argument unfolds in three stages, the first (1:11—2:21) being a historical argument for the superior origin and nature of Paul's gospel over that of the Judaizers. Paul's gospel did not come from man but directly as revelation from God, yet that gospel was also confirmed by the apostles in Jerusalem. However, when Peter caved in to Judaistic pressure in Antioch and lived according to Jewish nomistic practice by refusing to eat with gentile Christians, Paul rebuked him publicly, for his hypocrisy was not in accord with the truth of the gospel.

Let us note at this point that Peter (and the Jewish believers with him who also refrained from eating with the gentiles) offers another example of one who distorted the gospel. Like the Galatians, as suggested above, the reality of Peter's faith is beyond question, but he nonetheless is carried away into hypocrisy for fear of the Judaizers, and so Paul rebukes him because he was not "walking straight in line with[43] the truth of the gospel" (2:14–21). It is clear that Peter is not teaching a false view of justification, but is distorting the gospel by his actions, by his ethical and relational behavior. It is also noteworthy that Paul accused Peter of compelling—probably in an implicit manner—gentiles to live like Jews (just as the Judaizers would do explicitly).[44] It is also significant that, although Peter was not teaching a false view of justification, in correcting him Paul appeals to a proper understanding of justification by faith, for its implications for our daily life are antithetical to nomistic observance[45] (and to said observance as a criterion of acceptance and fellowship); and, conversely, nomistic observance has antithetical implications for justification. If righteousness, or right standing with God,[46] could be attained through keeping the Law, it would render the grace of God and the death of Christ superfluous.

---

43. ὀρθοποδοῦσιν (*orthopodousin*), as translated by Barclay, *Obeying the Truth*, 77; cf. also Bruce, *Galatians*, 132; cf. also the alternatives in BDAG, s.v. ὀρθοποδέω.

44. Cousar, *Galatians*, 47–48; Bruce, *Galatians*, 132–33; Longenecker, *Galatians*, 78–80.

45. Cousar, *Galatians*, 49.

46. "Righteousness" (δικαιοςύνη) throughout Galatians is a forensic rather than ethical concept, a result from justification (δικαιόω, "to justify"), from which the term is derived. With the possible exception of 3:11, δικαιοςύνη speaks of our right standing with God as a result of justification through faith. See Moo, *Galatians*, 55–57; Schreiner, *Galatians*, 173–75; Bruce, *Galatians*, 147. Note, however, that Longenecker, *Galatians*, 95, argues that the forensic sense of δικαιοςύνη is intended in 2:15–16, but the ethical sense is intended in 2:17–20, while the summative 2:21 encompasses both senses. Similarly, cf. Witherington, *Grace in Galatia*, 193n80; Ziesler, *Galatians*, 30.

In the course of making this argument, Paul twice uses the term σάρξ, in 2:16 and 2:20. It may be the case, as Russell argues, that Paul is foreshadowing his antithetical usage with πνεῦμα, which he begins in 3:2–3, and continues to develop thereafter.[47] However, it is not possible to be certain, for the choice to employ the term σάρξ is contextually intelligible in each verse for its own sake, and it is not obvious that the use of the term itself in 2:16 and 20 does any work in establishing Paul's flesh-Spirit antithesis. Paul's πᾶσα σάρξ (*pasa sarx*) in 2:16 is a standard anthropological term inherited from the Old Testament. While Paul evidently is quoting Psalm 142:2 LXX (MT, ET 143:2), and substituting πᾶσα σάρξ for the LXX's πᾶς ζῶν (*pas zōn* [from the MT's כָּל־חָי] *kol-ḥāy*), this is not a surprising substitution given the rarity of πᾶς ζῶν (only here), and the ubiquity of πᾶσα σάρξ as an expression denoting "all flesh."[48] Paul's use of σάρξ in 2:20 is also easily explicable as a purely somatic use appropriate to the SH-Now life that Paul lives between his conversion and the parousia of Christ. Given the absence of an antithetical use of σάρξ in the passage, and the ease with which these occurrences are explained, it is impossible to be certain that Paul intended them to foreshadow or contribute to the flesh-Spirit antithesis beginning in 3:2–3. However, given the proximity of that passage, the possibility cannot be denied, either.

Paul's Series of Experiential and Scriptural Proofs (3:1—4:31)

The second stage of Paul's argument follows in 3:1—4:31, in which a series of six proofs of an experiential and Scriptural nature are given to establish the superiority of Paul's gospel over the Judaizers' non-gospel, in that only the former conveys true Abrahamic sonship and the Holy Spirit as the promised blessing of the Abrahamic covenant, which in turn makes them free sons of God. In contrast, the Judaizers' non-gospel of keeping the Law does not result in the reception of the Spirit, but shuts people up in bondage under sin, and identifies them as children according to the flesh who persecute Abraham's true descendants according to the Spirit.

Paul's first proof (3:1–5) consists of five rhetorical questions about their experiences of hearing the gospel and of the Spirit. This is a powerful argument because the questions are put forward in such a way that each only permits one answer in favor of Paul's gospel, while rendering the Judaizers'

---

47. Russell, *Flesh/Spirit Conflict*, 119–22.
48. Silva, "Galatians," 790.

gospel absurd.[49] For example, the first question in 3:1 initially appears to be a mere expression of vexation and disbelief that the Galatians could be falling for this non-gospel after Paul had so clearly preached the gospel of Jesus crucified. As such, it is typically treated in a hasty fashion so commentators can move on to the following questions. In fact, the commentators usually spend more time discussing witchcraft, magic, spells, and the evil eye than the rhetorical effect that the question likely had.[50] On closer examination, however, we see how tightly linked this passage is to the preceding one of 2:15–21, which not only clearly put forward Paul's gospel of justification by faith, but culminated in the centrality of Jesus Christ crucified. However, this gracious, loving, self-giving act of God is superfluous and vain if righteousness comes from the Law. With 3:1, Paul brings the Galatians face to face with the dilemma he had presented to Peter.[51] Paul confronted them with the absurd implication of the vanity of Christ's crucifixion and reminds them that they were evangelized by means of a dramatic proclamation of Christ crucified. Given the centrality of Jesus' cross, how could the Galatians even entertain the absurdity of seeking righteousness by the Law which would render it superfluous? How foolish indeed! The conceptual similarity of the vanity (δωρεάν, *dōrean*) of Christ's death in 2:21 and the vanity (εἰκῇ, *eikē*) of the Galatians' suffering in 3:4 is a second link between these two passages.[52] It seems that 3:1–5 depicts the Galatian temptation as an inversion of Paul's gospel and conversion as presented in 2:15–21. Both passages also make reference to the Law and faith. Clearly there are other parallel concepts at work though expressed in different terminology. Whereas Paul speaks of Christ living in him in 2:20, he speaks of the Galatians' experience of the Spirit in 3:2–5. However, whereas Paul died to the Law in order to live to God by means of faith in God's grace in the cross of Jesus, the Galatians

---

49. McKnight, *Galatians*, 135.

50. See, e.g., Witherington, *Grace in Galatia*, 201–3, and the literature cited there. (Witherington concludes Paul was speaking metaphorically, p. 203.) Cf. also Dunn, *Galatians*, 151–2; Moo, *Galatians*, 181. We would suggest that this is a misplaced emphasis at the cost of the neglect of Paul's rhetorical strategy in linking the passages 2:15–21 to 3:1–5 and its likely effect on the Galatians. This neglect is strange to account for, given the common recognition that the Antioch episode is to be applied to the Galatian situation; or, as Betz put it: "Paul addresses Cephas formally, and the Galatians materially" (*Galatians*, 114, quoted in Moo, *Galatians*, 154). Russell, *Flesh/Spirit Conflict*, 122, does note the linkage between the passages. This linkage also renders even more doubtful Cosgrove's claim that 3:1–5 is best interpreted apart from a consideration of 2:15–21 (*Cross and the Spirit*, p. 32).

51. This assumes that Paul's quotation of his challenge to Peter continues through 2:21; see Moo, *Galatians*, 153.

52. Cf. BDAG, s.v. δωρεάν; BDAG, s.v. εἰκῇ.

are contemplating an action that entails eschewing all that they have experienced of the Spirit through faith for the sake of the Law. Yet by means of 2:19—3:1, Paul has reminded them of the centrality of the crucifixion of Christ. He has also forcefully clarified the antithetical relationship between the Law and the cross of Christ by his statement that he died to the Law that he may live to God. This shows that Christ and the Law are antithetical, for either one makes the other superfluous. Furthermore, the passage makes clear that this antithetical relationship not only obtains for a past dying to the Law and coming alive to God through Christ; it also obtains for the continuing life of faith. The choice for the Galatians is the same as it was for Paul: they must either live by faith in Christ or by the Law. To do the former leaves no place for the Law, while to live by the Law is to nullify or set aside (ἀθετῶ [athetō], 2:21) the grace of God.[53]

Paul continues his series of rhetorical questions, twice moving from past to present:

"did you receive" (v. 2) → (having begun)
"are you now trying to finish" (v. 3)

"did you suffer" (v. 4) → "does he who provides you . . . do it by" (v. 5)

This reinforces the connection Paul makes between past justification by faith in Christ and continued Spirit-empowered living by faith in Christ. Where the latter is not evident, the former is very much in doubt. Accordingly, these are both concerns of Paul in the epistle to the Galatians,[54] for while the two may be conceptually distinguished in abstract consideration, they may not be separated existentially in the lives of would-be followers of Jesus.

Galatians 3:1-5 also introduces the antithetical use of σάρξ and πνεῦμα and embeds them in a set of conjunctive and disjunctive relationships with some other concepts of Pauline concern. Paul writes: "did you receive the Spirit by the works of the Law, or by hearing with faith? . . . having begun

---

53. Moo, *Galatians*, 154-55.

54. Contrary to interpreters who would insist that Paul is solely focused either (a) on justification to eternal salvation, or (b) present life in Christ through the Spirit and being victorious over the flesh. With reference to (a), see, e.g., Schreiner, *Galatians*, 184-85, 310-20. As for (b), see Russell, *Flesh/Spirit Conflict*, 83n72, 139n5; Witherington, *Grace in Galatia*, 214; Longenecker, *Galatians*, 103-4, 106-7. This is not to deny that (a) was a more pressing issue, for if (a) is not secured, (b) is moot in the long run. However, given the Judaizers' likely argument from "lawlessness," practical righteousness was probably a concern for the Galatians, and perhaps seen as an indication of the viability of the proposed means of justification. See Moo, *Galatians*, 19-22, 154-55, 340-41.

by the Spirit, are you now trying to finish (ἐπιτελεῖσθε)[55] by the flesh?" (3:2-3). This relates the Spirit-flesh antithesis to the faith-Law antithesis, and implicitly to the freedom-slavery and justified–not justified antitheses that Paul introduced in chapter 2:

Table 4: Antitheses in Galatians 2–3

Spirit	flesh
hearing with faith	works of the Law
freedom (2:4)	compulsion, slavery, subjection (2:3–5, 14)
justified (2:16)	not justified (2:16)

As Paul continues in the epistle, he will further develop this nexus by adding additional antitheses. We can already see that the flesh-Spirit antithesis is associated with the salvation-historical contrast between the Law and the gospel of faith in Christ. We have seen in every episode that Paul has recounted in his historical argument (1:11—2:21) a contrast with Judaism and some aspect of the gospel, and in the two episodes of chapter 2, the issue of compelling gentiles to Judaize or be circumcised drives the narrative. Given the background of the letter, and the context of Paul's discussion thus far, the Galatians would certainly see in the flesh-Spirit antithesis in 3:3 that the flesh would be a reference to their own attraction to the Jewish Law and circumcision.[56] Although Paul has not yet fully developed his salvation-historical contrast of flesh and Spirit, it is obvious that a deeper theological principle underlies the antithesis. He will go on to develop biblical and salvation-historical arguments in 3:6—4:31. In transitioning to them from his historical arguments, however, Paul initially addresses the Galatians purely at the experiential level in 3:1–5.[57] Given the biblical anthropological

---

55. See BDAG, s.v. ἐπιτελέω. I concur with BDAG that ἐπιτελέω (*epiteleō*) is most likely intended in the middle rather than passive voice. Thus also RSV, NRSV, NET, NIV (1984 and 2011), TNIV. This would avoid any suggestion of a "divine passive" behind the "being made complete" by the flesh. The connative rendering ("trying to finish," see NET, NIV [1984 and 2011], TNIV) makes a strong parallel with 5:4's "you who are trying to be justified by the Law."

56. Witherington, *Grace in Galatia*, 214; Ziesler, *Galatians*, 31–32; Schreiner, *Galatians*, 184–85; Moo, *Galatians*, 184–85.

57. Stanton, "Law of Moses and the Law of Christ," 103; Kruse, *Paul, the Law, and Justification*, 73–77. Russell stresses the salvation-historical import of the flesh-Spirit antithesis, but he seems to overstate the degree to which this is already explicit in 3:1–5,

THE *SARX*, THE *PNEUMA*, THE GOSPEL, & THE LETTER TO THE GALATIANS   169

background for σάρξ in contrast to πνεῦμα, it would most likely be clear to the Galatians that Paul is relegating the Law and circumcision advocated by the Judaizers to the realm of that which is merely human, weak, and ineffectual, as opposed to that which is of God's mighty Spirit. Verse 3's πνεύματι (*pneumati*) and σαρκί, most likely to be understood as datives of means, indicate two contrasting means of completing their Christian faith. From the Judaizing perspective, what Paul calls "the flesh" would be the means of truly entering into God's covenant people. For Paul, however, the Galatians are already in God's people in virtue of the Spirit that they have received, and by which they have "begun." Now the real question is whether or not they are going to continue, or whether they will now switch from a covenant relationship with God by means of the Spirit for one that is by means of the flesh.[58] Russell defines the flesh here as "bodily existence in its weakness and transitoriness under the authority of Judaistic constraints and in contrast to the working of God's Spirit."[59] This brings out the futility and absurdity of the Galatians finishing by means of the flesh.

In his second proof (3:6–14), Paul argues from Scripture that Abraham was justified by faith, and so, it is those who are of faith who are Abraham's sons; it is upon that basis that the gentiles are justified and receive the blessing of Abraham, and the promise of the Spirit.[60] In Paul's third proof (3:15–29), he offers a salvation-historical argument that the Abrahamic Covenant could not be set aside or altered by the Law which was given 430 years later as an interim measure, shutting all up under sin and keeping the Jews in custody as a guardian (παιδαγωγός, *paidagōgos*) until faith in Christ came; now all are sons of God through faith in Christ, and descendants and heirs of Abraham.

Paul's fourth proof (4:1–11) continues with the image of the child under the παιδαγωγός who is akin to a slave until he is of age to be adopted as a son. The work of Christ has accomplished the same for the Galatian believers, and now they have received the Holy Spirit, showing that they are sons and heirs of God. Paul marvels that they are being attracted back into a state

---

Flesh/Spirit Conflict, 122–24, 130–32.

58. Witherington, *Grace in Galatia*, 214; Bruce, *Galatians*, 149–50; Longenecker, *Galatians*, 103–4; Ziesler, *Galatians*, 31–32; Schreiner, *Galatians*, 184–85; Moo, *Galatians*, 184–85.

59. Russell, *Flesh/Spirit Conflict*, 136.

60. The precise relationship between these three things—(1) justification, (2) the blessing of Abraham, and (3) the promised Holy Spirit—is debated. While many scholars identify (2) and (3), Chee-Chiew Lee argues that Paul identifies (1) and (2), with (3) being the result and evidence of the other two, as well as the means by which they are perpetuated in the life of the believer, in Lee, *Blessing of Abraham*.

of slavery under the στοιχεῖα (stoicheia) again. Here he likens the Jews' existence under the Law, described as enslavement to the στοιχεῖα τοῦ κοσμοῦ (probably to be understood as "the fundamental principles of the world"),[61] to the pagan Galatians' former polytheism. They had been enslaved "to those which by nature are not gods" (v. 8), and now Paul marvels that they want to return back to slavery under the weak and miserable στοιχεῖα again (here also to be understood as "fundamental principles"). However, since the word could also refer to "elemental spirits" in a pagan context, when Paul uses the word so closely after the reference to polytheism in verse 8, it seems obvious that he is drawing a parallel and saying in effect that going after Torah is like returning to paganism—both are enslavement under στοιχεῖα, when Christ has set us free. In Paul's fifth proof (4:12–20), he uses a relational argument to contrast the love that has existed between himself and the Galatians with the ultimately selfish motivations of the Judaizers.[62]

Finally, in Paul's sixth proof (4:21–31), he uses a typological Scriptural argument to redefine those under the Law as the rejected slave children of the flesh akin to Ishmael, and like him, persecutors of those who are the free children of the Spirit, who are the heirs akin to Isaac. We have already seen that Paul redefined the identity of the true covenant people of God in Romans 2:25–29, and he does so here as well, albeit in a much more heated, polemical tone. In 4:21–31, Paul utilizes an "allegorical" or typological[63] argument

---

61. Bundrick, "*TA STOICHEIA TOU KOSMOU*," interprets both instances of the phrase (vv. 3, 9) as "the elementary or rudimentary religious teachings." In contrast, Arnold, "Returning to the Domain of the Powers," argues the opposite view, that both verses refer to demonic beings. For updated surveys and arguments supporting a third view that the term refers to the elemental components of the universe, see Moo, *Galatians*, 260–63, 271, 276–77; and Schreiner, *Galatians*, 267–69, 277–79. We find Bundrick's argument (pp. 361–63) persuasive that the "elementary teaching" interpretation is most applicable to the Jews under the Law. At the same time, the term's ambiguity still permits Paul to draw the polemical analogy described above.

62. However, Hansen, *Abraham in Galatians*, 27–33, 43–51, argues for a rebuke-request structure to Galatians, and that 4:12 marks a turning point to the request section, that prepares the reader for the paraenesis of 5:13—6:10. This would account for the marked difference in tone between 4:12–20 and the more expositional arguments of 3:6—4:7.

63. The meaning here of the *hapax legomenon* ἀλληγορούμενα (*allēgoroumena*) (from ἀλληγορέω [*allēgoreō*], "to use analogy or likeness to express [something], speak allegorically," see BDAG, s.v. ἀλληγορέω) is debated. Davis, "Allegorically Speaking," argues for an allegorical hermeneutic, but most scholars argue for the typological approach: Hanson, *Studies in Paul's Technique*, 91–103; see also Perriman, "Rhetorical Strategy," 27–28, who also lists other scholars as proponents of this view, including F. F. Bruce, E. E. Ellis, and C. H. Cosgrove. Caneday, "Covenant Lineage," concurs, although he rightly insists we should understand the OT as "typological revelation," rather than Paul and other NT writers as engaging in "typological interpretation." Karen Jobes

from Scripture to prove that the Galatian Christians are Abraham's sons κατὰ πνεῦμα, while the Judaizers are merely Abraham's sons κατὰ σάρκα.[64] Paul compares the slave Hagar to the Sinaitic Covenant, and her son Ishmael, who was born κατὰ σάρκα, to those who are slaves under that covenant. This draws on elements of Paul's previous arguments in 3:21—4:11,[65] in which the Jews, while under the Law, were like minor children kept in confinement under a guardian [παιδαγωγός], a circumstance which is phenomenologically equivalent to being a slave rather than a son.[66] The free woman (Sarah) is likened to the New Covenant, and her son (Isaac) who was born "through the promise" (δι' ἐπαγγελίας [di epangelias], v. 23) and κατὰ πνεῦμα (v. 29) is likened to Christians, including the Galatian Christians, who are "children of promise" (v. 28). Just as Ishmael (the slave child born κατὰ σάρκα) persecuted Isaac (the free child born κατὰ πνεῦμα) so now the Judaizers persecute those who are born κατὰ πνεῦμα but not κατὰ σάρκα (v. 29). But just as Scripture called for the son of the slave woman to be cast out so they would not be reckoned as heirs, so also now the Judaizers are not recognized as sons and heirs, but are to be expelled (vv. 30–31).[67]

To modern ears, this is a strange argument, but from a rhetorical point of view, it was most likely compelling to Paul and to his audience. First of all, the argument is supported by two key facts. (a) Paul and his contemporaries on all sides of the issue acknowledged that the Judaizers are children of Abraham κατὰ σάρκα, and the Galatian Christians are not. (b) Paul has established by a powerful experiential argument in 3:1–5 that the Galatians had received the Holy Spirit through faith. He followed this up with a Scriptural proof in 3:6–14 that those who are of faith as Abraham was are also sons of Abraham. Secondly, the placement of this allegorical argument in 4:21–31 suggests that Paul believed it would be persuasive for the Galatians. Paul placed this argument sixth and last in a series of experiential arguments intended to prove the Galatians' true sonship through faith. According to good rhetorical practice of the time, one's strongest arguments should

---

argues that Paul's meaning is not the same as the English "allegory," and so we should understand Paul's (and Isaiah's) hermeneutic as typological. See Jobes, "Jerusalem, Our Mother," 317–18. See also the comments of Silva, *Interpreting Galatians*, 162–65. The arc of typological exegesis that Jobes sees through Isaiah to Paul is akin to the typological treatment of the temple through the prophets to John's Gospel, see Hoskins, *Jesus as the Fulfillment of the Temple*, 18–36, 69–88, 103–7, 182–93.

64. Russell, *Flesh/Spirit Conflict*, 59–60, 80nn63-64.
65. Jobes, "Jerusalem, Our Mother," 312.
66. Lyall, *Slaves, Citizens, Sons*, 113.
67. Jobes, "Jerusalem, Our Mother," 312. Hansen, *Abraham in Galatians*, 145–50, argues that v. 30's veiled command to "cast out" the Judaizing troublemakers is the rhetorical point of the passage.

be at the beginning and end of a series of proofs in order to create a strong first impression, and a strong lasting impression. Weaker or more forgettable arguments offered some cumulative support, but were sandwiched in the middle of the stronger arguments.[68]

Third, Paul's argument most likely drew some blood, so to speak. It is not certain whether or not Paul was using and subverting Judaizer proof texts,[69] but it seems reasonably certain that Paul is addressing Judaizer *ideas* concerning their own identity and radically turning them on their head. This is powerfully evident in 4:21–31, where, allegorically speaking, the Judaizers are presented, not as Israelites, but as *Ishmaelites* who were merely born, like Ishmael, κατὰ σάρκα. In contrast, the Galatian Christians qualify scripturally as children of Abraham because, like Isaac, they are characterized by a supernatural birth as a result of faith.[70] Fourthly, Paul's exegesis was probably not so novel and unprecedented to the Galatians as it is to us. Karen Jobes has demonstrated the intertextual links between the theological themes of Genesis 16–17, 21, and Isaiah 54:1 (quoted in Gal 4:27), as well as a host of related Isaianic passages in which the themes from Genesis are redefined in a typological way that anticipates what Paul does with them in Galatians 3–4.[71] In fact, it was Isaiah who made the real leap in typological reasoning and hermeneutic applied to the Genesis chapters; Paul merely followed from the post-resurrection perspective. Jobes very plausibly conjectures that Paul had previously taught the Galatians when present with them and exegeted Isaiah in this fashion, such that now he gives a very abbreviated version of this argument which is nonetheless sufficient to recall to *their* mind his earlier teaching and thus fill any logical gaps *we* perceive in the argument as it stands in the epistle.[72]

---

68. Russell, *Flesh/Spirit Conflict*, 57–60, 79n61, 80n64; Jobes, "Jerusalem, Our Mother," 299.

69. As argued by Barrett, "Allegory of Abraham," 154–70, cited in Russell, *Flesh/Spirit Conflict*, 79–80n62. In Barrett's scenario, Paul is responding defensively to Judaizer arguments. However, if Jobes is correct, Paul has sufficient reason for presenting this argument regardless of whether the Jews had used proof-texts from Genesis 16–17, 21 or not. Of course, it is still possible that the Judaizers used these texts and Paul was prepared with this counter-argument for which his earlier oral teaching had primed the Galatian believers to hear.

70. Russell, *Flesh/Spirit Conflict*, 60, 79–80nn62, 64; Jobes, "Jerusalem, Our Mother," 299–300, 317–18.

71. Jobes, "Jerusalem, Our Mother," 309–18.

72. Jobes, "Jerusalem, Our Mother," 318–19.

Paul's Warning Against Circumcision and Torah, and the Ethical Superiority of the True Gospel (5:1—6:10)

The third and climactic stage of Paul's argument (5:1—6:10) brings to a head his case against the Judaizers' non-gospel of Torah observance and circumcision, and instead exhorts the Galatians to a Spirit-empowered life of voluntary loving service to one another. Strictly speaking, the passage is not a paraenetic section separate from Paul's theological argument, but is the necessary culmination of it. Nonetheless, Paul does include here a great deal of general and specific moral exhortation in content.[73] The passage contributes to Paul's argument against the Judaizers by demonstrating the ethical superiority of his gospel, while simultaneously charging the Galatians to live up to that standard. Whereas those who submit to Torah attempt to "do" the Law but fail to fulfill it, those who live free of the yoke of Torah but walk according to the Spirit, loving and serving one another, "fulfill" the Law.[74]

In 5:1-12, Paul exhorts the Galatians to stand firm in their freedom in Christ against the call to submit to the slavery of circumcision and Torah observance.[75] This is coupled with Paul's severe warning against accepting the Judaizers' gospel, the consequences of which we have already examined (5:2-4). Paul then supports the warning with a contrasting positive statement about the basis of the Christian's eschatological hope and life of faith (5:5-6): "For we ourselves, through the Spirit, by faith, are eagerly waiting for the hope of righteousness. For in Christ Jesus neither circumcision means anything, nor uncircumcision, but faith working through love." Paul uses an associative "we" to include the Galatians in this description, similarly to the way he includes them in the "us" of 5:1, and in keeping with his regard for them as true brothers in faith (v. 11), and his confidence in the Lord that they will accept his correction (v. 10).

What exactly is "the hope of righteousness" (ἐλπίδα δικαιοσύνης, *elpida dikaiosunēs*) for which those in Christ are eagerly waiting (5:5)? This is exceedingly difficult to identify with precision or certainty.[76] Many exegetes understand δικαιοσύνης to be an objective or appositional genitive, such

---

73. Russell, *Flesh/Spirit Conflict*, 61-62, 81n65; Matera, "Culmination of Paul's Argument," 79-88; Barclay, *Obeying the Truth*, 216-20; Fee, "Freedom and the Life of Obedience," 201, 212-13n4.

74. Duvall, "Identity-Performance-Result," 33-34; Kruse, *Paul, the Law, and Justification*, 103-4.

75. Russell, *Flesh/Spirit Conflict*, 61-62, 81n65; Matera, "Culmination of Paul's Argument," 79-88; Barclay, *Obeying the Truth*, 216-20; Fee, "Freedom and the Life of Obedience," 201, 212-13n4.

76. See Fung, *Galatians*, 224-27, for a brief survey of exegetical options.

that what is hoped for is "righteousness." Commentators are divided again over how to clarify what Paul means by "righteousness." Two things seem reasonably clear: (1) that from the contrast with "(seeking) to be justified" (δικαιοῦσθε) in 5:4, δικαιοσύνης here should also be understood as forensic, rather than ethical;[77] and (2) that "we are eagerly waiting for" (ἀπεκδεχόμεθα, *apekdechometha*) indicates an eschatological anticipation, as in all of its Pauline uses (Rom 8:19, 23, 25; 1 Cor 1:7; Phil 3:20).[78] Accordingly, Schreiner and Moo both argue that "righteousness" refers to the eschatological verdict of acquittal on the day of judgment as a future aspect of forensic righteousness or justification.[79] This is a very plausible integration of the relevant data, provided one accepts the notion of future justification. It is the rejection of this concept that leads Fung to deny this interpretation.[80] We share Fung's reservations regarding future justification.[81] Furthermore, while we agree that δικαιοσύνης is an objective or appositional genitive that those in Christ expect on the last day, the account given of it as a mere eschatological forensic declaration seems too thin. Paul's use of ἀπεκδέχομαι consistently has an object that is far more robust, and this suggests to us that "righteousness" in 5:5 is a sort of theological shorthand or metonymy that relates a host of soteriological benefits (obtained by faith but not circumcision or the Law, 5:2, 4) that will be realized on the last day. In every instance that Paul uses ἀπεκδέχομαι, believers (or in the case of Romans 8:19, the creation) are eagerly awaiting the return of Christ, the redemption of their bodies, and the complete transformation that it brings in terms of righteousness, life, power, and glory. To get at the fullness of what Paul means by "righteousness" in Galatians 5:5, we should especially consider Romans 8:18-25, with its threefold use of ἀπεκδέχομαι (8:19, 23, 25), which is also embedded in a larger passage (Rom 8:1-30, and even much of the surrounding context) having numerous parallels with the themes of Galatians as a whole. It seems that "righteousness" in Galatians 5:5 stands in for all the entailments of justification that culminate on that eschatological last day (as in Rom 8:30). Now we have the status as sons and heirs of God, but on that day, our sonship will be revealed, our bodies redeemed and adopted, that which we have hoped for will be seen, and we will be glorified (Rom 8:12-30).[82] This is the

---

77. Moo, *Galatians*, 327; Schreiner, *Galatians*, 316; Fung, *Galatians*, 225.

78. Moo, *Galatians*, 327; Schreiner, *Galatians*, 315-16; Fung, *Galatians*, 224.

79 Schreiner, *Galatians*, 315-16; Moo, *Galatians*, 327-29. Cf. also the tentative agreement of Witherington, *Grace in Galatia*, 369-70.

80. Fung, *Galatians*, 224-26, 232-35.

81. See also the arguments of Hill, *Greek Words and Hebrew Meanings*, 141-62.

82. Fung's view is similar, although he argues δικαιοσύνης is a subjective genitive (mistakenly, in our judgment), *Galatians*, 226-27. See also pp. 225-26, where Fung

fullness of salvation, which is also spoken of as the Christian's hope which he eagerly awaits (8:23–25). Accordingly, while it is no doubt true that this event constitutes a kind of vindication (or public revelation of justification and adopted divine sonship),[83] it seems that more than just the forensic eschatological verdict is the object of hope and expectation. This is similar to the conclusion of Hill and G. S. Duncan:

> The future consummation of "justification" is implied in Gal. 5:5, "For through the Spirit, by faith, we wait for the hope of righteousness": as G. S. Duncan has said, "Though the believer is 'accepted as righteous' here and now, he relies on Christ to complete the good work that has been begun in him and to make him righteous so that he can be accepted on the day of judgment."[84]

Therefore, in Galatians 5:5–6 Paul reorients the Galatians' gaze away from looking backwards to the weak, enslaving mode of life under the Law that fails to justify, and points them forward to the great hope of the culmination of their righteousness and justification that their faith has secured, which will be realized in the eschaton.[85] Furthermore, this forward-looking, eager anticipation for that reality gives some impetus to our moral transformation in the present.

The manifestation of true righteousness under the New Covenant is not circumcision or keeping Torah, but faith working through love (5:6), which will be elaborated upon in 5:13—6:10. Paul's two other "neither circumcision nor uncircumcision" texts in Galatians 6:15 and 1 Corinthians 7:19 shed further light on the ethical priorities of the New Covenant. Galatians 6:15 speaks of "a new creation," which Hubbard has persuasively argued is an

---

discusses and dismisses the similar view of Foerster (*TDNT* 7:992–93) that takes δικαιοςύνης as an objective genitive, and argues that it is a synonym for "salvation." The main basis for rejecting this view is that righteousness or justification cannot be identified with salvation. However, Foerster's view can be "saved" if we slightly loosen the relation between the terms. We would agree that strict identity is too strong a characterization of the relationship between these concepts. But they nevertheless are closely related such that one causes or entails the other, and thus the use of one of these terms can also refer to the related concepts through such devices as metonymy. This is exactly what we have argued above that Paul is doing in Gal 5:5.

83. Schreiner, *Galatians*, 316.

84. Hill, *Greek Words and Hebrew Meanings*, 151, citing Duncan, *Epistle of Paul to the Galatians*, 156. This quotation seems likely to both resonate with and provoke reservations for advocates of many perspectives.

85. 1 John 3:1–3 echoes the Pauline view on our eager hope for Christ's return and transformation of our bodies. John also asserts the present moral significance of this eschatological focus: "And everyone who has this hope *fixed* on Him purifies himself, just as He is pure" (v. 3, NASB).

anthropological and pneumatological conception of the converted person as a new creature with the long-promised Holy Spirit resident within to help, enable, and transform.[86] Accordingly, this text gives us the basis for the other "neither circumcision nor uncircumcision" texts: it is the Holy Spirit who enables "faith working through love" (Gal 5:6), and "keeping God's commands" (1 Cor 7:19). Furthermore, all of the virtues which do not run afoul of the Law in Galatians 5:22–24 are, of course, the fruit of the Spirit.

Let us quickly finish our survey of Galatians before analyzing Galatians 5:13–26 more closely. In 5:13–26, Paul teaches them how their freedom is meant for serving one another in love by walking by the Spirit, which both thwarts the desire of the flesh and fulfills the Law. However, those who are under the Law are in fact in the flesh, and hence, in opposition to the Spirit, and they exhibit an entirely different ethical and relational pattern—committing the works of the flesh which disqualify them as heirs to the kingdom of God. Those who live by the Spirit, on the contrary, are to walk by the Spirit, which results in a qualitatively different ethical and relational dynamic. In 6:1–10, Paul gives a few concrete examples. In 6:1–5, this dynamic takes the form of gently restoring those who fall into sin, and hence bearing one another's burdens; this is in contrast to the selfish, boastful, and envious competition that characterizes those in the flesh and under the Law. In 6:6–10, it takes the shape of generous sharing and beneficence, particularly to those of the household of faith, in contrast to selfishness.

Finally, Paul concludes with a *recapitulatio* in 6:11–18, in which he reiterates his main themes in an elliptical fashion. He stresses the irrelevance of circumcision to one's place in "the Israel of God" (i.e., the true covenant people of God). Our boasting is in Christ crucified, which results in one becoming a new creation (with the Spirit of God resident within), and hence, characterized by a qualitatively different walk.

Conclusion: The Σάρξ-Πνεῦμα Antithesis and Its Nexus of Associations in Galatians 1–4

By way of conclusion, let us revisit the chart we introduced in the discussion of Galatians 3:1–5, which illustrated the antithetical use of σάρξ and πνεῦμα and embedded them in a nexus of conjunctive and disjunctive relationships to other antithetical concepts. Now that we have completed our survey of the letter, we may fill out additional details of this antithetical nexus based on the contents of Galatians 1–4:

86. Hubbard, *New Creation*, 209–29.

Table 5: Living by the flesh vs. Living by the Spirit

(living) by the Spirit (3:2–3)	(living) by the Flesh (3:3)
hearing with faith (3:2)	works of the Law (3:2)
freedom (2:4)	compulsion, slavery, subjection (2:3–5, 14)
justified (2:16)	not justified (2:16)
sons of Abraham (3:7)	(implied) *not* sons of Abraham (3:7–10, 16)
Recipients of blessing (3:8–9, 14)	cursed (3:10–13)
heirs, by promise, of the blessing of Abraham, i.e., the Holy Spirit[87] (3:14, 18, 29; 4:6–7)	not of the seed of Abraham that inherits (3:16–18; 4:30)
sons of God through faith in Jesus (3:26; 4:5–7)	(implied) slaves under the elemental things of the world/ the Law (4:3–5, 8–9)
free sons of Abraham born of promise through the Spirit under the (new) covenant of the "Jerusalem above"	slave sons of Abraham born according to the flesh, under the Sinai covenant, who do not inherit (4:21–31)

From this set of associations, we glean a fuller picture of what it meant to be in the Spirit, and what it meant to be in the flesh by clinging to Torah, despite the work of Christ and the Spirit's advent. Thus far in Galatians, it is the salvation-historical sense of flesh that is in view, as we saw in most of the instances in Romans 6–8. Next we shall exegete Galatians 5:13–26 and examine the flesh-Spirit antithesis there.

---

87. Or, perhaps, the blessing is justification, which results in the Holy Spirit's presence. See Lee, *Blessing of Abraham*.

— 8 —

The *Sarx* and Walking by the Spirit in Galatians 5:13–26

Now that important preliminary issues of the wider context of the letter to the Galatians have been clarified, let us move on to take a closer look at Paul's central σάρξ-πνεῦμα passage in Galatians 5:13–26. Let us first observe the argumentative structure of the passage.

The Structure of Galatians 5:13–26: An Exegetical Diagram and Translation

The general flow of Galatians 5:13–26 has a chiastic structure in which verses 13–15 and verses 25–26 act as the outer brackets. Within the passage, verses 16–18 and verse 24 serve to bracket the central vice-virtue lists of the works of the flesh (vv. 19–21) and the fruit of the Spirit (vv. 22–23). After the outer bracket of 5:25–26, Paul charges the Galatians to cultivate in their communities the fruit of the Spirit he has described, as Hansen ably summarizes:

> Paul's ethical instructions in 6:1–10, it needs to be noted, spell out in concrete fashion how the moral qualities listed in 5:22–23 are to be expressed in practical ways for the welfare of the Christian communities in the province of Galatia—that is, how such moral qualities as "gentleness" (6:1), "love" (6:2), "self-control" (6:4), "patience" (6:9–10), and "goodness" (6:6, 10) are to be expressed in practical ways to build relationships within these communities. Sowing to the Spirit (6:8), therefore, means bearing "the fruit of the Spirit" within the relationships of the church. And those who choose to sow to the Spirit will from the Spirit reap eternal life.[1]

---

1. Hansen, "Paul's Conversion and His Ethic of Freedom," 235.

We shall not treat this passage in detail, but shall focus our attention on the immediately preceding text that provides its rationale.

Here is a basic diagram of the chiastic structure of 5:13–26:

Table 6: Chiastic Structure of Galatians 5:13–26

>A 5:13–15
>>B 5:16–18
>>>C 5:19–21
>>>C' 5:22–23
>>B' 5:24
>A' 5:25–26

Now let us take note of the exegetical diagram of Gal 5:13–26 (my translation, with * indicating plurals in the Greek):

Table 7: Exegetical Diagram of Galatians 5:13–26

Freedom to serve through love by the Spirit

A Called to be free to serve one another through love

13a	Explanation of 5:1	For you* were called for freedom, brothers;
b	13bc- Qualification of purpose of v. 13a- "only not"	only not freedom for an opportunity for the flesh,
c	Contrast v. 13b- "but," expansion of 5:6	but through love serve* one another.
14a	Basis of v. 13c	For the whole Law has been fulfilled by one word, by this:
b	Content- Command	you will love your neighbor as yourself.
15a	1st class Conditional prot., contrast of 13c	But if you* bite* and tear* one another to pieces*,
b	1st class Conditional apod., Warning	watch out
c	Purpose of 15b	lest you* are totally consumed by one another.

B Walk by the Spirit and you will not fulfill the desire of the flesh

16a	Exhortation; 16ab—expansion of 13	But I say, walk* by the Spirit
b	Result of 16a	and you certainly will not fulfill the desire of the flesh.
17a	17abc- Explanation of 16b; Problem	For the flesh desires against the Spirit and the Spirit against the flesh,
b	Explanation of 17a	for these are opposed to one another,
c	Result of 17ab	so that you* do not do whatever you* wish.
18a	18ab- Solution of 17abc; 1st class Conditional prot.,	But if you* are being led by the Spirit,
b	1st class Conditional apod., Inference of 18a	you* are not under the law.

C The works of the flesh

19a	Expansion of "flesh" of 16b–17a	Now the works of the flesh are evident, which are
19b–21a	List of 19a	fornication, impurity, licentiousness, [20] idolatry, sorcery, hostilities, strife, jealousy, rages, rivalries, dissensions, factions, [21] jealousies, drinking binges, revelries and things such as these,
21b	Warning (Reminder) of 19a–21a	which things, I warn you*, even as I warned [you* before], that
21c	Content of 21b, Consequence of 19a–21a	those who practice such things will not inherit the kingdom of God.

C' The fruit of the Spirit

22a	Expansion of "Spirit" of 16–18, Contrast of 19–21	But the fruit of the Spirit is
22b–23a	List of 22a	love, joy, peace, forbearance, kindness, goodness, faith, [23] gentleness, self-control;

23b	Consequence of 22a–23a, Restatement of 18b	against such things there is no law.

B' Christians have crucified the flesh with its desires

24	Conclusion of 16–23	Now those who belong to Christ [Jesus] have crucified the flesh with its passions and desires.

A' Keep in step with the Spirit (together)

25a	vv. 25–26—Conclusion of 13–24; 1st class Conditional prot.	If we live by the Spirit,
b	1st class Conditional apod., Exhortation	let us keep in step with the Spirit.
26a	Exhortation	Let us not become conceited,
b	Manner of 26a	provoking one another,
c	Manner of 26a	envying one another.

Immediately after this passage, Paul gives two means of serving one another through love and walking in step with the Spirit together (i.e., two applications of 5:13–15 and 25–26). First, in 6:1–5, he exhorts the Galatians to gently restore those overtaken by sin, keeping in mind their own susceptibility. Second, in 6:6–10, he exhorts the Galatians to give generous financial support to the ministry of the Word and Spirit, as well as benevolent support to people, believers in particular, rather than spending on themselves. This completes for us the argumentative structure of the passage with its applications. Now let us take a more detailed exegetical look at 5:13–26.

An Exegesis of Galatians 5:13–26 with a Focus on Critical Interpretive Issues and the Use of Σάρξ

A 5:13–15

Galatians 5:13–26 in general, and verse 13 in particular, explains the purpose and quality of the "freedom" of 5:1, namely, love (i.e., the love of 5:6) expressed in service to one another—a paradoxical form of "slavery" which is in contrast to the bondage of the yoke of slavery under Torah (5:1). One aspect of the paradox is that we are in slavery to "one another," for slavery is a hierarchical social structure with a unilateral flow of power and submission; it is not a relationship of mutual self-giving and love.[2] Under Paul's pen, both "freedom" and "slavery" are redefined in accordance with the paramount value of love.[3] In accordance with the teaching of Jesus regarding what God expects of us towards our neighbor,[4] Paul asserts that this loving service to one another fulfills the righteous intent of the whole Law (cf. Rom 8:4) even though believers are free of the Law (Gal 4:21—5:6). The exact meaning of this is debated, as well as its relation to Paul's insistence throughout Galatians that Christians are no longer under the Law or obligated to keep it (cf. e.g., 2:3-5, 11-21; 3:10-14; 5:1-6). The interpretive option that best seems to fit Paul's overall thought and the immediate context is that of Moo:

> On this view, the implied agent of the passive verb [πεπλήρωται (peplērōtai), "it has been fulfilled" or "it is fulfilled"] is Jesus Christ, who "fulfills" the whole law in his teaching by highlighting love for the neighbor as the true and ultimate completion, or "filling up," of the law—and in his life by going to the cross as the ultimate embodiment and pattern of sacrificial love . . . The fact that Paul refers to the "law of Christ" later in this section (6:2) would fit well with this focus on Christ's own teaching; and this interpretation would dovetail nicely with the claim Jesus makes in Matt. 5:17 about the "fulfillment" of "the law and the prophets."[5]

---

2. Barclay, *Obeying the Truth*, 108-9.

3. Bruce, *Galatians*, 240-41; Fung, *Galatians*, 244-45; Dunn, *Galatians*, 288; Witherington, *Grace in Galatia*, 378-79; Moo, *Galatians*, 345n6.

4. See Mark 12:31//Matt 22:39; Luke 10:27. Of course, Jesus spoke of two great commandments, but Paul has omitted Jesus' "greatest commandment" that speaks of love for the Lord God. Arguably he does so because this is taken for granted, and that what is at issue now is social relationships in the church. See Schreiner, *Galatians*, 335; Wenham, *Paul*, 255-58 (and nn106-7), 266-71.

5. Moo, *Galatians*, 348. See the wider discussion of options on pp. 346-48. Cf. also the discussion of Martyn, *Galatians*, 486-91, whose interpretation is similar to Moo's. However, we find Martyn's speculation (p. 486) about the Law's "cursing and enslaving voice" as opposed to its "promissory and guiding voice" to be dubious. Furthermore, we consider his elaboration, in Comment 48 on pp. 503-14, to be not at all representative of what Paul wrote. Martyn nearly admits as much when he suggests Paul could have made his intention plainer if he had written something akin to Martyn's own paraphrase—which Paul did not, Martyn reasons, for it would have given the Judaizers a rhetorical advantage (pp. 513-14).

Freedom from the Law is not lawlessness, nor is it to be an opportunity for the flesh,[6] which manifests itself in vicious competitive striving.[7] Verses 13–15 establish a clear emphasis on the relational dynamics among believers in community; although this does not preclude any application to Christians qua individuals, with such an emphasis on "faith working through love" and "serving one another through love," the aspects of righteous living that are stressed are the relational ones.[8]

B 5:16–18

The exhortation of Galatians 5:16 explains how the flesh is denied an opportunity (5:13). This denial is stated in confident, emphatic terms: οὐ μὴ τελέσητε (*ou mē telesēte*), "you certainly will not fulfill."[9] Galatians 5:17 plays some explanatory role, but there is great disagreement over its function and interpretation due to its ambiguous final clause (ἵνα μὴ ἃ ἐὰν θέλητε ταῦτα ποιῆτε [*hina mē ha ean thelēte tauta poiēte*], "so that/in order that you do not do whatever you wish").[10] There is a superficial similarity between Galatians 5:17 and Romans 7:15 that has led some to identify the circumstances described in them.[11] But note first of all that these cannot be parallel circum-

---

6. Fung, *Galatians*, 244–45; Martyn, *Galatians*, 479, 484–86, wastes no opportunity to heighten the apocalyptic, cosmic, militaristic warfare imagery in the passage. Hence, ἀφορμή (*aphormē*) is not just "an opportunity," but "a military base of operations for the Flesh," a translation that would be justified in a military or warfare context, but is arguably too exaggerated for this one (see Moo, *Galatians*, 343n2; Longenecker, *Galatians*, 239). Even worse, Martyn's descriptive translation "the Flesh, *active as a cosmic power*" (my emphasis) is completely gratuitous, and has no basis in the text.

7. Russell, *Flesh/Spirit Conflict*, 144. However, it seems Russell is deeply mistaken in his interpretation of "freedom as an opportunity for the flesh" as an "attempt to be perfected by the Judaizers' bodily emphases (3:3) by emphasizing birth into God's family (4:23, 29), which is wanting to be under Torah (4:21; 5:1)" including circumcision (p. 147, see also pp. 145–50). This is plainly contrary to Paul's description of the "freedom" of 5:1 and 13 as standing firm and not submitting to the yoke of Torah and circumcision. Therefore the "flesh" in view in 5:13 is the Galatians' own flesh, which desires the opportunity to do the "works of the flesh" of 5:19–21; it is not the "flesh community" of the Judaizers which desires an opportunity to subject the Galatians to circumcision. Schnelle, *Apostle Paul*, 294–95, seems to hold a view similar to Russell's.

8. Fee, *God's Empowering Presence*, 425; Martyn, *Galatians*, 482, 485, 486n48.

9. Barclay, *Obeying the Truth*, 111; Ridderbos, *Epistle of Paul to the Churches of Galatia*, 203n6; Martyn, *Galatians*, 492; Hansen, "Paul's Conversion," 225.

10. Barclay's discussion of the interpretive options is most helpful in *Obeying the Truth*, 110–16. See also Russell, *Flesh/Spirit Conflict*, 154–59; Schreiner, *Galatians*, 343–45; Moo, *Galatians*, 354–56.

11. E.g., Dunn, *Theology of Paul*, 477–82; Dunn, *Galatians*, 297–300; Longenecker, *Galatians*, 245–46; Ridderbos, *Epistle of Paul to the Churches of Galatia*, 203–4; George,

stances. Romans 7:14–25 depicts someone who is under the Law, enslaved to sin, with the Spirit totally absent from the picture, and without any hope of victory.[12] But in Galatians 5:16–17, the flesh and Spirit are present and in conflict. This is a situation involving Christians. To see it otherwise is to interpret these passages in an atemporal, ahistorical manner that fails to note the eschatological distinction between them that results from the advent of the Spirit. Despite his overheated tone and exaggerated apocalypticism, Martyn is certainly correct to reject such a view when he states (against Longenecker), "This war is not, therefore, a timeless anthropological rivalry, a struggle that has been raging in the heart of the human being since the dawn of time. On the contrary, it is the apocalyptic battle of the end-time, the war that has been declared by the Spirit, not by the Flesh."[13]

Another difference between these passages is that in Romans 7:15, the thing that the person wants to do but cannot do is more specified (τοῦτο, *touto*), viz., the good things of the Law (see 7:16). But this is not the case in Galatians 5:17, where the "these things" (ταῦτα) you may not do is plural and more relativized by the relative pronoun ἅ, the particle of contingency ἐάν, and the verb θέλητε. Coming after a relative pronoun, the particle ἐάν is most likely equivalent to ἄν,[14] resulting in the following translation for the clause: "so that, whatever things you wish, these things you may not do," or in a smoother English translation: "so that you may not do whatever you wish."[15]

Barclay's explanation of 5:17's role as an explication of 5:16 seems to be the simplest and yet most satisfactory way to account for all the evidence of the passage. Walking by the Spirit means that you will not fulfill the desire of the flesh simply because the Spirit opposes the flesh. The two are opposed to one another:

Galatians, 387–88. Note also the similarity between Gal 5:16–18 and the Gethsemane saying of Matt. 26:41//Mark 14:38. David Wenham has speculated whether Paul may have been influenced by this saying in *Paul*, 275–80. It is impossible to determine the extent to which this is the case; while Paul certainly must be familiar with the traditions of Jesus' arrest in Gethsemane, there are significant differences in the flesh-spirit antithesis of the Gethsemane saying and the flesh-Spirit antithesis of Paul. In the former, the "spirit" is not the Holy Spirit, but the "inner man" of Rom 7:18–24, and like that passage, describes a pre-Pentecost experience for believers.

12. Hansen, "Paul's Conversion," 225–26.
13. Martyn, *Galatians*, 494.
14. BDAG, s.v., ἐάν, definition 3.
15. The open-endedness resulting from ἅ ἐάν, "whatever things," is not reflected in the translations or typically discussed in the commentaries, except Moo, *Galatians*, 352, 354–56. Bruce, *Galatians*, translates it this way on p. 244, but then proceeds to ignore this feature of the text in his commentary.

> Such mutual opposition clearly implies mutual exclusion and thus satisfactorily explains why the Galatians' walk in the Spirit will not fulfil the desire of the flesh (5.16). But this also means that their "freedom" in the Spirit should not be taken to mean freedom to live however they like. Warfare excludes some options and necessitates others. If they walk in the Spirit they are caught up into this conflict, which means that they are not free to do whatever they want—ἵνα μὴ ἃ ἐὰν θέλητε ταῦτα ποιῆτε (5.17). Such conflict ensures that their freedom is not absolute, for their walk in the Spirit will set them against the flesh and thus define the moral choices they must make.[16]

This interpretation of "so that you may not do whatever you wish" strikes the precisely correct nuance. Some scholars misunderstand the open-endedness of the phrase to mean that believers cannot do anything, no matter what they wish to do, good or bad. In that case, the believer's agency is nullified, and is essentially usurped by either the flesh or the Spirit, with supremacy passing to that one to which the Christian submits.[17] Actually, this is not what the phrase means. Since verse 17 is clearly intended to explain the frustration of the flesh's desire in the life of the one walking by the Spirit (5:16), this view must be precluded.[18] Rather, the implication of "so that you may not do whatever you wish" is that walking by the Spirit in freedom apart from the Law does not mean that you are completely unrestrained in living however you desire. That is to say, the "whatever you wish" is not to be taken as all-inclusive, but as *excluding particular things*—those desires of the flesh (v. 16) for which the flesh would abuse our freedom from the Law as an opportunity (v. 13), those works of the flesh which lead to death (vv. 19–21), to which the Spirit is opposed. For believers to walk in the Spirit entails that they are not open to the option of the flesh's desires, but that they themselves have joined the Spirit's warfare against them, and have committed themselves to using their freedom for some activities (i.e., the fruit of the Spirit, vv. 22–23) and against others (i.e., the works of the flesh, vv. 19–21).[19]

On this view, whether the final clause of 5:17 is a purpose or a result clause is immaterial, because the result is that the purpose is achieved—Christians do not just do whatever they want, and the flesh does not succeed in taking advantage of the Christian's freedom (5:13). The subject who

---

16. Barclay, *Obeying the Truth*, 112.

17. E.g., Moo, *Galatians*, 354–56 (esp. 356). Moo mistakenly attributes this position to Barclay (*Obeying the Truth*, pp. 113–14), whose interpretation of the phrase is actually much narrower, as is evident from p. 115.

18. Rightly, Hansen, *Galatians*, 170.

19. Barclay, *Obeying the Truth*, 115; so also Witherington, *Grace in Galatia*, 393–95.

is "purposing" is not clear, but, if this interpretation is correct, the implicit agent who is intending this outcome would be God or the Spirit.[20]

Accordingly, 5:18 indicates that being led by the Spirit replaces being under the Law. "Christians are no longer 'under the law', that is, under its restraining, disciplining and directing influence (cf. ὑπὸ παιδαγωγόν [*hypo paidagōgon*], 3.23–5) because the Spirit provides all the necessary guidance in the fight against the flesh."[21]

Given the uniform biblical depiction of the strength of the Spirit in contrast to the weakness of the flesh, it is not necessary for Paul to spell out beyond verse 16 that this conflict between flesh and Spirit will end in victory for the Spirit. However, this should not be taken for granted. The fact that Paul warns his readers against allowing the flesh to exploit their freedom, and commands them to mutual loving service, and couches the certain promise of victory as a result of obeying the command to walk by the Spirit (5:16), indicates that this is not something that the Spirit does to believers as they sit back passively. Victory by the Spirit presupposes believers' participation in the Spirit's warfare against the flesh. The Christian can still live a fleshly life, even though this is antithetical to life in Christ—for a time. However, continued practice of such a life results in death—i.e., not inheriting the kingdom (Gal 5:21)—thus indicating that any profession of Christ was actually in vain. The Christian must "be led" (ἄγω [*agō*], 5:18) by the Spirit, which is most likely equivalent to "walk (περιπατέω [*peripateō*]) by the Spirit" (5:16), and "follow (or, walk according to the standard of/in conformity with; στοιχέω [*stoicheō*]) the Spirit" (5:25).[22] This suggests that what is necessary for the Christian to prevail beyond a mere stalemate of some kind, or to be made complete (ἐπιτελέω, Gal 3:3), is cooperation with the Spirit in the pursuit of self-discipline for the sake of God and brethren. As we shall elaborate below, this involves renewing the mind unto God's will, making the body the slave of that mind, and hence the slave to God, righteousness, and neighbor, such that we, through love, serve one another (Gal 5:13–14).

However, this mode of discipleship is impossible to combine with life under Torah, which involves depending upon the flesh for righteousness. This puts one in the situation described in 5:1–4, in a state of apostasy, voluntary enslavement to the Law (and hence, to the flesh), and cut off from Christ and his righteousness that is ours through faith and the Spirit.

20. Barclay, *Obeying the Truth*, 115n23.

21. Barclay, *Obeying the Truth*, 115–16.

22. For other Pauline uses of στοιχέω, see Gal 6:16; Phil 3:16; Rom 4:12. All of them involve a sense of walking or living in accordance with a standard, rule, or pattern of life.

Accordingly, verse 18 says that if we are led by the Spirit, we are not *under the Law*. The phrase "under the Law" has been substituted for the phrase "in the flesh," which we would have expected from verses 16–17. However, to be (or to continue) under the Law *is* to be (or to revert to being) in the flesh (3:3), and so being freed from the Law and standing firm in that freedom is necessary to walking by the Spirit.[23] Hubbard notes that Paul often

> condenses the entire law, flesh, sin, and death scenario into a single term, and this goes some way toward explicating his use of law and flesh as synonyms. To be ὑπὸ νόμον [*hypo nomon*] (5.18) is to live in the unaided realm of the flesh, which inevitably results in the "works of the flesh" (5.19). To be led by the Spirit is to be enabled to produce its fruit (5.23), which Paul earlier sums up with the word 'righteousness' (3.21).[24]

C 5:19–21

Given the centrality of the virtue-vice lists to the passage as a whole, this is the appropriate time to address an argument raised by Russell regarding the function of the entire passage. A key question about the function of the passage is to what extent is it, according to the traditional interpretation, (A) an ethical exhortation of virtues to cultivate and vices to avoid (or a depiction of what should be typical of the Christian regarding said virtues and vices)? Or is it, according to Russell, (B) the culminating theological argument against circumcision and Torah as a mode of discipleship or means of constraining bodily behavior, an argument in which two different community dynamics are held up for comparison to show (by means of an effect-to-cause argument) that the Spirit produces righteousness, but circumcision and Torah does not?[25] Or perhaps is (C) some combination of the views, possible? In support of position (C), let us now analyze the strong points and limitations of (A) and (B).

In support of view (A) is (i) the prima facie reading of the passage, in which 5:13 is the prime exhortation to use our freedom from Torah to serve one another through love, with an expansion and secondary exhortation in 5:16 to walk by the Spirit to keep from fulfilling the desires of the flesh. While it is Paul's aim to persuade them not to submit to circumcision and Torah, 5:1–12 brought these issues to a climax (at least until the *recapitulatio*

---

23. Hubbard, *New Creation in Paul's Letters*, 208.
24. Hubbard, *New Creation in Paul's Letters*, 208.
25. Russell, *Flesh/Spirit Conflict*, 2–4, 61–64, 83–85 (nn74–76), 143–67.

of 6:11–18), and now in 5:13–26 the issue is presumed (for the sake of argument, at any rate) to be settled in favor of Paul's gospel. The pertinent question then becomes, How shall the Galatians live? If Torah is not the means to righteousness and restraining sin, what is? These are the questions Paul is attempting to answer by his exhortations in this passage.

Additionally, (ii) we have already seen that σάρξ is not just a salvation-historical term for Paul, but an anthropological one that is still true of believers in the new covenant era. There is still some struggle with the flesh for believers, and some reason for believers to be warned about it. There is still the potential for believers to fall into fleshly thought- and behavior-patterns that are antithetical to their life in Christ and the Spirit. A noteworthy example is Peter in 2:11–21, whose status as a Christian who was Spirit-empowered in his life and ministry is beyond question, and who was also wrong in this instance precisely in the sense of promoting a "discipleship after the flesh" (my characterization, cf. 2:14).

A final support for this reading comes from (iii) the close parallel passage of Romans 13:8–14.

> [8] Owe nothing to anyone except to love one another; for he who loves his neighbor has fulfilled *the* law. [9] For this, "YOU SHALL NOT COMMIT ADULTERY, YOU SHALL NOT MURDER, YOU SHALL NOT STEAL, YOU SHALL NOT COVET," and if there is any other commandment, it is summed up in this saying, "YOU SHALL LOVE YOUR NEIGHBOR AS YOURSELF." [10] Love does no wrong to a neighbor; therefore love is the fulfillment of *the* law.
>
> [11] *Do* this, knowing the time, that it is already the hour for you to awaken from sleep; for now salvation is nearer to us than when we believed. [12] The night is almost gone, and the day is near. Therefore let us lay aside the deeds of darkness and put on the armor of light. [13] Let us behave properly as in the day, not in carousing and drunkenness, not in sexual promiscuity and sensuality, not in strife and jealousy. [14] But put on the Lord Jesus Christ, and make no provision for the flesh in regard to *its* lusts. (Rom 13:8–14 NASB)

Despite the fact that arguing against circumcision and Torah is not as central for Paul in Romans, we have a passage here that is so remarkably similar to Galatians 5:13–26. It suggests that for both passages there is a common concern for righteous Christian living, regardless of the presence or absence of the threat from the Judaizers' non-gospel.

Regarding view (B) and its support, Russell argues that 5:13—6:10 is not a section of true paranesis, but is the culminating theological argument against circumcision and Torah as a mode of discipleship or means of constraining bodily behavior, an argument in which the community dynamics are held up to show that the Spirit produces righteousness, but circumcision/Torah does not. Certainly this would be a powerful capstone of his argumentative strategy.

By way of evaluation, a good case can be made for understanding this passage as a part of Paul's culminating theological argument, rhetorically speaking. Nonetheless, there is an undeniably exhortational aspect to it. So, while it is not akin to Paul's typical sections of paranesis in his epistles, view (A) is right that it has a strong aspect of ethical imperative and exhortation about it—there is a sense in which the danger of the flesh is real and present for Christians, and the counsel to walk by the Spirit is the means of avoiding the flesh, whether in terms of its nomistic thinking or its sinful works.

Secondly, Russell's view that Paul's main point in this section is to give a description of the "Spirit-community" and "flesh-community" rings false for a number of reasons—but not completely false. This cannot be the point of this section, because it is just not what the text says.[26] Recall that Paul has used "flesh" and "Spirit" throughout Galatians, and they never seem to be used as stand-ins for the ideas of "the flesh-*community*" or "the Spirit-*community*." There is no real signal here in this context that the terms take on this meaning as theological shorthand in verses 17, 19, or 22. Granted, Paul can speak euphemistically to refer to different people groups or sects,[27] but we are lacking any contextual clue that he is doing so here in his use of "flesh" and "Spirit."

---

26. I write this with a bit of fear and trembling, and one eye glancing at E. D. Hirsch's warning of how easily an interpreter can dismiss contrary interpretations of a text once he has become entrapped by his own conception of the text, in Hirsch, *Validity in Interpretation*, 166, quoted in Russell, *Flesh/Spirit Conflict*, 137.

27. E.g., "the circumcision" to refer to Jews (Gal 2:7-9), to Jewish believers generally (Rom 4:9; 15:8), and to the Judaizers (or circumcision party; Gal 2:12). Another euphemism used by Paul is "the mutilation" (Phil 3:2) to refer to the "circumcision party" or Judaizers. Finally, he employed terms like "the uncircumcision" (or more literally, "the foreskin") to refer to gentiles (Gal 2:7), and gentile believers (Rom 4:9), and "the (true) circumcision" (Phil 3:3) to non-Judaizing Christians. We see some of the same uses in the disputed Pauline epistles: "the circumcision" and "the uncircumcision" to refer to Jewish and gentile believers in Col 3:11 and Eph 2:11 (though here the context favors those who were *formerly* Jews or gentiles, but are *now* Jewish and gentile *Christians* together in one body); "the circumcision" is also used to refer to Jewish believers specified not to belong to the Judaizers (Col 4:11), and to gentile (Cretan) converts to the Judaizers (Titus 1:10). In all of these examples, the author always makes the euphemistic intent clear by some signal in the context, which is just not present here in Gal 5.

Furthermore, since the Judaizers' gospel and mode of discipleship was appealing to the Galatian believers, it is difficult to accept the idea that Paul's audience would have automatically and immediately perceived the vice list as a description of "the flesh community" without something more explicit to indicate it; nor is it likely that they would have found it an apt description. Can Paul really be claiming that the "Judaizer" or "flesh-community" is guilty of "immorality, impurity, sensuality, idolatry," and "sorcery" (Gal 5:19-20)? It seems this could not be a persuasive argument to Paul's audience if it were evidently false regarding the Judaizers that the Galatians knew by personal interaction.

This raises a further problem with Russell's appeal to "Spirit-" and "flesh-communities." He is somewhat unclear or inconsistent regarding what these communities *are*, and what Paul is claiming *about them*. As for the latter, Russell argues that Paul is contrasting the internal relational dynamics of the Judaizers' community with the dynamics of his own communities;[28] yet at the same time, he argues that Paul is *not* claiming that the list of the works of the flesh in 5:19-21 are specifically characteristic of the Judaizer community; rather, they are true of the broader category of those in the σάρξ, which includes Pagans, Jews, and Judaizers.[29] Certainly Russell is correct in this latter conception, but now one wonders what is gained by referring to a "community" at all.

Once again we are back up against the problem of defining a community. Russell seems to oscillate between referring on the one hand to real, discrete, flesh and blood communities (e.g., the Pauline churches, the Judaizer community), and on the other, to communities that are abstractions (e.g., the "flesh community," i.e., all who are in the flesh in a salvation-historical sense). The problem is that, in appealing to the first, he is mistaken, for two compelling reasons: (1) it is doubtful at best that Paul even refers to a "Judaizer community," and if he did he would most likely have been regarded as wrong by the Galatians because (2) there is no particular Judaizer community that could truly be characterized by this entire list of vices. In appealing to the latter, abstract conception of "community," Russell is closer to the intent of the passage, but the term "community" becomes misleading and inappropriate, for communities by definition cannot be abstractions; communities are real flesh-and-blood entities composed of persons who literally interact and share certain values. In that sense, the "flesh community" is somewhat a fiction of analysis, existing neither in the text of Galatians 5, nor out there in the social world inhabited by the Galatians.

---

28. Russell, *Flesh/Spirit Conflict*, 147.
29. Russell, *Flesh/Spirit Conflict*, 161.

This insistence on finding actual communities in Galatians 5 is unnecessary; to speak of community dynamics or relationships (which Russell, Fee, Hansen, Witherington, and Martyn are certainly correct to insist is true of Galatians[30]) does not require literal reference to some particular community where these dynamics are manifested. This is particularly true if the passage, as per view (A) above, is exhorting one pattern of life and its results (walking by the Spirit and producing its fruits) over another (living under the Law, by the flesh [3:3], and producing the works of the flesh).

However, having dispensed with the talk of communities, there remains a grain of truth in Russell's claim, as per view (B), that Paul is making an argumentative point and not just a paranaetic one. It seems that Paul is insinuating that the sinful "works of the flesh" are typical or common to those living under the Law generally, both in the past and today. Accordingly, the way of Torah, circumcision, and the flesh will not make you righteous; but the Torah-free way of faith, love, and the Spirit does. This is evident when we see the deeds of the flesh in practice.

So whom would Paul's audience perceive to be the practitioners of the deeds of the flesh? Let us take a brief survey of the vice terms to see with whom they would be associated.[31]

Certainly the stereotypical gentile sins of immorality and idolatry could be seen in contemporary times; however, such sins could also be seen in Israel's history. "Sexual immorality" (πορνεία, *porneia*) was applied numerous times to Jews and Israel in the LXX to describe both literal sexual immorality, and spiritual adultery. The verb form πορνεύω (*porneuō*) is also used with both senses in the LXX; Paul uses the verb form πορνεύω of the Israelites (with a literal sense) in 1 Corinthians 10:8. Of course, literal sexual immorality and adultery among the Israelites is routinely referred to in the OT with more generic language, such as "to lie with" (שָׁכַב [*šākab*], κοιμάω [*koimaō*]) or "to go in to" (i.e., to enter a room to meet someone for the purpose of sexual relations; בּוֹא [*bô'*], εἰσέρχομαι [*eiserchomai*]). "Impurity, uncleanness" (ἀκαθαρσία, *akatharsia*) was a constant ineliminable concern of the Torah in Leviticus, and moral impurity is criticized in the Prophets (esp. in the LXX). "Sensuality" (ἀσέλγεια, *aselgeia*) was more characteristic of gentiles and associated with them. "Idolatry" (εἰδωλολατρία, *eidōlolatria*) is of course a characteristic sin of the gentiles. In 1 Corinthians 10:7, Paul refers to the Israelites as "idolaters"(εἰδωλολάτρης, *eidōlolatrēs*), although in the OT itself, the language of fornication and adultery is more often used in

---

30. See Fee, *God's Empowering Presence*, 425; Hansen, *Galatians*, 175–76; Witherington, *Grace in Galatia*, 397–403; Martyn, *Galatians*, 482, 485–86 (and n48), 496.

31. For brevity's sake we will not list examples of verses for most of these vice terms and their uses. Examples can be readily seen in their respective entries in BDAG.

a metaphorical way to depict idolatry. "Sorcery" (φαρμακεία, *pharmakeia*) was applied to Egyptians and Babylonians in the LXX.

"Enmities, hostilities" (ἔχθρα, *echthra*) was used also as a synonym for the substantival use of the adjective ἔχθρος (*echthros*, "enemy"), which is applied to Israel in LXX Micah 2:8; 7:8, 10; or to God as Israel's enemy in LXX Isaiah 63:10; ἔχθρα was also used in the sense of "enmity" between Israelites in Jeremiah 9:1-8 (specifically, verse 8); Paul uses it with the sense of "hostility" toward God in Romans 8:7, speaking of those whose minds are set on the flesh. In Ephesians 2:14-16, the author uses it to speak of the enmity between Jews and gentiles that is removed in Christ.

With "strife" (ἔρις) and "jealousy" (ζῆλος [*zēlos*], and also the cognate verb ζηλόω [*zēloō*]), Paul begins employing terms that may evoke for the audience traits of the Jews, the Judaizers, and of the pre-Christian Paul himself. "Strife," or "quarrel" (ἔρις) is applied to gentile unbelievers in Romans 1:29; believers in Rome are exhorted to shun it or avoid it in Romans 13:13; the Corinthian believers are rebuked as fleshly because of their quarrels in 1 Corinthians 1:11 and 3:3; Paul worried that there would be quarrels with the Corinthians when he visited them in 2 Corinthians 12:20; Paul says that some preach Christ out of strife (and envy) in Philippians 1:15, most likely referring, not to Judaizers, but to Jewish Christians who disagreed with Paul, and who were evangelizing Jews.[32] Finally, believers are exhorted to avoid strife in 1 Timothy 6:4 and Titus 3:9, and in the latter passage the author also connects the term to disputes about the law.

"Jealousy, zeal" (ζῆλος) is a term that can be a virtue or a vice, depending on the context. In the OT it is used overwhelmingly in the virtuous sense, usually to describe the jealousy of Yahweh for his people as his prized possession. It is only on occasion used negatively of a person's jealousy (e.g., Eccl 4:4). It signifies a vice in Acts 5:17, describing the attitude of the high priest and his Sadducee associates towards the apostles and the early Christian movement; and in Acts 13:45 it describes the attitude of the Jews of Pisidian Antioch against Paul and Barnabas. While of course this is not Pauline usage, it is likely that it reflects an early Christian conception of the Jewish attitude, and Luke's source of information for 13:45 could very well have been Paul himself.[33] Paul uses the word with a negative connotation of jealousy in

---

32. Fee, *Philippians*, 118-23. O'Brien, *Philippians*, 103, concurs that they are not Judaizers. This is evident from the different way Paul speaks of the Judaizers in Phil 3:2 (and perhaps 3:18-19—cf. Silva, *Philippians*, 179-82).

33. The plausibility of this claim is inextricably bound with one's general views of the Lukan authorship of Acts, Luke's intent and competence in writing reliable history, and one's particular view of the "we-passages" of Acts. If criticisms of Luke on these matters are unconvincing, then a strong prima facie case stands that Paul would have

several passages: Romans 13:13; 1 Corinthians 3:3; 2 Corinthians 12:20. An interesting case occurs in Philippians 3:6, where Paul cites as an instance of his virtue as a Jew his *zeal*, to the degree of persecuting the church; but this modification of the "virtue" (as the cause of his persecution of the church) already is tipping Paul's hand that it was really a vice, which is then explicitly subverted into a vice in 3:7–8. Paul has deconstructed a traditional Jewish hallmark of righteousness that was rooted in the OT accounts of Phinehas (Num 25:6–13; Ps 106:30–31; Sir 45:23–24), and subsequently magnified in the Maccabean revolt against militant Hellenism, in which fervent devotion to the Law could take the form of suffering martyrdom or inflicting death on the pagan oppressors and Jewish collaborators (1 Macc 2:1–70; 4 Macc 16:1–25; 18:1–24). Paul had previously embodied this highly revered trait, but jettisons it in favor of devotion to Christ and conformity to the pattern of Christ's life, death, and resurrection.[34]

The uses of the cognates of ζῆλος are similar. The use of the verb form ζηλόω parallels that of the noun. In Acts 7:9, Joseph's brothers were jealous of him; in Acts 17:5, the Jews were jealous of Paul and Silas in Thessalonica; and in 1 Corinthians 13:4, love is not jealous. In Galatians 4:17, the Judaizers zealously desired to win over the Galatians, but not commendably, so that the Galatians will be zealously devoted to the Judaizers (the latter use may have a positive connotation). We see similar uses with the substantival form ζηλωτής (*zēlōtēs*). Though it can be a virtuous term, it is used negatively in Acts 21:20 to describe the Judaizers as "zealots for the law." In Acts 22:3, Luke's Paul describes himself as a pre-Christian as a "zealot for God." The real Paul says of himself in Galatians 1:14 that he was "even more a zealot for his ancestral traditions" than his contemporaries.

"(Outbursts of) anger" (θυμοί, *thumoi*) could also be a virtuous response to wickedness, as it is used of God's wrath in the LXX; or in other contexts it could be an expression of sinful anger motivated by unrighteousness and envy. As examples of the latter, we have Luke 4:28 (the rage of the

---

been a source for Luke regarding the Jewish zeal he faced. Luke apparently first appears in the "we" of 16:10, in the context of the second missionary journey, in which Paul was delivering the verdict of the Jerusalem council (16:4) and circumcising the half-Jewish Timothy as a prudent mission strategy because of the Jews in the region (16:1–3). Surely the recent history of the Judaizing conflict would have been frequent topic of conversation. On this reading, Luke was also present at several foreboding statements anticipating Jewish zeal and persecution (20:14–17, 19–24; 21:10–13, 17–24). Subsequently, Luke saw Jewish zeal in action against Paul firsthand. For fuller discussion and argumentation on Luke's historiography and the "we-passages," see Bock, *Theology of Luke-Acts*, 31–54; and Hemer, *Book of Acts*, 308–64, esp. 329–36, 346–51.

34. O'Brien, *Philippians*, 374–76; Dunn, *Theology of Paul*, 349–54; Hansen, "Paul's Conversion," 216; Cummins, *Paul and the Crucified Christ*.

Jews in the Synagogue at Jesus' teaching); Acts 19:28 (the rage of the Ephesian gentiles at Paul's successful evangelization efforts); 2 Corinthians 12:20 (Paul's fear that there will be rage or anger when he visits the Corinthians); and in Ephesians 4:31 and Colossians 3:8 (in which believers are exhorted to put aside wrath).

"Rivalries" (ἐριθεῖαι, *eritheiai*) refers to selfishness or selfish ambition, probably in a context of dispute or in such a manner as to foment contention; Paul applies the term to both Jews and gentiles. In Romans 2:8, it is true of both Jews and gentiles, but Paul underscores the application to the Jews; in 2 Corinthians 12:20, Paul fears there will be selfish ambition or rivalry when he visits the Corinthians; in Philippians 1:17, some preach Christ out of selfish ambition as rivals to Paul. In Philippians 2:3, Paul exhorts the Philippian Christians not to live by selfish ambition, a trait very much endemic in Roman Philippi.[35]

Paul also exhorts against "dissensions" (διχοστασίαι, *dichostasiai*) in Romans 16:17. The term for "factions, parties, sects" (αἱρέσεις, *haireseis*) was used in Acts 5:15 of the faction of the Sadducees who rose up with the high priest, filled with jealousy; in Acts 15:5, it refers to those among the believers who were of the party of the Pharisees—i.e., the Judaizers. In 1 Corinthians 11:19, Paul speaks ironically about the factions among the Corinthians. As for the term "envies" (φθόνοι, *phthonoi*), the Jews handed Christ over to Pilate out of envy (Mark 15:10 and Matt 27:18). Stereotypically, the gentiles are filled with envy (Rom 1:29). In Philippians 1:15, some preach Christ out of envy towards Paul; in 1 Timothy 6:4, the author warns against dissenters who provoke envy; and in Titus 3:3, envy is a characteristic of our former life before Christ's regeneration and renewal of us. Finally, Paul also uses the verb form φθονέω (*phthoneō*) in Galatians 5:26 to enjoin the Galatians against envy.

"Drunkenness" (μέθαι, *methai*) is forbidden by Paul to the Romans also (Rom 13:3). The term μέθη (*methē*) is used in the OT prophets (LXX) as symbolic of men reeling under judgment. However, it is also used for literal drunkenness in the LXX as well (e.g., Prov 20:1; Joel 1:5; Hag 1:6; Isa 28:7). Accordingly, while drunkenness would not be considered particular to the Jews, it was certainly not unheard of among them. The use of the verb form μεθύω (*methuō*) parallels that of the noun: it is used in 1 Samuel 1:13; 25:36; 1 Kings 16:9; and 21:16 for literal drunkenness; and there are many instances in the prophets where it is symbolic of men reeling under judgment. In Matthew 24:49, the wicked servant beats others, eats and gets drunk, and is caught unaware by the master's return. In Acts 2:15, Peter

---

35. Hellerman, *Reconstructing Honor in Roman Philippi*.

tells the Jews: these men are not drunk. In contrast, in 1 Corinthians 11:21, Paul upbraids the Corinthians for being disorderly, selfish, and drunk at the Lord's Supper. Finally, he teaches in 1 Thessalonians 5:7 that getting drunk is a deed of darkness, unfit for children of the light.

"Excessive feasting, carousing, revelries" (κῶμοι, kōmoi) was also forbidden by Paul to the Romans (Rom 13:13). This vice appears to be more associated with the gentiles. First Peter 4:3 explicitly links it to the gentiles.

The table below summarizes the vices and their characteristic practitioners:

Table 8: The Vices of Galatians 5:19-21

Vice	Characteristic of gentiles	Characteristic of OT Jews	Characteristic of first-century Jews or Judaizers
Immorality (πορνεία)	Yes (stereotypically so)	Yes (metaphorically, for idolatry; and literally, though usually expressed in different language)	No
Impurity (ἀκαθαρσία)	Yes (stereotypically so)	Yes, a constant Levitical concern of Torah	Yes, a constant Levitical concern of Torah
Sensuality (ἀσέλγεια)	Yes (stereotypically so)	No	No
Idolatry (εἰδωλολατρία)	Yes (stereotypically so)	Yes (before the exile, but usually depicted in language of "adultery") cf. 1 Cor 10:7; No after exile	No
Sorcery (φαρμακεία)	Yes—Egyptians and Babylonians in LXX	No	No
Enmities (ἔχθρα)	Yes	Yes	Yes
Strife (ἔρις)	Yes	No	Yes (Judaizers)
Jealousy (ζῆλος)	No	No (not in the vicious sense)	YES—Paul too
outbursts of anger (θυμοί)	Yes	Yes	Yes

Vice	Characteristic of gentiles	Characteristic of OT Jews	Characteristic of first-century Jews or Judaizers
Selfish ambition (ἐριθεῖαι)	Yes		Yes
Dissensions (διχοστασίαι)	[General exhortation to avoid this vice—not clearly directed against any particular group]		
Factions (αἱρέσεις)	Yes		Yes
Envying (φθόνοι)	Yes		Yes
Drunkenness (μέθαι)	Yes	Yes	Yes
Carousing (κῶμοι)	Yes	No	No
TOTALS (out of 15)	13 Yes, 1 No, 1 Unclear	6 Yes, 5 No, 3 Unclear	9 Yes, 5 No, 1 Unclear

The resultant tally of the chart above contradicts the idea that Paul's main point in the passage can be a depiction of the vices particular to the Judaizer community. Of course, the gentiles, the Jews under the Mosaic Law, and the first-century unbelieving Jews and the Judaizers depending upon the Torah and the flesh are *all* indicted in this vice list as manifesting the works of the flesh. Therefore, we would expect the Galatian believers to hear charges against their pagan past, against OT Israel, against the Judaizers, and some that were true of Paul in his former manner of life. Those who practice the works of the flesh show that they are not heirs or sons, and will not inherit the kingdom of God.

This final note recalls Romans 7:5, in which Paul describes the former time "when we were in the flesh" that the sinful passions were at work "in the members of our body *to bear fruit for death*" (my emphasis). The reference to the evil works as "fruit" is the antithesis of the fruit of the Spirit in Galatians 5:22–23, and the description of them as "fruit *for death*" corresponds to the warning in Galatians 5:21 that those "who practice such things will not inherit the kingdom of God." Accordingly, in his elaboration of Romans 7:5, in the passage 7:14–25, Paul cries out for deliverance from "this body of death" in 7:24. By contrast, in Romans 8:11, those who by the Spirit put to death the practices of the body "will live," which should be taken in its ultimate sense of eternal life—they are sons and heirs of God's kingdom (8:14-17).

C' 5:22-23

We shall not dwell on the fruit of the Spirit, for it is fairly obvious that these are manifested through the indwelling Spirit in the lives of Christians, i.e., of sons of God and heirs of his kingdom. Let us also note that, while the virtues of individual personal holiness are not unimportant, the importance of relational virtues is preeminent here,[36] just as the sins which fractured community were an overriding concern above. Accordingly, love is the paramount virtue, driving the others (5:6, 13-15). Though Christians are not under the Law and therefore do not *do* or *keep* the Law in terms of nomistic observance, they nonetheless *fulfill* its righteous purpose in their loving service to one another (5:14). In verse 23, we have the same general thought stated negatively—that the virtues listed as the fruit of the Spirit do not violate the Law.

Barclay is most likely correct in his suggestion that Paul is drawing on OT eschatological prophecies such as Isaiah 32:15-16 and Joel 2:18-32 that predicted great fruitfulness for Israel because of the Spirit.

> Paul's reference to the "fruit of the Spirit" may therefore be intended to evoke the prophetic statements on Israel and the promise of her future: such fruit is what God has always demanded of his people and what was promised for the "age to come." Now, in "the fullness of time" (Gal. 4.4) as "the Spirit is poured out from on high" (Is 32.15), the people of God are able to produce the "fruit" which was expected of them. By choosing a word with these rich associations, Paul is able to provide his appeal with further support: if the Galatians will only continue to walk in the Spirit, they will actually produce the sort of behaviour which God requires.[37]

Accordingly, the promise of the fruit of the Spirit demonstrates the superiority of the way of the Spirit over that of Torah and flesh, and thus

---

36. So Witherington, *Grace in Galatia*, 407-9; Martyn, *Galatians*, 498-501; Hansen, *Galatians*, 178-79.

37. Barclay, *Obeying the Truth*, 121-22. N.B., "age to come" is Barclay's characterization, not the language of Isaiah 32, Joel 2, or Paul. See also 122n46 for Barclay's interesting and plausible suggestion that the "blessing of Abraham" of Gal 3:14 refers to Gen 28:3-4, which is fulfilled literally through the inclusion of gentiles, and metaphorically through the "fruit of the Spirit." See also Beale, "Old Testament Background."

functions argumentatively, as per view (A). However, at the same time, the fruit represent the normative virtues that are expected of God's people. There is no middle ground for the Galatians: they will either proceed by the flesh, under the Law, doing the works of the flesh, thus incurring the condemnation of the Law and failing to inherit the kingdom; or they will walk by the Spirit, producing its fruit which are not proscribed and condemned by the Law. Accordingly, Paul exhorts them to walk by the Spirit. Although the passage is not in the form of typical Pauline paranesis, its ethical function and content is undeniable, in accordance with view (B). Therefore, view (C) is correct in acknowledging both functions in this passage.

As we continue to exegete 5:24–26, a more precise picture of the ethical content will emerge, as the exact meaning of "walking by the Spirit" is clarified.

B' 5:24

Taken on its own, this is a most enigmatic text. However, it is accompanied by many parallels, some of which are also equally enigmatic on their own, yet when taken together they are mutually illuminating and reveal a coherent Pauline thought-pattern. We shall first look at the texts in Galatians and see what pattern emerges, and then look for parallels from Romans for confirmation.

The first category of texts from Galatians includes those of Pauline autobiography. This is actually one lengthy text from 1:10—2:21, plus a recapitulation of the theme in 6:14. Paul's autobiography plays a big role in the argument of Galatians, and is clearly meant to be paradigmatic (see 4:12), for Paul offers up an autobiography of reversal in which he is decisively turned from his former manner of life centered around the Torah to a new life by faith centered on Christ. The second class of texts includes those featuring a "formerly-now antithesis": 1:10; 1:13–17; 2:19–20; 4:3–7; 4:8–10, 19, and 6:15. These texts either explicitly or implicitly contrast the "before-Christ" life and the "since-Christ" life. The third class is composed of the "co-crucifixion" texts (which are part of a more general pattern of "death-life" texts): 2:19–20; 5:24; and 6:14. Fourth, and finally, we have the "Jesus-in-Paul" texts: 1:16; 2:20; 4:6 ("Spirit of his Son into our hearts"); and 4:19 ("until Christ is formed in you"). There are many connections between these themes, but the one passage that unites all of these categories of texts, pulling them into a coherent pattern, is 2:19–20.[38] This may be demonstrated graphically as follows:

---

38. Hubbard, *New Creation*, 191–95, 225–26.

Table 9: Galatians 5:24 and Its Intra-epistolary Parallels

Paradigmatic autobiography of reversal	1:10—2:21 (*including 2:19–20*)						6:14
Formerly-now	1:10	1:13–17	2:19–20	4:3–7	4:8–10, 19		6:15
Co-crucifixion			2:19–20			5:24	6:14
Jesus in Paul		1:16	2:20	4:6	4:19		

Galatians 2:20 introduces a series of three co-crucifixion texts in which Paul speaks in some way of the crucifixion of the believer: "I" have been crucified with Christ (and died to the Law and now live to God) (2:19–20); "the flesh" has been crucified, with its passions and desires (5:24); and "I" and "the world" have been crucified to each other (6:14). In 2:20 and 6:14, Paul's "I" is both personal and paradigmatic.[39] As so often in this letter, he writes of his own experiences as a pattern to be applied to the Galatians, and so he writes in 5:24 that "those who belong to Christ Jesus" have crucified the flesh. Hansen has noted that all three texts speak of the identification of the believer with the death of Jesus Christ on the cross.[40] Furthermore, Paul's two references to his own crucifixion (2:20; 6:14) are expressed in the perfect tense as a once-for-all, decisive identification with Christ and a simultaneous death to the Law, and to "the world" (a term that must be clarified momentarily).[41] The remaining text that speaks of believers generally (5:24) expresses the crucifixion by means of an aorist verb, but it is most likely to be taken as a consummative aorist and therefore semantically equivalent to a perfect tense, which is how it is uniformly rendered in the translations.[42] Paul's paradigmatic "crucifixion with Christ" is the turning point of the pattern that incorporates the thematic categories of texts noted in table 9.

The pattern that results from these texts can be summarized as follows: Paul formerly lived as a people pleaser (1:10), in his former manner of life in Judaism, in which he was advancing beyond many of his contemporaries, zealous for the ancestral traditions, even persecuting the church of God

---

39. Gaventa, "Galatians 1 and 2."
40. Hanson, "Paul's Conversion," 221–22.
41. Hanson, "Paul's Conversion," 221–22.
42. Wallace, *Greek Grammar*, 559–60. Pace Witherington, *Grace in Galatia*, 412, who interprets ἐσταύρωσαν (*estaurōsan*) as an ingressive aorist signifying an event which began in the past, but continues into the present, and thus speaks of the believer's continuing battle with the flesh. Hansen, *Galatians*, 180–81, seems to oscillate between these two views.

(1:13–14). Yet, when he was under the law (2:19), he was actually in bondage under the law as though a small child or slave (4:3–5). But then comes co-crucifixion with Christ! This crucifixion is described in three different ways— "I" am crucified with Christ (2:20), "the flesh with its passions and desires" is crucified (5:24), and "I" am crucified to the "world" and the "world" to "me" (6:14). This threefold crucifixion is one event that occurs for the believer at the time of his conversion, but joins the believer's life with the life, death, and new life of Jesus. The "flesh" of 5:24 and the "world" of 6:14 are very much related to the "I." The "world" of which Paul speaks is his former manner of life in Judaism and all of the sarkic values associated with it: boasting in the flesh, in circumcision, and competitive striving with others to advance over them.[43] Paul can speak of this threefold crucifixion as having the following implications: I no longer strive to please man, but God (1:10); I died to the law (2:19), and now I live to God (2:20); I am not under the law (5:18), but live by the Spirit (5:25); neither circumcision nor uncircumcision is anything, (6:13, 15; cf. 5:6), but new creation is what matters, and faith working through love (6:15; cf. 5:6). New creation is to be taken in an anthropological (not cosmological) sense, with a strong pneumatological component. That is, it speaks of the Christian convert as a new creature with the promised Holy Spirit resident within to enable and empower the believer to live a new life to God and in loving service to others. This is seen in the texts that speak of Jesus or the Spirit in the believer (1:16; 2:20; 4:6, 19).[44]

This understanding of "a new creation" establishes it as the antithesis of the "flesh" of 5:24.[45] The "flesh" is on the "death" side of Paul's death-life texts, while the Spirit and "new creation" are firmly on the "life" side of those texts (see 5:24–25; 6:14–15). Accordingly, Russell is right to emphasize the salvation-historical sense of the σάρξ that is used in 5:24 when he defines it as "bodily existence in frailty and weakness *apart from God's indwelling Spirit*, particularly in the circumcised state under Torah, when referring to Judaizers."[46] That entire mode of existence and life for the believer ended decisively at conversion. Old things have passed away, and now he is a new creation, with the Spirit who is life resident within.

Paul says something very similar in Romans that confirms what we have seen in Galatians. Recall in Romans 6 that Paul teaches that we have died with Christ, and thus have died to sin, and so are no longer mastered

---

43. Hubbard, *New Creation*, 215–18; Hansen, "Paul's Conversion," 216, 219–20, 222–23.

44. Hubbard, *New Creation*, 218–28; Hansen, "Paul's Conversion," 224.

45. Cf. also Ridderbos, *Paul*, 104.

46. Russell, *Flesh/Spirit Conflict*, 158 (emphasis mine); see also 165–67.

by sin, but instead serve God. In this context, Paul writes "our old man [ὁ παλαιὸς ἡμῶν ἄνθρωπος, ho palaios hēmōn anthrōpos] was crucified with [him] so that the body of sin might be nullified so that we would no longer be slaves to sin" (Rom 6:6).[47] Whether considering "(being in) the flesh" or "the old man," or their positive antithetical counterparts "being in the Spirit," "the new man," or "a new creation," we should not think of these as *natures*, but as whole persons considered in relation to the work of Christ and the enabling presence of the Spirit.[48]

The flesh (Gal 5:24) or the "old man" (Rom 6:6) was crucified so that the "body of sin" could be done away with (καταργηθῇ, katargēthē). The "body of sin" is not to be identified with the flesh in the salvation-historical sense as the "old man" is. The "body of sin" is a reference to one's bodily self as ruled by sin, and in this verse it is potentially applied to believers in the present time after conversion, yet the circumstance of sin's rule *has been negated* because of the crucifixion of the flesh/old man and the presence of the indwelling Holy Spirit. Therefore, Romans 6:11–13 charges believers to live in accordance with this fact: though their body is "mortal" and subject to the weakness and death characteristic of this age, it is no longer a "body of sin," such that sin is to rule their bodies no longer (v. 12). Rather, the "members of our body" are now to serve as instruments of righteousness for God (v. 13).[49]

Romans also confirms the picture of "the flesh" from Galatians regarding the key issue of the absence or presence of the indwelling Holy Spirit. We have seen this in the two texts in Romans: 7:18, in which the wretched man confesses that "nothing good dwells" in "my flesh"; and the contrasting circumstance in 8:11, in which the Holy Spirit indwells those who belong to Christ.

---

47. Hubbard, *New Creation*, 96–99. Note that the phrase (with its opposite "the new man") is used in the disputed Pauline letters in Col 3:9–11 and Eph 4:22–24 in a similar but not quite identical fashion (Moo, *Romans*, 373; Hubbard, *New Creation*, 96–98). In Rom 6:6 and Col 3:9–11, "the old man" is something that has been definitively crucified or laid aside in the past in favor of the new man who has been assumed; while in Eph 4:22–24, the laying aside of the old man and putting on of the new man is apparently something to be done as a continuing practice of Christian character formation. In this way, "the old man" is similar to "the flesh," which is depicted as definitively crucified in Gal 5:24, and yet the flesh is also a continuing concern, as we have noted above. The other side of the "flesh"-"a new creation" antithesis is also paralleled by "the new man" of Col 3:10; however, "a new creation" is only used in a definitive, once-for-all sense, not as something to be "put on" regularly as "the new man" of Eph 4:24.

48. Moo, *Romans*, 373–74; Russell, *Flesh/Spirit Conflict*, 154–56.

49. Moo, *Romans*, 382–85.

A' 5:25-26

These verses form a transition, with verse 25 drawing together the passage of verses 16–25 with its repeated idea of walking by the Spirit, and verse 26 picking up the themes of verses 13–15 again while simultaneously preparing for the application in 6:1–10. The entire passage from 5:13—6:10 is about how loving service to one another is the ethical dynamic that, though free of the Law, fulfills the righteous intent of the Law, or the law of Christ (6:2). At the heart of this ethical dynamic is a mode of discipleship that drives it, namely, walking by the Spirit, or being led by the Spirit (vv. 16, 18, 25). "Walking by the Spirit" is the means to the end of loving service to one another.[50] However, the content of walking by the Spirit is not elaborated. Assuming believers are not totally passive in this process, what exactly do they *do* to carry out Paul's exhortation to walk by the Spirit?

Russell gives some insight noting the different verbs in the three "walk/be led by the Spirit" verses:

> **Galatians 5:16** But I say, walk* by the Spirit [πνεύματι περιπατεῖτε, *pneumati peripateite*], and you* will certainly not carry out the desire of the flesh.
>
> **Galatians 5:18** But if you* are led by the Spirit [πνεύματι ἄγεσθε, *pneumati agesthe*], you* are not under the Law.
>
> **Galatians 5:25** If we live by the Spirit [ζῶμεν πνεύματι, *zōmen pneumati*], let us also walk by the Spirit [πνεύματι καὶ στοιχῶμεν, *pneumati kai stoichōmen*].

Περιπατέω already has a moral significance and is used as an idiom for living one's life a certain way, and ἄγω is also used for moral leadership.[51] However, στοιχέω is much more explicit in its moral connotation, indicating conformity to a standard or rule. Though it can also be used to mean "to walk," it retains its moral force, and implies something more like "follow" or "walk in step with."[52] Because of the use of στοιχέω in 5:25, Russell assimilates the πνεύματι περιπατεῖτε of 5:16 to the same general meaning by interpreting the πνεύματι in both verses as "a dative of rule."[53] So Paul is exhorting the Galatians to walk "by the rule or standard of the Spirit" in

---

50. Russell, *Flesh/Spirit Conflict*, 150–51.
51. BDAG, s.v. περιπατέω; s.v. ἄγω.
52. BDAG, s.v. στοιχέω.
53. Russell, *Flesh/Spirit Conflict*, 150–53. The categorization of πνεύματι as a "dative of rule" is an ad hoc one that is derived from the meanings of the verbs that it is attached to: περιπατέω, στοιχέω, and ἄγω (in v. 18).

accordance with the pattern or *typos* that Paul lived and taught among them. Accordingly, for the Galatians, this phrase must have had more clear content for them because of his oral teaching than it has from the letter alone. We are faced with the question: what exactly is this pattern? Russell defines walking by the rule of the Spirit as refusing to submit to Torah and circumcision, and remaining committed to the "Spirit community" rather than the "flesh community."[54] Aside from reservations about "flesh" and "Spirit" standing in for, respectively, a "flesh community" and "spirit community," this is doubtlessly true, as far as it goes. However, it does not seem to go nearly far enough, for it seems like more than this is needed in order for a Christian community to be healthy and characterized by a spiritual relational dynamic of mutual loving service. After all, the Corinthian community was able to become quite "fleshly" apart from any Judaizing controversy.[55] This reading of "walking by the Spirit" understands Paul to be instructing the Galatians on something that the passage has already assumed: 5:1 and 13–15 assumes for the sake of argument that the Galatians have stood firm in their freedom and refused to submit to the enslavement of Torah. The question to be addressed at this point is, ethically speaking, *now what?* If the Galatians are not to be made righteous by Torah, then how? Russell's interpretation stops well short of addressing the pertinent question.

Thankfully, by comparing what Paul wrote to the Galatians to other portions of the Pauline corpus, we may derive a fuller picture of what he meant when he exhorted the Galatians to walk by the Spirit. Recall, first of all, the circumstances of a human being according to Paul's salvation-historical argumentation in Romans 6–8. When they were "in the flesh" under the Law, they were enslaved to sin, apart from the Holy Spirit's indwelling or enablement, and their mind or inner man was a prisoner of the law of sin at work in their body, such that their body served the law of sin and produced fruit for death, or works which earned eternal death (Rom 7:5, 14–25; 6:16–19). Then they were united with Jesus in his death, and their old man was crucified with him, such that they died to the Law and to sin, and are now united with Jesus in his resurrection life; they are no longer slaves to sin, but slaves to God and to his righteousness so that they may bear fruit for God as they serve in the newness of the Spirit rather than the oldness of the Law. Accordingly, they are exhorted to consider themselves as dead to sin and alive to God, and not to allow sin to rule their bodies, but to present themselves to God as his slaves (Rom 7:4, 6; 6:1–23).

---

54. Russell, *Flesh/Spirit Conflict*, 158–59.

55. Note as well the observation by Hansen, *Galatians*, 80–81, footnote 3:3, especially the paragraph beginning "'Flesh' (NIV: *human effort*) in 3:3 . . ."

Now, even though set free from the Torah (Rom 8:4), and the law of sin and death that had formerly taken advantage of it to imprison them, those who walk in the Spirit may *fulfill* (πληρόω, *plēroō*) *the requirement* (δικαίωμα) of the Law—the content of which is unspecified, but note Galatians 5:14 and 6:2, and the contrast between *fulfilling* the Law (Rom 8:4) and *doing* (ποιέω, *poieō*) (all) the Law (Gal 3:10; 5:3). (Note also Romans 2:26, in which the uncircumcised keep (φυλάσσω, *phulassō*) the δικαίωμα of the Law.) This is contrasted in Romans 8:5-8 with those who are in the flesh, who set their minds on the things of the flesh. For examples of Jewish things of the flesh, consider Paul's criticisms of Judaism as practiced by himself formerly and by his Judaizing opponents (Gal 1:13-14; 4:9-10; 5:2-3, 6; Phil 3:2-6, 18-19). For examples of gentile things of the flesh, consider the sophistic cultural values of Corinth (1 Corinthians 1-4), the Roman social values of status in Rome and Philippi.[56] Both among Jews and gentiles, setting the mind on these "things of the flesh" resulted in a competitive striving in which one sought to advance over others, and to subject others to oneself. Accordingly, those who thought this way could not subject themselves (ὑποτάσσω [*hypotassō*], see Rom 10:3) to the law of God that commands that you should love your neighbor as yourself (see Gal 5:14). Therefore we are not surprised when Paul writes in Galatians 6:13 that the circumcised do not actually keep (φυλάσσω) the Law—in contrast to the uncircumcised of Romans 2:26 who do keep (φυλάσσω) the δικαίωμα of the Law, which suggests that the idea in Galatians 6:13 is that the circumcised do not keep *the* δικαίωμα of the Law. This is borne out by Paul's comments regarding the motives of the Judaizers (Gal 2:5; 4:17; 6:12-13).

But those who belong to Christ are not in the flesh, but in the Spirit, and the Spirit dwells in them (and through the Spirit, Christ dwells in them) (Rom 8:9-11), and even though their bodies are still mortal because of sin, the indwelling Spirit gives them life. Therefore (8:12-14), they are not debtors (ὀφειλέτης [*opheiletēs*]—cf. Gal 5:3) to the flesh to live κατὰ σάρκα (which leads to death, cf. Gal 5:21). Rather, they are obligated to live κατὰ πνεῦμα, which entails putting to death the deeds of the body (cf. the works of the flesh, Gal 5:19-21).[57] Those who are led by the Spirit are sons of God (cf. Gal 5:18).

56. Hellerman, *Reconstructing Honor in Roman Philippi*.

57. David Wenham entertains the possibility that Paul could have been influenced by Jesus traditions eventually recorded in Matt 5:29-30 and 18:8-9 (//Mark 9:43-47) when he wrote Gal 5:24 and Rom 8:13 (*Paul*, 274-75). In our judgment, while the language is similar in Gal 5:24, the concept is different, since this passage seems to refer to the once-for-all nullification of believers' old identity, and not to the daily mortification of the flesh. On the other hand, one aspect of our argument in this chapter is that this daily "putting to death the deeds of the flesh" is a conceptual component of "walking according to the standard of the flesh" in Gal 5:25-26, even though the language is

In a similar fashion, Paul writes in Galatians, "since we live by the Spirit, let us walk according to the standard of [στοιχέω] the Spirit" (Gal 5:25).

There are other instances in which στοιχέω denotes the idea of walking (i.e., living) according to a pattern, standard, or rule. In Acts 21:24, we have a negative example in which Paul is exhorted to show to the Judaistic Jews of Jerusalem that "you yourself walk in observance of the Law [στοιχεῖς καὶ αὐτὸς φυλάσσων τὸν νόμον (stoicheis kai autos phulassōn ton nomon)]." Paul also uses στοιχέω to speak of walking in conformity to a pattern that he advocates in Romans 4:12; Galatians 6:16; and Philippians 3:16. In Romans 4:12, Paul cites Abraham as "the father of circumcision to those who not only are of the circumcision, but who also follow in the steps [τοῖς στοιχοῦσιν τοῖς ἴχνεσιν (tois stoichousin tois ichnesin)] of the faith of our father Abraham which he had while uncircumcised" (NASB). In the *recapitulatio* at the end of Galatians, Paul reiterates his opposition to circumcision, nomistic observance, and Jewish boasting in such things. Instead he boasts in the cross of Christ by which the entire nomistic and "sarkic" value system he had held formerly was crucified and replaced by one centered in Christ and his cross which has resulted in the Spirit dwelling within (6:13–15). Verse 15's "neither circumcision" phrase recalls 5:6 about the importance of faith working through love, which is in turn picked up in 5:13–15 in the command to serve one another through love. Then in Galatians 6:16, Paul writes: "And as many as will walk by this rule [τῷ κανόνι τούτῳ στοιχήσουσιν (tō kanoni touto stoichēsousin)], peace be upon them, and mercy upon the Israel of God" (Gal 6:16, my translation).

Clearly, Paul had imparted to the Galatians, by his teaching and example, a pattern of belief and living that was to be the standard according to which they were to walk. Although it is not fully fleshed out in his epistle to the Galatians, there are sufficient indications in the letter that the Galatians were aware of this pattern, and there are enough conceptual connections with other Pauline epistles to enable us to sketch out its content. In that regard, the occurrence of στοιχέω in Philippians 3:16 is enlightening. The entire chapter 3 of Philippians is the relevant context, which shares many common themes with Galatians. In that chapter, Paul warns the Philippians to watch out for the Judaizers and their gospel of (false) circumcision in the flesh. In contrast, Paul and his followers are of the true circumcision and put their confidence in Christ and the Spirit rather than the flesh. Paul also contrasts himself with the Judaizers' fleshly mindset by means of an autobiography of reversal and formerly-now contrast, in which he describes his former life as the Jew *par excellence*, which he discounted and discarded

---

absent in these verses since Paul does not elaborate here on the content of the "walking."

in favor of righteousness through faith in Christ, and in order to know Jesus and be united to him in his suffering, death, and resurrection. Paul presses on to obtain the prize, and encourages his audience to have the same attitude, and exhorts in verse 16: "let us walk according to [στοιχεῖν, stoichein] what we have attained." He then continues, "Brothers, become fellow imitators of me, and observe those who walk in this way, even as you have us for an example" (v. 17). Paul had given a very clear pattern of the Christian life to the Philippians in which believers were to lower themselves in order to serve one another in love and humility so that they could stand firm together for the gospel. In giving this exhortation, Paul offered many models or examples to follow, including Timothy (2:19–22), Epaphroditus (2:25–30), and himself (1:12–16; 3:2–14), but the ultimate paradigm was of Jesus Christ himself, who humbled and lowered himself to the position of a slave, and died a shameful death on the cross for our interests rather than his own advantage (Phil 2:1–11). Paul exhorted them to live in accordance with this pattern: "The things you have learned and received and heard and seen in me, practice these things, and the God of peace will be with you" (4:9). Because of the connections between Galatians and Philippians, we may be reasonably confident that this is the pattern or standard according to which Paul expected the Galatians to walk (στοιχέω). Furthermore, a similar ethos is expressed in 2 Corinthians 4:5: "For we do not preach ourselves, but Jesus Christ as Lord, and ourselves as your slaves for Jesus' sake."

Therefore, to walk according to the standard or rule of the Spirit is to walk according to a pattern of Christlike love and service towards others. This gives us the τέλος of walking by the Spirit. What about the μορφή (morphē)? How did Paul instruct his disciples to walk by the Spirit so that this pattern would be inculcated into their lives? Paul does not present this systematically in his letters, but his exhortations are consistent enough that we can derive a coherent picture of Paul's program of spiritual formation. Many of the connections are present in the passages we have already looked at. We have seen that before, believers were slaves of sin, with their minds or inner persons as prisoners of the law of sin in their flesh or body. Now in Christ they are slaves of God and his righteousness, and are to live purposefully as such, and in loving servitude to others, especially other believers. In order to make this a reality, they must, by the Spirit's enablement, "roll back" or reverse their enslaved condition, beginning with their minds.

Romans 6 and 12 both instruct believers to *present* (παρίστημι, *paristēmi*) themselves to God for his service, and at the same time exhort them regarding the disposition of their minds. Romans 12:1–2 communicates this idea using the language of cultic temple service:

> Therefore I urge you, brethren, by the mercies of God, to present [παραστῆσαι, *parastēsai*] your bodies a living and holy sacrifice, acceptable to God, *which is* your spiritual service of worship [λατρείαν, *latreian*]. ² And do not be conformed to this world, but be transformed by the renewing of your mind, so that you may prove what the will of God is, that which is good and acceptable and perfect [τέλειον, *teleion*]. (Rom 12:1-2, NASB)

This results in right thinking about themselves in relation to others in the body of Christ, and loving service to them (Rom 12:3-16). Similarly, throughout Romans 6:12-22, Paul calls his readers to present (παρίστημι) themselves as slaves for obedience, not to sin any longer, but to God and righteousness. Just as insistent in this chapter is the need to have the right mindset: Paul appeals repeatedly to what they *know* or *believe* (or ought to), or to how they are to *consider* or *think* of their situation (6:3, 6, 8-9, 11, 16). Paul gives thanks that they were "obedient from the heart to that form [τύπος, *tupos*] of teaching to which you were committed" (6:17, NASB).

We see a similar prominence given to having the right mindset in several other passages. "Setting our minds on the things of the Spirit" as opposed to things of the flesh in Romans 8:5-9 is necessary to serve others in love, for the flesh is self-seeking, does not submit to others, but seeks to compel them to submit. Note also from 1 Corinthians 2:6-16 that Paul preaches a wisdom that must be received by the Spirit, not by natural wisdom. It is the Spirit that enables Paul's hearers to welcome or receive this wisdom because it is humbling and antithetical to human pride. The content of this wisdom, with its focus on the cross, does not appear to be solely the gospel in terms of justification, but also the gospel in terms of the thought and lifestyle of discipleship, for Paul is countering the fleshly and worldly attitudes of the Corinthians. Finally, Paul prefaces the great Christological passage in Philippians 2 with pointed exhortation regarding the mindset and attitude of Christ that believers were expected to cultivate; this is the point of the passage, with Philippians 2:6-11 serving as the illustration in support of this idea.[58]

Having renewed the mind and presented the body for service, believers must finally discipline the body. We have already looked at Philippians 3, a

---

58. Hellerman provides the cultural background of the Roman *cursus* ideology necessary to understand the significance of Jesus' condescension to the "form of a slave," even to death on a cross, in *Reconstructing Honor*, 129-66. For a survey of views on this contested passage, see Martin and Dodd, *Where Christology Began*. Richard Bauckham surveys the interpretive issues briefly (and navigates them correctly, in our judgment) in describing the divine identity of the humiliated Jesus in *God Crucified*, 56-61. See also O'Brien, *Philippians*, 186-271; Fee, *Philippians*, 39-46, 191-229. The classic treatment of Martin, *Carmen Christi*, is strongly challenged by the recent scholarship listed above.

passage that had links to Galatians 3:3 and 5:25 in terms of maturity and walking according to the standard that Paul had taught. The passage also has a strong emphasis on discipline in verses 12–16:

> [12] Not that I have already **obtained** *it* [ἔλαβον (*elabon*), cf. 1 Cor 9:24] or have already become **perfect** [τετελείωμαι (*teteleiōmai*), cf. Gal 3:3], but I press on so that I may **lay hold** [καταλάβω (*katalabō*), cf. 1 Cor 9:24] of that for which also I was **laid hold of** [κατελήμφθην (*katelēmphthēn*), cf. 1 Cor 9:24] by Christ Jesus. [13] Brethren, I do not regard myself as having **laid hold** [κατειληφέναι (*kateilēphenai*), cf. 1 Cor 9:24] of *it* yet; but one thing *I do*: forgetting what *lies* behind and reaching forward to what *lies* ahead, [14] I press on toward the goal for the **prize** [βραβεῖον (*brabeion*), cf. 1 Cor 9:24] of the upward call of God in Christ Jesus. [15] Let us therefore, as many as are **perfect** [τέλειοι (*teleioi*), cf. 3:12; Gal 3:3], have this attitude; and if in anything you have a different attitude, God will reveal that also to you; [16] however, let us keep **living** [στοιχεῖν (*stoichein*), Gal. 5:25; 6:16] by that same *standard* to which we have attained. (Phil 3:12-16, NASB, my emphases)

The above passage is connected to 1 Corinthians 9:19–27.[59] In 9:24–27, Paul disciplines his body and enslaves it (δουλαγωγῶ [*doulagōgō*], 9:27—a word also used in Romans 6:18, 22 to say we have become enslaved to righteousness and God); this is most likely a conceptual parallel to the idea of putting to death the deeds of the body in Romans 8:11–14. And subsequently (in terms of logic if not order of mention), Paul uses his freedom, not for himself, but makes himself a slave to others for their sakes and the gospel's sake (1 Cor 9:19–23).

In sum, the picture Paul presents is as follows: present the body for service to God as a slave, while renewing the mindset according to Christ; discipline the body to make it your slave; and finally, offer yourself and your body as a slave to serve others in love. This is what walking according to the standard of the Spirit looks like in practical terms. It fulfills the righteous intent of the Law through its selfless love and service to others, and it does not fulfill the desire of the flesh.

---

59. Interestingly, Paul also uses a "running" metaphor drawn from the world of athletic racing in Gal 5:7. See Longenecker, *Galatians*, 230.

— 9 —
Conclusion

Summing Up the Argument

In chapter 2 we surveyed the range of Old Testament meanings for "the flesh" and saw how it was used as an anthropological term of great depth which speaks profoundly of man's mortal and moral weakness before God. We also saw the strong connotations of sinfulness that the term suggests by its use in the flood narrative, in which "all flesh had corrupted their way upon the earth," and "the wickedness of man was great on the earth, and that every intent of the thoughts of his heart was only evil continually." In the light of the way the author of Genesis uses the term "flesh" in this context, it would seem that the distance between the Old Testament and Paul's strongly antithetical passages is overestimated by some commentators.

In chapter 3 we examined two of Paul's uses of κατὰ σάρκα. First, we saw how Paul contrasted natural κατὰ σάρκα relationships with relationships rooted in spiritual or divine realities. The latter were consistently valued more highly than the former. Thus Paul wrote that it was far more significant to count Abraham as our father in virtue of our common faith than to count him as our father κατὰ σάρκα. Similarly, while Paul acknowledged the Israelites as his brothers κατὰ σάρκα, he stressed that it was more important to be brothers by the Spirit, adopted by God the Father, and fellow heirs together with Christ. Secondly, Paul warned believers not to live by a κατὰ σάρκα value system that in the past had led them to view Jesus with contempt, and that was leading them to treat his messengers the same way. For the believer, the κατὰ σάρκα wisdom of the world is nullified, and Jesus crucified and risen is now the basis of our wisdom and righteousness, and our new standard of values.

In chapter 4 we advocated four stances on four theoretical questions that affect our reading of the σάρξ-πνεῦμα antithesis. Namely, we argued for the need to interpret Galatians in the light of Romans given the difficulties of mirror-reading. We also suggested that the theological coloring of the discussion of σάρξ in the lexicons needs to be critically evaluated, not just accepted as the definition of the word. Most importantly, we argued that Paul situates the σάρξ-πνεῦμα antithesis in two key theological frameworks: an anthropological one and a salvation-historical one, and that both together are necessary and sufficient to rightly interpret Paul's view of the flesh and its conflict with the Spirit. Finally, we argued that the flesh-Spirit conflict is a dynamic that is at work both at the individual level and at the community level.

In chapter 5 our analysis of Romans 6–8 established that Paul is employing a salvation-historical framework for σάρξ and πνεῦμα. The time "in the flesh" describes the historical time before Jesus came, when Jewish believers lived under the Law without the indwelling Spirit and experienced frustration and futility; despite their attempts to obey the Law, they were enslaved by sin. Now that Christ has come, and the Spirit has come, believers are no longer "in the flesh" but "in the Spirit" in a salvation-historical sense. The Spirit dwells within and gives life, and sets believers free from the Law and sin, such that they are now slaves to God and righteousness. However, despite the fact that we are no longer "in the flesh" from a salvation-historical perspective, anthropologically we are still "flesh," with the human weakness that is implied. Therefore, Paul gives warnings and commands that are pertinent to the weakness and lusts of the flesh. Thorough consideration of Paul's statements on flesh surfaced a tripartite salvation-historical schema behind Paul's statements. The "SH-Yesterday" corresponds to the time "in the flesh." The "SH-Now" corresponds to the subsequent time "in the Spirit" but before the parousia. Though we have the Holy Spirit dwelling within, with the life and power he gives, we are still "flesh" anthropologically, and our redemption is not complete. Therefore, it is appropriate that the term "flesh" and its attendant physical and moral weaknesses may be predicated to us. Finally, we anticipate the "SH-*Soon!*" when Christ will come back and complete our redemption with glorious, spiritual, bodies, no longer characterized as "flesh" in any way.

In chapter 6 we explored whether the flesh-Spirit antithesis and the tripartite salvation-historical schema corresponds in any way with the two ages of Jewish eschatology and the so-called "overlap of the ages" to which many Pauline scholars refer, and also to the idea of "new creation" in 2 Corinthians 5:17 and Galatians 6:15. We argued, first, against a rather large scholarly consensus, that the "overlap of the ages" is not an accurate description of Paul's eschatology. While we are in agreement regarding inaugurated eschatology and the eschatological tension of our incomplete redemption in the SH-Now between Jesus's two comings, we maintained that the "overlap of the ages" is not an exegetically warranted description. In Paul there is no "overlap of the ages," and therefore this construct does not correspond to the SH-Now. It seems clear the SH-*Soon!* describes the salvation-historical circumstances of the age to come, which is the age of consummation. Paul views the time which we are in currently, to which the designation SH-Now would be appropriate, as a continuation of the old age—"the present evil age." From a broader NT perspective we see that Jesus and the Spirit inaugurated "the last days" of the old age. This understanding coheres well with an anthropological and pneumatological view of Paul's "a new creation" references, which do not describe the beginning of *the* new creation, understood in a cosmological sense as a renewed cosmos or the turn of the ages and the abolishing of the old age. Rather, they describe the radical newness of the believer in Christ, in terms of his identity, and the transforming experience of the Spirit within.

In chapter 7 we surveyed the epistle to the Galatians as a whole and attempted to clarify some of its difficult issues. We argued that Paul's purpose was to prevent the Galatian believers from accepting the Judaizers' false gospel of circumcision and Torah, and that what was at stake was apostasy and the loss of the Galatians' eternal salvation. Galatians 5:2–4 makes this clear. Nonetheless, although the potential of apostasy was real, Paul was confident that these true brothers in the faith would heed his warning and the Galatians in fact would not apostasize. Essential to Paul's purpose was the need to explain the nature of justification through faith, which was antithetical to the "gospel" of circumcision and the Law, which rendered Christ's death superfluous. We argued that justification had a forensic sense of being declared righteous, as opposed to being made righteous, and that the righteousness Paul speaks of is that status, but also the robust fulfillment of that status when Jesus returns and consummates the salvation of his people. This kind of righteousness only comes through faith, not the Law. We also saw how the antithetical use of the flesh and Spirit was introduced in 3:1–5. Since the Galatians already possessed the Spirit, they had definite proof they were in a right standing with God based on faith in the gospel of the crucified Jesus that Paul had preached to them. There was no need to complete their faith by the fleshly means of circumcision and Torah. Finally, we saw how Paul's argument moved toward an ethical component that showed the superiority of his Law-free gospel over that of the Judaizers in the ethical sphere.

Finally, in chapter 8 we exegeted Galatians 5:13–26 and saw that Paul used his σάρξ-πνεῦμα antithesis both to demonstrate the ethical superiority of the true gospel over the Judaizers' gospel, and to exhort the Galatian believers to live up to that ethical superiority by walking according to the standard of the Spirit so that they do not fulfill the sinful desire of the flesh.

We saw that most occurrences of σάρξ in this passage had an anthropological sense that spoke of our natural human weakness that is inescapable prior to the parousia, and thus it is only by walking in the Spirit that we may live a life of love and service to others. Accordingly, the flesh is an appropriate subject of Paul's warnings and exhortations. Only 5:24 speaks of the crucifixion of our flesh in a salvation-historical sense, to speak of the once-for-all definitive end to our old identity at the cross. We then saw how this passage is related to the crucifixion of "our old man" in Romans 6:6, and our new status as "a new creation" in 2 Corinthians 5:17 and Galatians 6:15, a status that is defined by the indwelling Spirit of God within, who directs us into a walk of transformation unto Christlike love and service to others.

Question for Further Research

This thesis was originally conceived as a chapter exploring the antecedents to the use of σάρξ in John's Gospel. Though drawn inexorably deeper into and eventually captured by the tangled mystery of Paul's varied uses of σάρξ, the curiosity for John's use of the theme never departed. Looking forward, we are drawn to consider how John develops the theme of flesh, both for the intrinsic fascination of exploring the theme within the bounds of the Johannine literature, but also for the sake of comparing and contrasting the Pauline and Johannine development and use of the flesh.

Bibliography

Achtemeier, Paul J. "Finding the Way to Paul's Theology: A Response to J. Christiaan Beker and J. Paul Sampley." In *Pauline Theology, Volume I: Thessalonians, Philippians, Galatians, Philemon*, edited by Jouette M. Bassler, 25–36. Minneapolis: Fortress, 1991.

Arnold, Bill T., and John H. Choi. *A Guide to Biblical Hebrew Syntax*. Cambridge: Cambridge University Press, 2003.

Arnold, Clinton E. *Power and Magic: The Concept of Power in Ephesians*. Reprint, Eugene, OR: Wipf & Stock, 2001.

———. "Returning to the Domain of the Powers: *Stoicheia* as Evil Spirits in Galatians 4:3, 9." *NovT* 38.1 (1996) 29–46.

Ascough, Richard S. "Historical Approaches." In *Dictionary of Biblical Criticism and Interpretation*, edited by Stanley E. Porter, 157–59. London: Routledge, 2007.

Aune, David E. "Apocalypticism." In *DPL* 25–35.

Baird, William. *From C. H. Dodd to Hans Dieter Betz*. Vol. 3 of *History of New Testament Research*. Minneapolis: Fortress, 2013.

———. *From Jonathan Edwards to Rudolf Bultmann*. Vol. 2 of *History of New Testament Research*. Minneapolis: Fortress, 2003.

Balla, Peter. "2 Corinthians." In *Commentary on the New Testament Use of the Old Testament*, edited by G. K. Beale and D. A. Carson, 753–83. Grand Rapids: Baker, 2007.

Barclay, John M. G. "Mirror-Reading a Polemical Letter: Galatians as a Test Case." *JSNT* 31 (1987) 73–93.

———. *Obeying the Truth: A Study of Paul's Ethics in Galatians*. SNTW. Edinburgh: T. & T. Clark, 1988.

Barrett, C. K. "The Allegory of Abraham, Sarah, and Hagar in the Argument of Galatians." In *Essays on Paul*, 154–70. Philadelphia: Westminster, 1982.

———. *The First Epistle to the Corinthians*. BNTC. London: A. & C. Black, 1968.

———. *Freedom and Obligation: A Study of the Epistle to the Galatians*. Philadelphia: Westminster, 1985.

———. *The Gospel According to St. John: An Introduction with Commentary and Notes on the Greek Text*. London: SPCK, 1960.

Bauckham, Richard. *God Crucified: Monotheism and Christology in the New Testament*. Grand Rapids: Eerdmans, 1998.

———. *Jesus Among the Eyewitnesses: The Gospels as Eyewitness Testimony*. Grand Rapids: Eerdmans, 2006.

Baur, Ferdinand C. "Die Christuspartei in der korinthischen Gemeinde, der Gegensatz des petrinischen und paulinischen Christenthums in der ältesten Kirche, der Apostel Petrus in Rom." *TZT* 4 (1831) 61–206.

———. *Paul: The Apostle of Jesus Christ*. 2 vols. Translated by A. Menzies. London: Williams and Norgate, 1876.

Beale, G. K. *A New Testament Theology: The Unfolding of the Old Testament in the New*. Grand Rapids: Baker, 2011.

———. "The Old Testament Background of Paul's Reference to 'the Fruit of the Spirit' in Galatians 5:22." *BBR* 15.1 (2005) 1–38.

Beasley-Murray, G. R. *John*. WBC 36. 2nd ed. Nashville: Nelson, 1999.

Beker, J. Christiaan. *Paul the Apostle: The Triumph of God in Life and Thought*. Edinburgh: T. & T. Clark, 1989.

———. *Paul's Apocalyptic Gospel: The Coming Triumph of God*. Philadelphia: Fortress, 1982.

———. "Recasting Pauline Theology: The Coherence-Contingency Scheme as Interpretive Model." In *Pauline Theology, Volume I: Thessalonians, Philippians, Galatians, Philemon*, edited by Jouette M. Bassler, 15–24. Minneapolis: Fortress, 1991.

Betz, Hans Dieter. *Galatians: A Commentary on Paul's Letter to the Churches in Galatia*. Hermeneia. Minneapolis: Fortress, 1979.

Betz, Otto. *Offenbarung und Schriftforschung in der Qumransekte*. WUNT 6. Tübingen: Mohr-Siebeck, 1960.

Bird, Michael F. *The Saving Righteousness of God: Studies on Paul, Justification and the New Perspective*. Milton Keynes: Paternoster, 2007.

Bird, Michael F., and Preston M. Sprinkle, eds. *The Faith of Jesus Christ: Exegetical, Biblical, and Theological Studies*. Milton Keynes: Paternoster, 2009.

Birney, Leroy. "An Exegetical Study of Genesis 6:1–4." *JETS* 13.1 (Winter 1970) 43–52.

Bock, Darrell L. *Acts*. BECNT. Grand Rapids: Baker, 2007.

———. *A Theology of Luke-Acts: God's Promised Program, Realized for All Nations*. Biblical Theology of the New Testament. Grand Rapids: Zondervan, 2012.

Bonnard, Pierre. *L'Epitre de Saint Paul aux Galates*. Commentaire du Nouveau Testament 9. 2nd ed. Neuchatel: Delachaux & Niestle, 1972.

Bousset, Wilhelm. *Kyrios Christos: A History of the Belief in Christ from the Beginnings of Christianity to Irenaeus*. Translated by John E. Steely. Nashville: Abingdon, 1970.

Bowers, Paul. "Fulfilling the Gospel: The Scope of the Pauline Mission." *JETS* 30.2 (June 1987) 185–98.

Branch, R. G. "Zelophehad, Daughters of." In *Dictionary of the Old Testament: Pentateuch*, edited by T. Desmond Alexander and David W. Baker, 912–14. Downers Grove: InterVarsity, 2003.

Brandenburger, Egon. *Fleisch und Geist: Paulus und die dualistische Weisheit*. WMANT 29. Neukirchen-Vluyn: Neukirchener Verlag des Erziehungsvereins, 1968.

Bruce, F. F. *The Epistle to the Galatians*. NIGTC. Grand Rapids: Eerdmans, 1982.

———. "Galatian Problems: 2. North or South Galatians?" *BJRL* 52.2 (Spring 1970) 243–66.

———. "Galatians Problems: 4. The Date of the Epistle." *BJRL* 54.2 (Spring 1972) 250–67.

———. Review of *The New Testament World: Insights from Cultural Anthropology*, by Bruce J. Malina. *JSNT* 21 (June 1984) 111–13.

Brueggemann, Walter. *Genesis: A Bible Commentary for Teaching and Preaching*. IBC. Atlanta: John Knox, 1982.
Bultmann, Rudolf. *The Gospel of John*. Translated by G. R. Beasley-Murray. Oxford: Blackwell, 1971.
———. "New Testament and Mythology." In *Kerygma and Myth: A Theological Debate*, edited by Hans Werner Bartsch, 1–44. Translated by Reginald H. Fuller. New York: Harper & Row, 1961.
———. *Theology of the New Testament*. Translated by Kendrick Grobel. New York: Scribner's, 1951–55.
Bundrick, David R. "*TA STOICHEIA TOU KOSMOU* (GAL 4:3)." *JETS* 34.3 (1991) 353–64.
Burnett, Gary W. *Paul and the Salvation of the Individual*. Biblical Interpretation Series. Leiden: Brill, 2001.
Burton, Ernest De Witt. *A Critical and Exegetical Commentary on the Epistle to the Galatians*. ICC. Edinburgh: T. & T. Clark, 1921.
———. *Spirit, Soul and Flesh*. Historical and Linguistic Studies, Series 2, Vol. 3. Chicago: University of Chicago Press, 1918.
Caneday, Ardel B. "Covenant Lineage Allegorically Prefigured: 'Which Things Are Written Allegorically' (Galatians 4:21–31)." *SBJT* 14.3 (2010) 50–77.
Capes, David B., et al. *Rediscovering Paul: An Introduction to His World, Letters and Theology*. Downers Grove: InterVarsity, 2007.
Carson, D. A. *The Gospel According to John*. PNTC. Grand Rapids: Eerdmans, 1991.
Carson, D. A., et al., eds. *Justification and Variegated Nomism*. 2 vols. Grand Rapids: Baker, 2001–4.
Cassuto, Umberto. *A Commentary on the Book of Genesis, Part One: From Adam to Noah*. Translated by Israel Abrahams. Jerusalem: Magnes, 1961.
———. "The Episode of the Sons of God and the Daughters of Man." In *Biblical and Oriental Studies*, 1:17–28. Jerusalem: Magnes, 1973.
Chance, John K. "The Anthropology of Honor and Shame: Culture, Values, and Practice." *Semeia* 68 (1994) 139–51.
Chester, Stephen J. "The Retrospective View of Romans 7: Paul's Past in Present Perspective." In *Perspectives on Our Struggle with Sin: 3 Views of Romans 7*, edited by Terry L. Wilder, 57–103. Nashville: Broadman & Holman, 2011.
Chisholm, Robert B. "Flesh." In *NIDOTTE* 777–79.
Chisholm, Roderick. "Human Freedom and the Self." In *Free Will*, edited by Robert Kane, 47–58. Blackwell Readings in Philosophy. Malden, MA: Blackwell, 2002.
Ciampa, Roy E., and Brian S. Rosner. *The First Letter to the Corinthians*. PNTC. Grand Rapids: Eerdmans, 2010.
Cohen, Anthony P. *Self-Consciousness: An Alternative Anthropology of Identity*. London: Routledge, 1994.
———. *The Symbolic Construction of Community*. 2nd ed. London: Routledge, 1985.
Cole, R. Alan. *The Letter of Paul to the Galatians*. TNTC 9. 2nd ed. Grand Rapids: Eerdmans, 1989.
Congdon, David W. "Eschatologizing Apocalyptic: An Assessment of the Present Conversation on Pauline Apocalyptic." In *Apocalyptic and the Future of Theology: With and Beyond J. Louis Martyn*, edited by Joshua B. Davis and Douglas Harink, 118–36. Eugene, OR: Cascade, 2012.

Conzelmann, Hans. *1 Corinthians*. Translated by James W. Leitch. Hermeneia. Philadelphia: Fortress, 1975.

———. *The Theology of St. Luke*. Translated by Geoffrey Buswell. New York: Harper & Row, 1961.

Cosgrove, Charles H. *The Cross and the Spirit: A Study in the Argument and Theology of Galatians*. Macon, GA: Mercer University Press, 1988.

Cousar, Charles B. *Galatians*. IBC. Louisville: John Knox, 1982.

Craig, William Lane. *The Tensed Theory of Time: A Critical Examination*. Synthese Library 293. Dordrecht: Kluwer, 2000.

———. *The Tenseless Theory of Time: A Critical Examination*. Synthese Library 294. Dordrecht: Kluwer, 2000.

Cranfield, C. E. B. *A Critical and Exegetical Commentary on the Epistle to the Romans*. ICC. 2 vols. Edinburgh: T. & T. Clark, 1975.

Cranford, Michael. "Abraham in Romans 4: The Father of All Who Believe." *NTS* 41 (1995) 71–88.

Cullmann, Oscar. *Christ and Time*. 3rd ed. Translated by Floyd V. Filson. London: SCM, 1962.

Cummins, Stephen Anthony. *Paul and the Crucified Christ in Antioch: Maccabean Martyrdom and Galatians 1 and 2*. SNTSMS 114. Cambridge: Cambridge University Press, 2001.

Davies, W. D. *Paul and Rabbinic Judaism*. London: SPCK, 1948.

———. "Paul and the Dead Sea Scrolls: Flesh and Spirit." In *The Scrolls and the New Testament*, edited by Krister Stendahl, 157–82. New York: Harper & Row, 1957.

———. *Torah in the Messianic Age and/or the Age to Come*. SBLMS. Philadelphia: SBL, 1952.

Davies, W. D., and Dale C. Allison Jr. *Commentary on Matthew VIII–XVIII*. Vol. 2 of *The Gospel According to Saint Matthew*. ICC. Edinburgh: T. & T. Clark, 1991.

Davis, Anne. "Allegorically Speaking in Galatians 4:21—5:1." *BBR* 14.2 (2004) 161–74.

de Boer, Martinus C. "Paul's Mythologizing Program in Romans 5–8." In *Apocalyptic Paul: Cosmos and Anthropos in Romans 5–8*, edited by Beverly Roberts Gaventa, 1–20. Waco: Baylor University Press, 2013.

deSilva, David A. *Introducing the Apocrypha: Message, Context, and Significance*. Grand Rapids: Baker, 2002.

DeWeese, Garrett J. *God and the Nature of Time*. Burlington, VT: Ashgate, 2004.

Di Vito, Robert A. "Old Testament Anthropology and the Construction of Personal Identity." *CBQ* 61 (1999) 221–38.

Dorsey, David. "The Law of Moses and the Christian: A Compromise." *JETS* 34.3 (September 1991) 321–34.

Drane, John W. *Paul: Libertine or Legalist? A Study in the Theology of the Major Pauline Epistles*. London: SPCK, 1975.

Duncan, G. S. *The Epistle of Paul to the Galatians*. MNTC. London: Hodder & Stoughton, 1934.

Dunn, James D. G. *Beginning from Jerusalem*. Vol. 2 of *Christianity in the Making*. Grand Rapids: Eerdmans, 2009.

———. "Echoes of Intra-Jewish Polemic in Paul's Letter to the Galatians." *JBL* 112 (1993) 459–77.

———. *The Epistle to the Galatians*. BNTC. Peabody, MA: Hendrickson, 1993.

———. *The New Perspective on Paul*. 2nd ed. Grand Rapids: Eerdmans, 2008.

———. Review of *The Flesh-Spirit Conflict in Galatians*, by Walter Bo Russell III. *JTS* 52.1 (April 2001) 280–82.
———. *Romans 1–8.* WBC 38A. Waco: Word, 1988.
———. *The Theology of Paul the Apostle.* Grand Rapids: Eerdmans, 1998.
———. "Works of the Law and the Curse of the Law (Galatians 3:10–14)." *NTS* 31 (1985) 523–42.
Dunson, Ben C. "The Individual and Community in Pauline Scholarship," *Currents in Biblical Research* 9.1 (2010) 63–97.
———. "Individual and Community in Paul's Letter to the Romans." PhD diss., University of Durham, 2011.
Duvall, J. Scott. "'Identity-Performance-Result': Tracing Paul's Argument in Galatians 5 and 6." *Southwestern Journal of Theology* 37 (Fall 1994) 30–38.
Ebeling, Gerhard. *The Truth of the Gospel: An Exposition of Galatians.* Translated by David Green. Philadelphia: Fortress, 1985.
Erickson, Millard J. *Christian Theology.* 2d ed. Grand Rapids: Baker, 1998.
Erickson, R. J. "Flesh." In *DPL* 303–6.
Esler, Philip F. Review of *Portraits of Paul: An Archaeology of Ancient Personality*, by Bruce J. Malina and Jerome H. Neyrey. *Biblical Interpretation* 6.1 (January 1998) 113–15.
Fee, Gordon D. *The First Epistle to the Corinthians.* NICNT. Grand Rapids: Eerdmans, 1987.
———. "Freedom and the Life of Obedience (Galatians 5:1—6:18)." *RevExp* 91 (1994) 201–17.
———. *God's Empowering Presence: The Holy Spirit in the Letters of Paul.* Peabody, MA: Hendrickson, 1994.
———. *Pauline Christology: An Exegetical-Theological Study.* Peabody, MA: Hendrickson, 2007.
———. *Paul's Letter to the Philippians.* NICNT. Grand Rapids: Eerdmans, 1995.
Fitzmyer, Joseph A. "The Consecutive Meaning of EFV W in Romans 5.12." *NTS* 39 (1993) 321–39.
———. *First Corinthians.* Anchor Yale Bible Commentaries 32. New Haven, CT: Yale University Press, 2008.
———. *Romans: A New Translation with Introduction and Commentary.* AB 33. New York: Doubleday, 1993.
Flusser, David. "The Dead Sea Sect and Pre-Pauline Christianity." In *Aspects of the Dead Sea Scrolls*, edited by Chaim Rabin, 215–66. Scripta Hierosolymitana 4. Jerusalem: Magnes, 1958.
France, R. T. *The Gospel of Mark.* NIGTC. Grand Rapids: Eerdmans, 2002.
Frey, Jörg. "The Impact of the Dead Sea Scrolls on New Testament Interpretation." In *The Bible and the Dead Sea Scrolls, Volume 3: The Scrolls and Christian Origins*, edited by James H. Charlesworth, 407–61. The Second Princeton Symposium on Judaism and Christian Origins. Waco: Baylor University Press, 2006.
———. "The Notion of 'Flesh' in 4QInstruction and the Background of Pauline Usage." In *Sapiential, Liturgical and Poetical Texts from Qumran: Proceedings of the Third Meeting of the International Organization for Qumran Studies, Published in Memory of Maurice Baillet*, edited by Daniel K. Falk et al., 197–226. Studies on the Texts of the Desert of Judah 35. Leiden: Brill, 2000.
———. "Die paulinische Antithese von 'Fleisch' und 'Geist' und die palästinisch-jüdische Weisheitstradition." *ZNW* 90 (1999) 45–77.

Friberg, Timothy, et al. *Analytical Lexicon of the Greek New Testament*. Baker's Greek New Testament Library. BibleWorks 8. Norfolk, VA: BibleWorks, 2009.
Fung, Ronald Y. K. *The Epistle to the Galatians*. NICNT. Grand Rapids: Eerdmans, 1988.
Garland, David E. *1 Corinthians*. BECNT. Grand Rapids: Zondervan, 2003.
Gathercole, Simon J. *Where Is Boasting? Early Jewish Soteriology and Paul's Response in Romans 1–5*. Grand Rapids: Eerdmans, 2002.
Gaventa, B. R. "Galatians 1 and 2: Autobiography as Paradigm." *NovT* 28.4 (1986) 309–26.
George, Andrew, trans. *The Epic of Gilgamesh: A New Translation*. New York: Barnes & Noble, 1999.
George, Timothy. *Galatians*. NAC. Nashville: Broadman & Holman, 1994.
Gingrich, F. Wilbur. *A Shorter Lexicon of the Greek New Testament*. 2nd ed. Revised by Frederick W. Danker. BibleWorks 8. Norfolk, VA: BibleWorks, 2009.
Goff, Matthew J. *The Worldly and Heavenly Wisdom of 4QInstruction*. Studies on the Texts of the Desert of Judah 50. Leiden: Brill, 2003.
Grenz, Stanley J. *Theology for the Community of God*. Reprint, Grand Rapids: Eerdmans, 2000.
Grimshaw, James P. Review of *Portraits of Paul: An Archaeology of Ancient Personality*, by Bruce J. Malina and Jerome H. Neyrey. *Encounter* 58.3 (Summer 1987) 317–18.
Grudem, Wayne. *Systematic Theology: An Introduction to Biblical Doctrine*. Grand Rapids: Zondervan, 1994.
Gundry Volf, Judith. *Paul and Perseverance: Staying in and Falling Away*. WUNT 2 Reihe 37. Tübingen: Mohr, 1990.
Gunkel, Hermann. *Zum religionsgeschichtlichen Verständnis des Neuen Testaments*. Göttingen: Vandenhoeck and Ruprecht, 1903.
Hafemann, S. J. "Paul and His Interpreters." In *DPL* 666–79.
Hagner, Donald A. *The New Testament: A Historical and Theological Introduction*. Grand Rapids: Baker, 2012.
Hamilton, Peter. "Editor's Foreword." In *The Symbolic Construction of Community*, by Anthony P. Cohen, 7–9. 2nd ed. London: Routledge, 1985.
Hamilton, Victor P. *The Book of Genesis, Chapters 1–17*. NICOT. Grand Rapids: Eerdmans, 1990.
Hansen, G. Walter. *Abraham in Galatians: Epistolary and Rhetorical Contexts*. JSNTSup 29. Sheffield: JSOT, 1989.
———. *Galatians*. IVPNTC. Downers Grove: InterVarsity, 1994.
———. *The Letter to the Philippians*. PNTC. Grand Rapids: Eerdmans, 2009.
———. "Paul's Conversion and His Ethic of Freedom in Galatians." In *The Road from Damascus: The Impact of Paul's Conversion on His Life, Thought, and Ministry*, edited by Richard N. Longenecker, 213–37. McMaster New Testament Studies. Grand Rapids: Eerdmans, 1997.
Hanson, Anthony T. *Studies in Paul's Technique and Theology*. Grand Rapids: Eerdmans, 1974.
Harink, Douglas. "Partakers of the Divine Apocalypse: Hermeutics, History, and Human Agency after Martyn." In *Apocalyptic and the Future of Theology: With and Beyond J. Louis Martyn*, edited by Joshua B. Davis and Douglas Harink, 73–95. Eugene, OR: Cascade, 2012.

Harris, Horton. "Baur, Ferdinand Christian (1792–1860)." In *Dictionary of Biblical Criticism and Interpretation*, edited by Stanley E. Porter, 34–35. London: Routledge, 2007.

Harris, Murray J. *Jesus as God: The New Testament Use of Theos in Reference to Jesus*. Grand Rapids: Baker, 1992.

———. *The Second Epistle to the Corinthians*. NIGTC. Grand Rapids: Eerdmans, 2005.

Hawthorne, Gerald F. *Philippians*. WBC 43. Waco: Word, 1983.

Hays, Richard B. *The Faith of Jesus Christ: An Investigation of the Narrative Substructure of Galatians 3:1—4:11*. SBL Dissertation Series. Chico, CA: Scholars, 1983.

———. "'Have We Found Abraham to Be Our Forefather according to the Flesh?' A Reconsideration of Rom 4:1." *NovT* 27 (1985) 76–98.

Hellerman, Joseph H. *Reconstructing Honor in Roman Philippi: Carmen Christi as Cursus Pudorum*. SNTSMS 132. Cambridge: Cambridge University Press, 2005.

Hemer, Colin J. "Acts and Galatians Reconsidered." *Themelios* 2.3 (May 1977) 81–88.

———. *The Book of Acts in the Setting of Hellenistic History*. Winona Lake: Eisenbrauns, 1990.

Hendel, Ronald S. "Of Demigods and the Deluge: Toward an Interpretation of Genesis 6:1–4." *JBL* 106.1 (March 1987) 13–26.

Hengel, Martin. *Judaism and Hellenism: Studies in Their Encounter in Palestine during the Early Hellenistic Period*. 2 vols. Translated by John Bowden. Philadelphia: Fortress, 1974.

Héring, Jean. *The First Epistle of Saint Paul to the Corinthians*. Translated by A. W. Heathcote and P. J. Allcock. London: Epworth, 1962.

Herzfeld, Michael. "Honour and Shame: Problems in the Comparative Analysis of Moral Systems." *Man* 15.2 (June 1980) 339–51.

Hill, David. *Greek Words and Hebrew Meanings: Studies in the Semantics of Soteriological Terms*. SNTSMS 5. Cambridge: Cambridge University Press, 1967. Reprint, Eugene, OR: Wipf & Stock, 2000.

Hirsch, E. D., Jr. *Validity in Interpretation*. New Haven: Yale University Press, 1967.

Hoegen-Rohls, Christina. "Κτίσις and καινὴ κτίσις in Paul's Letters." In *Paul, Luke, and the Graeco-Roman World: Essays in Honour of Alexander J. M. Wedderburn*, edited by Alf Christopherson et al. and translated by Linda Maloney, 102–22. JSNTSup 219. Sheffield: JSOT, 2002.

Hoehner, Harold. "Chronology of the Apostolic Age." ThD diss., Dallas Theological Seminary, 1965.

Holsten, Carl. *Das Evangelium des Paulus*. 2 vols. Berlin: Reimer, 1880–98.

———. *Zum Evangelium des Paulus und des Petrus*. Rostock: Schmidt, 1868.

Holtzmann, H. J. *Lehrbuch der Neutestamentlichen Theologie*. 2 vols. Freiberg: Mohr, 1897.

Horrell, David G. "Models and Methods in Social-Scientific Interpretation: A Response to Philip Esler." *JSNT* 78 (2000) 83–105.

———. "Social Sciences Studying Formative Christian Phenomena: A Creative Movement." In *Handbook of Early Christianity: Social Science Approaches*, edited by Anthony J. Blasi et al., 3–28. Walnut Creek, CA: Alta Mira, 2002.

Hoskins, Paul M. *Jesus as the Fulfillment of the Temple in the Gospel of John*. Paternoster Biblical Monographs. Milton Keynes: Paternoster, 2006.

Hubbard, Moyer V. *New Creation in Paul's Letters and Thought*. SNTSMS 119. Cambridge: Cambridge University Press, 2002.

Hübner, Hans. *Law in Paul's Thought*. Translated by James C. G. Greig. SNTW. Edinburgh: T. & T. Clark, 1984.
Huppenbauer, H. "Fleisch in den Texten von Qumran." *TZ* 13 (1957) 298–300.
Jackson, T. Ryan. *New Creation in Paul's Letters: A Study of the Historical and Social Setting of a Pauline Concept*. WUNT 2 Reihe 272. Tübingen: Mohr Siebeck, 2010.
Jewett, Robert. *Paul's Anthropological Terms: A Study of Their Use in Conflict Settings*. Arbeiten zur Geschichte des antiken Judentums und des Urchristentums 10. Leiden: Brill, 1971.
Jobes, Karen H. "Jerusalem, Our Mother: Metalepsis and Intertextuality in Galatians 4:21–31." *WTJ* 55 (1993) 299–320.
Johnson, Aubrey R. *The Vitality of the Individual in the Thought of Ancient Israel*. 2nd ed. Cardiff: University of Wales, 1962.
Johnson, D. H. "Flesh." In *DLNT* 374–76.
Johnson, Elliott E. *Expository Hermeneutics: An Introduction*. Grand Rapids: Zondervan, 1990.
Johnson, Roger A. *Origins of Demythologizing: Philosophy and Historiography in the Theology of Rudolf Bultmann*. Leiden: Brill, 1974.
Käsemann, Ernst. *Commentary on Romans*. Translated by Geoffrey W. Bromiley. Grand Rapids: Eerdmans, 1980.
———. *New Testament Questions of Today*. Translated by W. J. Montague. London: SCM, 1969.
———. "On Paul's Anthropology." In *Perspectives on Paul*. Translated by Margaret Kohl, 1–31. Mifflintown, PA: Sigler, 1996.
Keener, Craig S. *The Gospel of John*. 2 vols. Peabody, MA: Hendrickson, 2003.
Kennedy, H. A. A. *St. Paul and the Mystery-Religions*. New York: Hodder and Stoughton, 1913.
Kim, Seyoon. *The Origin of Paul's Gospel*. Grand Rapids: Eerdmans, 1982.
———. *Paul and the New Perspective: Second Thoughts on the Origin of Paul's Gospel*. Grand Rapids: Eerdmans, 2002.
Kline, Meredith G. "Divine Kingship and Genesis 6:1–4." *WTJ* 24.2 (May 1962) 187–204.
Koester, Helmut. *History, Culture, and Religion of the Hellenistic Age*. Vol. 1 of *Introduction to the New Testament*. 2nd ed. New York: de Gruyter, 1995.
Kok, Ezra Hon-Seng. *"The Truth of the Gospel": A Study in Galatians 2:15–21*. Jian Dao Dissertation Series 7 / Bible and Literature 5. Hong Kong: Alliance Bible Seminary, 2000.
Köstenberger, Andreas J. *John*. BECNT. Grand Rapids: Baker, 2004.
Kreitzer, L. J. "Eschatology." In *DPL* 253–69.
Kripke, Saul A. *Naming and Necessity*. Cambridge: Harvard University Press, 1972.
Kruse, Colin G. *Paul, the Law, and Justification*. Peabody, MA: Hendrickson, 1996.
Kuhn, Karl George. "New Light on Temptation, Sin, and Flesh in the New Testament." In *The Scrolls and the New Testament*, edited by Krister Stendahl, 94–113. New York: Harper & Row, 1957.
Kümmel, W. G. *Das Bild des Menschen im neuen Testament*. Zurich: Zwingli, 1948.
———. *Römer 7 und die Bekehrung des Paulus*. Leipzig: Hinrichs, 1929.
Ladd, George Eldon. *The Presence of the Future*. Grand Rapids: Eerdmans, 1974.
———. *A Theology of the New Testament*. Edited by Donald A. Hagner. 2nd ed. Grand Rapids: Eerdmans, 1993.

Lagrange, Marie-Joseph. *Saint Paul: Epître aux Romains*. Etudes bibliques. Paris: Gabalda, 1950.

Lake, Kirsopp. *The Earlier Epistles of St. Paul: Their Motive and Origin*. London: Rivingtons, 1914.

Lambrecht, Jan. *The Wretched "I" and Its Liberation: Paul in Romans 7 and 8*. Louvain Theological and Pastoral Monographs 14. Louvain: Peeters, 1992.

Lee, Chee-Chiew. *The Blessing of Abraham, the Spirit, and Justification in Galatians: Their Relationship and Significance for Understanding Paul's Theology*. Eugene, OR: Pickwick, 2013.

Lincoln, Andrew T. *The Gospel According to Saint John*. BNTC. London: Hendrickson/Continuum, 2005.

———. *Paradise Now and Not Yet: Studies in the Role of the Heavenly Dimension in Paul's Thought with Special Reference to His Eschatology*. SNTSMS 43. Cambridge: Cambridge University Press, 1981.

Litfin, Duane. *St. Paul's Theology of Proclamation: 1 Corinthians 1-4 and Greco-Roman Rhetoric*. SNTSMS 79. Cambridge: Cambridge University Press, 1994.

Longenecker, Richard N. *Galatians*. WBC 41. Dallas: Word, 1990.

Lüdemann, Hermann. *Die Anthropologie des Apostels Paulus*. Kiel: Toeche, 1872.

Lull, David J. *The Spirit in Galatia: Paul's Interpretation of PNEUMA as Divine Power*. SBLDS 49. Chico, CA: Scholars, 1980.

Lyall, Francis. *Slaves, Citizens, Sons: Legal Metaphors in the Epistles*. Grand Rapids: Zondervan, 1984.

Lys, Daniel. "L'arrière-plan et les connotations vétérotestamentaires des *sarx* et de *sōma* (étude préliminaire)." *VT* 36 (1986) 163-204.

Machen, J. Gresham. *The Origin of Paul's Religion*. New York: Macmillan, 1921.

Malina, Bruce J. *Christian Origins and Cultural Anthropology: Practical Models for Biblical Interpretation*. Atlanta: John Knox Press, 1986.

———. *The New Testament World: Insights from Cultural Anthropology*. 3rd ed. Louisville: Westminster John Knox, 2001.

Malina, Bruce J., and Jerome H. Neyrey. *Portraits of Paul: An Archaeology of Ancient Personality*. Louisville: Westminster John Knox, 1996.

Martin, Ralph P. *Carmen Christi: Philippians 2:5-11 in Recent Interpretation and in the Setting of Early Christian Worship*. Grand Rapids: Eerdmans, 1983.

Martin, Ralph P., and Brian J. Dodd, eds. *Where Christology Began: Essays on Philippians 2*. Louisville: Westminster John Knox, 1998.

Martyn, J. Louis. "Apocalyptic Antinomies in Paul's Letter to the Galatians." *NTS* 31 (1985) 410-24.

———. *Galatians*. AB 33A. New York: Doubleday, 1997.

———. *Theological Issues in the Letters of Paul*. Nashville: Abingdon, 1997.

Matera, Frank. "The Culmination of Paul's Argument to the Galatians: Gal. 5.1—6.17." *NTS* 32 (1998) 79-91.

Mathews, Kenneth A. *Genesis 1-11:26*. NAC 1A. Nashville: Broadman & Holman, 1996.

Matlock, R. Barry. *Unveiling the Apocalyptic Paul: Paul's Interpreters and the Rhetoric of Criticism*. JSNTSup 127. Sheffield: Sheffield Academic, 1996.

Matthews, Victor H. "Family Relationships." In *Dictionary of the Old Testament: Pentateuch*, edited by T. Desmond Alexander and David W. Baker, 291-99. Downers Grove: InterVarsity, 2003.

McGrath, Alister E. "Justification." In *DPL* 517-23.

McKnight, Scot. *Galatians*. NIVAC. Grand Rapids: Zondervan, 1995.

McRay, John. *Archaeology and the New Testament*. Grand Rapids: Baker, 1991.
Meggitt, Justin L. *Paul, Poverty, and Survival*. SNTW. Edinburgh: T. & T. Clark, 1998.
Metzger, Bruce M. *An Introduction to the Apocrypha*. New York: Oxford University Press, 1957.
———. *A Textual Commentary on the Greek New Testament*. 4th rev. ed. Stuttgart: Deutsche Bibelgesellschaft, 1994.
Meyer, R. "Fleisch im Judentum." In *TWNT* 8:109–18.
Michaels, J. Ramsey. *The Gospel of John*. NICNT. Grand Rapids: Eerdmans, 2010.
Michel, O. "καταντάω, ὑπαντάω, ὑπάντησις." In *TDNT* 3:625.
Montefiore, C. G. *Judaism and St. Paul: Two Essays*. London: Goschen, 1914.
Moo, Douglas J. "Creation and New Creation." *BBR* 20.1 (2010) 39–60.
———. *Encountering the Book of Romans*. Grand Rapids: Baker, 2002.
———. *The Epistle to the Romans*. NICNT. Grand Rapids: Eerdmans, 1996.
———. *Galatians*. BECNT. Grand Rapids: Baker, 2013.
———. "Israel and Paul in Romans 7:7–12." *NTS* 32 (1986) 122–35.
Morris, Leon. *The Apostolic Preaching of the Cross*. 3rd ed. London: Tyndale, 1965.
———. *The Gospel According to John*. 2d ed. NICNT. Grand Rapids: Eerdmans, 1995.
Moule, C. F. D. "Jesus, Judaism, and Paul." In *Tradition and Interpretation in the New Testament: Essays in Honor of E. Earle Ellis for His 60th Birthday*, edited by Gerald F. Hawthorne and Otto Betz, 43–52. Grand Rapids: Eerdmans, 1987.
———. "'Justification' in its Relation to the Condition *kata pneuma* (Rom 8:1–11)." In *Battesimo e Giustizia in Rom 6 e 8*, edited by L. De Lorenzi, 177–201. Rome: Abbadiza S. Paolo, 1974.
Moulton, J. H., and W. F. Howard. *A Grammar of New Testament Greek*. 4 vols. Reprint, Edinburgh: T. & T. Clark, 1990.
Mussner, Franz. *Der Galaterbrief*. Herders theologischer Kommentar zum Nuen Testament 9. Freiberg: Herder, 1974.
Neill, Stephen, and Tom Wright. *The Interpretation of the New Testament, 1861–1986*. 2nd ed. Oxford: Oxford University Press, 1988.
Neyrey, Jerome H. "Bewitched in Galatia: Paul and Cultural Anthropology." *CBQ* 50 (1988) 72–100.
———. "Reading Paul in Social Science Perspective." In *Paul in Other Words: A Cultural Reading of His Letters*, 11–20. Louisville: Westminster John Knox, 1990.
Noetscher, Friedrich. *Zur theologischen Terminologie der Qumran-Texte*. BBB 10. Bonn: Hanstein, 1956.
O'Brien, Peter T. *The Epistle to the Philippians*. NIGTC. Grand Rapids: Eerdmans, 1991.
———. *The Letter to the Ephesians*. PNTC. Grand Rapids: Eerdmans, 1999.
Orr, William F., and James Arthur Walker. *1 Corinthians*. AB 32. New York: Doubleday, 1976.
Peristiany, J. G., and J. Pitt-Rivers, eds. *Honour and Shame: The Values of Mediterranean Society*. Chicago: University of Chicago, 1966.
Perriman, Andrew. "Rhetorical Strategy of Galatians 4:21—5:1." *EvQ* 65 (1993) 27–42.
Pfleiderer, Otto. *Paulinism: A Contribution to the History of Primitive Christian Theology*. Translated by Edward Peters. 2 vols. London: Williams and Norgate, 1877.
Piper, John. *The Future of Justification: A Response to N. T. Wright*. Wheaton: Crossway, 2007.
Rad, Gerhard von. *Genesis: A Commentary*. OTL. Translated by John H. Marks. 2nd ed. Philadelphia: Westminster, 1972.
Räisänen, Heikki. *Paul and the Law*. Minneapolis: Fortress, 1986.

Reitzenstein, Richard. *Die hellenistischen Mysterienreligionen*. Leipzig: Teubner, 1920.
Ridderbos, Herman. *The Epistle of Paul to the Churches of Galatia*. The New London Commentary on the New Testament. London: Marshall, Morgan & Scott, 1953.
———. *The Gospel of John*. Translated by John Vriend. Grand Rapids: Eerdmans, 1997.
———. *Paul: An Outline of His Theology*. Translated by John Richard de Witt. Grand Rapids: Eerdmans, 1976.
Robinson, H. Wheeler. *The Christian Doctrine of Man*. Edinburgh: T. & T. Clark, 1911.
Robinson, John A. T. *The Body: A Study in Pauline Theology*. London: SCM, 1952.
Russell, Walt. "The Apostle Paul's Redemptive-Historical Argumentation in Galatians 5:13–26." *WTJ* 57 (1995) 333–57.
———. "The Apostle Paul's View of the 'Sin Nature' / 'New Nature' Struggle." In *Christian Perspectives on Being Human: A Multidisciplinary Approach to Integration*, edited by J. P. Moreland and David M. Ciocchi, 207–28. Grand Rapids: Baker, 1993.
———. "Insights from Postmodernism's Emphasis on Interpretive Communities in the Interpretation of Romans 7." *JETS* 37.4 (December 1994) 511–27.
———. "Who Were Paul's Opponents in Galatia?" *BSac* 147 (July–September 1990) 329–50.
Russell, Walter Bo, III. *The Flesh/Spirit Conflict in Galatians*. Lanham, MD: University Press of America, 1997.
Ryken, Leland, et al., eds. "Body." In *Dictionary of Biblical Imagery*, 102–11. Downers Grove: InterVarsity, 1998.
Sand, Alexander. *Der Begriff "Fleisch" in den Paulinischen Hauptbriefen*. Biblische Untersuchungen 6. Regensburg: Verlag Friedrich Pustet, 1967.
Sanders, E. P. *Paul and Palestinian Judaism*. Philadelphia: Fortress, 1977.
Sarna, Nahum M. *Genesis: The Traditional Hebrew Text with the New JPS Translation*. JPS Torah Commentary. Philadelphia: Jewish Publication Society, 1989.
Schlier, Heinrich. *Der Brief an die Galater*. Kritisch exegetischer Kommentar über das Neue Testament 7. 5th ed. Göttingen: Vandenhoeck & Ruprecht, 1971.
Schnelle, Udo. *Apostle Paul: His Life and Theology*. Translated by Eugene M. Boring. Grand Rapids: Baker Academic, 2005.
Schoeps, Hans Joachim. *Paul: The Theology of the Apostle in the Light of Jewish Religious History*. Translated by Harold Knight. Philadelphia: Westminster, 1961.
Schreiner, Thomas R. *Galatians*. ZECNT. Grand Rapids: Zondervan, 2010.
———. *The Law and Its Fulfillment: A Pauline Theology of Law*. Grand Rapids: Baker, 1993.
———. *New Testament Theology: Magnifying God in Christ*. Grand Rapids: Baker, 2008.
———. *Paul, Apostle of God's Glory in Christ: A Pauline Theology*. Downers Grove: InterVarsity, 2001.
———. *Romans*. BECNT. Grand Rapids: Baker, 1998.
Schweitzer, Albert. *The Mysticism of Paul the Apostle*. Translated by William Montgomery. Reprint, Baltimore: Johns Hopkins University Press, 1998.
———. *Paul and His Interpreters: A Critical History*. Translated by William Montgomery. London: A. & C. Black, 1912.
Schweizer, Eduard. "σάρξ, σαρκικός, σάρκινος." In *TDNT* 7:98–151.
Seebass, H. "Flesh." In *NIDNTT* 671–78.
Schulz, Siegfried. "Zur Rechtfertigung aus Gnaden in Qumran und bei Paulus." *ZThK* 56 (1959) 155–85.
Silva, Moisés. *Explorations in Exegetical Method: Galatians as a Test Case*. Grand Rapids: Baker, 1996.

———. "Galatians." In *Commentary on the New Testament Use of the Old Testament*, edited by G. K. Beale and D. A. Carson, 785–812. Grand Rapids: Baker, 2007.

———. *Interpreting Galatians: Explorations in Exegetical Method*. 2nd ed. Grand Rapids: Baker, 2001.

———. *Philippians*. 2nd ed. BECNT. Grand Rapids: Baker, 2005.

Skinner, John. *Genesis*. ICC. Edinburgh: T. & T. Clark, 1910.

Snaith, John G. *Ecclesiasticus*. CBC. Cambridge: Cambridge University Press, 1974.

Soards, Marion L. *1 Corinthians*. NIBCNT. Peabody, MA: Hendricksen, 1999.

———. *The Apostle Paul: An Introduction to His Writings and Teachings*. New York: Paulist, 1987.

Stacey, W. David. *The Pauline View of Man*. London: Macmillan, 1956.

Stanton, Graham. "The Law of Moses and the Law of Christ: Galatians 3:1–6:2." In *Paul and the Mosaic Law*, edited by James D. G. Dunn, 99–116. WUNT 89. Tubingen: Mohr, 1996.

Strack, Hermann L., and Paul Billerbeck. *Das Evangelium nach Matthäus*. Vol. 1 of *Kommentar zum Nuen Testament aus Talmud und Midrasch*. Munich: C. H. Beck'sche Verlagsbuchhandlung, 1922.

Stuhlmacher, Peter. *Gerechtigkeit Gottes bei Paulus*. Göttingen: Vandenhoeck & Ruprecht, 1965.

———. *Paul's Letter to the Romans: A Commentary*. Translated by Scott J. Hafemann. Loiusville: Westminster/John Knox, 1994.

Thackeray, Henry St. John. *The Relation of St. Paul to Contemporary Jewish Thought*. London: Macmillan, 1900.

Thayer, Joseph. *A Greek-English Lexicon of the New Testament (Abridged and Revised Thayer Lexicon)*. Ontario, Canada: Online Bible Foundation, 1997. BibleWorks 8.

Thiselton, Anthony C. *First Corinthians: A Shorter Exegetical and Pastoral Commentary*. Grand Rapids: Eerdmans, 2006.

———. *The First Epistle to the Corinthians*. NIGTC. Grand Rapids: Eerdmans, 2000.

———. "Flesh." In *NIDNTT* 678–82.

Thrall, Margaret E. *The Second Epistle to the Corinthians*. 2 vols. ICC. Edinburgh: T. & T. Clark, 1994.

Tobin, Thomas H. "What Shall We Say That Abraham Found? The Controversy behind Romans 4." *HTR* 88.4 (1995) 437–52.

Vos, Geerhardus. *The Pauline Eschatology*. 2nd ed. Grand Rapids: Eerdmans, 1961.

Wallace, Daniel B. *Greek Grammar Beyond the Basics: An Exegetical Syntax of the New Testament*. Grand Rapids: Zondervan, 1996.

Waltke, Bruce K. *Genesis: A Commentary*. Grand Rapids: Zondervan, 2001.

Waltke, Bruce K., and Michael O'Connor. *An Introduction to Biblical Hebrew Syntax*. 2nd ed. Winona Lake, IN: Eisenbrauns, 2004.

Walton, John H. *Genesis*. NIVAC. Grand Rapids: Zondervan, 2001.

Weiss, Johannes. *Der este Korintherbrief*. Göttingen: Vandenhoeck & Ruprecht, 1910.

Wenham, David. *Paul: Follower of Jesus or Founder of Christianity?* Grand Rapids: Eerdmans, 1995.

Wenham, Gordon J. *Genesis 1–15*. WBC 1. Waco: Word, 1987.

Westerholm, Stephen. *Perspectives Old and New on Paul: The "Lutheran" Paul and His Critics*. Grand Rapids: Eerdmans, 2004.

Westermann, Claus. *Genesis 1–11: A Commentary*. Translated by John J. Scullion. Minneapolis: Augsburg, 1984.

Wilder, Terry L., ed. *Perspectives on Our Struggle with Sin: 3 Views of Romans 7*. Nashville: Broadman & Holman, 2011.
Wilkens, Steve, and Alan G. Padgett. *Faith and Reason in the Nineteenth Century*. Vol. 2 of *Christianity and Western Thought: A History of Philosophers, Ideas and Movements*. Downers Grove: InterVarsity, 2000.
Williams, Demetrius K. *Enemies of the Cross: The Terminology of the Cross and Conflict in Philippians*. JSNTSup 223. Sheffield: Sheffield Academic, 2002.
Winter, Bruce W. *After Paul Left Corinth: The Influence of Secular Ethics and Social Change*. Grand Rapids: Eerdmans, 2001.
———. *Philo and Paul Among the Sophists*. SNTSMS 96. Cambridge: Cambridge University Press, 1997.
Witherington, Ben, III. *Conflict and Community in Corinth: A Socio-Rhetorical Commentary on 1 and 2 Corinthians*. Grand Rapids: Eerdmans, 1995.
———. *Grace in Galatia: A Commentary on Paul's Letter to the Galatians*. Grand Rapids: Eerdmans, 1998.
———. *New Testament History: A Narrative Account*. Grand Rapids: Baker, 2001.
———. *Paul's Letter to the Philippians: A Socio-Rhetorical Commentary*. Grand Rapids: Eerdmans, 2011.
Wolff, Hans Walter. *Anthropology of the Old Testament*. Translated by Margaret Kohl. London: SCM, 1974.
Wright, N. T. *The Climax of the Covenant: Christ and the Law in Pauline Theology*. London: T. & T. Clark, 1991.
———. *Justification: God's Plan and Paul's Vision*. Downers Grove: InterVarsity, 2009.
———. "The Letter to the Romans: Introduction, Commentary, and Reflections." In *The New Interpreter's Bible*, edited by Leander E. Keck, 10:393–770. Nashville: Abingdon, 2002.
———. "Romans and the Theology of Paul." In *Pauline Theology, Volume 3: Romans*, edited by David M. Hay and E. Elizabeth Johnson, 30–67. Minneapolis: Fortress, 1995.
———. "The Shape of Justification." *BR* 17 (April 2001) 8, 50.
———. *What St. Paul Really Said: Was Paul of Tarsus the Real Founder of Christianity?* Grand Rapids: Eerdmans, 1997.
Yamauchi, Edwin M. *Pre-Christian Gnosticism: A Survey of the Proposed Evidences*. 2nd ed. Grand Rapids: Eerdmans, 1983.
Ziesler, J. *The Epistle to the Galatians*. Epworth. London: Epworth, 1992.
Ziesler, J. A. *The Meaning of Righteousness in Paul: A Linguistic and Theological Enquiry*. SNTSMS 20. Cambridge: Cambridge University Press, 1972.

Author Index

Achtemeier, Paul J., 90
Allison, Dale C., Jr., 39
Arnold, Bill T., 28, 39
Arnold, Clinton E., 128, 170
Ascough, Richard S., 7, 8
Aune, David E., 13

Baird, William, 6, 7, 8, 14, 17
Balla, Peter, 117
Barclay, John M. G., 3–6, 11, 14–15, 17–19, 77, 88–89, 118, 128, 152, 154, 157, 164, 173, 182–86, 197
Barrett, C. K., 13, 34, 132–33, 172
Bauckham, Richard, 75, 85, 107
Baur, Ferdinand C., 3–5, 8
Beale, G. K., 138–39, 141–42, 144–46, 197
Beasley-Murray, G. R., 34
Beker, J. Christiaan, 18, 90, 130, 135
Betz, Hans Dieter, 13, 148, 152, 163, 166
Betz, Otto, 19
Billerbeck, Paul, 39
Bird, Michael F., 104, 107, 153, 155
Birney, Leroy, 51
Bock, Darrell L., 134, 193
Bonnard, Pierre, 13, 15
Bousset, Wilhelm, 7
Bowers, Paul, 100
Branch, R. G., 149
Brandenburger, Egon, 19
Bruce, F. F., 13, 88, 97, 149, 152, 158–60, 163–64, 169–70, 182, 184
Brueggemann, Walter, 56
Bultmann, Rudolf, 8, 13–17, 34, 85

Bundrick, David R., 170
Burnett, Gary W., 97–98, 100
Burton, Ernest De Witt, 8–10, 12, 159–60

Caneday, Ardel B., 170
Capes, David B., 104
Carson, D. A., 34, 153
Cassuto, Umberto, 55
Chance, John K., 98
Chester, Stephen J., 110–11
Chisholm, Robert B., 26, 46–47, 62–63
Chisholm, Roderick, 100
Choi, John H., 28, 39
Ciampa, Roy E., 133
Cohen, Anthony P., 97–100, 112
Cole, R. Alan, 13
Congdon, David W., 14
Conzelmann, Hans, 128, 132
Cosgrove, Charles H., 13, 158, 166, 170
Cousar, Charles B., 164
Craig, William Lane, 133
Cranfield, C. E. B., 116, 161–62
Cranford, Michael, 70
Cullmann, Oscar, 128, 141
Cummins, Stephen Anthony, 157, 193

Davies, W. D., 8, 11–12, 19, 39, 124
Davis, Anne, 170
de Boer, Martinus C., 16–17
deSilva, David A., 38
DeWeese, Garrett J., 133
Di Vito, Robert A., 112
Dodd, Brian J., 207

Dorsey, David, 115
Drane, John W., 90
Duncan, G. S., 175
Dunn, James D. G., 3-4, 7-9, 70-72, 78, 90, 93, 102, 104, 107, 111, 113, 115, 128, 132, 152-54, 157-59, 166, 182-83, 193
Dunson, Ben C., 16, 100
Duvall, J. Scott, 173

Ebeling, Gerhard, 13
Erickson, Millard J., 155
Erickson, R. J., 26, 40, 42, 46, 62-63
Esler, Philip F., 97, 99

Fee, Gordon D., 70, 74, 84, 93, 96, 102, 114-16, 118, 122-23, 128, 173, 183, 191-92, 207
Fitzmyer, Joseph A., 102, 110-11, 132, 161
Flusser, David, 19
France, R. T., 66
Frey, Jörg, 3-5, 7-8, 14, 19
Friberg, Timothy, 26, 33, 40, 42, 46, 62-63
Fung, Ronald Y. K., 13, 156, 158-60, 173-74, 182-83

Garland, David E., 85, 132-33
Gathercole, Simon J., 107
Gaventa, B. R., 199
George, Andrew, 52
George, Timothy, 13, 183-84
Gingrich, F. Wilbur, 26, 33, 40, 42, 46, 62-63
Goff, Matthew J., 19
Grenz, Stanley J., 155
Grimshaw, James P., 97
Grudem, Wayne, 155
Gundry Volf, Judith, 154-55, 157-60, 163
Gunkel, Hermann, 6-7

Hafemann, S. J., 3, 6, 8, 18
Hagner, Donald A., 128, 135
Hamilton, Peter, 99
Hamilton, Victor P., 51-53, 55, 58, 60
Hansen, G. Walter, ix, 13, 118, 148-49, 152, 154, 158-59, 163, 170-71,
178, 183-85, 191, 193, 197, 199-200, 203
Hanson, Anthony T., 170
Harink, Douglas, 21
Harris, Horton, 3
Harris, Murray J., 74-76, 141
Hawthorne, Gerald F., 118
Hays, Richard B., 70, 108, 115
Hellerman, Joseph H., 194, 204, 207
Hemer, Colin J., 88, 193
Hendel, Ronald S., 53, 55-56
Hengel, Martin, 11
Héring, Jean, 130-31, 133
Herzfeld, Michael, 98
Hill, David, 156, 161-62, 174-75
Hirsch, E. D., Jr., 189
Hoehner, Harold, 89
Holsten, Carl, 5
Holtzmann, H. J., 5-6
Horrell, David G., 99
Hoskins, Paul M., 171
Howard, W. F., 161
Hubbard, Moyer V., 78-79, 83, 86, 89, 102, 137-39, 141-45, 149-50, 175-76, 187, 198, 200-201
Hübner, Hans, 90
Huppenbauer, H., 19

Jackson, T. Ryan, 138, 142-43, 145
Jewett, Robert, 4-9, 11-12, 14-17, 19, 89, 118, 128
Jobes, Karen H., 70, 170-72
Johnson, Aubrey R., 37, 42-43, 54
Johnson, D. H., , 26, 35, 42, 62
Johnson, Elliott E., 25
Johnson, Roger A., 14
Johnson, Sherman, 19

Käsemann, Ernst, 13-14, 16-18, 21, 111, 130
Keener, Craig S., 34
Kennedy, H. A. A., 8
Kim, Seyoon, 111, 117, 119-20, 153, 160
Kline, Meredith G., 51-52
Koester, Helmut, 11
Kok, Ezra Hon-Seng, 157
Köstenberger, Andreas J., 34
Kreitzer, L. J., 130

Kripke, Saul A., 53
Kruse, Colin G., 152, 163, 168, 173
Kuhn, Karl George, 19
Kümmel, W. G., 15-16, 112

Ladd, George Eldon, 12-13, 128, 131, 133-35, 155
Lagrange, Marie-Joseph, 70
Lake, Kirsopp, 7
Lambrecht, Jan, 110-11
Lee, Chee-Chiew, 169, 177
Lincoln, Andrew T., 34, 128-29, 135
Litfin, Duane, 80
Longenecker, Richard N., 13, 88, 149, 158-60, 163-64, 167, 169, 183-84, 208
Lüdemann, Hermann, 5-6
Lull, David J., 13
Lyall, Francis, 171
Lys, Daniel, 60

Machen, J. Gresham, 8
Malina, Bruce J., 96-99, 108
Martin, Ralph P., 207
Martyn, J. Louis, 18, 21, 89, 128, 130, 143, 147-48, 152, 182-84, 191, 197
Matera, Frank, 151, 173
Mathews, Kenneth A., 53-55, 61
Matlock, R. Barry, 5-6, 11, 14, 16-18, 130
Matthews, Victor H., 46, 149
McGrath, Alister E., 155
McKnight, Scot, 166
McRay, John, 80
Meggitt, Justin L., 81-82
Metzger, Bruce M., 38, 74-75, 134
Meyer, R., 19
Michaels, J. Ramsey, 34
Michel, O., 131
Montefiore, C. G., 7, 11
Moo, Douglas J., 21, 69-72, 78, 102-3, 107-8, 110-13, 115-19, 122-23, 128, 138-40, 142, 146-50, 152, 155-56, 159-60, 163-64, 166-70, 174, 182-85, 201
Morris, Leon, 34, 155
Moule, C. F. D., 108
Moulton, J. H., 161

Mussner, Franz, 13, 15

Neill, Stephen, 3-4, 6-8, 11, 14, 17
Neyrey, Jerome H., 96-99
Noetscher, Friedrich, 19

O'Brien, Peter T., 118, 136, 192-93, 207
O'Connor, Michael, 39
Orr, William F., 133

Padgett, Alan G., 4
Peristiany, J. G., 98
Perriman, Andrew, 170
Pfleiderer, Otto, 5-6
Piper, John, 152
Pitt-Rivers, J., 98

Rad, Gerhard von, 55
Räisänen, Heikki, 90, 106
Reitzenstein, Richard, 7-8
Ridderbos, Herman, 2-8, 20-21, 34, 78, 94, 121, 128, 183, 200
Robinson, H. Wheeler, 8-10
Robinson, John A. T., 8, 12-15, 85
Rosner, Brian S., 133
Russell, Walt (Walter Bo Russell III), 5-6, 8, 10, 13-14, 20-22, 28-29, 89, 92-93, 95-96, 98, 102, 110-15, 118, 128, 149, 151-52, 154, 157-59, 165-69, 171-73, 183, 187, 189-91, 200-203
Ryken, Leland, 26, 29, 35, 37-38, 40, 42, 46, 62-63

Sand, Alexander, 13, 15
Sanders, E. P., 124, 152
Sarna, Nahum M., 55
Schlier, Heinrich, 13, 15, 128
Schnelle, Udo, 7-8, 11, 183
Schoeps, Hans Joachim, 124, 128
Schreiner, Thomas R., 21, 78-79, 88-90, 93, 102, 104, 106, 110, 113-17, 122-24, 151, 153, 155-56, 158-59, 163-64, 167-70, 174-75, 182-83
Schweitzer, Albert, 6, 8-9, 16, 124
Schweizer, Eduard, 13, 15, 39
Seebass, H., 26, 31, 35, 40, 42, 46, 62-63
Schulz, Siegfried, 19

Silva, Moisés, 21, 88-90, 95, 165, 171, 192
Skinner, John, 55
Snaith, John G., 39
Soards, Marion L., 130, 132
Sprinkle, Preston M., 107
Stacey, W. David, 5-12, 15
Stanton, Graham, 168
Strack, Hermann L., 39
Stuhlmacher, Peter, 18, 111

Thackeray, Henry St. John, 8
Thayer, Joseph, 33, 39-40, 42, 46, 62-63
Thiselton, Anthony C., 15, 26, 40, 63, 80-85, 130-32
Thrall, Margaret E., 141
Tobin, Thomas H., 70-71

Vos, Geerhardus, 128

Walker, James Arthur, 133
Wallace, Daniel B., 28, 199
Waltke, Bruce K., 39, 55-57
Walton, John H., 51-52, 55-56

Weiss, Johannes, 130-31
Wenham, David, 117, 125, 132, 149, 182, 184, 204
Wenham, Gordon J., 47, 51-52, 55, 57
Westerholm, Stephen, 90, 107, 124, 153-54
Westermann, Claus, 55
Wilder, Terry L., 64, 110, 143
Wilkens, Steve, 4
Williams, Demetrius K., 118
Winter, Bruce W., 79-85
Witherington, Ben, III, 80, 118, 133, 146, 149, 152-53, 163-64, 169, 174, 182, 185, 191, 197, 199
Wolff, Hans Walter, 27-28, 32, 34, 44, 46-48, 60
Wright, N. T. (Tom Wright), 3-4, 6-8, 11, 14, 17, 23, 90, 104-9, 152-53, 155

Yamauchi, Edwin M., 7-8

Ziesler, J. A., 152, 160-61, 164, 168-69

Subject Index

Abraham as forefather of the Jews according to the flesh, 70–72
apocalyptic views of Paul, 16–18, 21, 100, 130, 132, 142, 147–48, 152, 183–84
apostasy in Galatians, 154–63

circumcision in the flesh, 77–79
community (corporate) vs. individual emphasis, 95–100
Corinth, 79–86

flesh, lexical treatment of, 91–92
flesh, salvation-historical sense/framework of, 102–120
flesh as body in part or in whole, 35–41
flesh as family, relatives, kin, 46–48
flesh as genitals or sexual urge, 33–35
flesh as literal flesh, skin, and muscle, 26–31
flesh as man, humanity, living things, in contrast to God (anthropological sense), 1–2, 4–6, 9–13, 16–18, 20–24, 49–66, 87–88, 93–94, 109, 120–26, 136, 165, 168–69, 188, 209–212
flesh as meat, 31–33
flesh as person, 42–45
fruit of the Spirit, 197–98

Galatians, Paul's argument in, 163–76
Galatians, purpose of the epistle, 151–63
Galatians as a warning, 151–63

Gnosticism, 6–8

heart of flesh, 66
Hellenistic mystery religions, 6–8
history of religions school, 6–8
history of research on Paul and the flesh, 2–21

inaugurated eschatology, 127–50
Israel according to the flesh, 77–79
Israelites as the source of Christ according to the flesh, 74–76

Jesus as the fleshly descendant of David, 69–70
Jews as Paul's brothers and Abraham's children according to the flesh, 72–73
justification, 70–71, 104–9, 151–57, 162–69, 173–75, 207, 211

masters according to the flesh, 76–77
men of flesh, fleshly men, 84–85
mirror-reading Paul's letters, 88–91
models in social-science research and biblical studies, 96–100, 105–9

new creation, 137–50

"overlap of the ages", 127–50

Paul, spiritual formation in, 202–8
Paul's eschatology, 127–50

Paul's tripartite salvation-historical temporal schema, 123–26

Qumran, 19–20

regarding people according to the flesh, 85–86

relationships according to the flesh, 68–77

Tübingen school, 3–4

walking by the Spirit, 202–8
wisdom according to the flesh, 79–85
works of the flesh, 187–97

Ancient Document Index

Old Testament/ Hebrew Bible

Genesis

1:2	54n57
1:26–31	51
1:26–28	50
1:28	51
2–3	111
2:7	39n28, 49, 51, 54, 56, 61
2:17	50, 59
2:18–24	51
2:21	27, 59
2:23	46, 60
2:24	48
2:25	60
3:6	51
3:14–24	59
3:14	39n28
3:16	39n28
3:17–19	61
3:19	50–51, 59
3:22–24	59, 61
3:22	50, 56
4	50
4:8–15	52
4:8–16	59
4:17–24	51
4:23–25	52
5:1—6:8	49
5	50, 59
5:5	50
5:8	50
5:11	50
5:14	50
5:17	50
5:20	50
5:27	50
5:28–32	50
5:31	50, 54, 60
5:32	50
6–8	49
6–7	61
6	26, 49, 60
6:1–8	93
6:1–4	49–50, 53, 58
6:1–2	54
6:1	57
6:2	51–52
6:3	22, 49, 53–63, 93
6:4	52–53, 57–58
6:5–8	49–50, 54
6:5–7	60–61
6:5	12n45, 54, 58
6:6	58
6:7	54, 58
6:8	50, 59
6:11–12	60–61
6:11	53–54, 58
6:12–13	61
6:12	49, 58, 61–62, 93
6:13	53, 58
6:17	54, 58, 60–61
6:19	58, 61
7:3	58
7:4	58

Genesis (continued)

7:6	58
7:10	58
7:12	58
7:14	58
7:15–16	58, 61
7:15	54, 58
7:17	58
7:18–20	58
7:18	58
7:19	58
7:20	58
7:21–23	58
7:21–22	60–61
7:21	58, 61
7:22	54, 58, 61
7:23	58
7:24	58
8:1	58
8:3	58
8:7	58
8:9	58
8:11	58
8:13	58
8:14	58
8:17	58
8:19	58
8:21–22	50
8:21	12n45
8:22	58
9	31
9:1	58
9:2	58
9:7	58
9:10	58
9:11	58
9:13	58
9:14	58
9:15–17	58
9:16	58
9:17	58
9:18–28	59
9:19	58
12	52
12:3	152
12:11–13	52
12:11	52
12:12	52
12:14	52
12:15	52
12:17	52
12:18	52
12:19	52
15	78
15:2–4	149
15:6	70–71n7
16–17	172
16	51
17	70–71n7, 78, 156
17:11	27
17:13	118
17:14	27
17:24–25	27
18:3	70–71n7
19:29	59
19:30–38	59
20	52
20:2	52
20:3	52
20:10–11	52
21	51, 172
21:10	149
26	52
26:7–9	52
26:7	52
29–30	51
29:14	46
37:27	47
40:19	29
41:2–4	27
41:8	27
41:19	27

Exodus

4:7	28
12	32
12:9	33
12:46	33
16	31
16:3	31
16:8	32
16:12	32
21:28	32
22:31	32
28:42	33
29:14	32
32:8	154

Leviticus

4:8–10	29
4:11	29
6:27	32
7:15	32
7:17–20	32
8:17	32
8:31	32
8:32	32
9:11	32
11	32
11:8	32
11:11	32
13	27–28n6
13:2	40
13:3	40
13:4	40
13:10	28
13:11	40
13:13	40
13:14–16	28
14:9	40
15	34, 40
15:2	34
15:7	34
15:13	34
15:16	34, 40
15:19	34
16:4	40
16:24	40
16:26	40
16:27	32
16:28	40
17:16	40
18	28, 48
18:6	46n38, 47
21:5	28
22:6	40
25:49	47
26:29	29

Numbers

11	32
11:4	32
11:13	32
11:18	32
11:21	32
11:33	32
13:33	53
19:5	32
19:7–8	40
25:6–13	193
27:1–11	149
36:1–13	149

Deuteronomy

5:26	62
9:16	154
10:16	78
12	32
12:15	32
12:20	32
12:23	32
12:27	32
14:8	32
21:15–17	149
25:11	33
28:52–57	30
28:53	30
28:55	30
30:6	78
32:42	37

Joshua

15:49	55

Judges

6:19–21	32
8:7	29
9:2	46

1 Samuel

1:13	194
17:44	30
25:36	194

2 Samuel

5:1	46
17:25	46n39
19:12	46
19:13	46

1 Kings

16:9	194
21:16	194
21:27	41

2 Kings

5:10	28
5:14	28
6:30	41
9:36	30

1 Chronicles

2:13–17	46n39
11:1	46

2 Chronicles

32:8	63

Nehemiah

5:5	47

Job

2:5	35
4:15	28
10:11	29
13:14	36
14:22	36
19:20	29
33:21	29
34:15	60
41:23	27

Psalms

1	64
16:8–11	42–43, 45
16:9	45
27:2	30
30:13	42n34
56:1–2	64
56:4	63
56:5–7	64
57:9	42n34
63:1	36, 43
65:2	62
67:19–20	75n20
78:27	32
78:39	64
79:2	30, 38n24
84:2	37
90	57
102:4	28
102:5	28
104:29–30	54n57, 56
106:30–31	193
108:2	42n34
142:2	165
145:21	62

Proverbs

3:22	36
4:22	43, 45
5:11	44
14:30	35
20:1	194
23:20	32

Ecclesiastes

1:2–3	44
1:8	44
1:13–18	44
3:19–21	54n57
4:4	192
5:6	44
11:10	41
12:8–12	44
12:12	44

Isaiah

2:2	134
22:13	32
28:7	194
31:3	64
32	197n37
32:15–16	197
40:5	62–64
40:6–8	64–65
42:5	54
43:18–19	139, 145

45:21–25	74n21	21:4–5	62
45:23–24	75	23	34
49	30	23:20	33–34
49:26	30, 37	32:5–6	37
53:11	161n33	36–37	119
54:1	172	36:26–27	78, 117
58:7	47, 48n42	36:26	66, 117–19
63:10	192	36:27	117
65:17	145	37:4–14	117
66:16	62	37:6	29
		37:8	29
		38:16	134
		39:17–20	39

Jeremiah

4:4	78	39:17–18	30–31, 37
9:1–8	192	40:43	32
9:8	192	44:7	37
9:22–25	78, 83	44:9	37
9:25–26	78		
10:19–22	112		

Daniel

11:15	32		
17:5–6	64	1:15	27
17:6	64	4:33	37
17:7–8	64		
19	30		

Hosea

19:3	30		
19:9	30	3:5	134
23:20	134	8:13	32
25:31	62		
31:27–34	134		

Joel

31:27	134		
31:29	134	1:5	194
31:31–34	78, 117	2	197n37
31:31	134	2:18–32	197
31:34	134	2:28–29	134
		2:28	62–63

Lamentations

Jonah

1:9–22	112		
2:20–22	112	3:4–10	58–59

Ezekiel

Micah

10:12	41	2:8	192
11:19–20	78, 117	4:1	134
11:19	66, 117–19	7:7–10	112
11:20	117	7:8	192
16	34	7:10	192
16:26	34		

Zephaniah

1:17	38

Haggai

1:6	194
2:12	32

Zechariah

3:7	55n60
11:9	30
11:16	30
14:12	29

Apocrypha

Baruch

2:3	31

1 Maccabees

2:1–70	193
7:17	38

2 Maccabees

7:24	154
9:9	27
11:24	154

4 Maccabees

6:6	27
7:18	35
9:17	27
9:20	27
9:28	28
10:8	27
15:15	27–28
16:1–25	193
18:1–24	193

Sirach

1:7–8	63
14:7—15:1	38
14:17–18	65
14:18	38
17	38
17:1	39n28
17:30–32	38–39
17:31	38, 65
19:12	27
23:16–17	48
25	45
25:26	45
28:5	64
30:21—31:6	45
30:21–24	45
31:1	45
31:2	45
31:5	45
31:6	45
38:28	28
44:20	28
45:23–24	193

Wisdom of Solomon

12:5–6	33
12:5	38

Pseudepigrapha

Psalms of Solomon

1:1—2:6	112
4:19	27

New Testament

Matthew

3:9	70–71nn7–8
5:17	182
5:29–30	204n57
16:17	39, 65
18:8–9	204n57

ANCIENT DOCUMENT INDEX

19:5-6	48	12:35-45	85n46
22:39	182n4	15:22-24	85n46
24:22	63	19:31-37	85n46
24:49	194	20:8	85n46
26:41	65, 183-184n11	20:28	74n14
27:18	194	21:4	85n46
28:20	133	21:7	85n46

Mark

9:43-47	204n57
10:7-8	48
10:17-30	134
10:17	134
10:23	134
10:30	134
12:31	182n4
13:20	63
14:38	65, 183-184n11
15:10	194

Luke

1:55	70-71n7
1:73	70-71n7
3:6	63
4:28	193
10:27	182n4
24:39	27

John

1:1	74n14
1:11	34n17
1:12	34n17
1:13	34
1:14	85n46
1:18	74n14
3:6	54n57
6:60-64	85n46
6:63	54n57
8:15	85n46
8:33-40	70-71n7
8:39	71n8
8:53	70-71n7
9:35-41	85n46
11:40	85n46

Acts

2:15	194
2:17-21	134
2:17	63, 134
2:25-28	45
2:26	45
5:3-4	74n14
5:15	194
5:17	192
7:2	70-71n7
7:9	193
13-14	88
13:15-16	73
13:26	73
13:38	73
13:45	192
15	88
15:5	194
17:5	193
18	80
19:28	194
20:28	74n14
21:20	193
21:24	205
22:1	73
22:3	193
23:1	73
23:5-6	73
28:17	73

Romans

1-4	6
1:1-5	152
1:3-4	69-70
1:3	69-70n3
1:5-7	113
1:13	113

Romans (continued)

1:16–17	152
1:18—2:12	93
1:29	192, 194
2	107
2:8	194
2:13	155n13
2:14–15	107
2:21–22	107
2:25–29	22, 77, 170
2:25–27	107
2:25–26	78
2:26	204
2:28–29	78–79
3:9–18	93
3:9	115
3:19–31	77
3:19–20	115
3:20–22	106–7
3:20	63, 93
3:21–22	107
3:21	106–7
4:1	70–71
4:2–5	71
4:4–5	160
4:5–11	155n13
4:9–12	78
4:9–11	71
4:9	189n27
4:11–12	71
4:12	186n22, 205
4:13–16	71, 77
4:15	111
4:22–25	71, 155n13
5–8	6
5:1	155n13
5:2	160
5:5	138
5:9	155–156n13
5:12–23	102, 111
5:12–21	93, 111n32
5:12	102n2
5:13–14	111
5:13	111–12
5:19	155n13
6–8	23, 102–126, 135, 177, 203, 210
6	109, 125, 200, 206
6:1–23	103, 203
6:3	207
6:4	79
6:6–7	114
6:6	24, 201, 207, 212
6:8–9	207
6:11–14	114
6:11–13	201
6:11	207
6:12–22	207
6:12	201
6:13	201
6:14	104, 109, 115, 159
6:16–22	114
6:16–19	203
6:16	207
6:17	207
6:18	208
6:19	109n27, 121, 124
6:22	208
7–8	12n51, 23, 104–6, 109
7:1—8:4	77
7	10, 109–110, 111n32, 112n34, 113
7:1–6	110
7:1	159
7:2	159
7:4–6	102–5, 109, 114–15
7:4	103, 125, 203
7:5	103, 124, 196, 203
7:6	79, 103, 111, 125, 138, 159, 203
7:5–25	103n4
7:7–25	103, 110, 113, 128n2
7:7–12	110
7:7–11	113
7:8–10	111–12
7:8	110–11
7:9–10	110
7:9	110
7:13–25	105, 110
7:13	110
7:14—8:11	10

7:14–25	103, 113–14, 115n48, 122, 124, 125n70, 184, 196, 203	8:12–17	73
		8:12–14	204
		8:12–13	122–23
		8:13	122–23, 204n57
7:14	103, 110, 115	8:14–17	197
7:15–21	103	8:14	117
7:15	183–84	8:18–25	126, 144, 174
7:16	184	8:19–39	155–156n13
7:17–18	116	8:19	174
7:18–24	183–184n11	8:23–27	125
7:18	66, 110, 201	8:23–25	123, 175
7:20	113	8:23	174
7:21–25	103, 114	8:25	174
7:21	106n15, 110	8:26	124
7:22	105	8:30	155n13, 174
7:23	103, 105, 106n15	9:1–8	72–74
7:24–25	114	9:3	72
7:24	103, 113, 196	9:5	74–76
7:25	103n4, 110, 113	9:6–8	73
8	107, 117, 122, 125n70	10:3	204
		11:14	48
8:1–30	174	12	206
8:1–17	103, 125, 138	12:1–2	206–7
8:1–14	120	12:2	79, 129, 138
8:1–11	20	12:3–16	207
8:1–9	122	13:3	194–95
8:1–4	109	13:8–14	188
8:1–3	115	13:13	192–93
8:1	105, 122, 155n13	13:14	15, 91–92, 123
8:2	105, 106n15, 114	14:17	135
8:3–9	15	14:21	33
8:3–4	108, 117	15:8	189n27
8:3	103, 105, 108	16:7	72
8:4	108, 117n53, 182, 204	16:11	72
		16:17	194
8:5–11	105, 122	16:21	72
8:5–9	125, 207		
8:5–8	204		
8:7	107, 192		

1 Corinthians

1–4	204
1–3	86, 129
1:4–7	80
1:7	123, 174
1:10—3:4	135–36
1:10–31	86
1:10–13	84
1:10–12	79

8:8–9	122
8:9–11	116, 204
8:9	91–92, 109, 117, 122
8:10–13	122
8:10	122
8:11–14	208
8:11	117, 122, 196, 201
8:12–30	174

1 Corinthians (continued)

1:11	84, 192
1:13–25	80
1:17–18	80
1:18–25	80
1:20	80, 129, 138
1:26–31	80–81
1:26–30	82
1:26	81–82
1:27–30	82
1:27–28	81–82n36
1:29	63, 93
2:1–5	83
2:6–16	207
2:6–11	83
2:6–8	129
2:6	138
2:8	138
2:12–15	84
2:12	129
2:13	85
2:14	85
2:15	85
3:1–4	84
3:1–3	91–92
3:1	84–85
3:2	84
3:3–8	84
3:3	84–85, 192–93
3:4	84
3:18–19	129
3:18	129, 138
3:22	129
5:6–8	79
6:9	135
6:10	135
6:13–20	48
6:16	48
6:19	138
7:19	175–76
8:4–6	75
8:4–5	75n16
8:13	33
9:19–27	208
9:19–23	208
9:20	115
9:24–27	208
9:24	208
9:27	208
10:7	191, 195
10:8	191
10:11	129–33, 133n17, 141, 143
10:18	78
10:25	33
10:27	140
11:19	194
11:21	195
13:4	193
15:20–58	144
15:21–28	126
15:28	17
15:35–57	120, 126
15:39	27, 121
15:40–53	121
15:40	121
15:42	121
15:43	121, 124
15:44	121
15:46	121
15:48	121
15:50–53	91–92
15:50	39, 65, 121, 135
15:51	121
15:56	111

2 Corinthians

1:16–17	45
1:22	138
1:23	45
2:1–13	45
3	117, 120
3:2–3	119
3:3–6	79, 117n54
3:3	120
3:6	54n57, 120, 138
3:7	111, 120
3:9	120
3:12–18	54n57
3:14	120
3:16–18	74n14, 120
3:18	138
4:4	75n16, 129, 137

4:5	206	2:4	153, 168, 177
4:6	120	2:5	204
4:11	41	2:7–9	189n27
4:16	79, 138	2:7	189n27
4:18	86	2:11–21	182, 188
5:2	123	2:12	189n27
5:4	123	2:14–21	164
5:5	138	2:14	168, 177, 188
5:12	86	2:15–21	158n17, 166
5:14–15	139, 143	2:15–16	164n46
5:14	139	2:15	157
5:15	145	2:16–17	162
5:16	85–86, 139	2:16	93, 155, 157, 165, 168, 177
5:17	23–24, 79, 132, 135, 137–45, 210, 212	2:17–20	164n46
		2:17	155–156n13
7:1	10, 40	2:19—3:1	167
7:4–9	45	2:19–20	150, 198–99
7:5	45	2:19	200
7:13	45	2:20	41, 165–66, 198–200
12:20	192–94	2:21	107, 157, 164n46, 166–67

Galatians

		3–4	172
1–4	176	3:1—4:31	165–72
1:1–5	152	3	149
1:4	21, 129, 138, 141, 146–47, 152n4	3:1–5	158n17, 165–68, 171, 176, 211
1:6–10	152	3:1–3	157
1:6–9	118	3:1	166
1:6	150, 154	3:2–5	155, 166
1:8	153	3:2–4	138
1:10—2:21	150, 158n17, 163–65, 198–99	3:2–3	23, 165, 167–68, 177
1:10	198–200	3:2	167, 177
1:11—6:10	164	3:3	15, 158, 167–69, 183n7, 186–87, 191, 208
1:11—2:21	168		
1:11–16	150		
1:11	65, 155	3:4	163, 166–67
1:13–17	198–99	3:5	167
1:13–14	157, 200, 204	3:6—4:31	168
1:14	193	3:6—4:7	170n62
1:16	198–200	3:6–14	169, 171
1:23–24	150	3:6–9	155
2–3	168	3:6–8	155
2:3–5	168, 177, 182	3:6	155–156n13
2:4–5	157	3:7–10	177
		3:7	177

Galatians (continued)

3:8–9	177
3:8	152, 162
3:10–14	150, 157, 182
3:10–13	177
3:10	115, 204
3:11	155, 162
3:14	155, 177, 197n37
3:15–29	169
3:15	155
3:16–18	177
3:16	177
3:18	177
3:19	111
3:21—4:11	171
3:21	157, 187
3:22	111
3:23–25	186
3:23	111, 115
3:24	162
3:25	115
3:26–29	155
3:26	177
3:28	147–49
3:29	177
4	149
4:1–11	169
4:2–5	115
4:3–7	198–99
4:3–5	177, 200
4:3	170n61
4:4–7	155
4:4	69–70n3, 197
4:5–7	177
4:6–7	177
4:6	138, 155, 198–200
4:7–8	155
4:8–10	198–99
4:8–9	177
4:8	170
4:9–21	156
4:9–10	204
4:9	170n61
4:10–20	150
4:12–20	170
4:12	150, 155, 170n62, 198
4:17	193, 204
4:19	150, 198–200
4:21—5:6	182
4:21–31	153, 170–72, 177
4:21	115, 183n7
4:23	171, 183n7
4:27	172
4:28	171
4:29	138, 171, 183n7
4:30–31	171
4:30	171n67, 177
4:31—6:10	158n17
5–6	12n51, 135
5:1—6:10	173–76
5	20, 162, 189n27, 191
5:1–12	173, 187
5:1–6	182
5:1–4	156, 186
5:1	155, 160, 173, 183n7, 203
5:2–6	79
5:2–4	150, 157–63, 173, 211
5:2–3	204
5:2	158, 160, 174
5:3	156, 158, 160, 204
5:4	155–156n13, 157–60, 162, 168n55, 174
5:5–6	146–48, 160, 173, 175
5:5	123, 126n73, 155–156n13, 173–75
5:6	118n58, 146, 150, 175–76, 181, 197, 200, 204–5
5:7	208n59
5:10	163, 173
5:11	173
5:12	118
5:13—6:10	170n62, 175, 189, 202
5:13–26	1, 23, 69, 92, 151, 164, 176–208, 211
5:13–25	150
5:13–21	157

5:13–15	178–83, 197, 202–3, 205	6:4	178
		6:6–10	176, 181
5:13–14	186	6:6	178
5:13	92, 179, 181, 183, 185, 187	6:8	94, 178
		6:9–10	178
5:14	117n53, 179, 197, 204	6:10	178
		6:11–18	176, 188
5:15	179	6:12–18	146
5:16–26	10, 18, 20	6:12–13	118, 204
5:16–25	202	6:12	157
5:16–18	125, 178–79, 183–87	6:13–15	205
		6:13	28, 200, 204
5:16–17	184, 187	6:14–15	21, 137, 143–50, 200
5:16	92, 150, 180, 183, 185–87, 202	6:14	129, 136–37, 144, 146, 198–200
5:17	180, 183–85, 189	6:15–16	78
5:18	115, 180, 186–87, 200, 202, 204	6:15	23–24, 79, 132, 137–38, 139n17, 141n44, 144–48, 150, 175, 198–200, 205, 210, 212
5:19–21	10, 15, 94, 125n70, 153, 178–80, 183n7, 185, 187–97, 204		
		6:16	146, 186n22, 205, 208
5:19–20	190		
5:19	180, 187, 189		
5:21	135, 180, 186, 196, 204		

Ephesians

5:22–25	125, 150
5:22–24	176
5:22–23	178–80, 185, 196–98	1:13–14	138
		1:22	129
5:22	180, 189	2:1–7	129, 135–36
5:23	181, 187, 197	2:2	129
5:24–26	198	2:3	35
5:24–25	200	2:7	129, 135
5:24	24, 92, 178–81, 198–201, 204n57, 212	2:11	189n27
		2:14–16	192
		3:9	129
5:25–26	178–81, 202–8	3:11	129
5:25	138, 150, 181, 186, 200, 202, 205, 208	4:22–24	201n47
		4:24	201n47
		4:31	194
		5:5	135
5:26	157, 181, 194	5:31	48
6:1–10	176, 178, 202	6:5–9	76
6:1–5	176, 181	6:5	76
6:1	178	6:10	65
6:2	178, 182, 202, 204		

Philippians

1:12–16	206
1:15	192, 194
1:17	194
1:22	41, 91–92, 120
1:24	41, 91–92, 120
2	207
2:1–11	206
2:3	194
2:5–11	75
2:6–11	70n5, 207
2:6	74n14
2:19–22	206
2:25–30	206
3	135, 205, 207
3:2–14	206
3:2–9	118
3:2–6	204
3:2	118n58, 189n27, 192n32
3:3–9	15
3:3	189n27
3:6	193
3:7–8	193
3:12–16	208
3:16	186n22, 205
3:17	206
3:18–19	118, 192n32, 204
3:19	75n16
3:20–21	126
3:20	123, 174
4:9	206

Colossians

1:26	129
2:18	10
3:8	194
3:9–11	201n47
3:10	201n47
3:11	189n27
3:22—4:1	76
3:22	76
4:11	189n27

1 Thessalonians

1:10	155n13
2:12	135
4:4	33
5:7	195
5:9	155n13

2 Thessalonians

1:5	135

1 Timothy

6:4	192, 194
6:17	129

2 Timothy

3:1	134
4:10	129

Titus

1:10	189n27
2:12	129
2:13	74n14
3:3	194
3:9	192

Philemon

16	76

Hebrews

1:1–2	133
1:8	74n14
12:9	48

James

5:3	31, 134

1 Peter

1:23–25	65
1:24–25	65
4:1–2	41
4:3	195

2 Peter

2:10	34–35
3:3	134
3:15–16	92
3:18	35

1 John

2:16	35
2:18	134n19
3:1–3	175n85
3:3	175n85

Jude

7–8	35

Revelation

17:16	31
19:17–20	39
19:18	31
19:21	31

www.ingramcontent.com/pod-product-compliance
Lightning Source LLC
Chambersburg PA
CBHW050847230426
43667CB00012B/2188